WRITE TO LEARN

Harcourt College Publishers

Where Learning Comes to Life

TECHNOLOGY
Technology is changing the learning experience, by increasing the power of your textbook and other learning materials; by allowing you to access more information, more quickly; and by bringing a wider array of choices in your course and content information sources.

Harcourt College Publishers has developed the most comprehensive Web sites, e-books, and electronic learning materials on the market to help you use technology to achieve your goals.

PARTNERS IN LEARNING
Harcourt partners with other companies to make technology work for you and to supply the learning resources you want and need. More importantly, Harcourt and its partners provide avenues to help you reduce your research time of numerous information sources.

Harcourt College Publishers and its partners offer increased opportunities to enhance your learning resources and address your learning style. With quick access to chapter-specific Web sites and e-books . . . from interactive study materials to quizzing, testing, and career advice . . . Harcourt and its partners bring learning to life.

Harcourt's partnership with Digital:Convergence™ brings :CRQ™ technology and the :CueCat™ reader to you and allows Harcourt to provide you with a complete and dynamic list of resources designed to help you achieve your learning goals. Just swipe the cue to view a list of Harcourt's partners and Harcourt's print and electronic learning solutions.

http://www.harcourtcollege.com/partners/

WRITE TO LEARN
SEVENTH EDITION

DONALD M. MURRAY

Harcourt College Publishers

FORT WORTH PHILADELPHIA SAN DIEGO NEW YORK ORLANDO AUSTIN SAN ANTONIO
TORONTO MONTREAL LONDON SYDNEY TOKYO

To Minnie Mae

Who made soup of old bones
and mailed out manuscript
in which I had no faith

Publisher	Earl McPeek
Acquisitions Editor	John Meyers
Developmental Editor	Laurie Runion
Project Manager	Elaine Hellmund

Cover credit: Bill Brammer

ISBN: 0-15-506512-2

Library of Congress Catalog Card Number:

Address for Domestic Orders
Harcourt College Publishers, 6277 Sea Harbor Drive, Orlando, FL 32887-6777
800-782-4479

Address for International Orders
International Customer Service
Harcourt, Inc., 6277 Sea Harbor Drive, Orlando, FL 32887-6777
407-345-3800
(fax) 407-345-4060
(e-mail) hbintl@harcourt.com

Address for Editorial Correspondence
Harcourt College Publishers, 301 Commerce Street, Suite 3700, Fort Worth, TX 76102

Web Site Address
http://www.harcourtcollege.com

Harcourt College Publishers will provide complimentary supplements or supplement packages to those adopters qualified under our adoption policy. Please contact your sales representative to learn how you qualify. If as an adopter or potential user you receive supplements you do not need, please return them to your sales representative or send them to:

Attn: Returns Department, Troy Warehouse, 465 South Lincoln Drive, Troy, MO 63379.

Printed in the United States of America

1 2 3 4 5 6 7 8 9   0 6 6   9 8 7 6 5 4 3 2 1

Harcourt College Publishers

PREFACE TO THE SEVENTH EDITION

It is an honor and a delight to be able to produce the seventh edition of a work. How few writers ever have so many opportunities to try and get it right. Of course, in my sixty-one years of publishing, I have learned you never get it right. That is a blessing. I have been able to practice my obsession with the writing process seven times and each edition has been different. So will the eighth if I am fortunate enough to have the chance to contradict myself and learn by writing.

Each day I practice my craft. Well, let's be honest. I have only written 1,287 days out of the last 1,481, but in those four years and 20 days I have written 1,029,198 words for an average of 799.7 words per writing day. And day after day I have not only surprised myself by what I have written, but how I have written it. I continue my apprenticeship.

This edition is changed by what I have learned and by the wise counsel of many readers who have tested my ideas in their own classrooms and on their own pages.

Here is what is new in the seventh edition:

- Chapter 1, "Make Writing Easy," is new. It is designed to help the student enter the writing act immediately, using the skills they have at this beginning stage.
- Chapter 2, "Unlearning to Write," is the former first chapter with the addition of what I think is important—that we have to unlearn to write if we are to write well.
- There are now three new, short "Shoptalk" chapters designed to help students develop the all-important attitudes that make it possible for them to learn and practice the writing process and to help prepare themselves for common writing tasks they will have to perform: Chapter 4, "Shoptalk:

The Research Plan"; Chapter 7, "Shoptalk: Preparing to Revise and Edit"; and Chapter 8, "Shoptalk: Helping Each Other." This last chapter is especially important because it shows students how they can help their classmates—and be helped by their classmates—by responding to their drafts in pairs, small groups, or class size workshops.

- We have a new section on page 236 on writing e-mail at work that is meant to help students overcome some common mistakes when using this form of communication.
- The writing process itself is refined. In the sixth edition it was: FOCUS, EXPLORE, PLAN, DRAFT, and CLARIFY. In the seventh edition it is: FOCUS, RESEARCH, DRAFT, REVISE, and EDIT which we feel is more helpful to students and their teachers.
- One of the most important contributions to this edition are the essays "Lost and Found in Cyberspace" and "Assessing a World Wide Web Site" by Associate Professor Lisa Miller, an authority on Internet journalism and author of *Power Journalism: Computer-Assisted Reporting* (Harcourt College Publishers, 1998).
- I have taken the reader into my workroom with two new case histories. One weaves itself through the book, demonstrating how I work with voice. The other, in Chapter 12, shows how an essay can be written in small fragments of time.

PEDAGOGICAL FEATURES

Instructors and students will find the same useful pedagogical features as in the previous edition: writing using a daybook, writing with voice, writers' quotations, end-of-chapter questions and answers, and end-of-chapter activities. We have also continued the index, "Help for Your Writing Problems," on the inside front cover as well as a reference list of "Writing Techniques" placed on the inside back cover.

THE INSTRUCTOR'S MANUAL

I write the instructor's manual to help teachers with the practical problems of the classroom. It is based on my own experience as a teacher and on the experiences of instructors who have used *Write to Learn* in many different types of institutions and courses, with students at varying levels of accomplishment. It is specific, practical, and designed to help both beginning and experienced instructors in realistic teaching situations. This manual can be obtained by contacting your local Harcourt College sales representative.

───────── **ACKNOWLEDGMENTS** ─────────

I write each morning by myself but I am never alone. I am part of a writing community that inspires and supports me. Minnie Mae, who started mailing out the manuscripts that I was burning when we were first married, is my first reader and constant supporter.

Laurie Runion has again been involved in the conceptual development of this edition, as well as its chapter-by-chapter, page-by-page, paragraph-by-paragraph, sentence-by-sentence, word-by-word execution. She has suggested, commanded, demonstrated, supported, and corrected with perception, wisdom, and good humor. It is her book as much as it is mine and it is a joy for me to be allowed to collaborate with her.

I am still indebted to the questions and activities contributed by Mary Hallet, now assistant professor of English at Southeastern Massachusetts University.

Christopher Scanlan of the Poynter Institute in St. Petersburg, Florida; Donald Graves in Jackson, New Hampshire; Brock Dethier of Utah State University in Logan, Utah; Thomas Romano of the University of Miami in Oxford, Ohio; Elizabeth Cooke of the University of Maine at Farmington; Michael Steinberg of Michigan State University in East Lansing, Michigan; Lisa Miller of the University of New Hampshire and writer Ralph Fletcher of Durham, New Hampshire are as close as the telephone, e-mail, and fax. They always share, respond, listen, laugh, and understand.

The other members of my private writing community who appear behind my computer screen each writing morning, shaking their heads no and yes, smiling or frowning, include Driek Zirinsky of Boise State University, Bonnie Sunstein of the University of Iowa, Elizabeth Chiseri-Strater of the University of North Carolina at Greensboro, and Lad Tobin of Boston College.

I have been given wise counsel by those who reviewed the sixth edition and made valuable suggestions for the seventh, as well as those who have reviewed past editions: Ida Ferdman, Glendale Community College; Ray Moye, Coastal Carolina University; Lance Svehla, University of Akron; Larry Burton, University South Alabama; Sherie Coelho, Antelope Valley College; Bobbie R. Coleman, Moorpark College; Eileen Donovan-Kranz, Boston College; Marion Hogan Larson, Bethel College; Joan Spangler, California State University—Fullerton; Gil Tierney, William Rainey Harper College; and Karen Uehling, Boise State University.

I would also like to thank Carmen Sarkissian for her charming essay on becoming a writer and her instructor, Ida Ferdman at Glendale Community College, for sharing it with me.

I owe special thanks to the staff at Harcourt College Publishers: Michael Rosenberg, former Executive Editor for English; Julie McBurney, former Acquisitions Editor for English; Laurie Runion, Developmental Editor; Elaine Hellmund, Project Manager; John Meyers, former Market Strategist for English and now Acquisitions Editor; Nancy Marcus Land and the staff at Publications Development Company; and Steven Baker, copyeditor.

CONTENTS

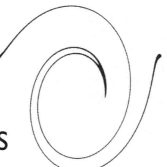

CHAPTER 3
FOCUS   57

....

CHAPTER 4
SHOPTALK: THE RESEARCH PLAN   9 1

....

CHAPTER 5
RESEARCH   97

....

CHAPTER 6
DRAFT   1 20

....

CHAPTER 7
SHOPTALK: PREPARING TO
REVISE AND EDIT   170

....

CHAPTER 8
SHOPTALK: HELPING EACH OTHER   176

....

CHAPTER 9
REVISE AND EDIT   184

....

CHAPTER 10
FIT YOUR PROCESS TO YOUR TASK   219

CHAPTER 11
LEARNING FROM WRITERS   242

AFTERWORD   315

INDEX   316

Other Books by Donald M. Murray

The Craft of Revision, Fourth Edition (Harcourt College Publishers, 2001)

My Twice-Lived Life: A Memoir (Ballentine, 2001)

Writing to Deadline—The Journalist at Work (Heinemann, 2000)

Crafting a Life in Essay, Story, Poem (Heinemann, 1996)

Read to Write, Third Edition (Harcourt College Publishers, 1993)

Shoptalk: Learning to Write with Writers (Heinemann, Boynton/Cook, 1990)

Expecting the Unexpected (Heinemann, Boynton/Cook, 1989)

Learning by Teaching, Second Edition (Heinemann, Boynton/Cook, 1989)

CHAPTER 1

MAKE WRITING EASY

Let's write together.

Write what?

I don't know. I don't need to know what I am going to write and neither do you. Writing produces writing.

I have come to appreciate the terror and emptiness I used to fear when I faced the blank screen and the insistent demand of the blinking cursor. Not knowing what I will write, or even if I can write, means I will not write what I have written before. I have begun a voyage of *discovery.* The initial satisfaction from writing is *surprise:* we say what we do not expect to say in a way we do not expect to say it.

Surprise is also essential when I do come to my desk with a writing assignment. I know the topic but not how I will approach it or what I will learn from the assignment. After sixty years of publishing, I am still an apprentice to the writer's craft, taking instruction from each morning's draft, the experiments in meaning writers use to discover what to say and how to say it. As Eudora Welty wrote, "The writer himself studies intensely how to do it while he is in the thick of doing it; then when the particular novel or story is done, he is likely to forget how; he does well to. Each work is new. Mercifully, the question of how abides less in the abstract, and less in the past, than in the specific, in the work at hand. . . ."

All writers are self-taught. Your instructor can help, your classmates can help, this book can help, but you still have to write to learn to write. As you read this book, stop the moment you feel like writing and write. This book should be a collaborative experience as we write together. If you write as you read, you will better understand what I am saying—and you will have the satisfaction and fun of discovering what you did not know about your life.

This morning, for example, I came to my desk to finish this chapter and just started to read through what I thought was the final draft, but after reading the first three words, the next two surprised me and I was off, writing what I did not intend.

· 1 ·

I sit back and let my mind drift. This is not the time for hard thinking, for concentration, for purpose, but the time for reflection, for patience, for accident. I remember what the poet William Stafford wrote:

> ". . . . one should lower his standards until there is no felt threshold to go over in writing. It's easy to write. You just shouldn't have standards that inhibit you from writing . . . . I can imagine a person beginning to feel he's not able to write up to that standard he imagines the world has set for him. But to me that's surrealistic. The only standard I can rationally have is the standard I'm meeting right now. . . . You should be more willing to forgive yourself. It doesn't make any difference if you are good or bad today. The assessment of the product is something that happens after you've done it."

I have presumed to write books to tell others how to write, but I have to remember that I must be willing to write badly to write well, that what I accomplished yesterday may be of no help today.

You mean you haven't learn to write and you write books on how to write? Yes, and I flunked out of high school and became a professor, was a fearful kid and was in combat as a paratrooper, said I'd never get married and have been married twice, never imagined I'd be a parent and am now a grandfather. Life is always unexpected and writing should be as well.

School emphasizes straight-line thinking, but writers and artists, scientists and marketing managers also practice a circular, drifty kind of associative thinking that connects what the logical mind would never connect. In beginning to write, I have to remind myself not to think too hard but relax, listen to what drifts through my mind.

Sometimes a stimulus—a sound, a smell, something I see—stirs memories. I see moonlight open up into the woods behind my house and remember how much we hated moonlight in the Battle of the Bulge in World War II when what would be a lovely night in peacetime exposed us as we tried to hide from the enemy. I hear an oboe being played on the radio and imagine it is my long dead daughter practicing her oboe in the next room. I smell the pine Christmas tree and travel in memory to summer camp years before.

If those connections interest you, if they seem to hold a mystery, a problem, a question, then write—but the topic does not have to be that clear. I particularly delight in the connections without immediate explanation. I sit back, try to make my mind blank when I remember a newspaper story I read the night before about the possibility of restoring passenger rail service through our town. The phrase "train to college" drifts into mind.

Try it. It is impossible to have a blank mind. Something will drift out of your memory or experience, something you see or hear, smell or touch or taste will come into your head. The important thing is not to strain at it but remain in a drifty, dreamy state, making notes on what appears on the stage in the theater of your mind.

Now let's stop talking about writing and write together. As Gertrude Stein said, "Any time is the time to write a poem." And I'd add, anything else. Let's get writing.

> Train to college ... doesn't run anymore ... north station ... boston bruins ... montreal train ... prep school kids ... how they dressed, talked ... moved ... walk up hill ... suitcase ... tie Windsor knot ... escape ... map on ceiling ... football ... high school flunk out ... away from home at last ... homesickness at home ... no away ... sickness ... trip to beg for father's pay ... war on ... roommate ... fist fight ... navaho blanket ... editor newspaper ... Mort Howell ... my second good teacher ... "you seemed to know how the world worked" ... draft notice ... no designer jeans ... designer person ... made myself up ... and didn't ... became what I was ... clipped on kick-off ... knee still hurts ... mort howell gives me papers ... Christian Science Monitor editorial ... you'll be a writer.

Try it. Don't worry about spelling, grammar, mechanics, rhetoric—not yet. And don't worry about revealing yourself. No one will see what you've written—not yet.

Next I look for the fragment in the freewriting I just did that surprised me or caught my interest at the moment. "My second good teacher" reminded me of my first good teacher in the sixth grade and my third good teacher in college after World War II, and that made me realize that three good teachers were enough. That leads me to want to figure out what made these three teachers good for me.

I hope you are moving between your draft and my page, moving back and forth, often discovering something unexpected, interesting, surprising, confounding, curious that may be worth exploring in writing. People—many teachers included—make writing a big deal. It is, on many levels, a very complex intellectual issue, the way designing a new downtown hotel, office, and shopping plaza can be for an architect. But I'm just a worker, a carpenter of prose, and my job is obvious and easy. I will start with my first good teacher and work my way to my third and I will start with description, making myself re-see (and eventually my reader see) that first teacher. In writing a specific description I often find revealing details appear that will lead toward meaning.

Where do I start? In the beginning.

> When I walked into my sixth grade classroom in September ...

> *What do I say next? It is obvious. What did I see that surprised me?*

> ... I saw a young man with glasses standing at the front of the room.

> *Now I am back in that classroom and my writer's memory has locked in. I started thinking what I would have thought when I was twelve years old.*

He must be a new principal. The only men in the Massachusetts Fields School were the principal or the janitor and this man wore a brown suit.

> *I am surprised I remember his brown suit.*
>
> *How do I write? Line by line. I am in a conversation with the reader. What does the reader want to know? What was a man doing in the classroom? I tell them. No mystery. The sentence written usually tells me the sentence that must be written next.*

"Good morning. I am Mr. Hamilton, your new teacher."

> *Now the reader needs to know why he was one of my best teachers. I have no choice. I can't go off and write about getting glasses that year or beating up Walter Almeda whose father played for the Red Sox, or paying a bribe to get a paper route and then having to fight a grown man who had paid the same bribe or what it was like to live during the Great Depression. I used to write like a puppy, running after every new scent but now the evolving draft tells me what I have to write next.*

The first thing that surprised me was that Mr. Hamilton let us know him as a person. He was married to a teacher and he talked about her. He was young and we didn't seem to learn from him as much as learn with him. His enthusiasm about learning was contagious and he was tough.

He demanded more of me than any teacher had before but he somehow communicated to me that he saw in me what no one else had seen, not at home, church, or school. He shared my secret ambition that I would be successful, possibly even be a published writer—if I worked hard—and I did work hard for him.

> *It is time for me to move on to the next teacher who made a difference in my life.*
>
> *It was six years later and grade 13, my first year of college, before I met another teacher, Mort Howell, who connected with me. I realize the reader is going to say, "What? There were no good teachers from grade seven through twelve?" and I have to ask the question the reader asks when the reader asks it. If I don't hear the reader's questions I get someone to read my draft and ask them what questions they would ask and where would they answer them. What do they need to know that I haven't told them?*

Of course there were other good teachers. North Quincy Junior and Senior High Schools had a good reputation, but the teachers I had didn't make a difference to me. Classes were large in the Great Depression of the 1930's, 45 to 60 in a classroom, and if you didn't learn the way the teacher taught, too bad. I was an A/F student doing well in the courses I liked, poorly in the ones that bored me. I didn't know I was bored. I thought I was stupid. But that didn't bother me.

I had good jobs for a teenager outside of school and I thought hard work would do it for me. And the future showed I was right in part. Hard work works.

> *I worry that I have gone off on a tangent, but to reveal my good teachers, I have to expose their challenge.*

I dropped out of school in the spring of my tenth grade, did it again next year, and in my senior year when I never went to school on Thursday but went to Boston to attend the 10 AM and noon shows of the big bands at the RKO in Boston.

> *Now I have to get myself to college and that is a story I have told many times. I don't want to get into it here but the reader will wonder how a high school dropout got to college. I'll plunge on, trying be as brief as possible, realizing I may have to do some cutting in this section but I can't cut until I know the length of the essay and can judge how much the reader needs to know against how long the reader will be patient and stick with me through the explanation.*

And then I stop. I have made the mistake my students make. Whether experienced or beginning writers, we have to keep learning. I decided to write about three good teachers in a 700 to 800 word essay. To do that I have to get from teacher to teacher and I'll have no space to reveal the teacher and show what a teacher can do to change a student's life. The experienced writer is always seeking limits.

Writers write less so they can write more. Instead of writing the story of the entire game, political campaign, courtship, scientific experiment, they focus on the critical moment and reveal it in great detail. If I am going to write about Mort Howell, the Freshman English teacher who changed my life, I will have to set up the scene when he works with me as adviser to the school newspaper.

> Mr. Howell came out from behind his desk and sat beside me in the empty classroom. We were colleagues, not teacher and student as we read the lead editorial I had written. He did not lecture me on the writer's craft, we read what I had thought was a final draft together, pausing to consider and reconsider each paragraph, sentence, word, working back and forth, cutting, adding, reordering, making a comma a semicolon, then a period as a long sentence became two sentences—for emphasis.
>
> There was always a reason for each change and if I didn't see it, I could ask him and he would bounce the question back to me, listen to my answer, modify it, agree with it or give his own answer.
>
> We read aloud, listening to the music of each line. We stood back and considered the line of logic that ran through each editorial. We played the role of reader to see if the meaning was clear and we read it as the subject to see if we were fair.

We sat side by side at the workbench practicing the craft I was to dedicate myself to for the rest of my life. Writing about this fifty-eight years later I am there and Mort Howell is here, still at my side as I write and rewrite these sentences. He never lived to see a computer, but I am not practicing electronics on my Dell, I am practicing the craft of writing he demonstrated hour after patient hour at my side.

——————— THE WRITER'S MEMORY ———————

The writer's memory is a powerful telescope to the past. I do not have a good memory in the quiz show sense and as I age I have increasing trouble with names. When I write, however, the flow of language takes me back and I remember what I did not know I knew.

I remembered Mort Howell who became a friend after the war and who gave me my own Freshman English papers when I started to teach the course at the age of thirty-nine! I did not remember the editing sessions that have been the center of my professional life until I started writing about his classroom and how he came out from behind his desk and sat with me when we worked together on the school paper.

You already have the concerns—the obsessions, fears, pleasures—that will color your life and your writing. As Willa Cather so wisely said, "Most of the basic material a writer works with is acquired before the age of fifteen." I remember trying to write words with a stick in the dirt before I could read. I have had a lifelong fascination with stories. My grandmother with whom my family lived and who really brought me up had a "shock" (a stroke) and was paralyzed when I was a child. I helped care for her and have been interested in chronic disease. I was a medical writer at one time, and the process of aging is often the topic of my weekly column in the *Boston Globe* today. My family was an unhappy one and I am still trying to figure out why. After experiencing war, I am still trying to comprehend what is within us that makes war possible. I was a bad student and thought my teachers could do a better job of teaching so I write books on teaching. Those are my writing territories in which most of my writing has grown: the writing and teaching process, sickness and aging, my family and my war.

Look within yourself by writing down what you think about when you are not thinking, what you notice out of the corner of your eye, what interests you, and then start writing about one of those subjects. Writing allows writers to stand back from personal experience the way an artist stands back from a painting and see their lives more clearly, and it is a tool for reflection. The great British poet William Wordsworth talked about "emotion recollected in tranquility," the need to reflect on incidents in life and discover their meaning by writing about them. Memory provides us with a perpetual double vision, the past illuminated by the present, the present illuminated by the past. The past adds texture and significance to the moment and the moment puts the past in a new perspective.

I recently had to call 911 for medical help for my wife and that made me go back and explore in writing the first time I had to call for medical help.

> Grandmother has fallen. It is the house on Vassall Street in Wollaston, Massachusetts. She is on the dining room floor. I see the Oriental rug, the sideboard, the china closet in which I saw my face in the house on Grand View Avenue. I help grandmother up into a dining room chair. Her right arm has a huge, round rising lump turning red. She does not cry. She would never cry but her face is fierce, her mouth set. I am six, maybe seven, wearing corduroy knickers. I know grandmother cannot hold the ear piece of the old fashion telephone with her left hand and dial with her swollen right arm. I go to the phone and ask the operator for Dr. Bartlett and I tell him what happens and he is on his way and I know I have been a good boy.

But as always, I can only write a small fragment of what I see: the door to the kitchen and the pantry where I spilled the huge crock of hot grape jelly, the window and the branches of the apple tree where I learned to climb, the dining room table whose underside I knew so well because I studied its construction while Grandma, Mother, and Uncle Will force open my mouth as I lay on the floor and gag at the hated oatmeal, thick skinned, gluey, cold, being forced into my mouth.

Each memory breeds other memories, long chains of memories that connect and branch off. The British novelist Graham Greene said, "When I construct a scene, I don't describe the hundredth part of what I see; I see the characters scratching their noses, walking about, tilting back in their chairs—even after I've finished writing—so much so that after a while I feel a weariness which does not derive all that much from my effort of imagination but is more like a visual fatigue: My eyes are tired from watching my characters."

And if I write the physical description it will reveal my feelings and my thoughts. My pride at calling the doctor, the terror I felt and the punishment I received from tipping over the hot jelly, the achievement of climbing the tree and what I saw when I spied on the second floor of my home, and the stubborn anger I felt at having the now cold hot oatmeal shoved into my gagging throat.

Of course the remembered experience is textured by all that I have done and felt and thought since.

I become the boy in the back of the classroom who will drop out of high school before the year is out, but now I am not only him, but a teacher who saw himself bored in his classroom. The memory is more complex than the original experience. I am the child who doesn't want to go to bed, the parent who had to make a daughter go to bed, the grandfather who sees himself in his daughter and in his reluctant granddaughter.

Memories also arrive at the most unexpected and often inappropriate times, delivered by each of my senses. My fingers touch a seersucker jacket and I am dressed in a sailor suit I haven't worn since I was five years old. I smell second-hand smoke and become the four-pack-a-day smoker I was as a teenager. I hear a door slam and jump at a bullet from a German sniper. I taste the delightfully bland tastelessness of mashed potatoes and am seated at the kitchen table in my Scots Yankee home.

THE WRITER'S VOICE

Voice is a mystery to beginning writers—and many English teachers. Voice may also be the most important element in writing, the one that seduces the reader, makes the reader trust the writer, makes the reader feel an individual relationship with the writer, forces the reader to turn the page.

The experienced writer may occasionally hear the voice of a piece *before* the draft is written. If that happens, it occurs in a fragment of language that launches a draft. I hear myself say, for no reason I understand, "the melancholy of a sunny day" and hear something that is akin to music. I know this is a personal essay, the way a musician hears a few notes and knows it is the blues, rock, folk, classical, a song, a symphony, rap.

So what did I hear? I hear the particular sound of the word "melancholy" which is a different sound than "sadness" or "unhappiness" or "the fear in" or "apprehension." All of those words could combine with "a sunny day" and make an essay, short story, a poem, a song for someone else, but the music in "the melancholy of a sunny day" is the voice I hear and I must follow the voice.

What else did I hear? I hear the surprise or tension or interaction that comes from the collision of the words "melancholy" and "sunny." The relationship is unexpected. It gives off sparks. The voice of the essay will come clear and strong as I write a draft. The voice arises from the writing. I listen as I write, hearing the writing in my ear before I see the writing on the screen. I tune the writing while I draft. In the voice sections of the chapters ahead this essay will evolve and I will point out the elements of voice as they appear. For now I hear the voice of that line "the melancholy of a sunny day" and that is enough for me.

THE WRITER'S DAYBOOK

My daybook is essential to easy writing. I don't know where I *first* heard the term daybook, but a number of years ago I found myself using the term and writing every day—well, almost every day—in a ten-by-eight spiral notebook filled with greenish, narrow-ruled paper, with a margin line down the left. This worked for me. I write on my lap, in the living room or on the porch, in the car or an airplane, during meetings, in bed, or sitting on a rock wall while resting during a walk. A bound book doesn't work for me. I find a spiral book convenient and easy to handle; and since I write in all sorts of light, indoors and out, I find the greenish paper comfortable. I chose the size because it fits in the outside pocket of the bag I carry everywhere. I tried to keep a journal, imagining I was Gide or Camus. But I wasn't either of those writers or anyone else famous. I was only myself, and what I wrote to imitate others was pompous, full of hot air, hilarious to read, and utterly useless to me as a writer. At other times I tried to keep a diary, but then I found myself recording only trivia—the temperature, or whom I met, or what I ate.

A few years ago, two composition researchers examined my daybooks. They were surprised to find no signs of struggle. I was not. I'm not fighting writing, I'm playing with writing. If it isn't fun, if nothing is happening, I stop and wait until the magic begins. The daybook also keeps my writing muscles in condition; it lets me know what I'm concerned with making into writing; it increases my productivity.

The organization is simply a day-by-day chronology. When I change the subject I write a code word—"novel," "poem," "talk at St. Anselm's," "children's book?"—in the left-hand margin. That way I can look back through the book and collect all the notes I've made on a single project or concern.

How I use my daybook varies from time to time. Since I now do most of my writing using a computer, my daybooks have pages or paragraphs I have printed out and pasted in so I can read, reconsider, and play with the writing during spare moments. All the writing in the daybook is a form of talking to myself, a way of thinking on paper. Much of my "spontaneous" writing can be tracked through years of daybooks in which I have thought and rethought, planned and researched, drafted and redrafted its movement from interesting fragment to possible draft. Here are some of the items you might see in my daybook:

- Questions that need to be answered
- Fragments of writing seeking a voice
- Leads, hundreds of leads, the beginning lines of what I may write
- Titles, hundred of titles
- Notes from which I have made lectures, talks, or speeches
- Notes I have made at lectures, talks, or speeches of others; also notes I have made at poetry readings, hockey games, and concerts
- Outlines

- Ideas for stories, articles, poems, books, papers
- Diagrams showing how a piece might be organized or, more likely, showing the relationships between parts of an idea
- Drafts
- A running commentary on my writing techniques, habits, problems and solutions
- Observations
- Quotations from writers or artists
- Newspaper clippings
- Titles of books to be read
- Notes on what I have read
- Pictures I want to save
- Writing schedules
- Pasted-in copies of interesting letters I've received or written
- Lists, lots of lists
- Pasted-in handouts I've developed for classes or workshops

I don't use the daybook in any single way. Anything that will stimulate or record my thinking, anything that will move toward writing goes into the daybook. When a notebook is filled—I am on number 110 at this writing—I go through it and harvest a page or two or three of the most interesting material for the beginning of the next daybook. When I'm ready to work seriously on a project, I go back through past daybooks and photocopy pages that relate to the subject I'm working on.

Make your daybook your own. Don't try to follow anyone else's formula. And don't write it for another audience. It's a private place where you can think and where you can be dumb, stupid, sloppy, silly; where you can do all the bad writing and bad thinking essential for those moments of insight that produce good writing.

Your daybook might not—should not—be like mine. It may be a file stored in a computer where I have a folder called DAYBOOK. The poet Mekeel McBride's daybook is a bound sketch pad in which she draws and paints as well as writes. I envy her and have tried to imitate her, but it doesn't work for me. I know other writers who use file cards, tiny pocket notebooks, huge accounting ledgers, scraps of paper stuck in file folders in a drawer, a paper compost heap that flows from desk to floor. And some writers keep only mental daybooks in which they make notes of the world and rehearse the writing they intend to do, trying out one approach and then another in their minds. There is no one way and no correct way to write well; there are many ways and it is your job to find what works for you and be ready to switch when it stops helping you write well.

IN THE WRITER'S WORKSHOP

When I was in ninth grade I accidentally found a book in the library that talked about the writer's life. I started writing down some of the quotations, then found another book on writing by another writer, then another. The writers did NOT say what my English teachers who were good critical readers of finished writing said about writing; the writers talked about the experience of making. I took down more quotations, then still more, and I have not stopped yet. Just this week I read an interview in *The New Yorker* on line (www.newyorker.com) with Alice Munro, who I think is the best short story writer publishing today, and I saved this:

> The first draft . . . I write may be quite sketchy and inadequate and banal—things about the people, about how they sounded or things they said or how they looked—and I'll know that isn't right, but I just go on, and then I get to know them, and I start getting to know them better just by something they say. I don't generally have this thing that these people come alive and dictate to me—I've never had quite that experience. But they do say something sometimes that I didn't expect, or they do something, or something happens that I didn't know was going to happen. But this generally comes to me the day that I'm writing it, I didn't know it when I planned the story.

I've just started a novel and feel my characters are one dimensional and don't know what to do about it. Alice Munro comforts, instructs, and inspires me. This book is based on a lifelong study of what writers say about their craft. In the Writer's Workshop you will enter into the conversation of craft I have with writers living and dead. And I hope you will find more quotations by writers and copy them into your notebook, laptop, or paste them into this text. Writing is not a mystery; it is a craft that can be learned and shared. You can learn with and from the best writers of today and yesterday.

> *When you first start writing—and I think it's true for a lot of beginning writers—you're scared to death that if you don't get that sentence right that minute it's never going to show up again. And it isn't. But it doesn't matter—another one will, and it'll probably be better. . . . I write out of ignorance. I write about the things I don't have any resolutions for, and when I'm finished, I think I know a little bit more about it. I don't write out of what I know. It's what I don't know that stimulates me. I merely know enough to get started.* TONI MORRISON

> *. . . one should lower his standards until there is no felt threshold to go over in writing. It's easy to write. You just shouldn't have standards that inhibit you from writing.* WILLIAM STAFFORD

> *It's like being on a high board, looking down to a cold, chilly pool. Then I give myself a little push. The water isn't as cold as I thought.* NEIL SIMON

Planning to write is not writing. Outlining . . . researching . . . talking to people about what you're doing, none of that is writing. Writing is writing. E. L. DOCTOROW

How do I know what I think until I see what I say? E. M. FORSTER

The first draft of anything is shit. ERNEST HEMINGWAY

In a very real sense, the writer writes in order to teach himself, to understand himself. ALFRED KAZIN

The beautiful part of writing is that you don't have to get it right the first time, unlike, say, a brain surgeon. You can always do it better, find the exact word, the apt phrase, the leaping simile. ROBERT CORMIER

To me, the greatest pleasure of writing is not what it's about, but the music the words make. TRUMAN CAPOTE

There's a common notion that self-discipline is a freakish peculiarity of writers—that writers differ from other people by possessing enormous and equal portions of talent and willpower. They grit their powerful teeth and go into their little rooms. I think that's a bad misunderstanding of what impels the writer. What impels the writer is a deep love for and respect for language, for literary forms, for books. It's a privilege to muck about in sentences all morning. It's a challenge to bring off a powerful effect. You don't do it from willpower; you do it from an abiding passion for the field. I'm sure it's the same in every other field.

Writing a book is like rearing children—willpower has very little to do with it. If you have a little baby crying in the middle of the night, and if you depend only on willpower to get you out of bed to feed the baby, that baby will starve. You do it out of love. Willpower is a weak idea; love is strong. You don't have to scrouge yourself with cat-o'-nine-tails to go to the baby. You got to the baby out of love for that particular baby. That's the same way you go to your desk. There's nothing freakish about it. Caring passionately about something isn't against nature, and it isn't against human nature. It's what we're here to do. ANNIE DILLARD

——— QUESTIONS ABOUT WRITING ———

I just wrote what came into my head and it looks like squashed bugs, run over skunk, and upchuck.

Ah, you think like a writer. I've often felt the same way. Those are good, strong images. If you can write like that you'll be able to write vigorous, interesting writing.

What I do with a discovery draft that doesn't seem to discover anything is to hold my nose and look for anything that surprised me, that I didn't think I would say. It may be a line, a word, an image, or just an attitude toward something, a feeling that may point to a topic you should explore. The hint of what you may have to write may also come from your tone of voice, the music you hear feebly rising from the ick as you read it out loud.

And you may have to start over, but I find that most upchuck drafts contain something that runs against what I have believed, thought, or felt, something that I need to think about—by writing.

I keep writing the same thing. I don't mean just the subject, but the same attitude toward the topic. It is borrrrring. Does this happen to you, and if it does, what do you do about it?

It does and I have some tricks to jar me out of the rut.

A. I change the point of view. If I've been writing about my grandson, I turn around and write from his point of view. How does he see the visiting giant with the white beard? I do this with ideas. I'm against capital punishment. What are the arguments for it? The story of a crime, for example, can be told from the point of view of the victim, the arresting officer, the officer who failed to arrest the perpetrator, the criminal, the EMT, an onlooker, the prosecuting and defense attorneys.

B. I move back in time or ahead to put the topic in a different historical perspective.

C. If the story is long, I write it short, which causes me to dig more deeply into it. If it is short, I write it long, which causes me to extend myself into an area of new knowledge.

D. I try a different voice, sounding angry, sad, amused, nostalgic, frustrated, doubting, believing, naïve, experienced.

Do writing tools make a difference in finding a subject to explore?

They sure do. The dip pen, the fountain pen, the typewriter, the dictating machine, the computer, and now the voice-activated computer all make it easier to write, to record the flow of information and language. Ease is important. If you have to focus your attention on getting each word down you will not develop the momentum that will carry you from what you know to what you may know that you don't know you know until it appears on the screen.

Does reading help in finding something to write about?

Of course. There is a whole genre of critical essays and reviews of books, but more than that reading allows you to find subjects that interest you and shows you how different writers view the same subject. My good writing friend Chip Scanlan will copy pages of another person's writing to better hear the writer's voice, to discover how that writer paces the text, how details are introduced, how language is used.

It is plagiarism if you put your own name on it, but good artistic practice to use imitation as a form of instruction. Most museums have many students making copies of great works, and musicians will study other performances by imitating them.

Someone has said that writing is a visual art. How can I improve my seeing?

I'm one of those someones. Seeing will improve your writing—and writing will improve your seeing.

I increased my ability to see by listing hundreds—thousands—of specific details. I made myself consciously see, looking for details that relieved how people's actions betrayed their words, revealed false fear, documented bravery in the face of limitations, exposed a conflict between people.

I not only looked for what was done, but what was not done. The unsaid often tells more than the said. I watched the world out of the corner of my eye, aware and alert to all that entered the increasing range of my vision. And the more revealing specifics I saw and used them in writing, the more I saw.

There's one big side benefit to the relationship of seeing and writing: I am rarely bored. Waiting in the doctor's office, ticket line, in the parking lot, air terminal, I concentrate on seeing. I watch how people walk, how they treat each other.

I'm not especially happy about it, but I seem to live life on the sidelines. I don't star on any team or get elected president of anything. Since I'm not on the inside with any group, how can I find something to write about?

Writers live on the sidelines. When others bustle about—busy, busy, busy—writers observe and reflect. Writers connect. Writers record and celebrate and analyze and explain.

I'm an engineering student, not one of those artsy people. Why do I have to write?

A study a few years ago revealed that engineering graduates wrote more than any other group of students. We live in a small world connected electronically. Writing isn't just novels and poems, writing is memos and proposals and reports and plans and agreements. Information is power and the people who can communicate information clearly and accurately will exert that power.

I have good ideas but they run down and I have nothing to say. Anything I can do?

Of course you can try another idea but if this is happening regularly I suggest you just force yourself to keep writing. That is what I do. When I can't think of what to say next, I realize I am thinking ahead of the writing. Writing is thinking and if I keep writing new ideas, new questions, interesting problems appear in what I am saying.

I have always been told I have to have a firm thesis statement before I can begin to write. Is that true?

No. In fact, writing a thesis statement first can produce bad writing, writing in which there is no discovery. There are times when it may be necessary to write from a firm conclusory statement, but I can't remember when I have had to do that. The thesis statement has been taught in traditional English classes because teachers who are not writers have been taught it is important. And writing a good thesis statement AFTER you have finished writing can be a challenging and productive intellectual exercise.

We write not to say what we know, but to learn, to discover, to know. Writing is thinking, exploring, finding out. The thesis statement imprisons the writer in previous thought.

Be honest, isn't writing just hard work?

It sure can be. The famous sports writer Red Smith said, "There's nothing to writing. All you do is sit down at the typewriter and open a vein."

But it doesn't have to be. I used to make writing hard, thinking it was virtuous, that writing should be a struggle. I bragged about how hard I worked and so did the other writers I knew. But they had all chosen a life of writing because it was easier than math or languages or science and, most of all, because it was fun. I became bored with their moaning—and with my own.

I studied what I did when the writing did come easily and then followed those methods to make it easy for me to write so that my writing would be easy for my readers to read.

Writing Activities

1. Take a regular or video camera and use it to focus at the familiar world around you—perhaps your room, a courtyard, a small piece of countryside, a

street corner. Zoom in close, move back to a distance shot, then zoom in close again. Write down the things you noticed that you hadn't seen before: the many colors in "ordinary" brick or a tree's bark, the pattern of roofs or windows, the casual way a seagull rose on an invisible wave of air, the wobbly step of a young teenager wearing grown-up shoes, how the fur of a frightened dog rose when someone approached.

2. Use a different sense—hearing, smell, taste, touch—to describe a place or person important to you. You will not only increase your sense awareness—and use other sense than visual when you write—you will stimulate your awareness in every sense.

3. Pick a news story—a basketball game, an election, a shooting—and put yourself in the story, telling it from your point of view to see how point of view can give you new ways to look at the world.

4. Go to an art museum and study the paintings, drawings, photographs, sculptures to see how the artist saw and revealed the word. What line, touch of color, shadow, or shape revealed the character of the person portrayed? Students at Cornell Medical School take part in a program at the Frick Museum that increases their powers of observation by careful study of works of art.

Imagine how Rembrandt, Munch, Degas, or other great artists would look at your world and you may see something to write—and a way of writing it. I recently visited an exhibition of portraits by Alice Neel, a powerful American painter, and learned a great deal about art, vision, the people she painted—and about writing. I again realized the importance of the dominant impression in writing, giving priority to the revealing detail.

5. Take a sketchbook or some art paper and draw a familiar place or location. You don't have to be good at art, but the discipline of trying to catch line, form, color will sharpen your visual skills for writing.

6. Writers, with their particular vision of the world, make me look at my world so that I see something to write about where I had seen nothing before. Become your favorite writer—I might choose Alice Munro or Sharon Olds—and tell your story in the writer's voice, using the way the writer looked at the world, what the writer saw, how it was seen, how it was revealed.

7. We live in a movie/TV age. Turn yourself into a screenwriter for a day and look for dramatic scenes in your life, places of conflict, change, resolution. Seeing the screen story you will discover a subject. Remember that movies and TV shows are written and it is the quality of the writing as much as the acting, direction, or photography that makes a fine drama.

8. Interview a family member, neighbor, friend to find out the turning points in their lives or what they have learned from life experiences. Interview me about my experiences in combat in World War II and you might find that I

wanted to go into battle with cowards, not heroes. By exploring what I mean you may realize you have a story to tell from your own life.

9. List the most important events or people in your life, then see how they connect, what the relationship is between, say, learning to swim and teaching handicapped children to swim and becoming an education major. The best writing comes when two events or people or ideas collide, sparking a story or essay.

10. Team up with a classmate and visit a familiar spot—the library, a hangout, a game, a coffeehouse, and point out to each other what you see and what it reveals. You won't see the same things the same and in the difference there may be a subject. As Sandra Cisneros said, "Imagine yourself at your kitchen table, in your pajamas. Imagine one person you'd allow to see you that way, and write in the voice you'd use to that friend. Write about what makes you different."

CHAPTER 2

UNLEARNING TO WRITE

Those mornings when I sit at my desk and no words come, when the draft staggers and stumbles to a halt, or I read what I have written with shame and disgust and punch "Delete," I often find I have been following the rules of the high school teacher I had in the eleventh and twelfth grade.

They were the rules I had been taught in elementary school, junior high school, and the first two years in high school, retaught and made absolute. When I wrote outside of class I often broke the rules or simply ignored them, but they sounded so certain, so logical, so authoritative—pun intended—that years later, like a forest fire that travels underground and suddenly bursts out unexpectedly, I find I am following one or more of them. I have to stop and once more unlearn the rules.

My teachers were well intentioned but they were readers who did not write themselves. They looked at published writing and imagined how it was made. These rules were often logical but wrong in practice. In my first book on writing I said their way of deciding how writers wrote was like trying to imagine a pig from sausage.

In this chapter you will be introduced to a process that published writers use to write and that you will be able to adjust to your way of thinking, your experience with writing, and to the writing task itself. But first you—and I—have to unlearn to write.

It might be fun for you to stop right now and write down the absolute rules you have been taught about writing to see if they match what I was taught and had to unlearn.

———— WHAT I HAD TO UNLEARN ————

I. KNOW WHAT YOU WANT TO SAY BEFORE YOU SAY IT

When I wrote in school the teacher would march up and down the aisles repeating, "Know what you want to say before you say it." Most of the time she would require that we write a thesis statement at the top of the page, telling what the writing we hadn't yet done would say.

Writers are writers, however, because the act of writing is a voyage into the unknown, an adventure in discovering what you know that you didn't know you knew, what connects in ways you haven't connected what you know before, what you need to know.

Once in a while I do know what I am going to say or have an assignment that limits discovery. In those cases I have to *unknow* to find my own way to the predicted meaning. The best writing is traitor to intent. It grows, line by line, from a terrifying emptiness when there is no purpose, no topic, no clear meaning. Writers write and discover what they have to say from the evolving drafts. It is the writing, not the writer that speaks. Novelist and short story writer Donald Barthelme explains:

> Writing is a process of dealing with not-knowing, a forcing of what and how. We have all heard novelists testify to the fact that, beginning a new book, they are utterly baffled as to how to proceed, what should be written and how it might be written, even though they've done a dozen. At best there's a slender intuition, not much greater than an itch. Art is not difficult because it wishes to be difficult, rather because it wishes to be art. However much the writer might long to be, in his work, simple, honest, straightforward, these virtues are no longer available to him. He discovers that in being simple, honest, straightforward, nothing much happens: he speaks the speakable, whereas we are looking for the as-yet unspeakable, the as-yet unspoken.

People ask, "Where do you get your ideas?" I answer, "I don't have ideas." I am terrified of ideas. I may have a shard of ancient Indian pottery, a fragment of bone that may be dog or dinosaur, a burr under the saddle, an answer that has not yet met its question, a contradiction to a certain belief, a fragment of language that contains a tension, a hint that there is an as yet unseen world around the next turn in the road that I must explore. As Graham Greene said, "The novel is an unknown man and I have to find him."

When I am lucky, I don't even have that. I have a panic nothingness and I start to describe something that I caught in the corner of my eye, not knowing I saw it, and as I write it the barely remembered scene becomes clearer—draft by draft— the way blank photographic paper slowly reveals its image in a tray of developer.

I have the world—memory and vision—and words. That is enough. I write and what I find myself saying reveals what I have to say.

2. FORM COMES BEFORE CONTENT

My teacher would assign the form—a literary essay, a personal essay, an argument before the topic. The form should grow organically as the writer writes to discover what to say and how to say it. The blueprint for an argument may come from a textbook as a blueprint for a bridge comes from a textbook on building bridges, but it must be adapted to the width of the river, the current, the makeup of the banks and the river bottom, the traffic it will bear. The form of the argument should grow according to the facts on both sides, the proponent and opposition, the place the case is being argued and the audience. The argument evolves as the writer gathers the facts and anticipates the reader's doubts and questions.

Writers should not build a form and then pour concrete into it, but write and then see what develops. In school we build walls between fiction and nonfiction, narrative and exposition, poetry and argument, but the writer breaks down those walls using dialogue and scene in nonfiction, argument and logic in fiction.

3. CORRECT SPELLING, GRAMMAR, MECHANICS ARE ESSENTIAL IN THE FIRST DRAFT

Ernest Hemingway said, "Prose is architecture not interior decoration." It is important for the accurate communication of meaning to follow the traditions of language on the final draft. They are the conventions reader and writer share. Most of the time, in fact, we will follow these conventions but if we concentrate on them while writing, our language becomes stiff and meaningless.

I am a terrible speller. I use a bad speller's dictionary, a word list book, my computer spellcheck, and my wife to correct my spelling before I submit a draft to an editor but if I stop to spell well as I write, I may lose the river of thought that is carrying me towards meaning.

The same is true of grammar and punctuation. In fact, if I am writing what I have not written before, my language often becomes awkward as I struggle to find what I want to say and then how to make it clear to me and then my reader. In fact, the breakthrough into a new meaning often comes when the syntax collapses and I find myself saying badly what I will later make clear.

4. LONG IS BETTER THAN SHORT

My teachers had good reason to teach us vocabulary through the grades, introducing us to longer and more complex words. They had to help us escape the limitation of brief subject-verb-object sentences, introducing clauses and complex sentence structures. The same thing was true of paragraphs and beyond. The unintended message was that longer is better and, in fact, those students who used big multisyllabic words, long mountain trails of sentences, huge overpacked paragraphs, page upon page saying what could have been said in a few words were rewarded with praise and *As*.

When these students, partly because they have gotten such good grades, try to become writers, they discover that short is better than long. Writers use the shortest words, shortest sentences, and shortest paragraphs they can. Since the ideas they have to communicate are often complicated, the shortest words that contain the appropriate meaning may be long ones and the shortest sentences may be full of clauses.

For the first two decades of my writing life I had a quote from the great essayist E. B. White's teacher Will Strunk over my desk:

> Vigorous writing is concise. A sentence should contain no unnecessary words, a paragraph no unnecessary sentences, for the same reason that a drawing should have no unnecessary lines and a machine no unnecessary parts. This requires not that the writer make all his sentences short, or that he avoid all detail and treat his subjects only in outline, but that every word tell.

5. DON'T WRITE AS YOU SPEAK

I was taught NOT to write as I spoke. I was instructed to follow the written style of the previous century and write in a formal style that often could not easily be read aloud. Speech and writing were taught to me as separate subjects by different teachers. We live, however, in an informal, dress-down age. We appreciate writing that gives the illusion of speech, good writing as conversation. Of course—uh—it isn't like—you know—uh—what I sorta, you know—uh—mean.

Graceful and effective writing today sounds like idealized speech, flowing naturally toward meaning. Readers want to hear the individual voice of the reader, the writer's way of speaking tuned to the meaning of what is being said and the audience to which it is aimed.

I write aloud as most writers do, hearing what I write before I see it. I can write with the screen turned off—try it. You should be able to write as well or better than when it is turned on.

6. ALWAYS OUTLINE FIRST

Not always. You can't draw a map of country you have never visited. If you are using writing to explore a new territory you probably can't write an outline until after the first draft, when it may be very helpful.

It depends, of course, on the form you are writing as well as your familiarity with the subject. In writing this edition of *Write to Learn* my editor and I have to agree on an outline. But even then the outline is not the rigid plan I was taught in high school but a sketch. The first chapter ended long before I thought it would, and all this business about unlearning to write which I had written in a different form years ago seemed a necessary if unexpected way to begin this chapter.

Later, on pages 124 to 136 we will introduce many ways to outline, but it does not have to come before the first draft.

7. THE FIRST DRAFT SHOULD BE THE LAST DRAFT

Sometimes that does happen. I have been writing a weekly newspaper column for thirteen years, more than 650 columns. I know the form, the length, the audience, my persona, and voice, and most of the time now I revise and edit as I go along and when I finish, but last week the editor—who was right—demanded three major revisions. For years when I wrote magazine articles I wrote three drafts of each one and revised each draft ten times. I went through the article thirty times.

Most of the time I have to write a *discovery draft* to find out what I have to say, a *development draft* to reveal and document what I have discovered, and a *clarifying draft* to make it clear to myself and the reader.

In school, I was only required to rewrite when I wrote a bad paper. If I was singled out to rewrite it was because the teacher felt I had failed. The same was true when I started working on a newspaper, but when I graduated to magazines and books, the first thing I had to learn was to rewrite. Not just because my first drafts failed—and they did—but because it took many drafts to discover and communicate my subject. For writers, writing is rewriting.

8. THERE IS ONE RIGHT WAY

I believed longer than I like to admit what my teachers seemed to believe: There is one right way. If I could find the one right word, the single right sentence, the only right paragraph, I would become a writer. What I have learned as a writer is that there are many wrong ways and many right ways. The way of the writer is selection and choice; the method, trial and error. Writing is an experimental science.

There are no rights and wrongs in writing. The standard is higher than correctness. You can be absolutely correct and write badly—many academics prove that. The writer confronts—word by word, line by line, paragraph by paragraph—the demanding questions: Does it work? Does it advance the meaning? Does it fit within the context? Is it accurate? Is it graceful? Is it clear?

James Thurber commanded, "Don't get it right, get it written."

When I fail, I go right back to first grade. Miss Kelly jams me in the wastebasket, my feet sticking out by my head like rabbit ears. I am humiliated. I despair. I want to quit but I have to remind myself that failure is essential. If I am not failing I am not writing, I am repeating what I have said before—in the way I have said it before.

The wrong word leads to the right word, the broken syntax points toward the phrase that clarifies. Writing is not stenography. Writing is thinking, a process of trial-and-error experimentation in which failure reveals what we cannot yet say but where the saying may lay hidden. Novelist John Fowles tells us, "Follow the accident, fear the fixed plan—that is the rule."

9. REVISION AND EDITING ARE THE SAME

In school I was told that when I finished a draft, I was to check the spelling, grammatical usage, and punctuation. Correctness was all.

As a writer I learned that writing was a search for a significant meaning and then communicating it. Correctness was the last part of the writing process, patting your hair in place, straightening your tie.

Revision is literally the process of re-seeing. When writers revise they reconsider the subject, the genre, the focus, its development, its voice. Writers revise first to discover and develop what they have to say and then to shape it so readers who have no interest in reading the message will read it.

Editing is the process of clarification. Writers go through the entire piece line by line, again and again, to make sure each detail is accurate, that every word or phrase that needs to be defined is, to cut what is unnecessary, to add what is necessary, to move words around to make the meaning clear, and to follow the conventions of language if they help the reader receive and understand the meaning.

10. SAY WHAT YOU ARE GOING TO SAY, SAY IT, SAY WHAT YOU'VE SAID

I can hear my teacher repeating this counsel again and again and again. She demanded an introduction, a repetitive body of prose, and a conclusion. It was once good advice, and in fact such an organization may be required in certain situations, in writing scientific papers, for example. But the general reader today does not have the patience to read the same thing three times.

In this book we will demonstrate the lede, or lead, that propels the reader right into the subject in the first paragraph, in the first sentences, in the first words. And the book will also show the conclusion that implies the meaning without insulting readers by telling them what to think or how to feel.

11. WRITE IN GENERALITIES FOR A GENERAL AUDIENCE

Makes sense, but it doesn't work. Universal writing rises from the specific, the resonating detail that sparks emotions, memories, thoughts in the mind of the reader. As novelist and essayist James Carroll says:

> The law of particularity forces fiction writers, poets, and dramatists to obsess over details, instances, and concrete images, while treating the experience of

one or two characters as if it matters as much as the sum total experience of the entire human race. To writers, a moment in time, properly rendered, is worth all time—a single, vividly imagined place is worth the cosmos.

The more particular I am—writing of my Scots Baptist grandmother, for example—the more readers read the memories of their Russian Jewish, Irish Catholic, Chinese Buddhist grandmothers. Accurate, resonating specifics makes readers read—and trust what they read.

12. TALENT IS RARE

Rare talent is rare. In each generation there are a few writers who practice their craft so well they will survive this century and perhaps the next. But talent is common. I once wrote with a class of elementary students so talented I asked them how they were chosen. They had IQs between 80 and 85—and a teacher who respected the stories they had to tell and their potential to tell them. Every class I taught had students that were more talented than I was. I did not have a freshman English class that had a student who could not become a professional—if they worked at it. I have had students who have careers in writing and editing with verbal scores in the 300s on their SATs.

What most of my students did NOT have was the desire to be published and the work habits to make it possible. The distinguished short story writer Andre Dubus declares, "Talent is cheap. What matters is discipline." Novelist E. M. Forster testifies, "The act of writing inspires me," and Graham Greene says, "I have no talent. It's just a question of working, of being willing to put in the time. . . . If one wants to write, one simply has to organize one's life in a mass of little habits."

13. EASY WRITING IS BAD WRITING

Writing should be easy. The cliché states, "easy writing makes hard reading." Just the opposite. Hard, constipated writing makes difficult reading, writing that is not read. We make writing hard out of displaced virtue.

I work hard to make writing easy, remembering the times when the writing went well and repeating those attitudes and conditions.

14. STUDY WHAT IS PUBLISHED AND IMITATE IT

Wrong. It is logical, but what is being published can be reproduced by staff members or experienced freelancers. Editors are looking for the voices they haven't yet heard telling the stories they don't know exist in ways they have not yet imagined. As Doris Lessing says, "You have to remember that nobody ever wants a new writer. You have to create your own demand."

How do you do that? By respecting your own vision of the world. Sandra Cisneros says it best:

> Imagine yourself at your kitchen table, in your pajamas. Imagine one person you'd allow to see you that way, and write in the voice you'd use to that friend. Write about what makes you different.

I have found that all the things that made me strange—even frightening—to my family, my neighbors, my pastor and my church members, my teachers and schoolmates, and continue to puzzle my wife and my children, colleagues and friends, and even myself are those things that I have to offer the world.

As my friend Chip Scanlan, writer and director of writing programs at the Poynter Institute says, "Do the writing only you can do."

15. DON'T MAKE MISTAKES

It is essential that writers make mistakes. Failure is essential to the writer. It is the failures that reveal the possibilities for good writing. We have to write badly to write well. Writers take risks, they take chances.

Be promiscuous—as a writer. Write in as many forms and voices for as many publications and readers as possible. Write what you know and what you need to know and what you will know only by writing. As Annie Dillard advises,

> One of the few things I know about writing is this: spend it all, shoot it, play it, lose it, all, right away, every time. Do not hoard what seems good for a later place in the book, or for another book; give it, give it all, give it now. The impulse to save something good for a better place later is the signal to spend it now. Something more will arise for later, something better. These things fill from behind, like well water.

John Jerome says, "Perfect is the enemy of good."

16. YOU CAN'T TEACH WRITING

Of course you can. My students taught themselves to write better in my classes than they wrote before the class. Take instruction from the writer Ursula Le Guin:

> If you want to be a tuba player you get a tuba, and some tuba music. And you ask the neighbors to move away or put cotton in their ears. And you probably get a tuba teacher, because there are a lot of objective rules and techniques to both written music and to tuba performance. And then you sit down and you play the tuba, every day, every week, every month, year after year, until you are good at playing the tuba; until you can—if you desire—play the truth on the tuba.

It is exactly the same with writing. You sit down, and you do it, and you do it, and you do it, until you have learned how to do it.

THE WRITING PROCESS

This book has been built on a single process. That sequence of writing tasks is based on my continuing study of the process of published writers in many different genres and a great variety of student writers, all tested against my own daily experience at the writing desk.

The writing process in this seventh edition of *Write to Learn* is:

FOCUS

RESEARCH

DRAFT

REVISE

EDIT

Then I have inserted a few minichapters to support that process:

SHOPTALK: THE RESEARCH PLAN

SHOPTALK: PREPARING TO REVISE AND EDIT

SHOPTALK: HELPING EACH OTHER

Focus

The writer finds or is assigned a territory to explore, then chooses one part of the territory that appears to be most significant.

Research

The writer scans memory, feelings, thoughts about that part of the territory, then uses the library and Internet, written and human sources, personal experience and observation to create an inventory of information from which to write.

Draft

The writer drafts quickly to outrun the censor and cause those instructive failures that reveal the meaning of the subject, surprising the writer—and the reader—with an unexpected insight.

Revise

The writer reads to discover the meaning revealed in the draft and then rewrites to develop the form, order, content, and voice of the draft.

Edit

The writer reads the draft line by line for accuracy, clarity, grace, and to make sure the conventions of spelling, mechanics, and grammar are ignored only when it is essential to communicate meaning.

WHY USE THE PROCESS APPROACH TO WRITING?

We take the mystery out of the craft of writing and reveal a process that writers use to produce their drafts. Here is why I use the writing process approach to writing.

To Work in an Effective Pattern

We may imagine that we just sit down and write, but we usually follow a process of preparation and execution based on our thinking style, our working habits, and our experience with the task. We should know and keep refining that process. If we do not know what we do and why, we may follow a procedure that is confused and inefficient. We may make writing harder than it needs to be and even practice a process that produces bad writing.

To Avoid Panic and Despair

When we sit down to write the task seems so overwhelming that we need a proven procedure, attitudes and habits, sequential acts, that have worked in the past so that we move into the unknown in a way that has brought us to the known in the past.

To Save Time

If we do not have a process, we jump around and perform tasks out of order that have to be done over. If we have no focus, then our research may be wasteful; if we correct the grammar before we have discovered a meaning, we are wasting our time.

To Write Effectively and Efficiently

Following a process that we have used successfully before, increases our effectiveness. We will, for example, have the documentation in inventory that we need when we develop what we have to say.

To Talk Effectively with Colleagues, Students, Teachers, Bosses

Most conflicts between writers and their readers—classmates or colleagues, teachers or bosses—come when the writer is at one stage in the process and the reader is in another. The writer may be seeking a focus and the reader may not be helping with that search but correcting spelling. A common understanding of the writing process will allow the reader to respond to writing in a way that is effective.

————THE PROCESS IS CIRCULAR————

Since we have introduced the writing process as a sequence or list, it appears linear with the writer following the first stage, then moving on through the second, third, fourth, fifth stages, following a straight line toward meaning; but, in practice, the process is circular. At each point the writer may move back through an earlier stage of the process.

- The need for a new focus may be revealed while you are doing research.
- As you write a draft, a new focus may be needed or you may need to do more research.
- When you revise you may have to re-focus, re-research, or re-draft.
- Even when you are editing, you may need once more to focus, research, draft, or revise.

Sometimes you may even start by researching, drafting, or revising something you have written before. The writing process should not be a series of rigid commands but a flexible strategy. As in war or sports an effective strategy must change as it confronts reality. Writing is never boring to me because I always find new opportunities and challenges when I begin to write and all the way along the road to meaning.

WHY THE PROCESS WILL CHANGE

Writers' processes will change for three principal reasons:

1. The way the writer's head works. I was just reading a book by a famous artist who pointed out that some painters will begin a portrait by sketching the whole head, others will start with a particular such as an eyebrow, and others will switch back and forth, according to how they see the subject. I write in the morning, others writers work at night; I write fast, others work slowly; I have to get the beginning right before I go on, others plunge in and write the final beginning later; I like to discover the end, others have to know the end before they begin.

2. The writing task. A newspaper article produced on deadline is a different task from a scholarly article written for a distant deadline. The recommendation letter requires that the audience be considered first while in writing a lyric poem, the reader may be considered last. A book written over two years is a far different task than a blue book exam finished in an hour.

3. The writer's experience with the task. In writing my first columns, I wrote many drafts, trying to feel my way into a new task. Now I usually write one draft, having rehearsed most of the writing that was once done on paper in my head. As we become familiar with a topic, a form, an audience, a voice our writing process may change.

Remember: there is not one writing process.
Repeat: THERE IS NOT ONE WRITING PROCESS.

I often make the mistake of applying the writing process or strategy that worked on the last writing project to a new one. It may work but it also may not work. Remember what I said earlier, the process will change according to the writer's way of thinking and working, the writing task, and the writer's experience with the task.

I have built this book on the writing process that my research and experience tells me is most often used by writers and is also a process that is easy to learn. It is not THE way to complete a writing task but A way. Once you become experienced with this process you have a basic approach to writing that is practical and logical. When you are stuck in writing you can go back to basics and begin the process anew, but as you continue to write you will keep adjusting the process to the challenge on the page.

Sometimes I write with a river flood of fluency, other days I build a draft slowly like a bricklayer. No matter. I am a writer. I write. And you should as well. I am however always using a process to write. The trick is to find the process that works and I find the one in this book—focus, research, draft, revise, edit—works most of the time.

FIND YOUR OWN WRITING TERRITORIES

When we write we explore personal territories, our experiences and our obsessions. Willa Cather said, "Most of the basic material a writer works with is acquired before the age of fifteen." Add in World War II in which I fought between the ages of 18 and 21 and it will certainly be true of me. Some of your best writing will come from these territories.

These territories—or themes—are the ones I keep returning to when I am alone. In mining these territories I have found a lifetime of writing:

School and writing. I was always fascinated by pen and paper, obsessed with the mystery of how words and lines could create and clarify a world. I read books, studied pictures, and did badly in school. I did not learn in the way that the "bright" kids learned and thought I was dumb. My motivation to become a teacher and to write books about writing and the teaching of writing came from my personal struggles in the classroom; I wanted to understand how writing was made so that I could help students like myself explore our world through writing.

Family. Like most families, mine had difficulties—problems, tensions, conflicts—I could not understand when I was young. Much of my writing today deals with family: my grandparents and parents who are dead, my daughters, their husbands, and our grandchildren; the daughter we lost when she was twenty. I keep writing about family to celebrate and to understand.

Sickness, aging, and death. I had a sickly childhood. The grandmother with whom I lived became paralyzed when I was very young, and I helped take care of her until I went to college. I wrote many magazine pieces about health issues, and now I write a weekly column for the *Boston Globe*—"Over Sixty"—that documents my own aging.

War. I was in combat as a paratrooper during World War II and am still trying to deal with the internal conflict of pride and shame experienced during my own months in combat. The Pulitzer Prize I received was for writing on military affairs, and my columns and poems constantly find their way onto the battlefield. The novel I am writing explores the effect of war on those who appear to survive it.

List the subjects that make you itch. What do you think about when you are driving alone in the car, taking a walk, tuning out the people you're with at dinner or a party, doing errands or the laundry, while listening to a boring lecture? What keeps you awake nights? What do you try to avoid thinking about? Donald Barthelme said: "Write about what you're most afraid of."

Of course much of the writing you do in school or at work concerns territories dominated by teachers or employers. It is important to try to make the territory your own, to turn any assignment so you can write with confidence—and to find an abundance of specific information on which you can draw.

FIND YOUR OWN MYSTERY

Our best subjects come from the mysteries in our lives or in the topics we are exploring with language. Grace Paley said, "We write about what we don't know about what we know." Many of us know a parent, uncle or aunt, teacher or neighbor whose life was changed by the Vietnam War or Gulf War, but often we do not know the details or the nature of the change. That individual's personal history is a mystery that might help us to understand them—and the nature of war—if we could explore it.

Seek and confront the mysteries in your life to find writing subjects. The mysteries may be personal: What was the influence of my parents' religion on my life? What explains the fact I flunked out of high school in June and led the class in junior college that October? How did winning an Associated Press award in my first year on a newspaper effect me as a writer?

Or they may be impersonal: What makes it possible for a heavy metal plane to fly? Why does one product sell while a similar one sits on the supermarket shelf? The mysteries may be small or large, personal or impersonal, but they engage our minds. They present problems we need to solve and provide us with unexpected answers as we watch our words appear on the page or screen.

TECHNIQUES FOR DISCOVERING SUBJECTS

There are many other ways to discover the mysteries that will produce effective subjects. Play with them to see what works for you.

Brainstorming

One of the best ways to discover what you already know is to brainstorm. When you brainstorm you write down everything that comes into your mind as fast as you can. You don't need to be critical; you do want to be illogical, irrational, even silly. You want to discover what is in your mind. You want to be surprised.

Here I have brainstormed about my childhood to see what topics I may have overlooked that need to be explored in writing. I'll start with the geography of childhood and see where it leads me as I list as fast as I can, not worrying if I am silly or stupid. Brainstorm beside me in the margin of the text. There's plenty of white space. You may discover a subject you want to explore through writing. My list is personal; I'm writing about my childhood. Your list doesn't have to be. Brainstorm any topic, personal or impersonal, with which you have some experience to see if there's something you wish to explore.

Now to brainstorm:

- Geography of childhood
- The block
- The vacant lot
- Empty stores
- Cellar hole
- Under the porch
- Playing doctor
- Sex mis-education
- Behind the garage
- Dogs, Airedale, Chow, scared
- Uncle

- Grandmother collapses
- Alien WASP—white Protestant in Irish Catholic neighborhood
- School
- Nearsighted
- Sat in back row
- Glasses
- "Four-eyes"
- Turn the other cheek—beaten up on playground
- Muddy Ducks
- Fights
- Seriousness of games
- Red Sox, Bruins
- Snow
- Sleighs
- Uncle Will's car up on blocks in winter
- His Buick
- The Sunday drive
- Almost drowning
- Fear of water
- Sickly childhood
- Days in bed—good
- Reading
- Friends who lived in walls
- Fantasy
- Temper—threw hammer at uncle, he fell
- Grandmother's paralysis
- Day I pulled hot jelly over me
- Wood stove
- Mystery of basement
- Mystery of attic
- Den
- Brown, color of my childhood

That took eight minutes. It's possible to brainstorm for a much longer time, but I find short spurts—fifteen minutes, ten minutes, five minutes—are more productive. You can also brainstorm together with another person or a group of people. The important thing is not to censor what you say, not to judge it, not to really understand it—but to let it come.

This brainstorming list is printed simply as it came. I didn't prepare for it, except by living with my grandmother until I went off to college. I had to let it come.

After you have brainstormed, look at what you've written to see what surprises you or which items connect. These surprises and connections remind you of what you know and make you aware of meanings you hadn't seen before.

It is important not to worry about how the brainstorming list is written. Don't worry about spelling or penmanship or sentences; it is a time to write in a sort of private language of code words that stand for particular meanings in your own mind. When the phrase "turn the other cheek" appeared on my brainstorming list, it reminded me of all the years—from grade one until grade six—when my mother would instruct me not to fight but to "turn the other cheek." If I really believed in Jesus, she said, the fists of the other boys would be held and they would not smite me. Apparently, I was never able to believe enough, because their fists kept hitting me and I lived in fear, humiliation, and guilt at my lack of faith. All that and much, much more would pour out if I wrote about that phrase in a column, novel, or poem; but the simple phrase "turn the other cheek" would be enough to hold it in reserve for another writing session.

I brainstorm before I write important letters or memos. I brainstorm class lectures and novels. I brainstorm articles and poems and textbooks such as this. I also brainstorm before I decide to buy a car or take a job or choose a vacation. Brainstorming shows me what I know, what I need to know, and what the connections are between what I know and don't know.

LOOKING FOR SURPRISE

I look at the list to see what surprised me. Whatever you are brainstorming—an academic paper or a job application letter—first go over the list to see what surprises you, to find out what discoveries you have made.

The surprise doesn't need to be enormous. I am surprised by:

- Under the porch
- Playing doctor
- Sex mis-education
- Behind the garage

I don't remember what happened behind the garage, and that's enough of a mystery for me to start to explore my childhood world when I first became aware of sex—I thought the facts of life ridiculous when I first learned them, and, in fact, they are—so this topic might be worth exploring.

I also note:

- Seriousness of games
- Red Sox, Bruins

That is all it takes to remind me of the importance of being a sports fan in a town like Boston. It was one of the few subjects that connected me with my father and my uncles—the world of men—and the emphasis on sports and competition probably marked me more than I know. If I write about that subject, I may discover its importance.

An old theme for me but a new twist:

- Sickly childhood
- Days in bed—good

What have we lost because of miracle drugs? Convalescence. I am nostalgic for the long, lonely weeks of fantasy and the reading that helped make me a writer.

LOOKING FOR CONNECTIONS

Next I look for connections between the items on my list. I draw lines connecting related entries, creating little bunches that may lead to a subject:

- The vacant lot
- Empty stores
- Cellar hole

Child's delight in playgrounds created by construction and business failures in the Great Depression.

- Alien WASP—white Protestant in Irish Catholic neighborhood
- Turn the other cheek— beaten up on playground
- Fights
- Seriousness of games
- Almost drowning
- Fear of water
- Sickly childhood

Might explore the terrors of childhood.

- School
- Nearsighted
- Sat in back row
- Glasses
- "Four-eyes"

Might reconstruct the school world of a nearsighted kid when you got beaten up for wearing glasses.

MAPPING

Another form of brainstorming that often works is mapping. You put the subject or topic you want to think about in the center of the page and then draw lines radiating out from it when another idea occurs to you. These lines branch off, capturing the fragments of information that you have unknowingly stored in memory.

A map of thoughts I have about my childhood follows.

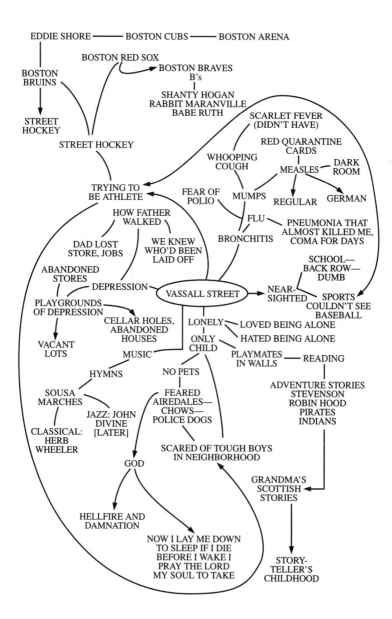

How Mapping Leads to Writing

That map took less than ten minutes to create, about the same time as the brainstorm list, but it produced different information. I rediscovered the red quarantine cards that were placed on the door when anyone had scarlet fever or measles; this memory might lead me into the territory of childhood disease before miracle drugs. The map also made me aware that much I had learned about the world had come in the form of stories—from the Bible, from Grandma and the uncles, from the street, from the classroom. Then there was the role of music—my family's hymns and Sousa marches, my jazz and the beginning of my interest in classical music—I could write a musical geography of my childhood.

MAKING A TREE

Another helpful technique to discover what you already know and don't know you know is to draw a tree. The figure on page 37 reveals the branches that can grow from a single idea.

This technique gives you a way of breaking down a subject or letting a subject expand. Some writers who use trees successfully place the central idea at the top of the page and let the tree grow down, whereas others place the central idea at the bottom of the page and let the tree grow up. Both produce excellent results.

This tree took five minutes to create, and it produced some new insights. I discovered the larger complexity of religions with which I grew up and their contradictions, the food myths that were important in my childhood, and the role of secrets in our family.

FREE WRITING

Another technique I have found productive is free writing. In brainstorming we work with lists. In free writing we depend on the momentum of narrative flow to force unexpected connections. To free write, sit down and let the writing flow; see if language will start to reveal something that unexpectedly interests you—an event, person, place, idea, feeling. Suspend critical judgment, as you do when brainstorming or mapping, and look for something to happen.

I'm never sure that anything will happen when I free write. But it really doesn't matter. Some days the writing comes, and some days it doesn't. If free writing doesn't work right away, I try brainstorming or mapping, or staring out the window, or turning to another project, or getting a cup of tea, or taking a walk, or otherwise creating an interruption. It is important in doing creative work to step back from the draft, the canvas, the score, the lab experiment—just far enough to gain perspective, to allow the subconscious to percolate. But in a few minutes I'll return to my desk, and something will work.

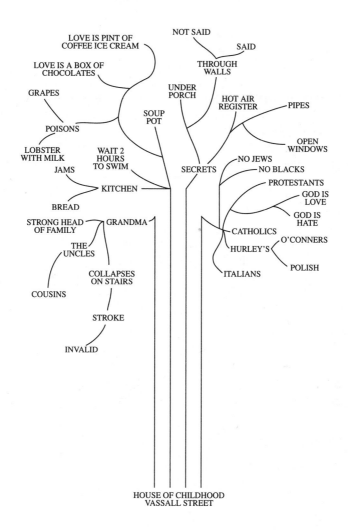

Now I'll free write, aware that my free writing looks more polished than the beginning writer's. It is. I refuse to fake it for the purpose of an example, but don't worry if your free writing is a lot sloppier than mine. It should be.

I don't think I was ever alone in that house of childhood. Mother was a woman of the streets, shopping, always shopping, chatting with friends, having lunch with them. She hated housework and cooking; she loved going out. And yet, although Grandma was there singing hymns in the kitchen; and Uncle Will was at his desk, keeping the books for one customer or another; or Father was at the dining room table organizing sales slips from the store and Mother was in the living room reading a woman's magazine; I remember being alone in that house. I had hiding places. My own room, under the dining room table, between the bushes and the house, behind the sofa, at the top of the stairs in the dark, in the empty coal bin.

I must have been a strange little boy, always listening, always making up stories, always trying to understand the tensions between the four adults with whom I lived. They were all so self-centered they gave me a lot of room—space, we'd call it today. I drove by the house and it is smaller, much smaller, than I remembered. I suppose I was never more than a few feet from anyone, and yet that loneliness is real. And the silence. We did all our hurting with turning away, what was not said, was our favorite weapon.

That few minutes of writing certainly took me where I did not expect to go, giving me a whole new vision of my childhood on Vassall Street.

Velocity in free writing is important; write fast so that you say what you do not expect to say. Also, note that free writing isn't really free. It starts to take you somewhere, to tell you what to say and how to say it. After free writing, look back to see whether you want to follow any of your paths, to explore them so the writing stops being private and can go public to readers. Decide whether you want to share with others what you are discovering. If you do, you'll find that the more personal the writing, the more specific and private, the more it will spark memories and ideas in your readers' minds.

Free writing is just as valuable a technique to use as a starting point for a term paper, a historical essay, or a review of scientific literature. It's a way of thinking in which you can preserve the flow of thought.

INTERVIEWING YOURSELF

Develop your own "itch list" to help you find a subject. Here are some of the questions I ask myself to discover what I want to "scratch" next:

- What has surprised me recently? What do I need to know?
- What would I like to know?
- How are things different than they used to be? How will things be different in the future?
- What have we lost?
- What have we gained?
- What do I know that others need to know?
- Who would I like to get to know?
- What's not happening that should?
- What's happening that shouldn't?
- Who would I like to see at work?

- What process do I need to know?
- What process would it be fun to observe?
- How can I switch my position so I will see my world differently?
- What have I read, heard, thought that confuses me?
- What connections are being made that surprise me?
- How are people's behavior changing?
- How are beliefs changing?
- What makes me mad?
- Sad?
- Happy?
- Worried?
- Frightened?
- Content?
- What do I expect to see, hear?
- Why?

——— START THE WRITING HABIT ———

The myth: Published writers—screenwriters, playwrights, novelists, poets, nonfiction writers, short-story writers, as well as composers and artists—lead lives of Bohemian excess, smoking stuff, drinking stuff, and chasing stuff all night long.

The reality: Writers write; the artistic life is a life of discipline. Gustave Flaubert said, "Be regular and ordinary in your life like a bourgeois so that you may be violent and original in your work." Flannery O'Connor testified, "Every morning between 9 and 12 I go to my room and sit before a piece of paper. Many times I just sit for three hours with no ideas coming to me. But I know one thing: If an idea does come between 9 and 12, I am there ready for it."

Sounds simple, doesn't it? It isn't. Getting the writing done day in and day out, despite interruptions, phone calls, obligations, duties, responsibilities, inertia, exhaustion, poor health, bad weather, invited and uninvited guests, too much drinking, too much eating or too little eating, wars, storms, births, deaths, marriages, divorces, travel, letters that come and letters that don't come, and a million other problems, is what separates the writer from the hope-to-be writer.

TIME

We have two kinds of writing times: fragmentary and insulated.

Fragmentary Time

The few minutes you have before a class begins, sitting in a doctor's office, waiting for a friend to show up for lunch, waiting for a bus, or during the commercials while watching TV.

The focusing and planning I do is performed mostly in small fragments of time that can be measured only in minutes, sometimes in seconds. This writing is done in my head and in my daybook. It isn't a question of hours but of minutes.

Try it yourself the next time you have a few extra minutes see how long it takes to brainstorm five essay titles, write a lead paragraph, draft a description, focus on a definition, sketch an anecdote, or even outline an article. I suspect you will find that when you thought you worked ten, or fifteen, or twenty minutes, you've worked two minutes, or four, or ninety seconds.

If you make good use of those fragments of time, then you'll be able to write when you have a stretch of uninterrupted time.

Insulated Time

The half-hours, hours, hour-and-a-halves, two hours you are able to shut out the world—in your room, the library, an empty classroom. Obviously, we have much more fragmentary time than we have insulated time, and it is important that we make use of both kinds of time. For most writers an hour is good, but not good enough. Two hours is plenty; three hours is heroic. During those times unplug the phone, lock the door; do not read, plan, edit, nap, or eat—just write.

The time of day is important. Most young writers start writing late at night but end up writing in the morning—the early morning—when their minds are fresh and the world is least likely to intrude. Goethe said, "Use the day before the day. Early morning hours have gold in their mouth."

The time of day, however, is not as important as habit. Most productive writers—there are exceptions—establish a routine and write at the same time every day. They know the time and the people around them know the time. Alberto Moravia says:

> When I sit down to write—that's between 9 and 12 every morning, and I have never, incidentally, written a line in the afternoon or at night—when I sit down at my table to write, I never know what it's going to be until I'm under way. I trust in inspiration, which sometimes comes and sometimes doesn't. But I don't sit back waiting for it. I work every day.

Do not attempt long, exhausting writing sessions. Few writers are productive in that way. Most writers write regularly for one to three hours every day, and those are considered full-time writers. You may have to try for half an hour to an hour a day.

Once you have produced a draft, fragmentary time can serve you again. I find it better to edit in short bursts. If I edit more than fifteen minutes at a run I tend to be kind, far too kind. In these slivers of time, early and late in the day, I can cut, insert, reorder, and perhaps decide that I need another draft when I have a few hours of insulated time.

PLACE

It helps to have a place where you go to write. It should be a place where you can leave your work lying out and come back to it later, where you have your tools at hand and you have the climate that you prefer.

Ross MacDonald said, "I took my lifelong tenancy in the bare muffled room of the professional writer where I am sitting now, with my back to the window, writing longhand in a spiral notebook." I like to look up from my writing and see a view. Other writers, such as Ross MacDonald, turn their backs to the view. I need music when I write; other writers need silence. Create a place of your own where you can shut the door and be alone.

That's an ideal many students can't achieve because they have families or roommates. It isn't easy to create that internal space, but it can be done, as Lois Duncan points out:

> Now I keep a typewriter with a sheet of paper in it on the end of the kitchen table. When I have a five-minute lull and the children are playing quietly, I sit down and knock out a paragraph. I have learned that I can write, if necessary, with a TV set blaring on one side of me and a child banging on a piano on the other. I've even typed out a story with a colicky baby draped across my lap. It is not ideal—but it is possible.

Writer Donald Graves has been able to write in a dormitory room with pneumatic drill construction going on next door or in a small summer cottage filled with family, friends, and dogs by using earphones and listening to Beethoven at top volume to insulate himself from the surrounding world.

Find ways to detach yourself from the world and go to that place where you can "hear" the writing. Depending on your personality, that place may not be the ideal artist's cabin high in the Rockies. I wrote most of one novel in a park, either sitting in the car or at a picnic table far out of the range of my mother-in-law's voice. I like to write in coffee shops and diners where no one knows me, and where there is a stimulating but unobtrusive background life that I can observe or ignore. When I was an undergraduate, my favorite writing places included the top row of the empty football stadium, a pleasing assortment of rocks on the Atlantic coast, a special table in the library, and an empty classroom late at night. Find the places where you can hear your voice as it speaks from the page.

— CONDITIONS THAT INVITE WRITING —

I have to cultivate conditions that encourage writing. I do this by looking at what conditions I experienced when the writing came easily, when I was ready to write and the writing flowed almost effortlessly. Yes, there are such days.

EXPECTATION

I expect to write. My attitude predicts my performance. The swimmer who goes to the starting block prepared to lose will lose; the writer who does not expect a draft will not write one. I have to recall when I have written easily before to expect that the draft will come.

DEMAND

External

A deadline helps—a line beyond which you are dead if you don't deliver. No excuses. I am lucky because I start the week with a Monday morning deadline on my column. All week I know that I will sit down Monday morning and produce a column, and I do. My editor expects it; I expect it. An external demand that requires a finished product can make all the difference between a published writer and a wish-I-were-published writer.

Internal

I also have an internal demand. I need to write to understand the life I have led and am leading. Catherine Drinker Bowen explains, "Writing is a kind of double living. The writer experiences everything twice. Once in reality and once in that mirror which waits always before or behind him." Compare it to what happens to you when you go over the family get together in your mind or in conversation with a friend, recreating what you did and didn't do, should have and should not have done or said to find out what it means. I write to discover who I am and what the life I am leading means. I must write.

It isn't just personal writing that causes significant discovery. Lawyers write briefs to find out how past judicial decisions impact their cases; businesspeople write reports to discover where profits are being made or lost; insurance investigators write to find out if their companies must pay claims; scientists and engineers write to find out what experiments taught them and what future experiments need to be performed.

REHEARSAL

Most times I come to my desk having rehearsed what I may say, the way I would rehearse an employment interview. I go over fragments of language, strategies of development and communication in my conscious and subconscious mind. I talk to myself, I dream, I imagine what I may say, sometimes making notes, often just letting the random fragments of writing circulate through my mind. It is all brought together as I start to draft.

FORGIVENESS

To write, I have to write as well as I can write today, accepting the fact that I cannot write as well as I'd like to or as well as I imagine other writers are writing. I keep rereading the wise counsel of poet William Stafford:

> I believe that the so-called "writing block" is a product of some kind of dispro-portion between your standards and your performance. . . . One should lower his standards until there is no felt threshold to go over in writing. It's easy to write. You just shouldn't have standards that inhibit you from writing.
> . . . I can imagine a person beginning to feel he's not able to write up to that standard he imagines the world has set for him. But to me that's surrealistic. The only standard I can rationally have is the standard I'm meeting right now. . . . You should be more willing to forgive yourself. It doesn't make any difference if you are good or bad today. The assessment of the product is some-thing that happens after you've done it.

VELOCITY

To balance a bike you have to pedal fast; and for writers to outrun the censor and cause the accidents of insight and language that mark good writing, you have to write fast. I usually do my best first draft writing when I am saying what I do not yet know. In writing fast, ideas appear, specifics connect, a voice begins to come clear. Some of them are good and some are very bad, but that will be taken care of in the revising. To get the good ideas, the ones worth developing, I have to force myself to push the writing beyond where it and I are comfortable.

EASE

I try to write with ease, relaxed, allowing the words to flow through me natu-rally. If I do this, the draft will instruct, telling me what I should say and how I should say it. The evolving draft will take its own course, exploring experience as it is relived. If I am patient, receptive, open to surprise, the draft will tell me what I have to say. E. M. Forster said: "Think before you speak, is criticism's motto; speak before you think is creation's."

Write easily. Relax. Allow the writing to pass through you. Do not force, strain, or intend, but receive. The cliché says, "Easy writing makes hard reading" but the experienced writer knows the opposite is true—graceful, fluid writing makes easy reading.

All of these conditions and attitudes help get me to start writing. They aren't all in place every day but enough are so that I begin each day writing, and that writing gives me the wonderful surprise of hearing what I didn't know I knew. That's what keeps me writing.

——— WRITE IN A DAYBOOK ———

When I sit down to write a newspaper column, a chapter in a book, a novel, a poem, a memo, a business letter, a note of sympathy, a complaint to a company, I have a history with that form. I know its traditions, the reader's expectations, how I have performed the task before, how writers I respect—E. B. White, George Orwell, Sharon Olds, Alice Munro, Paul Watkins, Joan Didion—have done it. Of course I need to know all that, but each time I begin to write I need to unknow it as well.

First, of course, I write in my head. When I hear something there that might be a piece of writing, I save it in my daybook. I can put it there in any form. I don't need paragraphs or complete sentences. I may draw a diagram or a sketch. I try to avoid, for the moment, what I know and ask myself:

What do I have to explore?

How can I best explore it?

And then, when I have found my territory and my subject within it, I can ask:

How best can I share it?

The daybook entries allow me to stand back, to catch ideas that are fragmentary, hardly able to be written, to extend them and hold them in place so I can return to them.

Reading back in my current daybook I find these lines I had forgotten:

Triangulation
I stood aside (a child)

Learning the geometry of my childhood

A triangle with mother's mother at the top

At the corners father, mother

(constellation)

(outside) Uncle Will who would take me into the backyard at night

This is unlearned writing. I don't know what it means. For example I have no memory of Uncle Will taking me out in the yard at night. No idea at all why I wrote that. I am excited by the line "learning the geometry of childhood." I can see that going in all sorts of directions. The geometry might be a rhomboid or a parallelogram, a rectangle, a box.

Today it seems to me to be about power. The child has to discover where the power is in the home in which he or she lives. I'm also interested that I am outside the triangle. The normal triangle would be mother-father-child, but of course that is not normal any more and never was. There are grandparents, uncles, and aunts that move in, stepparents. And when marriages break apart, the geometry changes, perhaps I need to consider matrixes, three-dimensional geometric patterns. This is the way one writer's mind works in his daybook. This may become a short poem, an essay, a novel, a screenplay. My notes have given me a way to look at the world, a way to make the familiar strange that may ignite a piece of writing.

The daybook is a breeding place for writing. It does not just allow, it encourages unexpected connections, previously unheard voices, relationships between genre. In school we concentrate too often on finished writing, prematurely finished writing. The daybook allow the unfinished, sometimes un-begun, writing that is essential for writing that allows the writer to learn, to say what hasn't been said before, and to share it with readers.

——— HEAR THE VOICE OF THE DRAFT ———

Voice is style and tone and more. It is the human sound that arises from a written page. Voice is rhythm and beat, inflection and emphasis, volume and pause; it is the manner in which the author speaks; it is the flow of what is spoken; it is the emotional content of writing; it is energy and force; it is the presence of an individual writer speaking to an individual reader. Voice is the most important, the most magical and powerful element of writing. During writing and revising, the writer hears the voice of the draft and tunes it to the meaning being developed and made clear.

One way to hear the voice of the draft is to speak aloud while writing. Then you will hear the tone of what you are saying, the background music that communicates mood and emotion. You can do this by "silently" speaking what you write, as I am doing now. Then you will be able to hear what you are writing—and tune the voice of the draft to what is being said.

Voice is magic but not mysterious. From another room, you can recognize the voices of those with whom you live; you know if they're mad, sad, having a good time, asking, rejecting, commanding, pleading. You can accomplish the same effect through your writing. You establish a voice that arises from the page.

Remember in Chapter 1 on page 8 when I wrote about voice, I mentioned the music in the phrase "the melancholy of a sunny day"? Now I will push that piece a bit further, writing aloud.

> On this sunny day I look out the window of the Florida condo and feel the pattern of the August sun passing through the leaves that arch over an abandoned road. I am here, now, an old man and simultaneously I am the fourteen-year-old boy exploring the New Hampshire villages abandoned during the Gold Rush of 1849.
>
> I am happy as I was that day so long ago, so immediate in memory, I realize my happiness is strange for it is accompanied by a melancholy for the villagers who followed their dream. That implies they found only fool's gold when they may have become rich. At least they escaped the hard work of farming in fields that grow granite ledges and stones the size of a pig.
>
> I wonder what my dreams were then. A life of arctic exploration? Playing for the Red Sox, the only first baseman who shut his eyes when he swung at the ball? A heroic role in the war that we would soon enter? Becoming a writer, the most impossible dream of all it seemed then?

What do I hear in those few paragraphs? A reflective voice speaking with long sentences. In the way of writers, the music of my brief description of that lost road, makes me see the whole village of cellar holes, fields turned to forest, a dam crumpled under the force of a flood river. I want to keep hearing that voice and to do that I will have to keep writing, keep listening to what I am writing.

Read aloud—and I mean right out loud—the first sentences of the following passages to hear the voices of each of these writers:

• THE JOY LUCK CLUB •
Amy Tan

> My father has asked me to be the fourth corner at the Joy Luck Club. I am to replace my mother, whose seat at the mah jong table has been empty since she died two months ago. My father thinks she was killed by her own thoughts.
>
> *Amy Tan's voice takes you right into her world. Her father's command establishes a new relationship with his daughter, who is "to replace my mother" (his wife). The next sentence explains why this new relationship and the last sentence creates a mystery; he does not have a conventional,*

1990s, American cause of death such as cancer or heart disease. The narrator's voice is direct, simple, spare of emotion, neither resentful of her father nor sad for the loss of her mother; it is the voice of a young observer of life who is recounting an event that has significance to discover its full implications.

• PROSPECT •
Bill Littlefield

Scouting was a funny thing for me to get into, the way both Alice and I felt about travel. But I'm damned if the business wasn't full of guys who didn't like to fly, even though there was an awful lot of flying involved, and guys who said they hated to drive, too, though sometimes they'd drive all day and all night. There were guys who said they got stomachaches when they had to sell a boy's parents on the idea of him signing, and others who claimed they'd rather go to the dentist than fill out all the paperwork their clubs required. But we will put up with almost anything for the chance to do something that offers us joy. And when you get older you will fly, or drive, or stand on your head to be in the presence of that thing, which is a fleeting thing.

This is the garrulous voice of an old baseball scout retired in Florida. We hear in this voice an old man who has spent his life sitting in the stands chatting with other old baseball players.

• THE REMAINS OF THE DAY •
Kazuo Ishiguro

It seems increasingly likely that I really will undertake the expedition that has been preoccupying my imagination now for some days. An expedition, I should say, which I will undertake alone, in the comfort of Mr. Farraday's Ford; an expedition which, as I foresee it, will take me through much of the finest countryside of England to the West Country, and may keep me away from Darlington Hall for as much as five or six days. The idea of such a journey came about, I should point out, from a most kind suggestion put to me by Mr. Farraday himself one afternoon almost a fortnight ago, when I had been dusting the portraits in the library.

Now we hear a radically different voice, the formal voice of a British butler, created by a young writer recognized as a master stylist.

• THE MERRY ADVENTURES OF ROBIN HOOD •
Howard Pyle

In merry England in the time of old, when good King Henry the Second ruled the land, there lived within the green glades of Sherwood Forest, near Nottingham Town, a famous outlaw whose name was Robin Hood. No archer ever lived that could speed a gray goose shaft with such skill and cunning as his, nor were there ever such yeomen as the sevenscore merry men that roamed with him through the greenwood shades.

This is the old-timey voice of one of my childhood's favorite books. It is a traditional storyteller voice that attempts to imitate a minstrel, preserving oral history.

• THE THINGS THEY CARRIED •
Tim O'Brien

First Lieutenant Jimmy Cross carried letters from a girl named Martha, a junior at Mount Sebastian College in New Jersey. They were not love letters, but Lieutenant Cross was hoping, so he kept them folded in plastic at the bottom of his rucksack. In the late afternoon, after a day's march, he would dig his foxhole, wash his hands under a canteen, unwrap the letters, hold them with the tips of his fingers, and spend the last hour of light pretending.

O'Brien, perhaps the best of the Vietnam novelists, uses a reportorial voice, somewhat detached, that allows him to reveal the horrors of war—in this case a soldier's loneliness and distance from the woman he loves.

• BELOVED •
Toni Morrison

124 was spiteful. Full of a baby's venom. The women in the house knew it and so did the children. For years each put up with the spite in his own way, but by 1873 Sethe and her daughter Denver were its only victims. The grandmother, Baby Suggs, was dead, and the sons, Howard and Buglar, had run away by the time they were thirteen years old—as soon as merely looking in a mirror shattered it (that was the signal for Buglar); as soon as two tiny handprints appeared in the cake (that was it for Howard). Neither boy waited to see more; another kettleful of chickpeas smoking in a heap on the floor; soda crackers crumbled and strewn in a line next to the doorsill.

Another storyteller's voice that recreates an oral tradition on the page. No reader can escape the power, energy, force of this voice by one of our most respected writers.

• WILDFIRE •
Richard Ford

In the fall of 1960, when I was sixteen and my father was for a time not working, my mother met a man named Warren Miller and fell in love with him.

Richard Ford, another of our most respected writers, has created a sentence of utter simplicity that reveals, in a few words, a very complicated story that would be told—and explored—by a sixteen-year-old narrator.

Each of these voices is different but each is true to the author and to the story the author is telling. Each one makes me want to listen, to read on. Each writer has an individual voice that comes from such influences as genes; ethnic, religious, and regional heritage; social and economic class; and educational background. The important thing is to take that personal voice and tune it to the meaning of the text. All of these examples of voice serve the meaning of the text. Think of a musical score that tells you when to be scared, when to laugh, when to be sad. The music of written language does the same thing: It tells you what to think and feel.

IN THE WRITER'S WORKSHOP

The hardest thing I had to do even to become a writer was believing that I had anything to say that people would want to read. ALICE MCDERMOTT

There is in you what is beyond you. PAUL VALERY

When my writing is going well, I know that I'm writing out of my personal obsessions. BHARTI MUKHERJEE

I never know what my stories are about until they are finished, until they choose to reveal themselves. I merely feel their power, how they breathe on me. I try not to write them. I prefer the rush of having them write me. KATE BRAVERMAN

That is the pure pleasure of creation—the not knowing that leads you to the knowing. BOBBIE ANN MASON

You always play the same way. You can't play different from who you are. Maybe you growl now, but your personality, intelligence, feeling, they don't change. I think it was Matisse who said, people have one idea and they're going to deal with it forever. WYNTON MARSALIS

I write every day, in the early morning. I become melancholy if I don't. Writing is really more of an obsession than a habit. WILLIAM TREVOR

If you want to be a writer, you have to write every day. The consistency, the monotony, the certainty, all vagaries and passions are covered by this daily reoccurrence. . . . The act of writing is a kind of guerrilla warfare; there is no vacation, no leave, no relief. WALTER MOSELEY

What I've found and what I believe is that everybody is talented. It's just that some people get it developed and some don't. STEPHEN SONDHEIM

For a couple of years I was waking up at five every morning to write for a few hours before going to work. That was when I knew what I wanted to say but didn't know how to say it. When I finally found the right voice, it took me only a month to write the novel. I'd take my eight-month-old son out in the stroller for a walk, and while he was looking around at the trees and grass in the park, I'd be thinking about what I was going to write next. Then I'd come home and write when he napped. I did exactly what a friend once told me to do—I never used my child's nap time for anything but writing. EVE HOROWITZ

I think I'm trying to keep myself from being bored. When I think about why I would be a writer, why I should continue to be a writer, it seems to me one of the few things you can do where you're never bored. GISH JEN

I don't plan my writing. What comes out is usually quite surprising. I write to find out what I'm thinking. JOHN ASHBERY

I have the feeling that if I don't write, the previous day disappears . . . one writes to recover what has been lost. ISABEL ALLENDE

QUESTIONS ABOUT LEARNING TO WRITE

Your writing seems awfully personal. Do I have to write about that kind of stuff, take off my clothes and dance around in public the way you do?

I hope not. It embarrasses me sometimes. I don't always feel comfortable running around in my birthday suit. And I don't always do it. I do it when it's the best way to help others or to say what I have to say. I never finished my Master's degree and I don't have a doctorate. My knowledge about writing comes primarily from personal experience. I'm also a pretty open person. I need to share my life with others and have them share their lives with me. It's my way to live but it doesn't need to be yours. Most writers I know are much more private than I am. You don't have to be an intellectual nudist to be a writer.

What is all this about a process for writing? I don't have a process and I still get As on my essays.

Everyone has a writing process, but the process is invisible since writers usually write alone. Because writing is a closed-door activity, we have no way of knowing the difficulty an author has with finding a topic or how many times she revises before publication.

We forget too that using a computer has made the process of writing less apparent, since we now can perform multiple tasks at one sitting: drafting, focusing, and drafting again; editing, deleting, and planning; revising, focusing, and drafting once more. When a writer finishes, we usually see only the result: a proofread product, typed, tidy, and ready for the reader's eye.

It's certainly true that some writers (and you may be one of these) can sit down at the computer and hammer out something worthwhile without much effort. But if asked to explain in detail how they compose, even these writers would define some sort of process. They sift through information and focus on an angle for their topic. They revise, insert, delete, and move text around, pausing to read what they have written before moving on. It is the rare, accomplished writer who does not finally read a printed copy of a draft with pencil in hand, looking for ways to make a story or essay even better.

If you are getting straight A's on all your writing, that's great! Your process is working for you. But you might want to ask yourself another question: Is your writing publishable? If the answer is no, it may be time to take your writing to the next plane, to push yourself beyond what is expected of you at school and to think of becoming the best writer you can on your own terms. Concentrate more on planning and revision. Write for yourself instead of for your teachers.

I've already explored my writing process in high school. Don't you think it's a waste of time to do it again in college?

No. Process means fluidity and growth, something that is always evolving, always in flux. While you are probably a more insightful writer from having paid attention early on to your writing process, you will never be finished exploring, changing, and improving the way you write until you draft your final sentence. Since you will be writing in one form or another throughout your life, that final sentence (we hope!) is a long way off.

You may want to think about it this way: You don't finish learning when you finish college. Each new experience becomes part of a longer, continuous process of analyzing and making meaning, of revising the way you view the world and the way you think about older experiences. Likewise, your experiences at college will be different from your high school experiences. You are probably already reprocessing what you know and what you think, even though you may have been at college for only a very short time. Since writing is a way of thinking, learning, and revising, your particular process will change as you change.

Besides, your writing assignments at college will most likely be much different from those in high school, and you will want to adapt your process accordingly. As you explore different disciplines and juggle an increasing number of deadlines, you will have to experiment with different processes. What worked for you in high school may not necessarily work for you now.

So if process means flexibility, why do I have to follow all the steps of the process in the order that you have them in this book?

You don't. Following a procedure is a good way to get started and move through a draft, and it's a good idea to work through the steps in the order you find them here as a way of beginning and thinking about your process. But it's not the only way. While you will probably complete each step of the process before you are through (and your teacher may insist on this), don't think of these steps as guideposts along a straight and narrow road. Think of them as points along a circle or spiral, sites that you will most likely revisit or pass again on your journey as a writer.

Writing should be an exciting, adventuresome activity. It should be full of surprises, unexpected opportunities, twists in the trail, surprising views, new challenges. You can always vary a method of working and go back to it when you need to. A writing method should never make a writer follow a discipline of writing that ignores the evolving life of a draft.

How about academic writing, essays I have to do for other classes? How will following a process help me if my teacher assigns a topic?

From a practical perspective, following a process of focusing, planning, drafting, revising, and editing will get you from Point A to Point B. It will force you to set a schedule and meet deadlines. Instead of writing your paper the night before class (or not turning it in at all!), you will have a polished product to hand in on the day it is due. This kind of agenda will also be helpful if you get a job that requires reports and other written products.

But aren't English teachers the only ones who use a writing process?

No. If you ask professors in different fields to talk about essays or books they have written, or if you see all their drafts, you will find that published writing evolves through an extensive process of focusing and revision. You will also discover that your professors rely on editors who proofread their work before it is published. None of these professors sits down at the computer and fires off a perfectly polished product the first time around.

What if my teacher won't let me write from my point of view or use the pronoun I when I write? What if she thinks it's too personal?

Even if you do not say I, you imply it in all your writing. It is the I who is behind every bit of information that goes into your paper and who makes the decisions regarding genre, focus, and angle. While the I may receive feedback and suggestions from other readers, that is the person who ultimately sits down to write the piece.

It would be great if you could come right out and say "I think . . ." in all of your papers. But if you can't, try not to distinguish too greatly between personal and academic writing when working through your writing process. All writing is revealing; all writing is personal. While a writer may be distant and detached, his or her choice of words, details, and focus can show what he or she thinks. Even the most "objective" academic writer reveals some sort of relationship with the people and ideas he or she writes about. The long and the short of it is, you don't need to say I to write from your own perspective or to make your writing your own.

Activities for Learning to Write

1. Start a writing process log or daybook, picking out a notebook that feels comfortable to you and is the right size so that you can have it with you most all the time. Doodle in it, write in it, paste things in it, record observations and thoughts, ideas and drafts for titles, leads, ends, middles. Create outlines and diagrams. Don't worry about neatness or correctness—this is a place to have fun. Talk to yourself, think to yourself, find out what you are seeing, hearing, feeling, thinking and what it means.

2. Select a writing partner in class and set aside a specific time, fifteen minutes to a half hour each day, to write one another via campus mail or e-mail. Make the main topic of correspondence the craft of writing, but don't be afraid to just talk about life in general; this is where good writing starts. Discuss subjects that you want to write about and ask questions about these subjects. Comment about the actual act of writing, too: where you sit, your ideal writing environment, when you are most productive, when you are not. Support each other through each stage of writing and help each other "power" through writer's block. Keep copies of your correspondence, and collect them in a binder at the end of the semester. Write a preface about your writing process and your semester as a "pen-pal."

3. Find a brainstorming "room": a cafe, dorm or bedroom, lounge area, or even a spot outside by a river or under a tree. Make it your own. Settle into your space with notebook or personal computer and reserve an hour or so each day just for free writing or brainstorming. Make a daily appointment with your spot, and commit yourself to keeping it for at least a month.

4. Come up with a list of five nouns and ask your writing partner to do the same. Exchange lists and write for five minutes apiece about each word, paying particular attention to sensory details and any memories the words evoke. Choose one of these and brainstorm with your partner about ways to expand it.

5. Ask a friend who uses an Internet bulletin board or newsgroup how to find groups to join and try one on for size. Explore the hundreds of topics these boards cover and choose two or three that interest you. Make a point to read and respond to the posted entries at least once or twice a week. Be attentive to

various "posts," jotting down what you agree or disagree with, what you learn from them, and what you can add. Then post your own thoughts.

6. Collaborate with a group of classmates on a TV script for a drama or sitcom. Look at the credits of your favorite shows and note how many writers collaborate together on a show. As an alternative, check network Web sites on the Internet, where you can find all kinds of information about popular programs. Decide how you will collaborate on the script, and elect a recorder who will keep a detailed record of the process you used in writing the script.

7. Invite a local writer—a newspaper columnist, poet, novelist, or essayist—into your classroom. Read selections from the writer's work, and ask the writer to bring in drafts and to talk about his or her writing process. Be prepared with questions about drafting, planning, focusing, and revising. Have on hand copies of publications by the writer, and refer to specific chapters and passages as you talk.

8. Visit the home or museum of a literary figure where drafts of the author's writing are on display, or check out a biography of an author from the library. Often such displays and biographies track the various stages of a famous work from beginning to end, from idea to publishing. Make a report to your group or class about the writer's composing process.

9. Check out the many writers' chat areas and bulletin boards on the Internet. "Listen" to the conversations among writers about drafting and revising, how they write, when they write, and where they write. Talk with them about your own processes, and choose a mentor from among them. You will find that most writers in these groups will be more than eager to discuss your work.

10. Write in your daybook about a project you have completed that made you proud. How about a speech you wrote and delivered in speech class? A car's engine you rebuilt during the summer? A dinner you cooked for your parents' wedding anniversary? The skis you refurbished last winter? When you have finished writing, list the steps you took in planning and carrying out your project. When did you first think of it? Did you have to gather information or do some research in order to complete it? Did you have to revise your plans as you went along? How much time did it take? Was the final product worth it? Was it well-received by others? When you have finished, compare the process of completing your project to the process of writing. How was it similar or different?

11. Choose a passage from a piece of autobiographical writing by a professional author, one that you think conveys a sense of his or her voice. Make copies and pass them around in a small group; ask your groupmates to do the same. Omit any information about the author or the title of the piece. Try to guess from the passage what the narrator is like. What kind of voice does the writer have? How old do you think the writer is? Is the writer male or female? Write up a profile of the narrator in your daybook.

12. Take a piece of your favorite writer's work and imagine the different stages it must have gone through before it was published. Try to step into your author's shoes and imagine how he or she got started. Pretend you're that author and plan the piece from beginning to end.

13. If your school has a writing center or lab, ask to sit in on a couple of tutoring sessions and listen to conversations about writing. If you can't actually listen in, then make an appointment with the director of the center or a writing tutor to talk about the various ways people go about writing and how tutors at the center help them through the process. Jot down your observations and then write an entry in your daybook comparing your own writing process with those of others.

14. Write a letter to a class partner about a writing project you have in mind and how you want to approach it. As you take the project through its various stages, write memos to your partner reporting on your progress. Pay special attention to the various phases of your writing process and how you move through, repeat, skip, or merge them. At the end of the semester, join with your partner in "publishing" a small book of your work.

15. Write a paper quickly the last minute before class. Don't bother to go back and reread, revise, or edit it. Make copies of your paper and pass them out in a small group. Read the paper aloud and then discuss what needs to be done with it. What process will your paper have to go through to make it better?

16. Hold a "bad" writing contest. With a group of classmates, write a short essay that you consider dull, unfocused, and . . . well . . . just generally bad. Exchange your bad essays with another group. Using the stages of the writing process outlined in this chapter, write up a list of suggestions for the authors of each essay and how you think they could improve it. Don't get stuck on grammatical and spelling errors at this point. Think about the gist of the piece, and read it with an eye toward planning, focusing, and drafting.

17. Imagine your writing as a house and draw a blueprint. Don't worry about being highly technical and accurate. Just divide the stages of writing into "rooms" (brainstorming, free writing, and mapping, for example, might be the doors and entrance ways to your house), and furnish the rooms with details about each step. As you write your essay, keep track of where you have to change your blueprint. Which rooms get the most use? Which do you visit the least?

18. Create the perfect writing area. Splurge on inspirational posters, artwork, a comfortable chair, the right pens and pencils and paper. Go to yard sales or flea markets to buy all the extras that will spiff up your special corner. Make it a place you will want to return to again and again. If you need music while you write, have your stereo and headphones nearby; if you like privacy, enclose the space with a screen. Post pictures of family and friends or of writers whom you admire around your computer or writing desk.

19. Talk to professors in your major or area of interest about writing in that discipline. Ask them to tell you about any articles they have written, how they went about planning and drafting them, and how they revised them. Find out what kind of feedback they got from friends, colleagues, and publishers that helped them put together their final drafts.

20. Retype a couple of pages from a published author's work on a typewriter or computer. Listen to the rhythm of the sentences as you rewrite them. Think of the words you are putting down and how the author chooses them. Pay attention to punctuation and the stylistic choices the author makes. Then rewrite the passage. Change or add punctuation or leave it out; drop or add details, or go off on a tangent of your own. Move the middle paragraph to the beginning or change the ending. Choose one scene or detail to write about extensively and omit others. Note when and how the focus of the essay shifts as you fiddle with it.

21. Make a list of teachers you remember. Next to their names, jot down writing assignments you associate with them. Select two or three names from this list and in your daybook write as quickly as you can about the teachers, what you learned about writing from each one, and how you began, sustained, and completed each writing assignment for that teacher. Be humorous or serious or reflective, but try to trace your writing process through each teacher and each writing assignment.

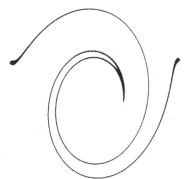

CHAPTER 3

FOCUS

I sit at my computer to start this chapter, my music playing on the CD, the sun bouncing off the leaves in my woods, rested, ready to write. On the screen the cursor blinks, blinks, blinks . . . Nothing.

I feel as if a giant vacuum cleaner has sucked out my brain. I have no memories, no thoughts, no ideas. The panic comes, the same terror I felt when I found myself over my head in the lake before I learned to swim and learned to take a deep breath, hold it, relax, and make myself calm so I could swim to where my feet at last touched bottom.

I have learned to accept the emptiness as part of the writing process. Do not struggle, flail about, but make myself calm, receptive.

A memory floats by like a lone cloud in an empty sky, then I hear my mother say something she said when I was a boy; I think of a line from an article I read the day before, then a question someone asked me the day before pushes its way into my mind, followed by an answer, and that causes another question. Suddenly my head is flooded with fragments of information, observations, memories, thoughts, ideas, and I am overwhelmed.

In minutes I have gone from hopeless emptiness to a drowning abundance. I have to remind myself that this is good, remember that Virginia Woolf said, "if there is one gift more essential to a novelist than another it is the power of combination—the single vision."

It is not just true of novelists and poets and screenwriters but also true of corporate memo writers, scientists writing up an experiment, social workers and lawyers, police and journalists, engineers, salespersons, everyone who has to put information in an order that the writer and then the reader can understand. The writer's artistic and intellectual challenge is to select significant information and connect it so it produces meaning.

The writer needs to collect far more than can be used so that the writer can make meaningful connections. As Elizabeth Bowen says, "The writer . . . sees what he did not expect to see. . . . Inattentive learner in the schoolroom of life, he keeps some faculty free to hear and wonder. His is the roving eye. By that roving eye is his subject found. The glance, at first only vaguely caught, goes on to concentrate, deepen; becomes the vision."

Writing doesn't begin with butt in the chair and fingers on the keyboard, but with eye, ears, nose, tongue, and skin making the writer aware of the world; and it doesn't end with a simple list of what the senses have delivered to the brain but a focused piece of writing. Writers need to focus, but there is no need to focus unless there is a glorious confusion of significant information.

SEE AND WRITE

If you ask young children to write a story, they are as likely to hand you drawings as bits of prose. They know instinctively what their teachers in the upper grades and college seem unable to understand: Writing is a visual art—writers see, then write. The few children who will become published writers continue, despite school, to see with the mind's eye, then write. They know from daily experience at the writing desk that writing is a special way of seeing.

Although published writers see what they write, I do not know of any composition textbook that connects writing and seeing. We are the victims of the academy, which separates the visual arts—drawing, painting, sculpture, photography—from the language arts of writing, reading, speaking.

THE CRAFT OF VISION

The writer's purpose, as novelist Joseph Conrad said, "is, by the power of the written word, to make you hear, to make you feel—it is, before all, to make you see." To make others see, writers must first see themselves. Each day I exercise my observation muscles. I watch the predawn light make black lace of the winter branches in the woods behind my house; on my morning walk I pay attention to how the faraway yellow day lily grows large as I approach it, until I can see the other colors that rise from its throat; I notice the young police officer's practiced, police-academy stroll up to the car he has just pulled over; I record the way my wife, as we watch the evening news, makes a sharp comment, then waits to smile until I get her double meaning; before falling off to sleep I walk down the path I took sixty summers ago to the lake, remembering how the water looked when I could not swim and feared the lake, and how the black water grew to a light bluegreen when I could dive, even swim all the way to the raft under water. I fall asleep swimming underwater with a bright ceiling of reflected sunlight above my head.

Specific sensory details that rise off the page and resonate in the reader's mind are vital to lively, effective writing. Listen to one of the best writers about the natural world, Diane Ackerman, who is also a novelist and poet:

[W]hen I go out on an expedition, I take with me small, spiral-bound yellow notebooks. They don't have very many pages in them, but that doesn't matter. If I fill one of those notebooks, I'll be able later to write something of 20 or 30 pages. All I put in the notebooks are sensory details. I don't put in what happened because I can remember what happened when, and I don't put in what people said, because I can always interview them later. The things I will not be able to remember are the sensory details—the color of the light on the water, the way the eyelashes flicked, how somebody walked across the sand, the sound of a mother seal calling to her young.

For years I would look at something ordinary, the parking lot uptown, my familiar rock wall, the people waiting for a concert to begin, and write down a hundred or a hundred and fifty specific details:

Old lady with tattoo

Ears pierced

Wrinkles

Silly?

Courageous?

Boots

Short, shuffly steps

Parkinson's?

Clerk's face changes when he sees a customer

Salesman's mask

Greedy smile

Slimy voice

Lady delighted

Coy

Sad

Lonely

Outside young woman rises from car as if she were rising from swimming pool

Liquid movement

She flows

Shy smile

But her eyes are not shy

Eyes like switchblade

Quick as a switchblade

Today I do not often formally write down such specifics. I don't need to because I have years of list making behind me. But you need to. Go to an ordinary place—where you are right now, where you would normally go next, where you waited for a friend yesterday. Start writing down specific, revealing details. You will discover that when you look at an ordinary place, event, or person and observe carefully, it becomes extraordinary.

I live my life collecting revealing details. I study my woods and pay attention to the dancing maple branch from which the squirrel has just leapt, then follow his acrobat course, racing along highways in the air only he can see. I pay attention to this morning's distance between the neighbor couple who first walked arm in arm laughing, then hand in hand listening to each other, now a yard apart, silent. Aging myself, I notice the signs of others' aging—the gray hair sneaking up under the dye job, the way a hand trembles, the step that is unsure, shuffling out ahead to find the curb.

I may still write down what I observe in my daybook, but most of the time I allow it to sift into memory unconsciously. It will remain there forgotten until it is recalled by my writing. Then it will appear on the page surprising me. The more I see, the more that is stored in memory like money in the bank, ready to be withdrawn when it is needed. I cannot promise you that if you develop the craft of vision that you will become a writer—or an artist—but I can promise you that you will rarely be bored.

THE SEEING I

The craft of vision begins with respect for your own point of view. This requirement sounds easy but it isn't. When I came into teaching, I was warned that my students would be selfish, self-centered, inflated with their own importance, and there were a few through the years that fitted that stereotype—but very few.

The biggest problem was a modesty so extensive, I thought it had to be false. It wasn't. Most of my students didn't believe they had anything worth saying. They didn't respect themselves and the individual points of view from which they saw their world; therefore, they didn't see or didn't pay attention to what they saw. If they saw—felt, thought—it, then it must not be special, yet to focus on your subject you need to respect your own eye.

Most of my students did not value their own experiences and their feelings and thoughts about their experiences, including the soldier wounded in Vietnam; the woman caring for her dying mother, her father, and her brothers and sisters—while going to school; the welfare mother of nine children who was returning to college; the man who left the ministry to become a writer; the professional fisherman; the victim of marital violence; the woman who was first mate on a three-masted schooner that had weathered a hurricane in the Caribbean; as well as all the other students who had lived their more quiet lives that were still filled with material for effective—and significant—writing.

The writer Sandra Cisneros tells us to, "Write about what makes you different." Wise advice that took me a lifetime to understand. All that made me strange—and sometimes frightening—to my family and weird to my teachers and classmates, made me a writer. I didn't know that as I stumbled through school, dropping out then flunking out of high school. I thought I was strange, different and yet dull, uninteresting, boring, blah. I did not know the importance of everyone's seeing I. You have already lived extraordinary lives. Take inventory:

What's your ethic background?

Racial?

Religious?

Are you adopted?

If so, what do you know about your background?

What don't you know?

What do you want to know?

What do you not want to know?

If you know your grandparents, write a line describing each one.

Do the same for your parents or stepparents.

Where did you grow up?

What do you know how to do?

What would you like to know how to do?

List your jobs.

List your skills.

Describe your world in a sentence.

What do you feel about your world?

What do you think about your world?

As you travel into yourself and your world, you will discover your personal angle of vision and be surprised at how much you know and how it influences your vision of the world. As you write, you will learn to respect your own individual way of looking at the world.

SEE WITH THE SEVEN SENSES

The writer needs to exercise the seven senses—sight, hearing, touch, taste, smell, memory, imagination. I'll pick a nearby subject, and while I'm recording it with my senses, you should pick your own subject and do the same. I look out my office window at the woods behind the house, the rock wall, the abandoned woodpile, the great tree stump that has become a banquet table for a huge pileated woodpecker, and then I spot my wife's compost piles just beyond the rock wall where she turns garbage into fertilizer to my disgust. It is such an unlikely subject, and I feel so strongly about it, I must pay attention.

Sight

My wife used to make a square of yard-long pieces of wood, stacked alternately so the garbage would be contained and yet receive the air essential to good rotting. Now the wood has rotted as well, and she just builds up circles of garbage—peels and shells and pizza crusts and leftovers, cooked zucchini and green, moldy bread, banana skins and apple cores and spaghetti and a green-spotted custard pie.

Hearing

I heard the "caw-caw" of the crows after a Wednesday dumping as they advertise what we had for Sunday dinner and before. We have no secrets from our gossipy crows.

Touch

One of my chores as a boy was to carry out what Uncle Will called "the swill"— the slimy, slithery ick in Mother's leaky sink garbage container. Now we have a garbage disposal unit in our sink, but my gardener wife keeps a plastic box in which she stores compost. When I have to carry it out, I do it at arm's length so I can't see the disgusting waste, what had to be cut away, what was rotting, what we weren't allowed to eat, what we refused to eat. I don't allow my fingers to touch the damp, gooey mess.

Taste

Taking out the compost, I taste last Saturday's supper—how great it had tasted at 7 P.M. and how it rose in my throat at 3 A.M., burning, sour, rancid. Its memory rises from the compost.

Smell

My wife lifts the cover off the kitchen compost box, and a stink, thick as pea soup, heavy as a wet tarpaulin, pushes down my throat then rises up inside my nose.

Memory

During one trip to the compost bins, a sweetish stench this time, I remember the afternoon in Berlin, at the end of the war, when they opened a subway where hundreds had been buried in an air raid months before—the sweet perfume of death spread across the city, street by street.

Imagination

I hate to garden, but I imagine I am a gardener and see in the death of plants, birth. At the top of the compost pile, a small green shoot, a single leaf, new life rising from what was discarded, tossed away to return to earth.

——————— WRITE TO SEE ———————

Wallace Stevens, the poet, wrote, "The tongue is an eye." When we write, we see. As the words spin forth, we discover scenes in memory that we had forgotten or only half-remembered. Language recovers vision.

I start thinking about my grandmother, with whom we lived and who was the most powerful person in my world until she had a stroke—we called it a "shock" then—that left her paralyzed and bedridden for the rest of her life. I remember the shiny gloss of the skin on the left hand she could not use and write that down, remembering in the writing the delicate colors of the skin, like the iridescent inside of an oyster shell.

I see her wispy crown of white hair and remember back until it was auburn and twisted into a knot on top of her head. She always said her hair was "not red but auburn" even when it was turning gray. How proud she had been of her hair, of her strength, widowed with five children and raising them in a foreign land. She told me stories of how, as a girl, a bull had attacked, and she drove sewing scissors up its nose, saving her companions and herself, and how, when her husband was alive but away on business and a robber with a six-gun wanted the mill's payroll, she broke his wrist with one stroke of her cane and got Alec, her oldest to run for the constable. But the woman I see is imprisoned in her bed, and I start to write what I do not know; my fingers on the keyboard become an eye. I do not think about writing but concentrate on seeing and recording what language sees.

> After school, I wash Grandma's legs that will never walk and, looking away, my hand moves upward, under the covers, following her geography, missing nothing.

> *As I write, I feel the experience of washing her in my right hand and feel her embarrassment and mine at our necessary intimacy. I go back to see more by writing, focusing on the action, not its meaning.*

> I dip the face cloth in the dishpan, rinse, return as she talks of washing the dead when she was a girl in the Hebrides.

*I remember more of the stories she told me when she was a girl on an is-
land off the western coast of Scotland, a girl who was old for her years
and trained by her mother, my great-grandmother, to care for the ill, the
dying, and the dead. I continue the interaction between memory and language by retelling her stories.*

A banging on the cottage door in the night and a shouted name, waking the
animals.

*I follow the story, traveling through geography to Scotland and through
time to the mid-1800s. I am surprised by what I write.*

Death always comes just before dawnlight, and she gathers her twice-
washed bindings, wraps herself in her Black Watch shawl.

*The dark, black-and-green shawl always lay on her bed. I was fascinated
by it. Her uncle, for whom I was named, had fought, according to family
legend, with the famous Scots Black Watch regiment against Napoleon at
Waterloo.*

To walk alone across the island's dark shadowed fields, watching out for
bulls.

*I remember that story of the long sewing scissors she jammed up an at-
tacking bull's nostrils when she was a girl, making her escape across a
stone wall.*

The closing of the eyes, the tying up of the jaw, the scrubbing away of all that
was soiled in the dying.

*My memory of what she said is woven together with what I have heard,
seen, read. This will be my duty to Grandma upon her leaving. Actually,
she died when I was overseas in combat, but as a boy I imagined I would
wash her after she died. It was not, as I remember it, a terrifying
thought, but an appropriate act of love and respect. I return to the simple description of my actions. That is where the power of writing often
stays.*

I empty the pan, fill it with warm water from the whistling kettle and attend
her other side.

*I am pacing out the story. I move from her paralyzed side to the side that
is still alive, and I am really surprised by what I write.*

My hand touches the foot that can still be tickled, then circles up.

*All that is unsaid, is said. All the times we laughed, all the times she
played with me when I was young, all the human caring that passed between us as I continue washing.*

What might be a paragraph in a social worker's report about a troubled teenager—which I was—who had to wash his grandmother becomes a celebration of living and dying in the writing. She had passed on her inheritance from her mother to me: I could do what had to be done. That act predicted some of what I had to do as I lived my life in the war and afterward, when I was alone with my other grandmother when she died, and when I had to give both my parents and a daughter the release of death after I made a lonely, necessary decision.

I find I have written a poem:

The Passing On of Care

After school I wash Grandma's legs
that will never walk and, looking away,
my hand moves upward, under the covers,
following her geography, missing nothing.

I dip the face cloth in the dishpan,
rinse, return as she talks of washing
the dead when she was a girl in the Hebrides:

A banging on the cottage door in the night
and a shouted name, waking the animals.

Death always comes just before dawnlight,
and she gathers her twice-washed bindings,
wraps herself in her Black Watch shawl
to walk alone across the island's
dark shadowed fields,
watching out for bulls.

The closing of the eyes,
the tying up of the jaw,
the scrubbing away
of all that was soiled
in the dying.

This will be my duty
to Grandma upon
her leaving.

I empty the pan, fill it with warm water
from the whistling kettle and attend
her other side. My hand touches
the foot that can still be tickled,
then circles up.

—————————— **THE FOCUSING LINE** ——————————

The focus is the point at which writers concentrate their attention so readers will also concentrate their attention. When we take a picture, we focus on the spot where the most interesting or revealing detail may be captured in a photograph. It is the same with writing. The writer may focus on an event, a moment in a person's life, a decision, an act, a discovery, a cause or an effect, a problem or a solution, but it always defines a place where the writer expects to find significance by writing.

My primary focusing technique is the *focusing line.* The focusing line is the words the writer uses to capture the focus, the starting point of the drafting process. It is more often a phrase—"an ordinary war"—than a sentence—"I write in my daybook that I had an ordinary war and think of the horrors that war makes ordinary." The sentence prematurely closes in on the subject, limiting what I may say; the phrase opens up the subject, stimulating me to think about unexpected connections and territories to explore.

The focusing line is often written in rather ordinary language, but it captures some tension, conflict, problem, irony, contradiction in the subject. This element gives the writer the energy to pursue the potential meaning that lies within the as-yet-unwritten draft.

The focusing line is often confused with a thesis statement; a lead, the first lines of a piece of writing; or an introduction. A thesis statement implies the final meaning of the writing to be written. A thesis statement may be helpful if the writer—and the instructor or editor—are willing to change it radically or abandon it when the draft contradicts it. Too often, a thesis statement implies that the thinking is done and the writer has agreed to a contract to deliver on the thesis statement. Writing is thinking; writing is discovery of new meaning. Therefore, I prefer the focusing line, which implies thinking during writing.

A *lead,* a journalistic term for the beginning or opening of a piece, often evolves from the focusing line but it doesn't need to. The focusing line inspires the piece of writing; the lead is designed to draw the reader into the text.

An introduction tells the reader what the text is going to say or why the writer has written the text or what methods the writer has used to research the subject. It places the cart before the horse for most readers, though. They will be put off by being given information they often do not know they need to know. The skillful writer weaves in the introductory information the reader needs to know at the moment in the text where the reader needs to know it.

IGNITION

The spark that starts my writing engine occurs when I translate the images and the specific information I observe, read, or remember—as well as my feelings and thoughts in reaction to them—into words in my head or in my daybook. I walk around, as we all do, talking to myself.

> Those kids are teasing the golden retriever tied to a long chain. The chain yanks him back. That must hurt. His tail is wagging and he seems to be barking happily but I wonder. They run into his territory, then dash away, offer him a stick, then pull it out of reach, never let him get the stick. What did that ancient Greek, Bion, say, let's see, "Though boys throw stones at frogs in sport; the frogs do not die in sport, but in earnest." I'd like to give that to the dog. He could put it up on the wall of his doghouse. I remember the uncles teasing me at family dinners, giving me a drumstick, pulling back when I reached for it. And tickling. I hated tickling but everybody laughed. I didn't laugh. They thought it was funny when I fell off the dock and almost drowned. Don't want to be a little kid again.

> *Maybe that last sentence is a focusing line. No, not for me. Not this time. It doesn't itch enough. I don't need to pursue it. I allow my mind to run its strange course, as erratic as a dog following this scent and then another and another.*

> Those kids teasing the dog are the same age as the kids I saw on the TV news last night. Was it the Middle East or Ireland? No matter. Their play is real. But childhood is tough. Learning about falling and the monsters in the closet at night and parents divorcing and pets dying and trying to figure out why people laugh at you when it isn't funny. Childhood—serious business.

> *There's a focusing line: Childhood—serious business.*

> Learning to walk is cute for grandfather, not for the kid. Falling down isn't funny. I remember . . .

Surprise is what tells us we have a focusing line. We think of something that is different from what we expect: Childhood is not all play for the child. The focusing line—childhood is serious business—has tension, conflict, surprise imbedded in it. We think—or try to think—of childhood as a happy time, but often it is not. When we smile at children at play, they may not be playing but tasting real terror, rejection, fear. It is hard work being a kid. I do not know what I have to say about this subject. I will only discover what I have to say if I write a draft. But I have the focusing line: Childhood is serious business.

That focusing line may not appear in the final draft, but it is the starting point. It is something I need to think about, something that may produce more thought, more surprise, first for me, then for the reader.

The focusing line often appears as ordinary language, as this one did, at first. It is the writing of the draft that reveals the extraordinary in the ordinary, but the line provides the energy that moves the writer and the writing toward meaning.

I write my newspaper column every week, work on a chapter of a nonfiction book or a novel, write poems, and they all start with a focusing line, an image, a mental picture that intrigues and haunts me, or a written line, a fragment of language that I know contains a piece of writing. Once I have the line, I can start writing immediately or wait until I have time. The spark will be there.

Most of the time, the focusing line is a response to life, but if I have a specific assignment, I still seek a line of my own. I continue to live my life in a state of passive awareness, a receptive alertness in which I absorb the life I am living and pay close attention to my reactions to that life. Certain signals within a line compel me to pay attention and to write.

Consider some of the elements in an effective focusing line that reveal the energy necessary to drive a draft forward.

CONFLICT

The most common beginning point is a conflict revealed by the line. Guilford College in North Carolina is a Quaker school, dedicated to nonviolence, but its football team is called the Fighting Quakers. I wrote in my daybook, "I had an ordinary war" and started writing a book about the extraordinary that becomes ordinary in war.

TENSION

A focusing line contains a conflict or problem that needs to be explored in writing. The quick note in my daybook reads "add/steele." Translation: "I must go back and read Addison and Steele to see how these eighteenth-century writers I once studied so carefully influenced me as a journalist. Might be a critical essay on how they relate to op-ed page pieces in papers like the *New York Times, Washington Post, St. Petersburg Times, Boston Globe.*"

MYSTERY

Usually there is a mystery in a focusing line, something I didn't understand and that I want—better yet, need—to understand. Line: "grdma tuff, kids weak." Translation: "My grandmothers lost their husbands early. They were immigrants with small children, and they had to be strong, but somehow their necessary strength made their children weak."

SURPRISE

I read what I do not expect. I write "they should stay in the graves" and report on a true and disturbing human feeling: my anger at those who I have loved and lost that will not be forgotten.

INFORMATION

Specific information reveals an issue or situation that demands attention and is full of implication. Line: "Est Ger Secpol." Translation: "The East German secret police 'consisted of a force of 85,000 regular employees, . . . 109,000 secret informers: that is, almost 1 of every 80 persons in the country. . . . The surveillance involved 1,052 full-time specialists who tapped telephones, 2,100 who steamed open letters, and 5,000 who followed suspects.'"

WORRY

I noted "My young daughters were proud" when I got out of the car and attacked a driver who had tried to run me off the road. Apparently, the girls saw a powerful man who could protect them. The police saw my attack and did not stop it. They even thought I was right to attack the other driver, but I felt within myself the paratrooper-trained ability to kill. Yes, I was proud that I could attack him, proud that I could win the male confrontation, but I knew that my hands—experienced in combat—could easily, almost casually, have killed him, and I wrote about my fear of what is within us.

JOY

I wake in the morning and take delight in "the coming of light." My writing celebrates the moment of waking—carpe diem, seize the day.

CONNECTION

I observe my grandson's "war games" and connect his play at war to my playing in war, when those who fell down dead did not jump up laughing. One of the most important things the writer does is to connect what is not usually connected so it reveals meaning.

PERSONAL TERRITORIES

Each of us has territories that we are compelled to explore, places where we find meaning. My personal territories are a childhood that was strange and full of questions I have not yet answered, a fascination with the creative process and language, the war, school where I did so badly and later returned as a teacher, my experience in combat and what I discovered about the enemy: myself. I read a story, for example, advocating the tracking of students—separating them by potential ability in high school; in response, I write down the single word line—*tracked*—and later write a column about how it felt to be categorized by a thirteen-track school system and how it marked my life in a bad way.

POINT OF VIEW

I write "skinny, bespectacled kid" and see myself as others saw me. As a grandfather, I also see myself when I was a boy or a young father. I see my daughters when they were the ages of their children, hear them saying now what we said to them—and I have a piece to write.

VOICE

The experienced writer hears the music that reveals the emotional content, or even the meaning of a piece, in just a fragment of language. You will too after you become used to listening to your language as you write. "I meet my cousin's son and am startled to see how much he looks like my father does in the snapshot of him taken before I was born. I feel I am meeting my father when he was young." I hear a reflective music in that line, a thinking back and musing music that makes me think of the childhood my father never had and how that experience shaped him—and perhaps me.

NEWS

On my friend Chip Scanlan's bulletin board I see a clipping from the May 1997 issue of *Mature Lifestyles* and copy it. Each item makes me see my world differently in a way that might lead to writing:

> If we could shrink the earth's population to a tiny village of exactly 100 people, and if we kept existing population ratios the same, our village would look like this:
>
> There would be 57 from Asia, 21 from Europe, 14 from North and South America, and 8 from Africa.
>
> 51 would be female; 49 would be male.
>
> 70 would be nonwhite; 30 would be white.
>
> 70 would be non-Christian; 30 would be Christian.
>
> Half of the entire wealth would be in the hands of only six people from the United States.
>
> 80 would live in substandard housing.
>
> 70 would be unable to read.
>
> 50 would suffer from malnutrition.
>
> One would be near death, and one would be near birth.
>
> One would have a college education.

SIGNIFICANCE

A focusing line has to reveal a subject that is potentially important. Line: "artists teach writers." Translation: "I'm going to write a scholarly essay [or book?] on what artists have to teach writers. I go to the art museum to learn to write. [Another essay on music? Interview my son-in-law, Michael Starobin, composer?]"

Other focusing lines might reveal a potential genre—a research paper, a memo, a short story—I should write. I might discover a need I have that others might need to know as well. I might see a pattern of behavior that should be exposed, an answer without a question or a question without an answer—until I write it.

———— FIND THE FOCUSING LINE ————

A focusing line is the product of all the observation and thinking that comes before writing: listing, brainstorming, mapping, freewriting. If I plunge ahead and write before finding the focusing line, it is usually a waste of time; if I have the line, however, the process of focusing, researching, drafting, revising, and editing usually goes well.

Of course, the focus of a piece changes as the writer gathers information and discovers its significance through writing. But without a draft focus, the writer wanders. I think the focusing line is one of the most important writing techniques I practice, and I learned it late in my life-long apprenticeship.

Here are some focusing lines from my daybook that have produced pieces of writing. These lines are similar to brief artist's sketches, notes in a private language that will spark my imagination at my writing desk. Note that without explanation, they may not mean much to an outside reader. Each one is not the end—a thesis statement—but a beginning—an ignition statement.

I always listened from the other room, learned the language of walls.

This line gave me a poem about the importance of stories in my childhood, how I lived by stories, trying to make sense of my world.

Saw old movie with Clark Gable. He yells, "Get me Rewrite" so he could dictate his story.

I was the rewrite man who was got when I first worked for a newspaper. This line could ignite an essay for college English on how dictation might help students to improve the effectiveness of their writing.

As I look back on my life, I visit the geographies that contained my world.

I haven't written a piece based on this line. It may be a poem, an essay, a short story. I visited a neighborhood where I had lived when I was in elementary school and became fascinated with the shrunken horizons of my world.

Editor tells me, "Cut it in half." Piece better.

Study the manuscripts of famous writers and see what they cut. Is there a pattern that would help apprentice writers? Article for **The Writer?**

Waking in the morning.

This private phrase inspired a proposal for my book **My Twice-Lived Life—A Memoir of Aging** *(New York: Ballantine, 2001) that explored the world of my aging, where waking in the morning is an exciting event.*

My father called in the middle of the night to ask, "How you doin'?"

I expected more from this first call from the dead, but all he wanted to know was the ordinary. Someday this thought will ripen into a poem.

Looks—was I somebody?

This note scribbled on a piece of paper in a Washington, D.C., restaurant led to an essay about the whole business of celebrity and personal identity.

WHAT THE FOCUSING LINE GIVES THE WRITER

We are all terrified when we begin a first draft and step off into the unknown, but the focusing line makes this step less terrifying. The focusing line solves a great many of my writing problems in advance. Let's look at one of the lines above and see how it helps as I begin a draft.

As I look back on my life, I visit the geographies that contained my world.

POSSIBLE DIRECTION

I have a strong indication of where my mind might travel in writing a draft.

RESEARCH

I could choose to research my childhood neighborhood and examine the political, economic, and sociological changes in that area.

REFLECTION

I could think back upon my childhood and how that geography affected my life.

DESCRIPTION

I could map my childhood world in words and see how our vision of an area changes as we grow old: my first trip around the block was more exciting than my first trip to Norway.

LIMITATION

What I write will not be about my high school neighborhood, the battlefields on which I fought, the neighborhoods in which my children spent their childhoods. The line helpfully excludes.

POINT OF VIEW

This can be thought of in two ways.

Angle of Vision

The point of view determines the place from which the writer and the reader observe the subject. The angle of vision includes everything that can be seen or known from that point. I may, for example, write from the point of view of an eight-year-old who has not yet questioned the prejudices of his parents, or I may write from the point of view of an adult critical of those prejudices. Sometimes point of view refers to first, second, and third person: I, you, he/she.

Opinion

Point of view also describes the opinion the writer has of the subject. It is important for the writer to have an opinion of the subject—my parents made the new neighborhood a fearful place because of their prejudices, an attitude that I as a child found unjustified.

VOICE

Voice is the word music that reveals and supports the meaning of the piece. We all respond to what is said to us and, especially, how it is said. Voice is the *how*. In the focusing line, the writer's trained ear often hears the music of the piece: "The first lesson of my childhood was, 'Stay on your own side of the fence.'" This statement has a different music than: "My parents talked about a God of love, but the God they described disliked more than loved, never reaching across the backyard fence to our neighbors."

FORM

Form is the type of writing: fiction, nonfiction, poetry, screenplay, argument, memo, lab report, book review. It includes the tradition of the type of writing;

the reader knows what to expect from a story, a poem, an argument. The line "The Good Book was, in my home, a Bad Book—full of what not to do" may ignite an autobiographical essay or a memo to a textbook publisher arguing for more positive approaches in textbooks.

STRUCTURE

Structure is the way I anticipate getting from the first line to the last; it is the trail of meaning I will follow as I produce a draft. Structure may take many forms. In a narrative, the actions and reactions between the characters create a chronological structure that pulls the reader forward; in an argument, the logic of one point leading to another may drag the reader toward the writer's conclusion. The line "I read Hazlet before Orwell or E. B. White" implies a chronological survey of essay writing, going back to the nineteenth, and perhaps the seventeenth, century.

OPENING

The focusing line often becomes the first sentence or paragraph of what I write. This lead leads—draws, entices—the reader into the writing. A focusing line like "my neighborhood had fences to keep out those who were different" might develop into the following lead: "Recently I visited the Land of Prejudice, the geography of my childhood where good fences did not make good neighbors."

Do I consciously march through all those elements when I develop a focusing line? Not always. But sometimes it helps to take apart what the cabinet-maker put together, to discover how she knew those pieces of burled wood could become a corner cabinet.

OTHER TECHNIQUES TO FIND A FOCUS

Here are some other techniques I use to find a focus.

THE STEINBECK STATEMENT

The great novelist John Steinbeck used to write down what a book was about on a single three-by-five card. He might write a five-hundred-page draft, but his focus would be on that sentence or two on the card. I have found it a valuable technique to do this when I have trouble with focus. That statement includes and excludes. It keeps my eye on target.

BUT—and don't forget this *but*—the statement will have to be revised as you write. You may know what you hope to write about when you start, but all writing is a voyage of discovery. You have to make course adjustments, refining and revising your initial statement as you discover what you have to say.

BEGIN BY ENDING

Many writers, including Truman Capote, Raymond Carver, John Gregory Dunne, William Gibson, Joseph Heller, John Irving, Eudora Welty, Toni Morrison, claim to know the end of a draft before they begin. They all have a destination that may be changed once they begin writing, but destination gives their first draft focus.

It may be helpful to write a dozen or two dozen last sentences. Once you choose one and know where you are headed, you may know where—and how—to begin.

A CONTROLLING IMAGE

When you started to write as a child, you sometimes drew a picture first, sometimes wrote the caption first. You worked back and forth calling both drawing and writing writing. I think writers still work that way. I see what I write, and many times the focus of my writing is an image: my mother and I are lifting my paralyzed grandmother in her bed and someone says something that makes us stop and laugh until we literally weep with humor; I see myself making a thick baloney and strawberry jam sandwich that I once thought tasty; I see myself driving along the road beside Wollaston Beach in the car five of us bought when we were in high school—for five bucks each—looking for girls.

Pay attention to what you see with your mind's eye—or with your real eye—as you research or think about what you are going to write. The focus may lie in that vision. You may have a controlling image that will give a landmark to guide you through the writing.

ANTICIPATE THE READER'S NEED

The focus of a piece of writing may come from the reader. In writing memos to a dean when I was English department chairperson, I knew what the dean wanted to hear and how he wanted to hear it—documented with statistics. My job was to focus a wandering discussion of our department needs in a way that would lead the dean to "buy" our argument and give us the fiscal support we needed.

Put yourself in the reader's place to see if you can understand what a particular reader needs to learn from the text. That may be your focus.

MOVE THE ANGLE OF VISION

When writing, the writer invites the reader to stand at the writer's side so the writer can point out the view and comment upon it. The place where the writer stands gives focus to the draft. In writing for teachers, I often ask them to stand beside me when I was a high school dropout. Many teachers were honor students and viewed school differently than I did, but if they want to reach all students, they need to see school as the less academically interested view it.

Often the writer moves the point of view or angle of vision, taking readers along as the view changes and their understanding of what they're seeing increases. It is where the writer and reader stop and what they pass by that keeps the writing in focus.

ADJUST THE DISTANCE

Distance is a key element in writing. Distance is how far the writer places the reader from the subject. Many writers always write close up; others always stand back at the same distance. Movies and television have made us all aware that the camera can put us on the mountain ridge watching the far-off cattle rustler and then move us in close to see one steer rolling its eyes in terror.

Move in close up, and you'll see in detail. The lens frames the revealing action, response, or object. You'll gain immediacy and intensity, but you can lose context, what the detail means. Stand way back and each detail is in context. Pun intended, you see the big picture. The frame extends so that you have a broad view, but you lose intensity.

The trick is to stand at a variety of distances, each appropriate to what is being said. The writer moves in close to increase intensity, then moves back to put what has been seen into context; the writer stands back to establish context, then moves in close to make the reader see, feel, think, care.

There is no ideal distance apart from subject. The craft is to always be at that distance that most effectively helps the reader see, feel, and understand. The skilled writer uses a zoom lens, adjusting the distance so that the reader experiences intensity without losing context, has enough detachment so that the reader has room to respond, is close enough so that the reader is forced to respond.

Play with distance as you focus and draft—describe your grandmother's hand as you held it in the nursing home, describe her in the group picture of the family arriving in America when she was the little girl in front—to see how it will help you explore your subject and communicate it.

ASK THE RESEARCH QUESTION

In the academic world, the focusing line becomes the research question, as we discuss in more detail on pages 100–110. The sociologist, historian, physicist, economist, literary critic, health ethicist, philosopher, biochemist, or member of any other intellectual discipline needs to learn how to ask a good research question. The research question is central to the term paper, the master's thesis, the doctoral dissertation, the grant proposal, the paper at an academic meeting, the scholarly article and book.

MAKE A THESIS STATEMENT

The thesis statement is a fully developed focusing line: "Toni Morrison reveals the tensions of small-city, Midwestern life for everyone, not just African Americans."

The advantage is that the thesis statement provides focus for the research and the writing. Academic writing in many disciplines has historically favored argument, and the thesis statement in such a piece provides the writer and reader with a clear debating point. It encourages, for example, the reader to say, "Whoa! I'm not so sure Toni Morrison does that. Let's see your evidence."

Many teachers demand, for these reasons, that writers articulate thesis statements before researching or writing papers. The great danger is that the scholars will only look to document those statements when, in fact, they might discover different critical views.

In that case, a writer should submit the revised thesis statement to the instructor: "Toni Morrison's novels document how different the small-city, Midwestern experience of African Americans is from that of their white neighbors."

START A NEW WRITING TASK

The writing process you are learning can be adapted to any writing task and to changing conditions. As you proceed through school and beyond, new classes and new jobs will demand new forms of writing: memos, reports, fund-raising letters, poems, case histories, theses or dissertations, sermons, police reports, book or literature reviews, grant applications, letters of sympathy, job or graduate-school applications, screenplays, scientific or laboratory reports, legal briefs or judicial decisions, marketing plans.

A particular type of task will require a long text or a short one, straight text or text coordinated with a complex graphic design, writing alone or with a partner or a committee, completion in a day or less or a month or more.

In every case you will be able to adapt your experience with the writing process. I've adapted that process to write radio scripts; ghostwrite political and corporate publications; create short poems and long books; write memos, applications, reports, and all sorts of other writing tasks. You build on what you know how to do.

MAKE AN ASSIGNMENT
YOUR OWN

The best strategy for dealing with any writing assignment effectively is to make it your own. The skilled writer shifts the ownership of the assigned piece of writing from the teacher or employer to the writer. There are guidelines for doing this:

READ THE ASSIGNMENT CAREFULLY

Go over the assignment several times to make sure you know what is expected of you. If the assignment has been given orally, write it out and read it over. Make sure you understand the purpose of the assignment, not just what you are expected to do, but why you are expected to do it. The reason for the assignment will often help make the assignment clear. If you don't understand it, read what you have written back to the instructor.

ASK QUESTIONS

If you have studied the assignment carefully and still do not understand it, ask for clarification. It may be appropriate to ask to see good examples others have done in the past or samples of published writing that practice the lessons being taught by the assignment.

STAND BACK

Once the assignment is clear, walk away from it. Study the assignment at a distance to see what comes to mind. The assignment should be given to your subconscious, which will play with it, making connections with what you know, have seen, experienced, thought about.

An assignment always increases my awareness. I'm told by an editor to do a story on street people, and I go to Skid Row, the streets and alleys I've always avoided where I confront the bag ladies, the young man mining the dumpsters in the alley, the woman talking to herself on the street corner, the late-afternoon line at the mission or soup kitchen, the early morning turnout of drifters at the church dormitory for the poor. I note how they dress, I record the wary looks they give people, the way they make themselves invisible, the layers of clothing they wear, the bottles ineffectively hidden in small paper bags, the shaking hands, the shuffling steps. Little of this is conscious observation; I've just been made aware. I begin to see connections with experiences in my past—the refugees who clogged the roads leading from the battlefields they were fleeing and to which we were advancing—and with what I'm reading—perhaps Steinbeck's account of those fleeing the Dust Bowl for California during the

Depression or John Berger's report on the guest workers imported to northern European countries from southern Europe.

It is often helpful to stimulate this essential circling of the subject by using the techniques of brainstorming or freewriting introduced on pages 31–33, 36–38. Don't just attack the subject the way you've attacked similar subjects; collect and recollect information from which you can discover the most effective way to deal with this particular assignment.

BE SELF-CENTERED

Look at the assignment from your own point of view. Don't begin writing from a point of weakness, saying to yourself that you know nothing about the topic. That is rarely true. Of course, you should do the academic work required by the assignment—read the book, survey the voters, perform the experiment, observe the patient—but go beyond that. Look at the assignment from a point of strength. Think about what you know that may connect with the subject. You may have job experience, for example, that will allow you to make a special connection with a character in a book who has moved to a new and alien place, discovered she or he is adopted, or is sent to a nursing home the way your grandmother was. A history assignment may connect with a novel you read in a literature course; a paper in business administration may make use of what you studied in a computer course. Look at the subject from your own point of view, so that you shift the position of authority from the teacher to yourself.

This principle does not mean that you have a license to be prejudiced, to present unsubstantiated opinions, to be unfair. It does mean that, in the process of thinking about the topic and writing about it, you should take advantage of what you know. If you are writing about the care of the elderly, you may use your experience in working as an aide in a nursing home, your family's guilt about sending a grandparent to such a home, your neighbor's reasons to stop working as a nurse for the elderly. Such information may give you a way to approach the subject or to document a point in your final draft.

LIMIT THE SUBJECT

Don't try to cover the history of medicine for the elderly in Western civilization since 1600 in five pages. Instead limit the subject—perhaps concentrating on one nursing home, one disease such as Alzheimer's, one day, or even one patient. Limiting the subject allows it to be developed properly, so that one single point can be developed and documented in a way that satisfies the reader's hunger for meaning and information.

Remember the significant relationship between the words *author* and *authority.* Whenever possible, try to become an authority on the subject on which you are writing. You can do this by taking advantage of what you know, by researching the subject, and by exercising the muscle between your ears and thinking about the subject before you write. Thinking through your writing for each draft should be a way of discovering meaning.

──────── **FOCUS IN THE DAYBOOK** ────────

My daybook encourages the play that is essential in finding focus. It allows this process to happen when I'm waiting for my wife in a parking lot, watching the Celtics on TV, waiting for a friend to show up for lunch. I use these fragments of time to perform the brainstorming, mapping, listing, and other activities described in Chapter 2.

Here are some examples of focus-seeking play in my current daybook:

Poem?

in war he's at home

at home he's at war

This fooling around will become a poem.

The toy I remember best from my childhood was an empty Quaker Oats box. I hated porridge but I loved my drum, my castle tower, my wheel, my echo box, my cave.

This note did become a column.

When you age, your nose gets bigger—and your ears. We all become more of what we are.

This fragment became a television commentary.

On the ten o'clock news

a soldier peers over the edge

of the TV screen . . .

This became a poem.

──────── **FOCUS WITH VOICE** ────────

From the moment a subject occurs to me, I listen to the voices within the potential draft. I listen to the fragments—the lines—that pass through my mind and across my daybook page.

I have trained myself to hear the voice of the final draft in a fragment of language, the way an archeologist can examine a pottery shard and describe a civilization. The voice doesn't just lead to how the writing will be presented; it tells me what the as-yet-unwritten draft may be. It tells me what I think about the subject when I write about it. Voice leads to focus.

I rewrite the piece on the melancholy of a sunny day that I have worked on on pages 8 and 46.

> On this sunny day I look out the window of the Florida condo and feel the pattern of the August sun passing through the leaves that arch over an abandoned road. I am here, now, an old man and simultaneously I am the fourteen-year-old boy exploring the New Hampshire villages abandoned during the Gold Rush of 1849.
>
> I am happy as I was that day so long ago, so immediate in memory; I realize my happiness is strange for it is accompanied by a melancholy for the villagers who followed their dream. That implies they found only fool's gold when they may have become rich. At least they escaped the hard work of farming in fields that grow granite ledges and stones the size of a pig.
>
> I wonder what my dreams were then. A life of arctic exploration? Playing for the Red Sox, the only first baseman who shut his eyes when he swung at the ball? A heroic role in the war that we would soon enter? Becoming a writer, the most impossible dream of all it seemed then?
>
> *I listen for the place in the draft where I hear the possibility of a voice. It lies somewhere between the description of the road and the cliché "the villagers who followed their dreams." I sense a richness of image and language there and a connection I do not expect between the villagers and the life I have left. I will try to improvise on that music.*
>
> Now older than I ever expected to be I look back on the road of my life and meet a skinny fourteen-year-old boy in cutoff shorts, no shirt, walking down a woods road on a July day in New Hampshire. He keeps looking up and I remember he is looking for the younger trees that have grown where a road once cut through the woods. It is a road out of town, a windy woods road leading from the abandoned village behind him to California in the Gold Rush of 1849.
>
> The entire village followed the dream and he imagines he is one of them, and watching him I wonder if that was the moment he decided to follow his dream of becoming a writer, a destination further away than California at the time.
>
> *I hear music I can follow like a dance or marching band far in the distance, faint but clear. I have my focus: my boyhood dream now come true.*

IN THE WRITER'S WORKSHOP

I wanted to quit my job writing promotional copy, but I had a wife and two kids to support. I wanted to do another novel but had no ideas. I was worried. Then two sentences came to me: "In the office in which I work, there are five people of whom I am afraid. Each of these five is afraid of four people." In a dream, a kind of controlled reverie, I quickly developed the characters, the mood of anxiety, the beginning, the end and most of the middle of Something Happened. *And I knew Bob Slocum, my protagonist, intimately. Eventually, a better opening line came to me: "I get the willies when I see closed doors," and I wrote the first chapter around that line. But I kept the original to lead off the second part.* JOSEPH HELLER

All I ever know is the first line, the first sentence, the first page. ERSKINE CALDWELL

I had a line—"I wonder will it strike us over here"—that I thought would be the last line of As If It Matters. *When I had that line, I knew the book was finished, but I hadn't got the poem to go with it. So I kept mulling that over, and then eventually I sat down and pushed around a poem. It works like that, by accretion. You turn yourself into some kind of magnetic field so that things stick, and then you sit down—and the hard part is—push it out, and then you revise it.* EAMON GRENNAN

I've always been highly energized and have written poems in spurts. From the god-given first line right through the poem. And I don't write two or three lines and then come back the next day and write two or three more; I write the whole poem at one sitting and then come back to it from time to time over the months or years and rework it. A. R. AMMONS

What I do at the end of an afternoon's work is write two or three lines on what I think is the direction of the narrative, and where we might logically go the next day. CAMILO TOSE CELA

It was with that book [The Alleys of Eden] *that I finally figured out where a literary writer has to write from. That is, where I dream from, instead of where I think from. The hardest thing for me to learn as a writer was that I could not will my work into being. I learned I should not think about it. I should not abstract it and try to understand it in an intellectual way. I had to go to the dream place, into my unconscious, my artistic unconscious, and focus on the moment to moment flow of sensual experience to articulate my vision of the world. This was the fundamental thing and once I figured out how to go to that place consistently, everything else followed.* ROBERT OLEN BUTLER

You don't have to outline the play, it outlines itself. You go by sequential activity. One thing follows the other. But it all starts with that first seed, conflict. NEIL SIMON

I understand only particles. I understand the characters, but the novel itself is not in focus. The focus comes at random moments which no one can understand, least of all the author. For me, they usually follow great effort. To me, these illuminations are the grace of labor. All of my work has happened this way. It is at once the hazard and the beauty that a writer has to depend on such illuminations.

After months of confusion and labor, when the idea has flowered, the collusion is Divine. It always comes from the subconscious and cannot be controlled. For a whole year I worked on The Heart Is a Lonely Hunter *without understanding it at all. Each character was talking to a central character, but why, I didn't know. I'd almost decided that the book was no novel, that I should chop it up into short stories. But I could feel the mutilation in my body when I had that idea, and I was in despair. I had been working for five hours and I went outside. Suddenly, as I walked across a road, it occurred to me that Harry Minowitz, the character all the other characters were talking to, was a different man, a deaf mute, and immediately the name was changed to John Singer. The whole focus of the novel was fixed and I was for the first time committed with my whole soul to* The Heart Is a Lonely Hunter. Carson McCullers

The problem of creative writing is essentially one of concentration, and the supposed eccentricities of poets are usually due to mechanical habits or rituals developed in order to concentrate. Concentration, of course, for the purposes of writing poetry, is different from the kind of concentration required for working out a sum. It is a focusing of the attention in a special way, so that the poet is aware of all the implications and possible developments of his idea, just as one might say that a plant was not concentrating on developing mechanically in one direction, but in many directions, towards the warmth and light with its leaves, and towards the water with its roots, all at the same time. Stephen Spender

I remember that I started writing Sleepless Nights *because of a single line. The line was: "Now I will start my novel, but I don't know whether to call myself* I *or* she.*"* Elizabeth Hardwick

I replied that I could no more define poetry than a terrier can define a rat but that I thought we both recognized the object by the symptoms which it provokes in us. . . . Experience has taught me, when I am shaving of a morning, to keep watch over my thoughts, because, if a line of poetry strays into my memory, my skin bristles so that the razor ceases to act. A. E. Housman

——— QUESTIONS ABOUT FOCUSING ———

I went to a great concert this weekend, and I want to write about it from beginning to end so I can remember all of it. I don't want to leave anything out. So why should I try to focus?

One of the best things about writing is that it is something you can do by yourself and for yourself. That's why many of us keep diaries that list sequences of events and activities we don't want to forget. We want to look back on these entries years from now to remember an incident that seemed significant to us at the time of writing. And that's okay.

But writing for a class or group is always a negotiating process between making personal meaning and making meaning purposeful; while you will want to be true to your own experiences when you write, you will also want to convey those experiences in a way that will entice your reader, make him or her want to dive into your essay and follow it through to the end.

Just because your reader may not have been present at the event you describe doesn't mean that he or she craves a blow-by-blow account of the entire day. What your reader is looking for is something that makes your experience at the concert different from the experiences of the thousands of others who also attended.

Getting down every detail in your first draft is a great first step; you can always keep this draft as your own personal record of the event. But your next step should be to find a focusing line, something that will label the experience as your own and give your reader something to think through. You may, for example, choose to focus on a chance meeting with an old friend at the concert, or the interactions between particular groups of people, or even the outrageous clothing that many of them wore. Whatever your focus, it should convey a sense of your unique perspective and experience, the ingredients that make you different from other people and other writers.

What if I don't have a unique perspective? How can my focus possibly be interesting to other people?

New writers often think they have nothing different or important to say to an audience. They are afraid that their experiences are so insignificant that they will never fill up the number of pages required for any one writing assignment. So instead of narrowing their focus and going for depth, they broaden their focus and skip across the surface, filling up as many pages as they can.

Finding a focus doesn't mean writing about experiences no one else has had or ever will have; it doesn't mean being a genius or clever or breaking new ground. If you think in these terms, you will be afraid to write at all! What finding a focus means is locating a significant or provocative corner of your larger experience, then making yourself at home in it, furnishing it with vivid details, and inviting your readers to occupy that corner with you.

If a television or movie director were to film a single event in your life, he or she would certainly not film every single person you met, every meal you ate, your entire drive to or from the event, or every conversation you had. A good director would highlight only particular moments, scenes that convey a sense of who you are and how you relate to your world.

Let's take MTV's *The Real World* program as an example. A documentary about young adults living together, the show gives viewers glimpses into—not a panoramic view of—its characters' lives. While we see the young stars engaging in everyday activities, we view those activities through a very selective lens. The camera crews may very well film hours and hours of interactions and conversations among these people, but the directors edit the film so that we see only bits and pieces of it.

Include all the details you want about a day or an event when you write in your diary or when you draft an essay. Then go back and choose a handful of interesting images and try condensing them into one focusing image. If you want, arrange particular images, lines, or sentences from your draft into a poem that will help you focus. Use this focusing poem as a kind of outline for your draft.

What if what I want to focus on isn't what my readers think is most important?

Getting feedback from readers while you are drafting is an important step in writing. Reader feedback helps you see around corners and uncover blind spots in your essay; it lets you know when your writing is engaging and when it is just plain boring—when you could say more and when you've simply said enough!

But sometimes you can reach an impasse in your relationship with your readers. When you find yourself being tugged and pulled between your own ideas and theirs, you may have to clarify your focus so that your readers can understand it better, or you may need to gather more information and develop your own ideas.

At times like this, don't automatically dismiss the reactions of other readers. At the same time, feel free to take a risk and try out the focus you want. You may find that the tension between your readers' wishes and your own will forces you into a deeper exploration of your ideas.

What if my readers want me to focus on one thing only and I want to focus on several?

Don't be surprised if the more you explore, the more complicated your focus becomes; what may seem like a single focal point at the start of your draft may quickly turn into several. It's okay to write about two or three things that are equally important. But then you have to find a way of making the combination of them most important. For example, "Most law school professors agree that there are three qualities an effective courtroom lawyer needs," or "there are four equal forces that came together and led us into the Vietnam War."

Some of the greatest books were written by writers who hardly left their rooms! Everything they wanted to write about they already had in their heads. So why make such a big deal out of seeing, touching, and experiencing the world?

Because the image of the solitary writer in the garret, oblivious to life, is largely a myth. Sure, some writers like to cultivate this image—it makes the rest of us think they are geniuses, and it puts a romantic spin on the actual hard work of planning, drafting, revising, and editing. These writers would like us to believe that composing is purely a matter of inspiration, of becoming attuned to the world through the mind's eye alone rather than through all seven of the writers' senses—seeing, hearing, touching, tasting, smelling, imagining, and remembering.

But even these writers usually keep some sort of journal or notebook in which they record their observations and jot down the details of everyday life. If they don't, you can bet that they have perfected their writers' senses through years of using them, of honing them through the experience of writing itself.

Don't be fooled by the myth. If you decide to isolate yourself and write from the mind alone, you will cut yourself off from the richness of living, not to mention writing. When you experience your environment through your senses, you are fully embodied; when you write through your senses, you embody the world.

If I want to write a poem or story, I can see where the craft of vision is useful, but if I want to write scholarly essays, how will "seeing" help?

Whether you are writing an analytical essay or a personal narrative, as you engage in the process of composing, you will find yourself using terms that refer repeatedly to seeing: Point of view, perspective, angle, focus, and revision are just a few of these terms. If you think of these words, they don't always literally mean using the eyes to see; they also mean envisioning or revising, seeing the world afresh through concepts and theories. Most of all, seeing through imagining.

Most of the world's greatest contributors to science, religion, and history were revolutionary "see-ers." When talking about people such as Albert Einstein, Marie Curie, Mahatma Ghandi, Martin Luther King, Jr., Susan B. Anthony, or Rosa Parks, we often use the term *visionaries*. We praise these figures for their "foresight" or their "fresh outlooks" on life. We discuss the ways in which they "opened our eyes" to new ideas and "revised" our ways of thinking. We refer to them as "far-seeing" people who refused to turn "a blind eye" on the world's injustices. We recognize them as people who argued ideas, took stances, and persuaded others through speaking and writing.

When you look deeply into concepts and theories, you become a visionary of a sort, an *insightful* writer who brings new perspectives to old ideas and issues—a thinker who sees in order that others may see.

But how can research involve new ways of seeing? Doesn't research, by its very name, mean that someone else has already searched my topic and found all the answers?

That's one way to look at it, especially if you are writing a research paper that involves only gathering specific facts and figures about your topic. But if you want to write a paper that allows you to think through data and come up with your own opinions and ideas, you will understand research as a way of bringing new perspectives and insights to a particular issue or problem.

Think of the term *research* itself, a word that suggests re-seeing. When thinking innovatively about your subject, you will find yourself using words and terms that reinforce this idea of seeing. You'll want to *re-view* your topic and what has already been written about it. You'll begin to see the issues involved from different *perspectives* and perhaps develop a whole new *outlook* on the problem. As you discuss your topic with classmates or your teacher, you'll probably respond in terms implying sight: "Now I see . . ." "This author opened my eyes to the fact that . . ." "This writer overlooked an important idea." Research in this sense doesn't mean reporting. It means re-visioning through writing.

I'm visually impaired. I literally cannot see very well. Does this mean that my writing will lack a particular richness?

No. It means that your writing will be enriched, because you have learned to "see" through your other senses. Fully sighted people who are inexperienced writers often rely too much on their eyes at the expense of hearing, touching, and tasting. You, however, have probably learned to use all your senses: You hear the rise and fall of conversation, smell the fragrances of seasons, taste the nuances in flavors of food, and test surfaces with your hands. This too is seeing. This also is writing.

In fact, your "limited" or "distorted" sight may give you a personal and artistic vision of our world. I have a book by a famous British ophthalmologist, *The World through Blunted Sight,* by Patrick Trevor-Roper and Allan Lame (London: Penguin Press, 1970, 1988) that documents how nearsightedness, farsightedness, astigmatism, color blindness, cataracts, glaucoma, muscular dystrophy, and degrees of blindness have affected great artists and, in effect, contributed to production of great art. These artists, because of "defects" in vision, have made it possible for us to see the world anew in their work.

Focusing Activities

1. Brainstorm a list of subjects that entice you, confuse you, anger you, please you. When you finish your list, jot down one word next to each item that you feel sums it up. Choose three words from this list and write them on the board. After all your classmates have done the same, choose six words from the entire list. There may be no rhyme or reason why you choose the words: they may remind you of something, or you may simply like the way they sound. Beginning with the first word, freewrite on each. Then choose one freewrite you'd like to expand and with the help of a writing partner, list three more words about that topic. Repeat the process until you have narrowed your focus and gathered plenty of details.

2. Draw a map of a place you like or dislike. Be as creative as you wish, but don't worry if your map isn't artistically beautiful. When you have finished drawing, freewrite about your place, what it means to you, why you drew it the way you did, what memories you have of it. Then trade maps with a writing partner and freewrite about each other's maps. What do you think the space you see represents for your partner? What does it say about him or her? Brainstorm a list of questions about the maps and when you have finished, read your questions to one another. Using these questions, freewrite about your own place again, and read your freewrites to one another.

3. Take a writing partner on a personalized "tour" of your hometown, city, or neighborhood. Begin by quickly listing in your notebook all of the "hot spots" or places that have meaning for you. Skip over the spots you consider dull and move from one hot spot to another. Jot down stories about each spot, and then read your list and stories to your partner. Ask your partner to draw a map of your hometown based on what you have read and then have your partner choose a spot on the map he or she would like to return to. Freewrite about that spot.

4. Wander out into the hallway or situate yourself at the busy entrance of a building. Record the conversations of passers-by. Freewrite about these conversations, imagining what they mean to the participants, or write about similar conversations you have had with friends.

5. Solve a mystery. Join a group of classmates in ferreting out information about a local issue or problem. Focus solely on that issue. Interview people and read up on the problem in newspapers and other media. How did the labor dispute at the local factory begin? Why do coaches earn more than faculty at some schools? Who painted the classrooms in your buildings institutional green? Collaborate on a draft, and in your daybook keep track of who does what and your collective writing process.

6. Brainstorm a list of relatives and freewrite about each. Choose one or two whom you want to learn more about and focus on them, or choose a couple of relatives you know well and want to write about.

7. Visit the library reference room with a partner and split up. Browse through the many specialized encyclopedias, dictionaries, and bibliographies. Select those that interest you and record their titles in your daybook. Look through these books and select three entries or topics that you want to know more about, or that you already know something about, and write them down. When you get back to class, compare lists. Choose four of the topics—two from your list and two from your partner's—and freewrite about each.

8. Make an authority inventory, listing all the things you're an expert on, that you have focused on: the jobs you can do, the things you can repair, the places where you've lived or visited, the problems you can solve, the hobbies you enjoy, the people you know, your family background. Each of us is an authority on

many things, and our best writing usually comes from what we know and care about.

9. Freewrite on any topic you want and read it aloud to the class. Ask your classmates to go to the board and write down one word, sentence, or fragment that they remember from the freewrite. Have them explain their choices and how these pieces of your essay can help you focus. Then write about your topic again, choosing a focusing point from their suggestions.

10. Draw a line down the middle of a page in your daybook. While watching a suspenseful movie or television show, sum up on the left-hand side what happens in each scene. Record on the right-hand side all that you think is left out of the filming. What don't you see during the show? What does the director include or omit? When you finish, go back over your list and in a few sentences describe the focus of the show, trying to sum up the main point.

11. Choose a favorite sitcom or drama on television and videotape at least one scene. Returning to that scene as often as you need, jot down all the details of setting, dialog, and acting. Rethink the scene from the perspective of a writer and reader rather than as a viewer. Write it up in your daybook not as a script, but as a passage in an essay or story. Since your assumed reader cannot see the scene as it was shown on television, adjust your focus and flesh out the details.

12. List songs that you love and that evoke a certain moment in your life. What memories do these songs bring back to you? Think of all the sensory details you associate with these songs and the events they represent—the taste of fruit punch at the junior prom, the fragrance of your crumpled corsage, the smooth wooden pew at your friend's memorial service, the grief-stricken look on her mother's face, the feeling of cold water cascading over your body at the shore, the odor of hot dogs steaming on the vendors' carts. Come up with all the memories and sensory details you can for each song.

13. Join a group of classmates in choosing a campus issue to research. Conduct interviews and gather information, and then exchange topics and notes with another group. Research your new topic using the information you have been given. Find out at least three new things about your topic that the previous group missed. Practice seeing beyond the data for what is missing instead of what is there.

14. Look in a mirror and sketch a portrait of yourself. Then in your daybook describe your portrait and the process of drawing it. Did sketching your likeness help you see yourself differently? What details did you notice that you may not have noticed before?

15. Visit a room or spot you go to everyday and see it anew. List as many details as you can, from the unusual to the ordinary. Then circle the details that you noticed for the first time. Return the next day and notice what you didn't notice the last time.

16. Try some intergenerational seeing. If you are a young student, think of an issue or topic that an older relative or friend might view differently from you; if you are older, choose a young friend or relative. Write your viewpoint in your daybook and then interview your friend to get his or her perspective. Describe how your ways of seeing are similar or different and why.

17. Go to a newsstand and examine the covers of one kind of magazine—news magazines, for example, or beauty, men's fitness, or home decorating magazines. List the various story titles and kinds of images the magazines feature on the front. What patterns do you see? What do they say about the particular genre of magazine? What do they say about our culture?

18. Pause at intervals and at different times of the day or night along your daily route home to your dorm, apartment, or house. Look and listen for what you have overlooked or never heard before. Note details in your daybook and describe how they change or remain the same.

19. Go to a particular site with a writing partner and write about it separately, each from your own viewpoint. Compare notes and discuss the differences and similarities in the way each of you viewed the same space.

20. Visit an isolated or quiet spot, such as a church or wildlife sanctuary. Sit still and listen for at least fifteen minutes. Write down in your notebook everything you hear. Then add a layer of details by describing what you see and then what you smell. Finally, note everything you feel—cold, wind, snow, rain, sun, or heat on your skin. Then write a short descriptive essay about the spot using these details.

21. See an argument from different cultural perspectives. With a group of classmates, choose a topic, such as affirmative action or immigration, and find one article each about the subject, making sure to include all perspectives, especially those of minority groups whose opinions may not be represented in mainstream publications. Be as objective as you can in your search, and when you have finished, list and compare the main points of each argument. Don't debate these points; discuss what they say about different cultural viewpoints and modes of seeing.

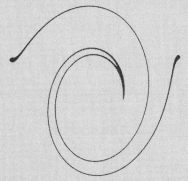

CHAPTER 4

SHOPTALK: THE
RESEARCH PLAN

Now that you have a focus, you must decide how to explore the topic and discover the significant, revealing, specific information on which effective writing is built. Exploring starts with an intention to travel into the unknown and the wise writer develops a research plan. That plan may—will—change during the research process as the explorer's plan changes when there are unexpected rivers to cross, unexpected cliffs to climb.

Each focus breeds specific questions. If the writer has an unfocused territory to explore in writing—the cost of a university education—the writer's questions will be global. How much does it cost to go to college in the United States? Who pays? How do they pay? And the answers will be general, abstract, almost impossible to turn into an interesting, reader-attracting piece of writing. If the writer has a good research plan—how are five single mothers paying for their college education?—the information with be filled with the significant, unexpected details that are essential to lively, convincing writing.

The effective writer plans. We all know that plans do not always work out in sports, business, war, and love, but the plan is the intelligent starting point. Having no plan equals chaos. We write—and our readers read us—to bring order out of chaos. That is the reason that underlies every writing act. We don't know, so we write to know. We need to achieve in our writing at least the great poet Robert Frost's "momentary stay against confusion."

Planning, of course, becomes easier when we are familiar with the task and the territory. The first plan is based on a guess about the unknown, all following plans are based on experience. The writing problems presented by the form in which we write, such as argument, critical review, proposal, personal essay, each provides its own individual need for information that lies within the sources appropriate to the topic.

——— THE RESEARCHER'S ATTITUDE ———

The attitude we bring to a task influences the results we achieve. We all know that attitude wins games, but we should remember that attitude also determines academic accomplishment.

CURIOSITY

Research begins with the insatiable curiosity of the child: "Why is the sky blue? Where does time come from? Can dogs talk to each other?" The questions continue until our parents shut us up. The good researcher/writer never really shuts up. The why's are not spoken out loud and they are not just addressed to parents, but the why's are there.

We want to know all—and more—that can be known about a subject that fascinates us. My curiosity about the writing process began in elementary school. I did not only want to know the story, I wanted to know the storytellers. Why did they tell stories? Where did they find their stories? What do you mean they made them up? How? Where did they start? How did they continue? How did they know the end? And on and on. Every answer I discovered brought an explosion of new questions and this fierce burning curiosity has continued into my seventies and I now know it will continue as long as I can listen, read, watch, and make up stories.

RESPECT FOR SPECIFICS

The writer has respect for concrete, accurate information and the sources of such information. The writer values the revealing detail. I remember when I learned as a soldier that the rifleman did not yank on the trigger but had to squeeze it, gently, softly, caressingly, so the weapon remained steady as I aimed. From that single detail I discovered that the soldier in the heat and confusion of battle had to be calm, quiet, detached, the opposite of what I had thought a good soldier would be.

The writer respects good sources: libraries, books, documents, Web sites, authorities that, in turn, seek and respect truth, or the information that will bring them as close to truth as they can get.

RESPECT FOR CONNECTIONS

As the child has an instinct for connecting blocks so that they make walls and towers, writers have an instinct for connection. They take the details they discover and connect them into meaning. Driving near my home in New Hampshire yesterday I felt a new respect for the rolling, empty fields that were left—so far—from the reach of the expanding suburbs. But then I connected those fields with the fact that American Indians who had lived on this land when it was forest must have resented the fields settlers carved out of the woods as I resent the developers who fill the fields with houses. And then I connect that resentment with the irony that I live in a developer-built house. I want to save New Hampshire from me. I am the enemy, the city dweller who moved to the country. I am always connecting what I discover and observe into meanings that seem new, at least to me.

SKEPTICISM

The great novelist and short story writer Ernest Hemingway said, "The most important essential gift for a good writer is a built-in, shock-proof shit detector."

The effective writer/researcher is not cynical, saying that there is no truth, that all people and institutions lie, but develops a healthy skepticism, questioning, doubting, checking and rechecking, applying common sense to each piece of information. Novelist Graham Greene asked, "Isn't disloyalty as much the writer's virtue as loyalty is the soldier's?"

It certainly is. If the writer's mission is to deliver truthful information to the reader, then each piece of information and every pattern of meaning must be subjected to ruthless scrutiny. And those beliefs and ideas and facts the writer has always held demand the greatest disloyalty.

—— CREATING THE RESEARCH PLAN ——

Remember that we do not write with words, we write with information. The words represent information, the way writing a check represents the money we have in the bank. No money in the bank and the check is worthless; no information on hand and the most skillful writing is worthless.

The reader demands information that is specific, clear, and accurate. The writer has to plan on how to get the information the reader demands.

Research plans will change with the personality, work habits, experience, and abilities of the writer; with the nature of the information that needs to be collected; with the writing form which is going to deliver the information to the reader.

My plans start on my shirt-pocket lined cards, on the pages of my daybook, on my computer screen. At first they are sketchy but they become clear and ordered as I work on them.

The stages I go through to create an effective research plan include:

OVERVIEW

First I step back mentally and think about the territory I am going to explore in writing. I am looking for the furthest horizons, seeing what lies within the greatest limitations and what comes to mind or eye from this distance.

I make mental and then written notes, sketches for a map of the territory that will reveal a way to approach and limit the subject. Many times I make important discoveries at this stage.

I might, for example, decide to discover why local control of schools, which is a basic tenet in our political system, advocated by all candidates of all parties in every election, so rarely works. I would think about my local school board and its jumping-bean response to immediate issues that appear and disappear in a year but block long-term professional curriculum planning.

Then I would make notes about other school systems and the way in which school systems are established in other countries, especially in Denmark, Canada, and Great Britain, with which I am most familiar. I would list the advantages and disadvantages of both local and national or regional systems.

ANTICIPATION

I try to anticipate the ways the reader will challenge what I have to say, what questions I must answer to persuade the reader. These are not the questions I want the reader to ask but the questions I *don't* want the reader to ask, that the reader will inevitably ask.

I might make a list in my daybook as a reminder to keep during my research and writing:

- What's wrong with the present local-school-control system?
- What system are you suggesting?
- How will it work?
- What problems will it solve? Produce?
- How much will it cost?

STRATEGY

I usually decide on the genre or form of writing, such as narrative, exposition, report, critical essay, that will help me explore the subject most effectively. Genre to me is a lens, and each genre has its own advantages.

In this case, poetry, fiction, and drama are not appropriate to the territory— local control of schools—that I intend to map. I am going to write nonfiction.

Now that I know that, it is clear that I must identify the sources of specific, authoritative, and accurate information. I list the categories of sources:

- Federal and state boards of education
- Organizations of superintendents and school board members
- Teachers' organizations
- Faculties of colleges of education
- Local school boards and school-district superintendents

TACTICS

I continue to narrow my focus. Now that I have decided I should use nonfiction, I consider a few of the alternatives: argumentative essay, analytical article, survey, the profile of a school board, the narrative history of a school board.

Now I have to find a school board that has been subject to radical changes because of political pressures that have influenced school board elections. I will have to:

- Read back issues of the locals newspapers that have covered the school board.
- Read the official minutes of the school board.
- List past and present school board members and their public positions.
- Interview school board members—past, present, and announced candidates for the next election.
- Talk to school administrators and teachers, past and present.
- Interview students, parents, and spokespersons for groups interested in education.

TOOLS

We have an increasing number of tools for research: libraries and the Internet, official records and newspaper files, interviews in person, by telephone, and e-mail, scanners and photo copy machines which can copy documents, fax and mail, and observation of school board meetings.

In researching my narrative history I will depend largely on local written records and interviews.

ACHIEVABILITY

I must always ask myself if I can fulfill the research plan. The biggest mistake I see graduate students make in designing their research projects relates to the question of achievability. Can I get the information I need within practical limitations of time and support?

I cannot, for example, afford to visit school boards in California, Arizona, Florida, Minnesota, New York, North Carolina. I must focus on a school board I can reach within an hour's drive of my home.

I cannot cover the history of the school board from eighteenth century to the twenty-first. I must limit my territory to the last thirty years, twenty, ten. It has to be long enough to document many changes, short enough so that I can finish the task.

And I can't cover every school board issue: school construction, curriculum, school superintendent hiring, sports. I decide to focus on the continual concern about sex education and limit it again to middle school.

FLEXIBILITY

The good plan is flexible. Once the researcher begins, the subject may change, or the sources, or the strategy, or the tactics. Nothing in research is stable.

I may find that the school system I chose will not cooperate but a neighboring system will; that the problem there is not in middle school but elementary school; that the strongest political pressure did not come from those who opposed sex education as I imagined, but those in favor of it.

We must always, as effective researchers be aware of our prejudices, or assumptions, our beliefs, our own vision of the world. Research is learning and learning causes change.

The joy of research comes from the discovery of information that surprises, challenges, questions, makes us reconsider, reflect, revise. The novelist E. L. Doctorow has said, "Every time you compose a book your composition of yourself is at risk. You put yourself further away from whatever is comfortable to you or you feel at home with. Writing is a lifetime act of self-displacement." Writing is revision and so is research, a re-seeing of the world.

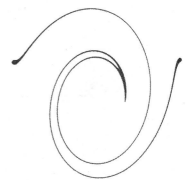

CHAPTER 5

RESEARCH

Research was an intimidating word for me. I imagined unhealthy-looking people working in geeky labs, all head and no body, whom I wouldn't want to have lunch with. They wore lab coats and happily performed dull tasks with complicated machines. In science classes, the work was rigid and predictable: I had to get the right answer on every experiment and the right answer was the one that had already been discovered. Although I was a reader and haunted libraries, library research was bibliographies, footnotes, and formal note taking.

And yet there were times when I sought out information I needed to know and found what I didn't expect, questions that brought new questions, answers that needed questions, trails of information I had to follow. Once I had to do a two-class period oral report for Mr. Donohue, the football coach and history teacher we called Moose out of his hearing. He assigned me the late-19th-century "Blood & Iron" Chancellor *Bismarck* and told me I would have to fill the two fifty-minute periods, no excuses, with my report. I groaned but for some reason found myself fascinated with the German leader and his Germany.

This wasn't research. This was fun. I trotted after one fact and then another discovering patterns of meaning in material I had thought dull. I remember the class paying attention, Moose nodding approvingly. I even remember an *A.* I could have used three class periods.

Research is adventure, trips into the unknown. Writers are the explorers society sends out to describe our public and private worlds. They use language to capture in words the not-yet-thought, the not-yet-said. They make the unknown known through language; they make the unspoken heard through voice. They live at the far and close edges of our lives, revealing what others have not seen—or not understood—in the world around them and have not seen within them.

Writers work at this exploration all the time: It is their blessing and their curse. They examine what others overlook; they reflect on what they see—and their reactions to it. They are blessed in never being bored, always remaining aware of the drama of the ordinary and the internal drama of trying to accept and understand what they have seen. They are cursed in always being aware of what is painful in life and aware of their own pain in observing it. The novelist Somerset Maugham explains, "The author does not only write when he is at his desk, he writes all day long, when he is thinking, when he is reading, when he is experiencing; everything he sees and feels is significant to his purpose."

The explorer first seeks information. Writers write with information—the specific, accurate information that readers need. Readers read to satisfy their hunger for information—specific, accurate information they can use. The writing act begins with the accumulation of the raw material of writing. The act of writing gives that information meaning: Writing is thinking.

——————— THE WRITER'S EYE ———————

Central to exploration is the writer's eye. The writer's eye sees what is, what isn't, what was, what may be. An athlete's eye is inherited. For years I went to an eye doctor who treated many players on the Boston Celtics basketball team, and I asked him if their eyes, not just their height and jumping ability, differ from those of the rest of us. He held up a finger far out of my peripheral vision and explained that all the Celtics could see the finger that I could not.

The athlete's eye is genetic, but the writer's eye can be developed. You can train yourself to see revealing specifics. A revealing specific is a detail, fact, quotation, word, phrase that gives off extra meaning. The male politician on the platform may pay close attention to a series of speakers, then look away, paying no attention, when the next speaker is a woman. It is an accurate detail that gives a clue to his attitude toward women. The screaming of the basketball coach that confuses his own players, the students who sit together at lunch and the ones who want to sit with them but don't, the trustees' decision to spend money for a hockey rink but not for faculty salaries are all revealing specifics.

The writer's eye collects the concrete information that readers like: a statistic, a fact, a direct quote, a specific act. Concrete details give a draft liveliness and authority—readers believe, often in error, that more specific detail makes a more authoritative author. Writing seems to ring with authority just because it is specific.

The writer's eye gathers information, using all the senses—the way the overhead light glints off the surgeon's scalpel, the eyes that reveal so much—and so little—above the surgical masks, the smell of medicine and sterilizing steam, the brass taste of fear, the feeling of helplessness a patient experiences when lashed down on a surgical table, the comfort of the nurse's touch.

Lying there, with part of your body asleep but your brain wide awake, you hear what isn't said, see what doctors don't do as well as what they do, the looks that pass from doctor to nurse to technician. You feel something of what it must have been like to have surgery before modern anesthesia, what surgery may be like with the further development of the laser. You see what is, what is not, what was, what may be.

The writer's eye sees patterns. Specifics have to add up, to lead the reader toward a conclusion, to answer the tough question, "So what?" You see the way the police stop the driver of a Lexus that goes through a red light but treat her with courtesy. Then you see the police stop a battered Chevy for the same offense, make the driver get out of the car and slam him up against the hood, while another officer calls in to see if the car is stolen or if the driver has a record. You are aware of the skin color of the second driver and begin to remember your father's prejudiced comments at the dinner table when you were a child, how the teacher commented when an African American student showed up in an elective math class—"No special treatment here, Darius,"—what the history textbook said about the Holocaust. You connect all such specifics into a pattern of prejudice.

E. M. Forster said, "Only connect," wise instruction for the writer, who deals with context and implication. Specific details are not enough by themselves. The way the police handle a suspect must be connected with a pattern of police brutality, training, prejudice, whether or not the treatment is appropriate or excessive.

The writer sees past and future. My mind turned backward in a recent "Now and Then" column, when I wrote of looking out at snowy woods and seeing snowball fights when I was a boy, and firefights during the Battle of the Bulge in World War II when I was a young paratrooper; I recalled my first sled rides with Uncle Will and a snow hut I built as a boy. I walk by a new building on campus and see within it the memory of the old building on the same spot that was torn down. Cows turn into parked cars, and I see the future shopping mall destroying the farm. The writer is always looking backward and forward, studying the present to discover the causes of events and to imagine their effects. The writer lives in a changing world, seeing what is, what was, what may be. As Robert Cormier says,

> What if? What if? My mind raced, and my emotions kept pace at the sidelines, the way it always happens when a story idea arrives, like a small explosion of thought and feeling. What if? What if an incident like that in the park had been crucial to a relationship between father and daughter? What would make it crucial? Well, what if the father, say, was divorced from the child's mother and the incident happened during one of his visiting days? And what if . . .

The writer's eye instructs; it sees meaning where the writer did not see meaning. Writers write from what they don't know as much as from what they do know.

As I write about my war experience—how much distance there had to be between us when we dug in along the front line, how we kept from getting to know replacement soldiers because most of them would be wounded or dead soon, how we could not admit our terror to those around us—I begin to remember how lonely infantry combat was, how little comradeship there was at the front lines. Language defines, develops, and changes my world.

The writer's eye provides the abundance the writer needs during writing. When you write about a person, place, or event important to you, you begin to remember details you didn't know you had stored in memory years before. I start to describe my first car and remember the high, crooked gearshift, the feel of the accelerator pedal; I hear the rasp when I apply the hand break; I smell the oil and gas and exhaust and the city smell in the wind that strikes my face. The more details I write, the more I have to write. This marvelous eye gives the writer a resource of revealing detail. What is most magical to me is that my writer's eye saw all sorts of specifics of which I was not aware until I wrote.

Stop reading, and take a piece of paper. Return in your mind to an important experience in your life, and list using all your senses the details you remember. Soon your writer's eye will reveal what you didn't know you saw at the accident scene, in the locker room, on the first day of school in a new town, last Saturday night.

THE RESEARCH QUESTION

The research question is central to effective research. Beginning researchers usually wander about in a subject without direction or they take on too grand a subject—the influence of oil on the politics of the Middle East—that would be too large for a book. The research question gives the researcher direction and limits.

The research question should:

- Be significant. Its answer should provide new insight or knowledge. How does the brain affect learning to write?

- Be limited. The answer should be accessible within the time available and other limits of the research—a semester, summer-school term, thesis or dissertation year, sabbatical. How did four stroke victims at the VA hospital relearn how to write?

- Demand a specific answer. The question should bring forth an answer that is not vague and general, but specific and informative. What were the three most important turning points experienced by the four stroke victims at the VA hospital as they relearned how to write?

- Be in a specific context. The question should be connected to an existing strand of knowledge; someone should need to know the answer. What are the implications for third-grade students with learning disabilities of the three most important turning points experienced by four stroke victims at the VA hospital as they relearned how to write?

THE INTERNAL SEARCH

School teaches us to look in the library, on a CD-ROM, on the Internet, in the laboratory, but the writer first looks inside at what is stored in memory. By writing, we make use of all that we have lived, felt, thought, know, if we respect and make use of what we have unconsciously stored in memory.

Remember

The first place from which to collect information is memory. You have recorded far more than you may realize on most subjects; unfamiliar subjects you can at least put in a context of memory. When I visit a new high school, I always remember North Quincy High School, failing grades, dropping out, returning until finally, flunking out. I collect information about the new school, first of all, in the context of my own autobiography.

Start your collecting process by listing in your daybook or journal, or on any piece of paper, code words and revealing specifics that remind you what you know about the topic. In remembering high school, I might list:

Mr. Collins, the principal

Bench outside his office

Day I goosed a teacher by accident

Miss Gooch, who had to jump to answer the phone on the wall

Teacher who took a swing at me because I was a Scot

Stack of forged hall passes I found when we moved

History report on Bismarck

Jobs more interesting than school

Class of 45+ students

Teachers condemned to teaching

Chicken game we played when writing in class

"Stardust" played last at ALL dances

Grade of 65, not a C or a D

I thought rich kids were born with slide rules

This is a private list, as yours will be. It will give you notes to yourself that may start a chain of memories. The more specific the items, the more memory will be triggered.

THE EXTERNAL SEARCH

The external search extends the internal one, reaching out to library and computer online sources, authorities that can be reached in person, by mail, e-mail, by phone, on the Internet. It combines all the normal techniques of the scholar with on-the-scene research and interview techniques of the journalist, sociologist, anthropologist.

Read

There are as many ways to read as there are to write, yet most people—prisoners of habit—usually read in the same way, at the same pace, no matter what the reading task. Never let school give you the impression that reading always has to be work, a purposeful job of collecting information. Reading can often be play: It is one of the best ways to leave the real world and escape to others.

Read Fast

Many people say that they read slowly but they remember what they read. The research I have read—and my own experience—denies this assertion. Of course, there are times when you have to—or want to—read slowly to savor or decode a text, but speed itself can be a benefit to reading. When you read fast, your effort concentrates the mind. You pay attention; your mind doesn't wander; you enter into the text and are carried along by the logic, the emotion, the music of language. Many times you have to read fast to allow the threads of the text to weave themselves into meaning. Read too slowly and you see only an individual thread or two, not the pattern evolving. Try it. Many schools teach speed-reading, but you can do it yourself by forcing yourself to read fast at the point of discomfort.

Stop here if you are a slow reader. Don't read each word individually but make yourself read in groups of words or lines, not single words. Move right ahead. See what happens.

Afterward, you may have to go back and read a selection again or study one passage carefully, but then your attention will be concentrated on what you know you need to understand—and I suspect you will remember more than you expected to remember.

Surface Reading

An expert fisherperson can scan the surface of a brook or inlet and sense where the fish are. The reader has to be able to skim the surface the same way. To collect information efficiently, the reader has to get through many books, articles, and reports to discover what needs close attention. Here's a checklist that may help you organize your reading by skimming.

- The title should suggest just what the book or article covers.
- A book's table of contents and an article's abstract may reveal their subjects.
- An author's biography may help you discover the relationship of the writer to your topic, as well as the author's authority to write on the subject.

- The index will lead you to discover specific references.
- The bibliography will send you to other sources to explore.
- Scan the text itself to find revealing section headings or key words.

The reading writer needs to develop these techniques, which, of course, may be applied to scanning newspapers or microfilm or files the writer finds through computer online research.

Interpreting   Once your eye has caught a key word or a specific revealing detail, interpret its meaning by putting it in the context of the piece you are reading or writing, or both. A college's brochure may boast, for example, that 60 percent of its student athletes actually graduate. One reader may be impressed by the statistic, while another may be appalled at the high percentage who fail to earn degrees.

Meaning never lies in isolated facts, but in context. It is the job of the reader to try to determine the information within the writer's context and then to use that information in a context that is appropriate and accurate.

Immersing   Fast reading can produce immersion in the text where you lose yourself in the mood, the poetry, the sweep of the account that puts you on a street in a strange city, in the hospital waiting room, in combat. By reading fast, you get the feel of a subject and the sense of the writing itself.

Connecting   Fast reading reveals information that connects with other information in the text, in other texts, in your notes and drafts, in your mind. Remember that you are writing to discover meaning, to allow specific pieces of information—represented by words—to arrange themselves in many patterns until one reveals significance.

INTERVIEW

The interview, in which you ask questions of an authority on your subject, is one of the basic tools for collecting significant information. Most people are shy about interviewing others. It helps to remember that the person who is being interviewed is being put in the position of an authority, and most people like to be authorities, to tell others what they know.

An interview can be informal—just a casual conversation—or formal—for which you make an appointment, prepare carefully, and probe deeply into the subject.

Prepare yourself for an interview by finding out as much as you can about the person you are going to interview. Prepare at least four or five principal questions you must ask in order to get the information you need. (Those are usually the questions the reader would like to ask if he or she were there.) Think of the reader; ask the reader's questions.

It's important to listen to what your interview subject has to say; don't go on asking the banker about interest rates after she has said the bank is closing. The interviewee may surprise you by what he or she says, and you have to decide on the spot which lead to follow.

Some interviewers take notes by hand, but it is more common to use a tape recorder. You should always ask permission to use a tape recorder on a telephone interview when the subject can't see the recorder. Face to face, when the recorder is visible, it is a courtesy, not a necessity, to ask permission to record. Most people prefer taped records to an interviewer's notes. Some even insist on the interviewer using a tape recorder—or make their own taped records of the interviews. You should, however, practice taking notes by hand, capturing the essence of what people say, even if you use a tape recorder. Sometimes the tape doesn't work, and if you're not taking notes yourself, you may become lazy and miss what's being said.

It's always best to interview a subject in person, so that you can see the expression on the face, the body language that emphasizes or contradicts what is being said, the environment in which the person lives or works, the way the person interacts with others. If you can't interview someone in person, then you may have to do so by telephone, mail, or even by e-mail.

How the Interview Can Lead to Writing   When you are researching any topic, from criminal justice to World War II to urban blight to environmental hazards, don't forget to use live sources. Talk to the people who are involved. They will not tell you the truth; they will tell you their own truths, and then you will have the challenge of weaving all the contradictions together into a meaning.

USE THE TELEPHONE AND THE MAIL

Organizations are also good sources of information. The library has directories of organizations that will help you find groups whose main function is distributing information on one side of a public issue—they are for or against abortion, distributing condoms to fight AIDS, allowing individuals to own handguns, saving wilderness areas from development. They will send pamphlets, brochures, or reports and answer your questions.

Governments—local, county, state, federal, and even international organizations such as NATO and the United Nations—have many groups that will provide you with reports, speeches, laws, regulations, proposals. Your local members of Congress can help you find the right agency and the office within the agency to contact.

USE THE LIBRARY

One of the greatest sources of material is the "attics" in almost every town, city, and state in the country, as well as in schools, universities, and the nation's capital itself. These attics collect books, magazines, newspapers, pamphlets, phonograph records, films, TV and audio tapes, photographs, maps, letters, journals—all the kinds of documents that record our past. We call these attics libraries.

Every library has a card catalog and/or computer file that identifies resources available there and gives their locations. Frequent more than one library, if you can. When I was freelancing, I found it a good investment to pay for cards in four library systems. Libraries are elemental sources for a writer, as important as wind is to a sailor.

If you are not yet familiar with your library, most have tours that will show you how they work. Take the tour. Most libraries also have pamphlets that help you find what you need to know. Study such materials. Most of all, use the library. Browse. Wander. Let the library reveal its resources to you. If you need help, ask for it. Cultivate a good working relationship with your librarian. Librarians are trained to be of service, and all of us who write are indebted to their patience and skills in finding information for us.

It's important when you find a reference in the library to make a note of all the essential information about it so that you can use the library easily the next time, and so that you can list the source in footnotes or a bibliography. Even if you write something that doesn't have footnotes or a bibliography, you should know exactly where you got the material so that you can respond to questions from editors or readers.

Usually you should record the author's last name first, then first name, then the middle initial, the title of the work (underlined if it is a book, or within quotation marks if it is an article), the publisher, the place of publication, the date, the page numbers, and, for your own use, the library reference number together with the name of the library.

Such notes tell you where the information is. It's important to keep a record of the books and other sources you found worthless, so you won't go over them again, as well as the ones that are particularly valuable. Most research doesn't result in big breakthroughs, but a slowly growing understanding of the subject.

USE THE INTERNET

The Internet today gives access to almost instantaneous contact with libraries around the world, as well as sources we can interview, organizations, government agencies, corporations, universities. I am continually astonished by the fact that I can enter a topic, a detail, a name, a category and have instant access to all sorts of references about it from all over the world.

As I read these days, watch TV, use e-mail, I keep seeing Web sites and ad-dresses that I record to investigate. Most sites have links with many other sites which, in turn, connect with others.

The Internet is such an important research tool that I have invited a friend and colleague to teach us some tricks of her trade. Lisa C. Miller, an associate professor and director of the journalism program at the University of New Hampshire, has published *Power Journalism: Computer-Assisted Reporting* (Fort Worth, TX: Harcourt, 1998). Professor Miller was a newspaper writer and edi-tor before she became a teacher and she has taught teachers and professionals.

LOST AND FOUND IN CYBERSPACE

BY Lisa C. Miller

The amount of information on the World Wide Web is dizzying: thousands of Web pages offer data both serious and silly, on subjects ranging from avi-ation to environmental conservation to the best recipes for chocolate chip cookies. The Web is one useful resource for research, but it's hard to know exactly where on the Web to look for what you need. Here are some tips that will make your research a little easier and more productive.

BEGIN WITH THE EXPERTS

If you have a topic in mind, start your research on a Web site put together by an expert or group of experts, or by an organization or museum that spe-cializes in that subject. For example, if you're investigating cancer treatments and research, you might start with the American Cancer Society (<http://www.cancer.org>). If you're looking at the history of rock 'n' roll, try the Rock and Roll Hall of Fame and Museum site (<http://www.rock-hall.com>). Try the White House site (<http://www.whitehouse.gov>) if you need the text of the president's most recent speech on education.

Or try sites such as the Librarians' Index to the Internet (<http://Aii.org>) or Voice of the Shuttle Web Page for Humanities Research (<http://voc.ucsb.edu>). These Web sites offer links to lots of other Web pages, with the links organized by subject. And since these pages are put together by in-formation experts, you can expect the links to take you to reliable and use-ful information.

HOW DO YOU FIND THESE SITES?

Books and magazines on the Internet often list the Web addresses of such sites, and sometimes you can take a wild guess on what the address might be by typing in whatever makes sense, such as <http://www.moma.org> for the Museum of Modern Art in New York. Otherwise, you might have to do a search using one of the tools discussed below.

SURF THROUGH A DIRECTORY OR SEARCH FOR AN ANSWER

Search tools called directories and search engines can help you find information on most any topic you choose. Directories sort Web pages into subject categories; you can go to the Web page of a directory, such as Yahoo! (<http://www.yahoo.com>) and browse through the categories, including Science, Health, Society & Culture, and Entertainment, looking for useful pages. You might browse through a directory like this if you have a general idea for your research, Shakespeare, say, but need to narrow your focus.

Search engines allow you to hunt through databases of Web pages using key words. You go to the home page of a search engine, such as Google (<http://www.google.com>), type in the words, and ask it to find Web pages that include those key words in their text.

Whether you're using a directory or a search engine, you're never actually searching the Web live; you're searching through a collection of Web pages, or databases, created for that particular search tool. The lines between directories and search engines are blurring. Many directories offer keyword searching, while many search engines offer directory listings of links.

One important difference between them is this: when you conduct a keyword search with a directory, the directory tries to match your key words with words in written descriptions of the Web sites in its database, and perhaps with words in titles or subject headings on the pages. Search engines, on the other hand, search for matches throughout the entire text of Web pages in their databases.

If you've got a pretty general topic to research, or you are looking to narrow down your topic, a directory might be your best bet. If you're searching for information on a very specific or obscure subject, you might need a search engine.

You'll also find some metasearch tools out there, such as MetaCrawler (<http://www.metacrawler.com>). These don't maintain their own databases of Web pages; instead, they search the databases of several other search tools at once. Whatever tool you choose, there are ways to make your search through the vast Web more productive.

SEARCH STRATEGIES

Choose your keywords carefully. Think about terms that might be commonly used. If your first search doesn't yield results, try different search terms, and broaden or narrow your search.

Look for tips on searching made available on each search tool's Web site. Look for a link labeled "Help," "Info," "Tips," "Advanced Search," or something similar. It's worth taking the time to read these—you'll get a sense of how the search tool works and how to best conduct your search, so you don't waste lots of time looking at pages about the Detroit Tigers when you really wanted information about tigers in the wild.

Make your search more specific by using symbols along with your key words:

- Many search tools allow you to put quotation marks around phrases you want to search for. If you just type in the keywords *campus* and *crime,* you'll get Web pages with both of these words, but you may also get pages that feature only campus or only crime. If you type in the phrase surrounded by quote marks—"campus crime"—the search tool will look for that phrase.

- Try putting a + sign in front of terms or phrases that absolutely must be included in your search: +"campus crime" +"New Hampshire."

- Some search tools also allow you to put a − sign right before a term you want excluded from the search. For example, you might type in + "key lime" -pie if you're not looking for recipes.

- Some search tools will allow you to do all of the above but may use different symbols or the words *and, or* and *not;* check the tips of help at each tool's Web site.

- Check your spelling if you're not getting any results. The computer can only do what you tell it to, not what you hope it will do (at least right now it can't. In the future, who knows . . .).

- Search tools rank results of a search from most relevant to least relevant, but they do this in different ways. Some determine relevancy by looking at how many times your key words appear on a Web page; some by how high on the page the words appear. Google looks at links from other pages to a page in its database. Usually you can find information about relevancy ranking on a search tool's Web site. No matter how it's done, if you don't find something relevant in the first twenty-five or so sites that come up after your search, you probably need to try a different search.

- Try more than one search tool. Their databases are different, they search in different ways, present results in different ways and don't all search the same number of Web pages.

And finally . . .

Remember that everything is not out there on the World Wide Web. If you can't find what you're looking for, you might need to leave cyberspace and look somewhere else. To make your research complete, you'll probably want to consult a wide range of sources, some online and some off.

My own problem during Internet research is not finding information but deciding what information is reliable. I have asked Professor Miller to address this problem.

ASSESSING A WORLD WIDE WEB SITE

BY Lisa C. Miller

Not all information on the World Wide Web is reliable or useful. Anyone with a computer and some basic software can create a snazzy Web page, but the content may not be what you need when you're doing research. You don't need to be more suspicious of information you find on the Web than you are of other information; just treat it as carefully as you would a magazine article or other resource you might use for research. Check the Web site out thoroughly, and look for the following clues about its content.

What does the address tell you about the origin of the information on the site? Look at the address or URL, the Universal Resource Locator. With this Web site address, <http://www.unh.edu>, the "edu" at the end indicates that this Web page is put up by an educational institution. The suffix "com" means a commercial organization; "gov" means the page is put up by a government agency; "org" means the page belongs to a nonprofit organization. This is one clue to whether a Web page offers reliable information. If you see a Web page address that includes a section starting with a title—like this: /miller/—this often indicates that this is an individual's Web page rather than a page put together—and sanctioned—by an organization.

Who is the author of the information on the page? What are his/her credentials? Can you figure out from information on the page if the author is affiliated with a school or official government agency or well-known organization? You should be able to figure out, by reading what's on a Web site, where the information presented there comes from. If there is no author or organization or government agency mentioned, and no official affiliation given, you probably don't want to take information from the site.

What is the purpose of the document? Is a specific point of view represented? If the information on a Web site seems biased, discussing only one view of a subject, or the sponsor of the site is a person or organization with a specific agenda, you need to take that into consideration. For example, if the information on the site supports only the view that Congress should repeal all gun control laws because people should not have to be licensed to own guns, you are probably reading someone's opinion on the subject. If you're seeking facts or want to explore different opinions on a subject, you may need to look elsewhere.

Does the Web document cover its subject in detail? Does it provide any supporting evidence? Does the author of the information presented on the Web site explain where that information came from? Are authorities cited in the document identified? Is there a list of works cited or bibliography? Look at assertions made on the Web site. Are examples or other evidence given to back these up? Suppose the document you are reading includes this statement: "Binge drinking is becoming a huge problem on college campuses." Are there statistics or examples or statements from experts to prove that? If not, how do you know the statement is true? And if you can't tell where information on the site came from, you won't know if it's reliable, and you'll have trouble citing it in your work.

Is the information presented accurate? Is the document free of grammatical and spelling errors? Look closely. If there are errors of fact, or many errors in grammar or spelling, you may be dealing with a less-than-reliable Web site.

When was the Web page last updated? Often you can find this information on the site. If you can't, you might not be getting the most current information.

Lisa Miller's advice has been very helpful to me as I search the Web for information I need for my own writing. The personal computer and the Internet have radically changed how we search for information for writing, but we shouldn't forget the important skills human beings developed long before the computer that are still valuable today.

OBSERVE

Don't overlook one of the writer's primary sources of information: first-hand observation. See how many of your five senses you can use to capture information—and to communicate that information to your reader.

Go to a place that is important to your topic. It may not be the place where you write. You may be writing about the Continental Congress in which our nation was born; you can't visit it, but you will understand that process better if you visit a legislature, a city council session, a town meeting.

AWARENESS INCREASES AWARENESS

As you train your writer's eye, you will discover how much you notice: the way an old lady dresses for her weekly trip out to the supermarket, how the candy and gum is placed so it can be grabbed by children riding high in their seats in supermarket carts, how the dignified, well-dressed man palms a candy bar and the look of shame on the face of the young boy who is with him. I am never bored because my eye makes the world interesting, exposes the extraordinary in the ordinary, the significant in the trivial.

——— RESEARCH USING THE DAYBOOK ———

When we search for information, we must both search the surface of our world and also dig deeply into the subject we are exploring. The daybook is essential for my way of performing these two contradictory-appearing tasks.

I am always noting things in my daybook that may be valuable later. In most cases these are specific details, images, thoughts, and as they accumulate in the daybook, the notes reflect my interests which seem very different from each other: college hockey, classical chamber music, the effect of war on combat veterans like myself, aging, why school doesn't work for many children, the craft of writing, the terrible loss of a child, the art of drawing, jazz. The daybook allows me to explore the many worlds I inhabit.

The daybook encourages the connections across these worlds that are vital for writing. Notes record the intimacy of listening to the late Beethoven string quartets, of studying the small sketches that led to Henry Moore's vast sculptures, of changing the bandages on my wife's head after a skin cancer operation, and I discover I have an essay to write on intimacy, celebrating small moments. And other notes lead me to discover the importance of being part of a community at a hockey game, a concert, a play, and a requiem mass. I use the daybook to circle my subject—downhill skiing—and see it from the point of view of the expert, the novice, the instructor, the equipment manufacturer, the safety patrol, the snowmaker, the orthopaedic surgeon.

But the daybook also encourages me to dig deeply into a narrowed topic making notes that explore the different kinds of physical pain and how we deal with it when we are young and old, when it affects our partners and children, how it is different on battlefield and football field. I find paragraphs I have written in the daybook while waiting in the hospital and discover that there are ways I deal with pain—and I have a column.

— HEAR THE VOICE WHILE RESEARCHING —

During exploration, the writer is alert for the voice of the material that may become the voice of the text. There is music in every piece of research you discover. Listen for the dancing avoidance in the presidential statement, the ponderous cadence of the scholarly tome, the rage in the voice of the dispossessed, the smug song from the fortunate, the drumbeat of damnation in the legal brief. Quotations from live interviews, phone calls, books, articles, memos, reports, papers help tell you of the significance of what you are hearing.

Voice is a clue to meaning the way movie music underlines the action on the screen. Often in writing you pick up the voice that is appropriate to the text from what is said by the research sources. Also, don't forget to listen to the voice of your own notes. You may, for example, make notes on how animals are tortured to test cosmetics and hear anger in your voice that will be tamed and made effective in your final written argument.

Never forget that writing is music. The melodies you hear rising from the page are vital to earning the reader's trust and to communicating the meaning of what you have to say. The music of your drafts—your voice—also helps to instruct you in the early stages of writing, telling you what you feel and think about the subject.

The voice of the essay on the melancholy of a sunny day I have worked on pages 8, 46, and 81 has come from the information stored in memory. The revision below calls on material from memory. It is important to recognize that remembering is research. But think how different my voice would be if the information came from such secondhand sources as Stewart H. Holbrook's *Yankee Exodus—An Account of Migration from New England* (New York: MacMillan, 1950) and even from firsthand state, country, and town sources. Each voice would be correct, that is, appropriate to the material discovered by personal or objective research—or even a combination of the two.

On this sunny day I look out the window of the Florida condo and feel the pattern of the August sun passing through the leaves that arch over an abandoned road. I am here, now, an old man and simultaneously I am the fourteen-year-old boy exploring the New Hampshire villages abandoned during the Gold Rush of 1849.

I have been told that if I look at the age of the trees and follow the younger, thinner ones, even if they are old, I will find I can follow a road through the forest abandoned almost seventy-five years before I was born. It wasn't easy. The forest was thick with summer foliage and I circled about before I could see what I had been told. The oldest trees were separated by a line of young ones.

I almost ran down this suddenly visible forest road until I heard a strange roar. I wondered if it was a train then realized it was the Asheolot River. I followed the curving road toward the sound and then I realized one road crossed my road, then another. The old moss-covered granite stones, half-hidden by saplings, bushes, underbrush were laid in a pattern.

These fields had been cleared. The rocks were walls. Then I found bigger rocks, great blocks of granite arranged in squares and rectangles, with a sagging in the middle. Trees grew up where once people lived. These were cellar holes, homes, barns, and at the edge of the roaring rapids, great stone slabs from which a mill had once grown.

~~I am happy as I was~~ I remember darting from one discovery to another, filled with an explorer's pride and delight. And then, on that day so long ago, so immediate in memory, ~~I realize my happiness is strange for it is accompanied by a~~ I felt a sudden melancholy for the villagers who followed their dream during the Gold Rush to California in 1849.

I stop here to stand back and listen to how my additional memories have shaped the essay. I'll let it sit overnight and return with a fresh eye and ear.

IN THE WRITER'S WORKSHOP

If you knew where you were going why would you bother writing? There'd be nothing to discover. JOHN GUARE

In Time Will Darken It *I couldn't decide whether the hero went to bed with the young woman from Mississippi or not, so I wrote it both ways, and continued to write it both ways, chapter after chapter after chapter. It was like a fork in the road. I finally faced the issue and decided that in the year 1912, he wouldn't have. So I threw away all the rest of it. It was a wasteful way of going about it, but I had to discover the form from the material. I didn't have a clear idea, usually, of what I was up to.* WILLIAM MAXWELL

As great architects and others have said, God lies in the details. I would say that art lies in the details and that the best skill that a writer can develop is an openness, a receptivity to life, at its most basic level, its most intricate details. There's almost nothing that can go wrong in a book that you can't fix with fascinating, riveting details of one sort or another. That's what life is; life isn't general. Life is texture, process, complexity. The intimate, sometimes terrifying, details of life are to my mind what make life so unexpected and breathtaking. If you can convey a scene in sensory detail, not only can you enter that scene yourself in your imagination or memory, but you can allow readers to walk into that scene also at the level of their senses.
DIANE ACKERMAN

The law of particularity forces fiction writers, poets, and dramatists to obsess over details, instances, and concrete images, while treating the experience of one or two characters as if it matters as much as the sum total experience of the entire human race. To writers, a moment in time, properly rendered, is worth all time—a single, vividly imagined place is worth the cosmos. History is the record of the causal link between human choice and consequence, and as the very word implies, history in that sense is the ground of story itself. JAMES CARROLL

The more particular, the more specific you are, the more universal you are.
NANCY HALE

[A]s you continue writing and rewriting, you begin to see possibilities you hadn't seen before. Writing a poem is always a process of discovery. You discover things about yourself as a poet, about language, about the nature of poetry. *I think it was W. H. Auden who once said to me that writing a poem is like solving for* x *in an equation.* ROBERT HAYDEN

That's not what writing is—writing what you know. You write in order to find things out . . . it's an act of discovery. GARRISON KEILLOR

To be a writer does not mean to present a truth, it means to discover a truth.
MILAN KUNDERA

For me, writing poetry is a series of bewildering discoveries, a search for something that remains largely unknown even when you find it. DAVID WAGONER

What discoveries I've made in the course of writing stories all begin with the particular, never the general. EUDORA WELTY

In travel you discover something and then go home and write about it. In fiction the discovery comes at the moment of writing. Halfway down the page you suddenly meet something unexpected. It's the surprise in writing that is the sustaining factor.
PAUL THEROUX

—— QUESTIONS ABOUT RESEARCHING ——

I'm okay with exploring my own life. That's no problem. But what about someone else's life? What right do I have to barge into their world asking questions?

Just thinking about this issue means that you have all your writer's senses attuned to the people around you, that you are being sensitive in the truest sense of the word! You are also feeling the full ethical weight of what it means to be a writer.

It's true. You certainly don't want to trample on someone else's privacy in search of material. But you don't want to look at people as completely isolated beings either. Lives bump up against one another. We make sense of our own lives by comparing them with others—by watching people live, solve problems, celebrate successes, and survive tragedies. Just because we observe, interview, and write about people doesn't mean that we are voyeurs or have a sadistic urge to see others exposed or in tears. It only means that we seek a common ground between our world and theirs, that we tread the terrain between one life and the next in search of what's similar and what's different.

Besides, writing is thinking, and thinking means asking questions. That's why good writing requires barging around a bit. Be sensitive. But also be inquisitive.

What if I don't get other people's lives right when I write about them?

There are no right or wrong ways to portray people; there are only different per-spectives. Certainly, you don't want to be vicious or uncaring in the way you gather information or write about others. As long as you are not consciously harming people, you shouldn't worry about asking questions or examining how other people live and what they think.

What if people won't give me information?

Give them a reason to give you the information. Flattery is a good reason. If that doesn't work, then you have to find another good reason: Do they want to help educate you? Do they want to persuade? Do they want revenge? Do they want to raise money for their cause? Do they want to defend themselves?

Some people simply want to talk. Many people go through their lives un-heard. This is often true of the elderly or people whose jobs or positions in society don't generally put them in the limelight. People like this are often thrilled that you consider their input significant, and they are usually happy to help you out.

There are many reasons why people will give out information; you just have to find the one that will unlock the information you need.

How do you know who's an authority and that what they tell you is true?

If you are interviewing people face to face, it's a good idea to find at least three sources for any important data. It's not so much that people lie as that they're uninformed; they believe what they're telling you, but it may not be true. As a researcher, you have to keep your common sense in good working order. When you are suspicious about a statement or a detail, pay attention to that hunch and check it out.

If you are getting your data from the Internet, checking sources may not be so easy. Web pages, chat rooms, bulletin boards—all of these sources may contain interesting information, but there is usually no single way of judging its accuracy. Always question what you read over the Internet (or for that matter in any printed text!). If you can, find information about the same issue from several different sources. You may also need to qualify your sources as you write up your data; let your reader know which you think are accurate and which you question.

So I should stick with only official sources, right? I should always go straight to the top for information?

If you want an expert on a particular subject, the best way to find the authority is to ask the people in that business who's the best. Ask nurses in the hospital, police officers on the force, teachers in the school, scientists in the lab whom you should talk to to find out about your subject. They work with all the authorities.

They are also authorities themselves, and this is an important point. Never underestimate the value of information you can get from those who are not "top dogs." These people have perspectives that may very well differ from those of official sources, and if you want to get a complete picture of an organization or site, you shouldn't forget these "everyday" people. They keep things running, and they also operate in the thick of activity instead of shutting themselves away in offices. While they may not be able to give you official documentation about your topic, they will certainly have an abundance of personal experiences to add to your information. Combined with other sources, interviews with these people will help you round out your research.

What if there are no books written on my topic?

That doesn't mean that your topic is not worth writing about or exploring. It may mean that you have a unique perspective on your topic.

Writers who are just beginning to explore often become discouraged when they find that no single "authority" has written about what interests them. They forget that exploring means searching and synthesizing clues and information. It means going on an adventure of discovery rather than a package tour of a well-known land. It means being a detective rather than a collector of facts and figures.

Rather than finding a single book that will cover your topic, find many different sources that refer to the subject you want to write about. You might check out data in magazines or newspapers, on the Internet, or in government documents, for example. You might interview people and send away for information from certain organizations.

Okay. I've gathered different sources and interviewed lots of people, but none of them agrees with any other on anything! Now what?

Don't be discouraged if all your sources don't say the same thing. Gather as many different perspectives as you can on your topic, and arrive at your own conclusions. That's the whole purpose of exploring. It's also one of the main reasons we write.

But first you will want to organize all your data so you can be clear about the issues and points of disagreement. To do this, draw a line down the middle of a page in your daybook. On the left, sum up very briefly all of the arguments of your various sources. Next to each argument on the right-hand side of the page, sum up in one word or sentence the main issue it addresses.

Now go back and organize your sources according to issues, making sure to note just how each agrees or disagrees with other sources. When it comes time to write your paper, you will have a clearer idea about the issues and the points of disagreement, and you will probably have formulated your own opinion from reviewing the issues and arguments.

Researching Activities

1. Go to the library and use Infotrac or a similar computerized database to track a story in newspapers and magazines. Use other databases to see what has been written about the story in literary and academic journals. Listen to various news broadcasts on the radio. Watch national news programs to see how they report the story. Gather as much information from as many different sources as possible, and keep track of which sources yield the most, and which the least. Pay particular attention to the different angles and perspectives each source takes.

2. Look in the class Book of Questions (created for Activity 10 in Chapter Four) and select one that intrigues you. Gather all the information you can to answer that question. Interview people, read city documents, check out library sources, and use your own eyes and other senses. Then with your partner or group, scan the information you have gathered and generate even more questions. Return to your sources or find new ones in order to answer those questions. Repeat the process until you have narrowed your focus and gathered all the information you will need to write about your topic.

3. Think of a famous or historical local figure you want to find out more about. Begin at the library with biographies about the person, and look in the online database or card catalog for general information on your subject. Ask reference

librarians what related materials are available. Then contact your local historical society and ask them where the personal papers and diaries of the person you have chosen are located and whether you can gain access to them. Such papers, called primary sources, are often housed in university or local town libraries or special museum archives. Sometimes you need official permission to read them, but most institutions will cooperate with you if you are doing research.

4. If you have older students in your class, explore an event or events that happened during their lives (such as the Vietnam war, the peace movement, the Kennedy assassinations). First write down in your daybook everything you think you know about the event, and then come up with a list of questions to ask your older classmates. Pay special attention to the language they use, listening for the slang or jargon of the period you are studying. Ask questions about things you don't understand, but also let your interviewees focus on whatever they want.

5. Access an Internet search engine, and type a word or words that sum up your topic. Browse at your leisure, moving from Web site to Web site according to your interests. Print out or keep a list of information that interests you and the addresses of the Web sites you consult.

6. With a group of classmates, take a sensory tour of a site—a favorite spot in the mountains, a beach, a town, a neighborhood, or perhaps a place of historical significance. Ask each person in the group to be responsible for one sense—seeing, hearing, tasting, smelling, or touching—and to record as many sensory details as possible. Reconvene as a group, and write up a portrait of the site.

7. Pick up a local newspaper, and focus on an issue being debated in your town. Research the issue by visiting government offices, Web sites, and local libraries. You might also want to check with the office of deeds, wills, and other records. Town libraries often keep extensive records on civic debates. Call the town or city hall and get a list of public offices, or look in the phone book under the listings for your town government. These sources will give you a better idea of where to start.

8. Visit a nursing home or senior citizen's apartment and ask to meet residents who want company. Meet them individually or invite them to gather as a group. Tell them that you are interested in hearing about their lives and the eras in which they lived. As you listen to their stories, jot down all the facts and details you can, asking questions as you go along. When your interviewees are comfortable with you, ask them if they would mind allowing you to see personal snapshots, letters, or diaries. Make a commitment to visit them once a week over a semester and offer them services in exchange for their time and stories, such as rides to church or the hairdresser, or a steady arm for a walk around the block.

9. Treat "invisible" people as significant sources of information. Such folks include custodians, food-service workers, clerical help in university offices, homeless

people on the street—people we often tend to dismiss as insignificant. Ask them questions about their lives, and invite them to tell stories about what they see, hear, and experience around them every day.

10. Explore your local or school government. Attend city council or student senate meetings, and keep up on the issues by looking in newspapers and listening to reports on local radio and television. Tune in to the local talk shows, and interview officials and citizens. Keep a log of issues that interest you and the details that pertain to them. Use your writer's eye and other senses to take in the whole scene and to analyze the people and debates involved.

11. Walk through a cemetery and observe and record as many details as possible: names and dates, sizes and condition of headstones, genders of the deceased, relationships, years lived, the vaults, statues, and tombstones, the cemetery landscape itself. Write a history of the cemetery just from what you observe. Do you think some "residents" were richer than others? Later, go to the church or public office that keeps the cemetery's records and read them for more information. Visit your local library, and check out newspaper stories and other printed sources about the cemetery and the deceased. Then revise your history according to the new details you gather.

12. Browse through bibliographies. These are lists of books and magazines by other authors whom writers consult when exploring and gathering information about their topics. Go to the library, and select a book about your topic; copy the bibliography (usually located in the back of the book or at the end of each chapter). Exchange bibliographies with a classmate and discuss the different angles and perspectives writers listed in the bibliographies have taken on your topic. Circle on the bibliographies a few of the books or periodicals you want to look at. Locate these materials and consult *their* bibliographies.

13. Choose three of the most helpful or unusual sources you have found, and write them on the board in class. When your classmates have done the same, go around the room and describe your sources and how you have used them. Choose six sources from the board that you have not yet used but would like to try.

14. Take your daybook to a public space, such as a restaurant or cafe. Write down as accurately as possible the conversations of people who pass by or converse at tables in your vicinity. Pay attention to the sound and rhythm of speech, and record as many comments and dialogues as you can. Don't worry about following any one conversation through from beginning to end. Just try to catch the gist of what people are saying.

15. Go to yard sales, and list interesting or unusual items you see for sale. Find out as much as you can about the histories of the objects, who they have belonged to and the people who are selling them. Observe the people who buy the objects, and listen in on the comments they make about them. Between sales, sit down somewhere and write about the most interesting items, people,

and conversations you've observed and listened to. Be on the lookout for humorous remarks, surprise purchases, and odd or interesting characters. List or write about as many of them as you can.

16. Visit the special collections departments, rare book rooms, or archives in your school or town library. These departments often house books and other materials pertaining to local or university history. Some include first editions of local authors' works or the letters and diaries of local literary and historical figures. Explore these collections by listing in your daybook as many of the resources they offer as you can and the possible topics for writing and research they suggest.

17. Paste interesting newspaper articles or personal artifacts in your daybook. Share your daybook with a writing partner, and ask him or her to choose at least three items from it and to interview you about their significance and what prompted you to choose them. Ask your partner to take notes while you talk, and get a copy for your daybook.

18. Write an exploratory draft on your topic and pass out copies in a small group. Ask your classmates to comment about the quality of information they find in your piece and where they want to see more. Have them suggest sources that might be useful to you.

19. Explore a topic through different genres of writing. If you are interested in football, for example, find novels, poems, movies, plays, essays, songs, newspaper columns, editorials, television shows, or public records that pertain to the game. Select three pieces written in three different genres, and report to the class about how they are different from or similar to each other.

20. Draft a family history. Interview relatives and family friends. Use the Internet to look up genealogies and Web pages of relatives, or go to the library's genealogy section. Make a family tree or start a family newsletter that focuses on a different aspect or branch of the family every month.

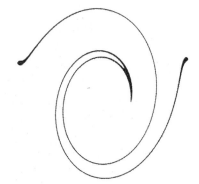

CHAPTER 6

DRAFT

Most mornings I come to my writing desk eager—well, ready—to write. My conscious and subconscious minds have been scribbling away since I left my writing desk the day before. I can hardly wait to see what my unconscious and subconscious have written. There is a sort of essential dumbness in my drafting: I write what I do not always know what I am saying. The draft reveals what I know, what I think about it, what I feel about it. I write for surprise, for the un-expected insight, voice, form, order, information, point of view that will appear on the screen.

This morning I came to my desk to draft this chapter and started by reading through what I had written yesterday morning, not intending to write anything new; but unexpectedly I found words rising between the sentences I had written the day before. I was surprised by "*a sort of essential dumbness in my drafting.*" The surprise of that fragment propelled me forward. I discover, by writing, what I didn't know I knew.

The other morning, however, I turned on my computer and my music and sat down, put my fingers above the keys. Nothing. I waited. Nothing. I started to panic, "Was this the last day of my being a writer?" but then remembered that when I have a writing—or a life—problem I find it helpful to write about it. I decided to write down the elements in a writing task that make me want to get to the task immediately—and keep going until I finish my daily quota—an av-erage 828 words a writing day over the past three years.

—— STARTING TO WRITE ——

These are some of the triggers that start me writing:

- A line (a fragment of language) or an image that contains an interesting conflict, contradiction, problem, point of view, question—or an answer seeking a question.

- A personal need to confront the issue: Donald Barthelme says, "Write about what you're most afraid of."
- A mystery, an intriguing not-knowing.
- A sense of private significance that may be important for others.
- A challenging combination of fear and confidence.
- A feeling that I may have something to say. Sandra Cisneros: "Write about what makes you different."
- A genre that may become a lens through which I can see the subject more clearly.
- An assignment. Somebody wants to hear what I have to say.
- A technical problem. Can I write this all in dialogue, can I write this backwards, can I show the humor in the tragedy, the tragedy in the humor?
- Achievability. Can I finish? In a large project, is there a way I can break it down into tasks I can complete in a single morning?

───────────── **KEEPING ON WRITING** ─────────────

Then I decided to list what keeps me going after I start:

- Surprise. Discovery. Learning. I am writing what I did not expect.
- A voice. In the line or soon after I hear a music in my voice that leads me toward meaning.
- A point of view from which to view the subject or an evolving point of view toward the subject.
- A sense of direction. I rarely know where I will end but I have a strong sense of moving toward an end.
- A reader who appears in my mind as I write. It is always good when I hear myself thinking that a particular writer friend or editor will appreciate the move my language is making.
- Play. The simple fun of making something I did not know I could make. I return to my childhood when a jumble of blocks becomes a tower, collapses and becomes a castle.

Make your own list and add to it as your experience in writing increases. This list will rescue you when you face the inevitable mornings of paralysis.

──── WRITING A DISCOVERY DRAFT ────

One way to start writing is to write. Just plunge in and start writing what I call a *discovery draft* that will reveal what you know and what you need to know. This is my favorite way to begin: off the pool edge and into the water.

No matter how familiar you are with the subject, no matter how well you have thought about and researched the topic, no matter how well you have planned solutions to the problems in the draft, you will be surprised by what appears on the screen or the page.

The first draft—the rough draft—does not say what you expected. Be thankful. The writing is instructing you, telling you what to say and how to say it. The first draft makes your argument stronger or weaker; it reveals a different problem or solution than you had intended to write about; it contradicts or deepens your previous beliefs; it reveals a new meaning or changes an old one; it speaks in an unexpected voice or grows into an unintended form. In these ways and others, the draft betrays the writer's intentions, and the inexperienced writer often believes that these surprises are failures.

Just the opposite. Writing is not what has been thunk, thought completed before the draft and transcribed to the page. Writing is thinking. As we think, our thoughts change. We use language to discover what we know, what it means, and how we feel about it.

A writer writes to see what the blank page reveals. Writers welcome—encourage, cultivate, even force—surprise, contradiction, the unexpected. Wallace Stevens said, "The tongue is an eye." We speak, and we see what we did not see before. Words hold meaning still, sentences clarify and connect, paragraphs develop and place in context, all revealing an evolving meaning that is more than we planned.

But as long as I have been writing I still often freeze before plunging in and starting the discovery draft. I want to know what I am going to say and how I am going to say it. I want neatness, order, correctness. We should be scared of the unknown. We will discover that we think or feel differently than we want. We will reveal ourselves to ourselves and others. We will write stupidly, clumsily, without apparent meaning. All this is essential to creativity but still we stand back and leave the page blank.

I treat this paralysis by listening to the counsel of writers I have collected to encourage and even to kick me off the edge of the pool.

I do a kind of pre-draft—what I call a "vomit-out." I don't even look at my notes to write it. It says, for example, "U.S. Journal, Chicago," followed by the title, and starts out, at least, in the form of a story. But it degenerates fairly quickly, and by page four or five sometimes the sentences aren't complete. I write almost the length of the story in this way. The whole operation takes no more than an hour at the typewriter, but it sometimes takes me all day to do it because I'm tired and I've put it off a bit. Sometimes I don't even look at the vomit-out for the rest of the week and I have an absolute terror of anybody seeing it. It's a very embarrassing document. I tear it up at the end of the week.

I don't write a pre-draft for fiction or for humor, but I can't seem to do without one for nonfiction. I've tried to figure out why I need it, what purpose it serves. I think it gives me an inventory of what I want to say and an opportunity to see which way the tone of the story is going to go, which is very important. Also, this is about the time that I begin to see technical problems that will come up—for example, that one part of the story doesn't lead into the next, or that I should write the story in the first person, or start it in a different way. And obviously, the most important and difficult parts of writing a piece of nonfiction are building the structure and setting the tone and point of view. In any case, almost always, I think, the first paragraph of the pre-draft has something to do with the story that I end up with.
CALVIN TRILLIN

If writing a book is impossible, write a chapter. If writing a chapter is impossible, write a page. If writing a page is impossible, write a paragraph. If writing a paragraph is impossible, write a sentence. If writing a sentence is impossible, write a word and teach yourself everything there is to know about that word and then write another, connected word and see where the connection leads. RICHARD RHODES

I believe that fiction feeds on itself, grows like a pregnancy. The more you write, the more there is to draw from; the more you say, the more there is to say. The deeper you go into your imagination, the richer that reservoir becomes. You do not run out of material by using all that's in you; rather, when you take everything that is available one day, it only makes room for new things to appear the next . . . You don't need to know a whole book in order to write the first page. You don't even need to know the end of the first page. You need only the desire to create something that will say what you feel needs to be said, however vague its form at the beginning. You need a willingness to discover the wealth and wisdom of your own subconscious, and to trust that it will tell you what to do and how to do it—not all at once, but as needed, step by step. You have to take a deep breath, let go of your usual control, and then begin walking in the dark. ELIZABETH BERG

Too often I wait for the sentence to finish taking shape in my mind before setting it down. It is better to seize it by the end that first offers itself, head and foot, though not knowing the rest, then pull: the rest will follow along. ANDRE GIDE

These writers console and instruct me. I leap into the discovery draft.

I write as fast as I can as long as I can. It is almost an unconscious act as I am carried along by the flow of language. I listen to what I am saying as I say it. I do not worry about typing, spelling, even getting the right word. I don't worry about sentence or paragraph structure, punctuation or documentation.

All those are matters for later. They must be dealt with in their time. They are important to make my meaning clear to others but now I am trying to discover my meaning. The draft will reveal my subject and my reaction to that subject to myself. If I am lucky I will surprise myself by how much I know, think, and feel—and I will discover what I have to do to clarify and document that meaning so others can stand beside me and see my vision.

——— WRITING AN OUTLINE ———

There are other forms of the first draft besides the unplanned, plunge-right-in discovery draft. The popular—and comforting—one is the outline that puts everything in its place. And that's the danger of all outlines: they keep everything in their place; they are so clear, so logical, that they are authoritative. They leave nothing to chance and chance is essential to good writing.

Sometimes I outline, sometimes I do not. I do not outline my columns; I do outline my textbooks; I outline some other nonfiction books and novels. And other times I do not. It depends on the task and the way my head responds to it.

Outline is a nasty word to many students, and I was one of them, for this method is often taught in such a rigid manner that it doesn't work. An outline is not a formal blueprint that has to be followed precisely; it is not a contract, and you can't be sued if you break it. An outline is a sketch, a guess, a scribbled map that may lead to a treasure. Writers may create outlines and then not refer to them during the writing, for what they learned by making the outlines allows them to get on with the writing. I am more likely to outline after the first full draft to see where I've gone and where I go, and at the end of the draft to see what I have discovered through the writing and how I have organized my material.

There are many ways to outline. This section shows eleven possible types. None of them is the way to outline. Develop your own system of outlining. Outline only if it helps you, and then outline in a way that provides that help.

I will demonstrate each outline on an assignment given by several freshman English instructors at the University of New Hampshire: Describe your hometown.

Outline 1

This one is my favorite form of outline.

> Title
>
> Lead
>
> Trail
>
> End

Demonstration of Outline 1

(**TITLE**)	My Hometown Was a City
(**LEAD**)	When other people talk of their hometowns, they mention lawns, trees that arch over streets, and backyard swimming pools. My hometown was a city. I remember alleys, boarded up stores, and vacant lots.
(**TRAIL**)	• But where I lived was neighborhood. • Geography of neighborhood. • Who lived there. • Games we played.
(**END**)	When I visited my roommate's hometown, it was like a movie set. I thought I'd be envious, but the streets were empty, I never saw his neighbors, I wondered how he could stand the quiet that kept me awake half the night.

Outline 2

My next favorite form of outlining is the one I use in my textbooks. It is the one I would most likely adapt in writing an academic research or term paper.

1. I write the chapter or section titles, playing with them until I get the wording right, until I see a clear line through the material.
2. I write the major headings for each section within the chapter, playing with them until I see a trail through the chapter or section.
3. I write the subheads for each section within the major section, ordering and reordering them.
4. I draft the text for each section, changing heads as the material dictates. Writing is thinking, and the order will change in the writing.

This procedure is a good technique for outlining a research paper, grant proposal, corporate annual report, brochure, any sort of writing that must communicate an abundance of information in an orderly fashion.

Demonstration of Outline 2

1. The title of my sociology paper will be "The Urban Neighborhood as Home Town."

2. The main sections will be:
   • Expanding Horizons
   • Worlds within Worlds [ethnic diversity]
   • Neighborhood Games
   • Neighborhood Ethics
   • Neighborhood Inheritance [Beliefs taken to suburbs]

3. The subsections within the section on Expanding Horizons will be:
   • Apartment
   • Stairway
   • Front stoop
   • Block
   • Back alley
   • Across the street and away

4. Draft a section within a section at a time. If one doesn't go easily, skip to the next. When you go back, many sections will not be needed, and the rest will be easy to write.

Outline 3

This formal outline style may be appropriate for a formal, very structured subject. It uses Arabic and roman numerals and capital and small letters to break a subject down into categories and subcategories in a logical sequence. Numerical outlines are also popular in some disciplines, and many computer software programs have a formal outline pattern built in.

The most formal outline style requires a full and complete sentence for each entry, but most writers just use fragments as signals for what will be said. Be careful in using the formal outline, because it may inhibit the search for and discovery of meaning that should come during the writing.

Demonstration of Outline 3

[One section of a sociology paper on urban neighborhoods]

III. Neighborhood games
  1. Importance of games
     A. Aldrich study
        a. LePage response
     B. History of games
  2. Nature of games
     A. Hiding
        a. Hide and Go Seek
        b. Ring-a-lievo
     B. Sports
        a. Stick ball
        b. Basketball
        c. Street hockey
        d. Soccer
     C. Gender differences
        a. Boys' games
        b. Girls' games
        c. Cross-overs
           1) Boys playing girls' games [rare]
           2) Girls playing boys' games [often]
     D. Ethnic differences
        a. White neighborhoods
        b. African American
        c. Latin American
        d. Asian

Outline 4

A writer friend of mine, Donald H. Graves, uses this outline form. He lists everything that might be included in the piece of writing in the left-hand column; then he moves items to the columns marked "Beginning," "Middle," "End."

Some of the things don't get moved, of course, and others come to mind as the outline is being made and go right into the appropriate columns. Some things in the left-hand column are not used. It's a brainstorming list, and it

Demonstration of Outline 4

Beginning	Middle	End	Brainstorming List
Home town urban	Qualities of neighborhood life:	How urban attitudes influence	Stick ball
Neighborhood urban unit	Ethnic comfort/ discomfort	How see suburban world through urban values	Latins played soccer
You are defined by your neighborhood	Diversity comfort/ discomfort		Blacks played basketball
	Fears		Whites played hockey
	Pleasures		Don't date X
	Games		Girls' games
	Family		Dress
	Dating + mating		Mixed families
			Loyalty to your own
			Food
			Racial myths
			My values today
			Alleys, loved alleys

becomes an inventory of material that may be used. Some items that are not on the list come to mind when the writer is working on the right-hand columns. The items are ordered—by number—within the columns after the writer has finished. Then the writer is ready to write.

Outline 5

A way to use the outline to dramatize the importance of certain parts of the piece of writing to the reader is to make a box outline in which the size of each box represents the importance of each part. The first paragraph, for example, is much more important to the reader than the pages that follow and might be two inches by four. The subject of the next four pages might be indicated in a phrase contained in a box only one-quarter of an inch by two inches. A main turning point might be in a box one inch by three, and then the rest of the piece might appear in another tiny box. Finally the closing might be in a box as large as—or larger than—the first paragraph. This can best be done with boxes, but it can also be done with typefaces.

This outline style really forces me to face up to the importance of the opening and the ending—to the importance of what I'm going to say and how I'm going to say it. It also forces me to see the structure of the piece in stark, efficient terms.

Demonstration of Outline 5

(OPENING)   Urban neighborhoods were home towns.

(BODY)   familiar geography
comfortable with fears
difference: dress
      food
      attitudes
values: loyalty to own kind (good and bad)
common games; different styles

(CLOSING)   Our suburban attitudes come from the home towns or neighborhoods where we grew up.

(**OPENING**) Urban neighborhoods were home towns.

(**BODY**) familiar geography
comfortable with fears
difference: dress
food
attitudes
values: loyalty to own kind
(good and bad)
common games; different styles

(**CLOSING**) Our suburban attitudes
come from the home towns
or neighborhoods where
we grew up.

Outline 6

A fine way to outline, especially on a complicated subject, is to brainstorm the questions the reader will ask and then put them in the order the reader will ask them.

There will usually be five questions—sometimes three or four, sometimes six or seven, but most likely five. You don't want to use the questions in the draft, but simply give the answers. The questions are in the reader's mind; the writer anticipates and answers them.

Outline 7

The writer can adapt outline forms from other disciplines. I often find it helpful to use a flow chart, similar to those used in systems engineering and business organization study. These charts are designed to show how a factory works, how materials flow from a natural resource to a manufactured product, how power

Demonstration of Outline 6

The questions are brainstormed, written down as they come to mind:

- Who were your neighbors? Did you get along with them?
- How can you have a home town when you lived in a city?
- How is a neighborhood like a small town?
- How does your home town, your urban neighborhood, influence your life today?
- What attitudes and beliefs did you take away from the neighborhood?
- What was life like in your home town [neighborhood]?

Now the questions are put in the order the reader will ask them and sharpened:

- How is a neighborhood like a small town?
- What was daily life like in your city neighborhood?
- Who were your neighbors?
- How did you get along with them?
- What attitudes and beliefs did you take away from the neighborhood?

flows in a corporation. Using this device, I can often spot a movement or force that can order my piece.

Demonstration of Outline 7

When we moved to city I discovered neighborhood was home town ⟶

Geography of neighborhood ⟶ Streets and blocks ⟶ Ethnic

boundaries ⟶ Playing and living within boundaries ⟶ Attitudes

and beliefs neighborhood taught me

Outline 8

A related outline form I find useful I've borrowed from computers. Computer users have developed a number of different forms of outlining that break down complicated subjects into their sequential parts. Most of these outlines flow from left to right.

At the left I state an issue: "The hometown in the city is the neighborhood." Then I give two extreme responses, one above the question and over to the right—"physical boundaries"—another below and over to the right—"ethical boundaries." I break down every answer this way until I see a pattern of potential meaning emerging.

Demonstration of Outline 8

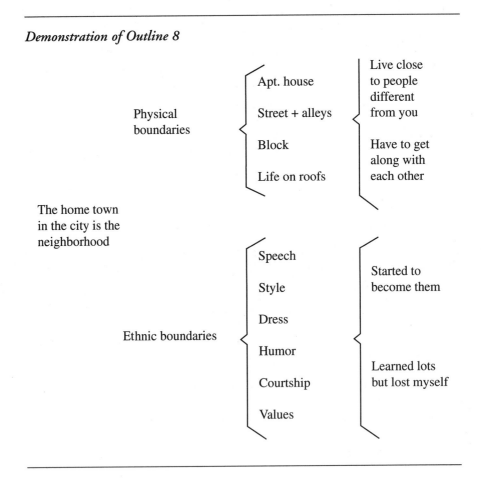

Physical boundaries
- Apt. house
- Street + alleys
- Block
- Life on roofs

Live close to people different from you

Have to get along with each other

The home town in the city is the neighborhood

Ethnic boundaries
- Speech
- Style
- Dress
- Humor
- Courtship
- Values

Started to become them

Learned lots but lost myself

Outline 9

In many effective pieces of writing, fiction as well as nonfiction, each chunk of writing—a paragraph, a page, a scene—answers a question and asks a new question. For example, will they get married? Yes, but will they be happy? Will the product sell? Yes, but will it bring a profit? You can create an outline by anticipating and listing these questions.

Demonstration of Outline 9

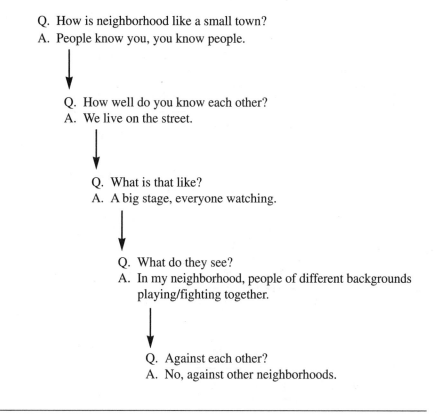

Q. How is neighborhood like a small town?
A. People know you, you know people.

Q. How well do you know each other?
A. We live on the street.

Q. What is that like?
A. A big stage, everyone watching.

Q. What do they see?
A. In my neighborhood, people of different backgrounds playing/fighting together.

Q. Against each other?
A. No, against other neighborhoods.

Outline 10

Many fine writers, such as John McPhee and John Gregory Dunne, use a card technique to outline. This is the most popular technique for movie scriptwriters.

Each scene or key topic in the writing gets its own card, sometimes using cards of different colors for different characters, or different kinds of material in nonfiction. Then the cards are pinned to a corkboard and moved around so the writer can see the pattern of the entire piece—book, movie, or article.

Demonstration of Outline 10

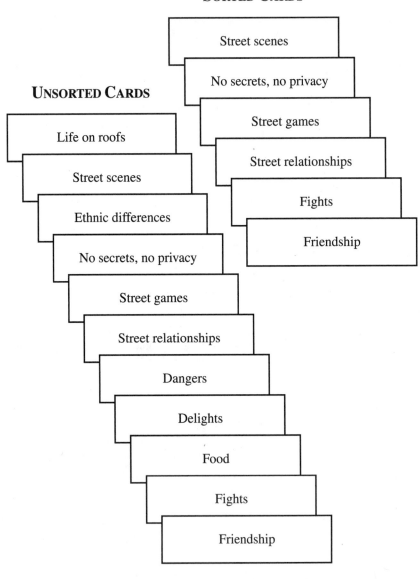

SORTED CARDS

Street scenes

No secrets, no privacy

Street games

Street relationships

Fights

Friendship

UNSORTED CARDS

Life on roofs

Street scenes

Ethnic differences

No secrets, no privacy

Street games

Street relationships

Dangers

Delights

Food

Fights

Friendship

Outline 11

Make a separate file folder for each topic within the piece of writing, a method that is helpful on a large project. You can renumber and move the file folders around, and you can put all your raw material—clips, photocopied articles, notes, photographs—right into a folder. When a folder is full, it may have to be

Demonstration of Outline 11

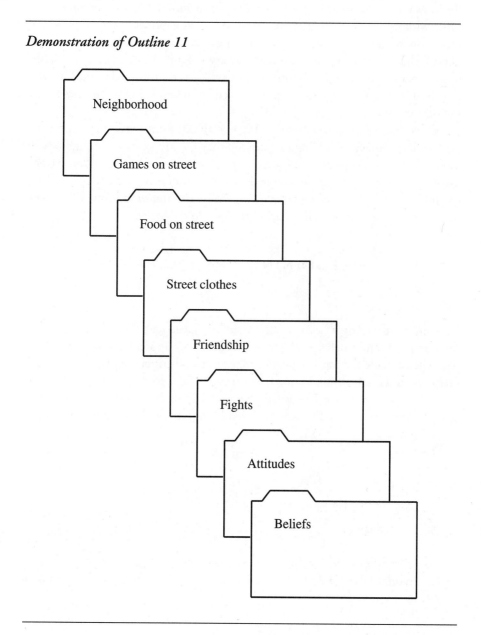

divided. When it has nothing in it, you may have to drop that topic or do more research.

Try out these outline forms, and then make up others that fit the way your mind works. There's no one way to outline, and no eleven ways to outline. But you should find some way of pre-seeing what you may write.

Yes, there are writers who say that they do not outline. But if you interview them, as I have, you find that most of them have outlined in their minds, sometimes without being aware they were doing it. That happens to me sometimes; I just know where the writing is going and how it is going to get there. It seems like a feeling, even though it's probably a very organized intellectual act. When this happens to me, I write. I don't outline unless I feel the need to outline. But I do find that most of the time, my drafts collapse unless I have outlines in my mind or on paper.

Of course, when you outline, you may realize that you need more information or that you need a different focus; you may have to go back through one or more of the earlier stages of the writing process. That isn't failure. You haven't made a mistake. That's one of the main reasons to outline, so that you will see the information you need to have before you write the draft. You will see, by outlining, if you have the information to develop the focus.

——————— BEGINNING THE DRAFT ———————

TITLE

I usually start writing a book or an article by drafting a title, first in my head, then on paper and finally on the screen. During my apprenticeship in my thirties, when I made the transition from first-draft newspaper writer to many-draft magazine and book writer, I drafted as many as 150 titles while I researched and thought about an article I planned to write. I scribbled titles in my daybook during commercials on TV, when a friend was late for lunch, while taking a break from another writing project.

Each title helps me:

- Refine the focus.
- Establish the voice.
- Target a reader.

I might, for example, work on an essay on football, a game I both enjoy and despise. Notice how my draft titles refine the focus, contain a voice, appeal to a reader:

To Hurt Is the Name of the Game

Football: America's War Game

Symbol of U.S. Militarism: Football

What I Learned by Playing Football

Hurt or Be Hurt

The Maim Game

Balance the University Budget: Junk Football

How to Exploit Students

Have You Ever Met a Scholar/Athlete?

My Knee Fifty Years after the Kick-Off

Do You Want Your Leg Straight or Bent?

Play with Pain

Hours of Commercials; Seconds of Action

Why I Love/Hate Football

None of these choices quite works, but you can see how each is a pre-draft of the text, and each demands a different text.

FIRST LINES

The first lines of any piece of writing are the most important to the reader and the writer. The reader is turned away from reading an article, book, or any other form of writing in seconds. Watch customers browse in a bookstore. They pick up a book, scan the first page—or less—and put it down or move toward the cash register.

When readers take the book home they feel the writer has made a promise to deliver information that the reader wants or needs. It promises clarity and grace; it promises surprise and satisfaction. Journalists use the term lead—sometimes spelled *lede* as it was in the days of the news ticker—for the first lines that should lead the reader into the story. The lead promises to satisfy the reader's expectations: A narrative lead should deliver a story; an argument lede follows with an argument.

The opening lines also establish a tension that produces the energy that drives the story forward. The beginning promises a resolution of that tension, a sense of completion at the end.

The first lines are equally important to the writer. They set the tone, the direction of the piece. Joan Didion reports, "What's so hard about the first sentence is that you're stuck with it. Everything else is going to flow out of that sentence. And by the time you've laid down the first two sentences, your options are all gone." Elie Wiesel adds, "With novels it's the first line that's important. If I have that, the novel comes easily. The first line determines the form of the whole novel. The first line sets the tone, the melody. If I hear the tone, the melody, then I have the book."

HOW TO WRITE THOSE IMPORTANT FIRST LINES

I never proceed with an opening unless I think it will produce a good piece of writing. That's the only "never" in my personal toolbox. An opening may not produce a piece of writing that works, and I may have to start over; what I discover in the writing may require a new opening; but I know only one place to start: at the beginning.

The search for the opening begins when I receive the assignment or when I realize I have a thought or idea that must be brought to paper. Sometimes the idea for a piece of writing comes to me in the form of the line or sentence or paragraph that becomes the opening.

In every case, I play with potential openings all during the research and planning process. I note possible openings in my head, in my daybook, in my file on the computer for that topic. When it is time to write, I play with openings. Play is important. I must be free to make discoveries, free enough to allow what I am writing to tell me what I need to say and how I need to say it. I used to write at least fifty to seventy-five first sentences or paragraphs for every article or book I wrote. After fifty years of writing, I am not that compulsive, and I don't keep count. Once every couple of years an opening will come to me that seems just right the first time, but most of my leads are products of word—and sentence and paragraph—play.

To show how much the first lines tell the reader, let's go back to my earlier football example and examine the first lines I might write in my daybook:

> Football prepared me for combat. My coaches were like infantry officers: loud, confident, and often dangerously wrong.

Now see what I can read in those two sentences:

Genre

It is an essay—perhaps an argument against the militarism and violence of football—in which I will explore the world of football in the context of my wartime experience. It is not a poem, play, short story, or news story about a football game, although I might explore this subject in those forms of writing another time.

Focus

The essay will focus on the relationship between football player and coach.

Context

The essay will be placed in the context of the beginning of another football season.

Voice

The voice is cynical, ironic, antiauthority, critical with a strong flavor of bitter humor.

Audience

Football fans who are not aware of how players are treated and what is wrong about a sport that encourages that treatment.

The Writer's Authority

The lead establishes the authority of the writer to speak as a former football player and combat veteran.

Angle of Vision

Coaches will be seen from the perspective of a player who later served in combat.

Opinion

The critical opinion of the essay will allow the possibility that the writing will make the writer see the issue in a different way.

Material

The lead makes the writer aware of the material in mental inventory for the task: I was a scholarship player kept on the field with injuries that bother me more than fifty years later. I also have a mental file full of wartime experiences—the lieutenant who caused his unit to mutiny, the stupid before-battle speech, the colonel who commanded U.S. troops to attack other U.S. troops.

Length

It's shaping up as a strong opinion piece based on autobiographical evidence, not a take-out that attempts to cover the whole story in detail and at great length or exposé. I'd better keep it to eight hundred to twelve hundred words if it is to be published and read.

Pace

Pace is the speed of the writing, which may accelerate when action is described and slow down when the writer reflects on the action. The voice of my first line tells me that the piece should move quickly to keep the reader involved and support the cynical, antiauthority voice. The beat is established in the voice. It should move rather quickly—a guerrilla attack, not a long campaign.

Proportion

Proportion is the effective balance between the parts in a piece of writing: pro as well as con, dialogue and description, action and reaction, statement and documentation, humor and seriousness. In this case, there had better be some objective, contemporary evidence to balance the autobiographical views of an old man.

Evidence Required

Play the devil's advocate to your own prose, doubting, questioning to discover the evidence you would need to believe and trust the writer. At some points as I read my draft, I hear myself responding, "Yeah? Who Says?" I then insert who says into the text, attributing the quote, citing the study, documenting the authority for what I have said.

Potential End

The closing will probably echo the lead and suggest that the writer was prepared for combat by football but not in the way expected.

DRAFTING FIRST LINES

When I write an opening, I am consciously trying to get at the essence of the story. I keep standing back and saying to myself:

What is the central tension?

What's new?

What is changed?

How is the reader affected?

What do I or the reader need to know?

What is the key problem?

What surprises me?

What question does the story answer?

What do I expect the reader to think, feel, do after reading it?

I have been involved in researching the details of the topic; now I have to stand back and see its significance.

Use the checklist that follows to find some effective ways to play with your own possible beginnings.

CHECKLIST FOR FIRST LINES

After you have written your final opening, read it again. Make sure your opening is:

- *Quick.* The reader will decide to read on—or not to read on—in a matter of seconds.

- *Accurate.* The reader who spots even a tiny error will refuse to believe anything you write.

- *Honest.* Don't hype an opening to tease the reader, because you must deliver what you promise.

- *Simple.* Cut back the underbrush. Use proper nouns, active verbs, and concrete details whenever possible.

- *Packed with information.* The effective opening gives the reader information, and that information makes the reader want to read on.

- *Heard.* The reader should hear an individual writer speaking directly to the reader.

CATEGORIES OF EFFECTIVE FIRST LINES

It may be helpful to take a piece of paper and list the kinds of openings you have in your writer's toolbox. Most writers have many more ways of beginning a piece of writing than they realize. Some of the openings in my toolbox are familiar ones.

News

Begin by telling what the reader needs to know in the order she or he needs to know it. Cover the five *W*s—who, what, when, where, why—especially why.

> The computer system at Western State University crashed when 2,500 students signed up for the same section of freshman English yesterday. They did it to protest new, adviser-free computer registration procedures.

Anecdote

The first lines tell a brief story that captures the essence of what you will be dealing with in the piece. It is the most popular magazine article opening, but watch out—if it's a good story but doesn't aim the reader in the direction you want to go, the whole piece may be lost.

> When Lorraine B. Well, registrar at Western State University, turned on her computer yesterday morning, she was surprised by a message in huge letters on her screen: "Tidal Wave."
>
> She didn't know what it meant until the university computer system crashed. More than 2,500 students had registered for the same section of freshman English to protest the adviser-free, computer registration program designed by Registrar Well.

Quotation

A quote is a good opening device, for it gives additional authority and an extra voice to the piece. Like the anecdotal opening, however, it must be right on target.

> "This human being heard the students," said Lorraine B. Well, Western State University registrar who developed adviser-free computer registration procedures. A student protest shut down all university computers.
>   More than 2,500 students registered . . .

Umbrella

This opening covers several equal, or almost equal, elements in the story.

> Registration procedures at Western State University are being reconsidered in an emergency meeting this morning after students—by computer—protested new adviser-free computer registration procedures.

Description

The writer may open by setting the scene for the story. Use specifics.

> Students at Western State University went online last night at the school's computer centers, from dorm rooms, from work stations, from their homes, from the library, even from bars and student hangouts where they could plug their laptops into phone lines.
>   They all—more than 2,500 of them—registered for Section 13 of freshman English to protest new adviser-free, computer registration . . .

Voice

Voice establishes the tone for communication between reader and writer. Read aloud and make sure that the voice of your opening is communicating information in the tone appropriate to that information.

> Civil war broke out on the campus of Western State University when computer fought computer.
>   Angry at a new, adviser-free computer registration system, students mobilized 2,500 computers and commanded them to attack.

Announcement

This lead simply tells the reader what you are going to say.

> Registration will be delayed at Western State University until a traditional faculty advising system is recreated. It will take the place of a computer registration system attacked by students armed with their own computers.

Tension

This opening reveals the forces of the story in action. They are coming together on a collision course or pulling against each other. The opening contains the forces, and makes the reader feel the tension between them.

> "Human Beings 2,500; Computer 0." That was the headline in the Western State University newspaper today when a protest shut down a new computer registration system.
>
> Philosophy Professor Owen Scanlan was not sure it was a victory for human beings. "They had to use computers to attack the university computer," Scanlan pointed out.

Problem

This kind of opening establishes the problem that will be solved, or not solved, in the piece.

> How could students protest an impersonal, computer-based registration system at Western State University? By computer.

Background

The writer first gives the reader the background of an event, argument, conflict, issue, or action.

> Students at Western State University have complained for years about their difficulties in making appointments with their faculty advisers. When Lorraine B. Well was appointed registrar last year, she was told to solve that problem.
>
> Registrar Well designed an adviser-free computer system that made students demand a return to the bad old days. More than 2,500 . . .

Narrative

This opening establishes that the story will be told in narrative form. Be careful not to start too early. Start as near to the end as possible to involve the reader in the story. Background information should not be delivered ahead of the story itself. The reader needs to be involved in the story first to know what information is needed—then the experienced writer delivers it.

> When Lorraine B. Well was a student at Western State University twenty years ago, she had to stand in line from 7 A.M. until after 4 P.M. one day each year to register for courses. In the years since then, she has been a graduate student, a corporate executive, a college professor. When she was appointed as registrar last year, Dr. Well believed that since all students had access to computers, she could design a humane, human-being-free registration system that would eliminate standing in line.

Question

This opening sounds like it should work, but it rarely does. The writer usually knows the answer to the question, and so it sounds patronizing, like the nurse who says, "Now we would like to take our medicine, wouldn't we?"

> How can registration lines at Western State University be eliminated? Not by computer, not yet.

Point of View

The writer establishes the position from which the reader will be shown the subject.

> I am a computer major, a hacker to be honest. I love computers, but I am writing this letter to protest the new computer registration system at Western State. I need a human being, not a computer, to give me advice on the courses I should take to study computers.

Reader Identification

The writer anticipates the reader's concerns and responds to them immediately.

> Western State University computerized registration advising, saying that all students today are used to computers. The administrators did not consider that students still would like to be advised by a human being. "Students won't use the computer advising system," predicted junior Minnie Mahler. "I'm a computer major and I'm going to talk to my professors face to face about what courses to take."

Face

A character is revealed in action. The reader becomes interested in the person and then the issue.

> Stanley Hunan was the first to hear the beeps and notice the blinking screens that signaled a major attack on the new Western State University computer advising system.
>
> A work study student at the computer center, his job was to monitor a registration system he resented.

Scene

The writer establishes a scene that is central to the meaning of the piece.

> A Western State University student with a baseball hat on backward rushed into Harry's bar last night, looking around wildly, "Need the men's room?" Harry asked.
>
> "No. A telephone," the student said, waving a laptop at the puzzled barkeep.

Dialogue

The reader hears one person speak and another react. It's not often you can use this opening, but when it's appropriate, it is dramatic and provides a lot of energy.

> "I wanted to eliminate lines," Registrar Lorraine B. Well told a Western State University sophomore yesterday.
>
> "You did," answered the student. "But you eliminated a human being, as well. I need a conversation, not 'if you are a liberal arts student, select Option 5.' I'm a dual biochem and forestry major, and the computer doesn't recognize that."

Process

A process central to the story is shown in action, and the reader is carried forward into the story.

> Students at Western State University who want registration advice have to boot a computer, click on "Regist" and hope they have a problem or conflict that has been programmed into the system.
>
> The following commands—a student pointed out that the word seems to contradict the principle of offering advice—reveal what it feels like to be a Western State student in need of registration counsel.

These are not all the possible ways to write openings. They are samples from my own toolbox. Make a list of the leads you like to write, and then look through periodicals and books to see other ways of writing them. Then steal the technique. Create your own museum of openings.

My museum of leads has an obvious one right inside the front door: "In the beginning God created Heaven and earth" (Genesis 1:1). I learn from leads by expert writers that I have collected. Here, for example, are many leads that introduce the same subject: New York City.

> *At the height of Harlem's nighttime fury a white police officer stood in the litter of glass and garbage that had come crashing down from the darkened rooftops and raised a bullhorn to his mouth. "Go home," he pleaded with the glowering Negro mobs that clustered along Seventh Avenue and atop the shabby tenements. "Go home," "Go home." From a man in the mob came a shout: "We are home, Baby."*
> *TIME, JULY 31, 1964*

> *I often feel drawn to the Hudson River, and I have spent a lot of time through the years poking around the part of it that flows past the city. I never get tired of looking at it; it hypnotizes me. I like to look at it in midsummer, when it is warm and dirty and drowsy, and I like to look at it when it is stirred up, when a northeast wind is blowing and a strong tide is running—a new-moon tide or a full-moon tide—and I like to look at it when it is slack. It is exciting to me on weekdays, when it is crowded with ocean craft, harbor craft, and river craft, but it is the river itself that draws me, and not the shipping, and I guess I like it best on Sundays, when*

there are lulls that sometimes last as long as half an hour, during which, all the way from the Battery to the George Washington Bridge, nothing moves upon it, not even a ferry, not even a tug, and it becomes as hushed and dark and secret and remote and unreal as a river in a dream. JOSEPH MITCHELL, "THE RIVER," *THE NEW YORKER*, APRIL 4, 1959

For more than half an hour thirty-eight respectable, law-abiding citizens in Queens watched a killer stalk and stab a woman in three separate attacks in Kew Gardens. Twice the sound of their voices and the sudden glow of their bedroom lights interrupted him and frightened him off. Each time he returned, sought her out, and stabbed her again. Not one person telephoned the police during the assault; one witness called after the woman was dead. MARTIN GANSBERG, *THE NEW YORK TIMES*, MARCH 27, 1964

The New York Giants, who overwhelmed two opponents at football last year, underwhelmed ten and whelmed two . . . RED SMITH, *NEW YORK HERALD TRIBUNE*

On any person who desires such queer prizes, New York will bestow the gift of loneliness and the gift of privacy. It is this largess that accounts for the presence within the city's walls of a considerable section of the population; for the residents of Manhattan are to a large extent strangers who have pulled up stakes somewhere and come to town, seeking sanctuary or fulfillment or some greater or lesser grail. The capacity to make such dubious gifts is a mysterious quality of New York. It can destroy an individual, or it can fulfill him, depending a good deal on luck. No one should come to New York to live unless he is willing to be lucky.
E. B. WHITE, "HERE IS NEW YORK," *HOLIDAY*, APRIL 1949

All of these writers deal with the same subject, but what a variety of approaches—and voices. Create your own museum for inspiration and instruction.

———— CONTINUING THE DRAFT ————

The novelist F. Scott Fitzgerald said, "All good writing is swimming under water and holding your breath," and finishing a draft often has that feeling to it. I find it wise to keep going as long as I can until I surface and take a break.

SPEED WRITING

Most writers of articles and short stories try to finish a draft at a sitting. They write as fast as they can, allowing the momentum of their writing to carry them forward. There are few things as exciting for me than to be carried forward by an evolving draft. I feel as if I am in a raft being carried through white water on a flood river.

To allow the flow of the text to carry you forward you have to disregard your handwriting or, in my case, my sloppy two-fingered typing. I have to ignore punctuation, sentence and paragraph length. At *Time Magazine* I learned not to stop the flow of the draft to look up a statistic, a reference, a quotation but to type *TK* in capital letters for TO KOME. I can go back and look up those pieces of information later. Nothing should slow the race toward meaning. Turn off the phone or use an answering machine, lock your door and hang a "Do Not Disturb" sign on the doorknob. The great nonfiction writer John McPhee tied himself in his chair with his bathrobe belt when he was a beginning writer.

The fast-written draft will help you outrace the censor who makes you doubt yourself, who focuses on the superficial aspects of writing, attempting to polish meaning before there is a meaning.

Speed, in some magic way I do not fully understand, becomes a magnet for information and language you did not know was in you. It draws on memory and voice so that you are saying more than you expected to say. Writing, for writers, proves how much they know, how much was hidden in the skull until a draft drew on it.

Drafting at top speed also connects what you have lived, heard and over-heard, researched, observed so that these fragments are woven into new mean-ings. Fluency is essential and it doesn't come from care, but from taking risks, writing what you do not expect, often what makes you uncomfortable because the racing draft escapes the prison of your preconceived knowledge, your beliefs, your prejudices. My metaphor: writing is like skating out on black ice, ice so thin it bends to your weight, so thin that water sprays from your skates as you skim along ahead of what you have known.

One way to gain speed in writing is to dictate. The first edition of this book was written in precomputer days when I dictated to my wife who typed on a lap desk we had in our van. We drove from New Hampshire to see her mother in Kentucky and back, then drove to Wyoming where I taught for a summer and a semester. When we arrived in Laramie, we had the draft of a book.

The biggest advantage of the computer for me is that I can write fast, that I can produce a sloppy draft that gets me from beginning to end. Then I can eas-ily revise and edit. If you can write fast enough, dictate your draft to a tape recorder or, better yet, try one of the computer dictating programs. I have used a Dragon program and will go back to that if I find I can't write at top speed.

BUILDING BLOCKS

If I can't write a draft at one sitting I break it down into chunks. I work on an ar-ticle's beginning, then the middle, and finally the end. I break a book down into chapters and then sections within the chapters, then develop that section that may be a few paragraphs or pages long or even a full chapter.

Then I build the entire draft from these blocks of writing, each one long enough to complete a specific topic, short enough to be done in the hours or hour I have available.

LAYERING

The technique I use most often to complete a draft is to layer my writing. Once I did quite a bit of oil painting, and my pictures were built up, layer after layer of paint, until the scene was revealed to me and a viewer. I write my books, articles, and poems the same way, starting each day at the beginning of yesterday's draft, reading and writing until my daily stint is finished. Each day I lay down a new layer of writing, and when I read it the next day, the new layer reveals more possibility.

There is no one way for writing to develop. As I layer, I may start with a sketch, other times the first writing feels complete. (The next day's reading usually shows it is not.) Sometimes I race ahead through the draft; other times each paragraph is honed before I go on to the next one. I try to allow the draft to tell me what it needs.

I start reading, and when I see—or, more likely, hear—something that needs doing, I do it. One day I'll read through all the written text and start writing where I left off the day before, another time I'll find myself working on dialogue; the next day I may begin to construct a new scene or argument; one time I'll stumble into a new discovery and have to go back and develop it, or weave references to it through the text; I may build up background description, develop the conflict, make the reader see a character more clearly; I may present more documentation, evidence, or exposition or hide it in a character's dialogue or action.

Layering is ideally suited for writing on the computer since it is easy to write over what you have written, but it can be done with typewriter or pen and paper as well. Part of the technique involves developing inserts that can be written or pasted within sentences or paragraphs, between paragraphs or sections, at the end, in the middle, or even before the beginning. Remember there are no rules; the draft leads and you follow.

The best way I know to get the feel of layering is to write a paragraph—perhaps of description—then to start again on a new page and write it again without reading the first one or, at least, only reading it loosely. Write easily. Relax. Let the draft lead. Then do it a third time, a fourth, perhaps a fifth. Does that mean you should always do it five times? No. The draft may call for three layers—or seventeen. Let me demonstrate and comment as I do. I chose this topic more from image and emotion than conscious thought. I saw through memory's eyes the long empty corridors of North Quincy High School with the shiny waxed floors and rows of lockers. I went back in time and felt the power of having a corridor pass and being allowed to travel the corridors when everyone else was in class. And I felt, like a dark, familiar ache, the loneliness of those corridors and the loneliness—the separateness, the being-differentness—of my high school years. I needed to explore this image and these feelings by writing.

Layer 1

When I think of North Quincy High School, I think of corridors more than classrooms. I expect to think of classrooms. Say "elementary school," and I think of the huge classroom clocks with roman numerals and waiting for the last clicks in the afternoon. Three minutes. Two. One. Escape.

I start by writing down my first thoughts about high school.

Layer 2

North Quincy High School. Not classrooms but corridors jammed with the hourly flood of teenagers. Beer jackets and saddle shoes, letter sweaters and girls with mysterious blooming sweaters. Sweater girls. Shouts and laughter, "swell" and "neat," the harsh, ugly south-of-Boston accent and the fastracingyankeetalk, the slamming of locker doors and the bells summoning the prisoners for lock-up.

I try to get into the text faster and, most of all, to develop the scene in my mind, to flesh it out with detail.

Layer 3

I heard myself say, "Everybody's alienated in high school" and was surprised I saw North Quincy High School and long, empty corridors.

I got into it slower so I could put it in context.

I would have expected to remember classrooms, hours that felt like whole lifetimes, clocks with huge roman numerals with hours between the click of the minute hand, teacher voices that used sarcasm like the flicking end of a bullwhip.

I transposed the material from elementary school. We had the same clocks in high school, and I waited for their clicks with the same desperation.

Or the flood of students between classes, beer jackets and sweater girls, "swell" and "neat," the slam of locker doors, peanut butter and jelly sandwiches, the perfume of sneakers and gym shorts.

I added detail, paced it a bit differently. All this detail I hoped would take me back to high school and lead me to meaning.

But what I remember, with something close to nostalgia, is the long, empty corridors with the classroom doors closed.

I develop the key image, the picture that haunts my memory.

Layer 4

We were talking about high school the other night, and I heard myself say, "Everybody's alienated in high school." I was surprised I saw North Quincy

High School—long, empty corridors—and felt something that felt like nostalgia. High school was not a good time for me. I dropped out twice and flunked out at the end. I would have expected anger, perhaps bitterness, even embarrassment, not nostalgia.

In the previous paragraph and the following one, I continue to develop with more detail, setting up the situation in the first paragraph, revealing the world of the school in the second.

I would have expected to remember classrooms, hours that felt like whole lifetimes, lectures on physics or algebra in which I lost any sense of meaning, clocks with huge roman numerals with hours passing between the click of the minute hand, teacher voices that used sarcasm like the flicking end of a bull whip. Or the flood of students between classes, beer jackets and sweater girls, "swell" and "neat," the slam of locker doors, peanut butter and jelly sandwiches, the perfume of sneakers and gym shorts. But what I remember, with something close to nostalgia, is the long, empty corridors with the classroom doors closed.

The floors gleamed with wax and the green locker doors were silent. The walls, I think, were stucco, and light fixtures hung from the ceiling. Inside the glass doors of the classrooms, I saw the tired gestures of the teachers and numbed faces of the students, faces that seemed drugged by information they did not want to know and would never understand.

Now I have placed myself—and, therefore, the reader—in the lonely corridor. As I distance myself from those locked into the classrooms, teachers and students alike, I am unknowingly taking a big step toward the meaning the next layer of text will reveal.

Layer 5

My wife and daughters and I were talking about high school the other evening—none of us wanted to return—and we laughed at someone who was still angry at being unappreciated and alienated in high school. I heard myself say, "Everybody's alienated in high school." As I spoke, I was carried back to North Quincy High School, with its long, empty corridors, and something that felt like nostalgia.

In the first paragraph I am extending the context a bit, setting the scene more completely. In these first paragraphs I am instinctively establishing mood, tone, pace; tuning my language to the evolving voice of the piece that will reveal meaning to me and will reveal and support meaning to the reader.

I was surprised. I have never felt nostalgic about high school before. It was not a good time for me. I won no letters, retained a virtue I desperately wanted to lose, dropped out twice, and flunked out at the end. I would have expected anger, perhaps bitterness, even shame, not nostalgia.

And I would have expected to remember classrooms, those educational cells to which I had been sentenced for hours that felt like whole lifetimes, lectures on physics or algebra in which I lost any sense of meaning, clocks with huge roman numerals with hours passing between clicks of the minute hand, teacher voices that used sarcasm like the flicking end of a bull whip. Or the flood of students between classes, beer jackets and sweater girls, "swell" and "neat," the slam of locker doors, peanut butter and jelly sandwiches, the perfume of sneakers and gym shorts. But what I remember, with something close to nostalgia, is the long, empty corridors with the classroom doors closed.

The floors gleamed with wax, and the green locker doors were silent. The walls, I think, were stucco, and orange-bulbed light fixtures hung from the ceiling. Inside the glass doors of the classrooms, I saw the tired gestures of the teachers and numbed faces of the students, faces that seemed drugged by information they did not want to know and would never understand. And I was alone in the corridor. I had escaped.

With the word escaped, the text has revealed its meaning to me.

Of course I remember those corridors with nostalgia. Just the other day I found stacks of forged corridor passes, stored away in case I returned to high school. I worked on the newspaper and the yearbook; I learned the system and then how to work it. I escaped homeroom and study hall, sometimes even class. I possessed the loneliness I had learned at home and the delicious egotism of alienation. I was an outsider, a writer before I knew I would become a writer, an almost man with forged corridor passes, documentation that I could escape high school, learn new systems and how, as a loner, to manipulate them. Those aged slips of paper were, I now realize, my diploma, and oh how I have used that education in the years since, walking so many corridors by myself, alienated and smug.

In the last paragraph I have explored, developed, examined, and extended the meaning I discovered, playing with it, turning it over, moving back to the slips, seeing their significance, delighting myself with the surprise of "smug," which gives me an insight about my lifetime of proud alienation. I have maintained the private illusion and arrogance of alienation even when I have earned awards, promotions, titles, tenure. I suppose that I am smugly alienated, secretly feeling superior to those around me. Too true, at times, but not all the time, I hope. This writing I did just to document a point has put me on the analyst's couch, revealed myself, and made me squirm; it has made me feel that I deserve a couple of good squirms.

In reading over all this, I am struck by my patience. Once, I would have wanted to know the meaning right away—or even thought I should have known the meaning before I wrote the first word. I would have sought meaning, panted after it. Now I am patient—and confident. Experience has taught me that if I keep writing, meaning will come. I will not think meaning. I will watch meaning arise from my page. The painter

William de Kooning once said, "I can't paint a tree but I can find a tree in my work," and Pablo Picasso testified, "To know what you want to draw, you have to begin drawing. If it turns out to be a man, I draw a man. If it turns out to be a woman, I draw a woman." They are patient, and I have learned patience as well. I have learned that I have learned it by rereading these drafts.

That was fun—and totally unexpected. The conversation took place and the image of the empty corridors came to mind, but I didn't begin to understand them until I completed this hour of layering, putting down text on top of text, revising to produce a first draft.

You will see other things I have done—good or bad—or should have done. You may make your own discoveries, comfortable and uncomfortable, as you live through my drafts. Mark them all down on my draft; try the same thing on yours.

What will I do with Layer 5? I don't know. Play with it perhaps. See if it grows into a column or a short story. It may pop up in the novel I'm drafting or turn into an academic article on layering, maybe even shrink to become a poem. Most likely it will remain what it is, a piece of writing that was fun to do because it captured an important part of my life and allowed me to examine it and come to some understanding I did not have before.

——— FINISHING THE DRAFT ———

When do you know the draft is done?

My answer always is, "When I meet the deadline." I've never finished anything without a deadline, a time when the final draft must be delivered to a teacher or editor.

That ending, however, should not just trail off. The ending is so important that many writers such as novelist and screenwriter John Irving know the ending before they begin and write to a specific destination. The ending is the last thing readers read and what they are most likely to remember.

The effective ending usually echoes back to the beginning, but only in some academic and scientific writing does the ending repeat what has already been said. The formal conclusion that tells the reader what has been said or how to think insults the general reader.

In essays, articles, and books for the general reader, the writer usually ends with a specific scene, quotation, anecdote, or detail that reminds the reader of what has been said without spelling it out. To find that ending I often use something that was a candidate for the beginning.

We all tend to run on too long and say too much. My *Boston Globe* editor, Irene Sege, more often than I like to admit, cuts the last paragraph of my column—and it always makes it better. To find that effective ending myself, I cover up the last paragraph and read to see if the next-to-last paragraph is the real ending. If not I cover up the third-from-the-last paragraph and keep moving back to a paragraph that can't be cut, and that becomes my ending.

—— UNBLOCKING WRITER'S BLOCK ——

It never gets easier to write. All writers are masters of avoidance. If interruptions don't occur, writers create them. They make phone calls, travel far on unnecessary errands, cut wood in July, buy snow shovels in August, play computer games, read and send e-mail, babble in a chat room, surf on the Internet. When it is time to write, writers read, attack the correspondence and the filing, sharpen pencils, buy new pens, change the cartridge in their printer, shop for a new computer, make coffee, make tea, rearrange the furniture in the office. When writers get together, they share, often shamefaced, new ways to avoid writing.

But some of that avoidance is good. E. B. White reminds us, "Delay is natural to a writer. He is like a surfer—he bides his time, waits for the perfect wave on which to ride in. Delay is instinctive with him." This waiting is purposeful, for most writers discover that starting a draft prematurely causes a total collapse three, five, or seven pages along, and it's harder to repair a train wreck of a draft than to start one along the right track.

Writers, of course, being writers, are never sure whether they are allowing their subjects to ripen properly or are just being lazy. This waiting is often the worst part of writing. It is filled with guilt and doubt, yet it is essential.

Then comes the time—often commanded by the deadline—when there can be no more delay, when the writing must be done. Here are some ways to overcome inertia and start writing:

1. Nulla dies sine linea. "Never a day without a line." Make writing a habit. Sit in the same place with the same tools every day and write until it becomes uncomfortable not to write. Then writing will come as a matter of course.

2. *Make believe you are writing a letter to a friend.* Put "Dear _____" at the top of the page and start writing. Tom Wolfe did this on one of his first *New Journalism* pieces. He wrote the editor a letter saying why he couldn't write the piece he'd been assigned. The letter flowed along in such a wonderful, easy fashion that the editor took the salutation off and ran it. It established a new style for contemporary journalism.

3. *Switch your writing tools.* If you normally type, write by hand. If you write by hand, type. Switch from pen to pencil or pencil to pen. Switch

from unlined paper to lined paper, or vice versa. Try larger paper or smaller, colored paper or white paper. Use a bound notebook or spiral notebook, a legal pad or a clipboard. Tools are a writer's toys, and effective, easy writing is the product of play. Sometimes I will change the font, the type size, the shape of the text on the page, allowing the computer to show me what I have said in a different form.

4. *Talk about the piece of writing with another writer, and pay close attention to what you say.* You may be telling yourself how to write the piece. You may even want to make notes as you talk on the telephone or in person. Pay attention to words or combinations of words that may become a voice and spark a piece of writing.

5. *Write down the reasons you are not writing.* Often when you see the problem you will be able to avoid it. You may realize that your standards are too high, or that you're thinking excessively of how one person will respond to your piece, or that you're trying to include too much. Once you have defined the problem, you may be able to dispose of it.

6. *Describe the process you went through when a piece of writing went well.* You may be able to read such an account in your journal. We need to reinforce the writing procedures that produce good writing. A description of what worked before may tell you that you need to delay at this moment, or it may reveal a trick that got you going another time. Keep a careful record of your work habits and the tricks of your trade, so that you have a positive resource to fall back on.

7. *Interview other writers to find out how they get started.* Try your classmates' tricks and see if they work for you.

8. *Switch the time of day.* Sometimes writing at night when you are tired lowers your critical sense in a positive way, and other times you can jump out of bed in the morning and get a start on the writing before your internal critic catches up with you.

9. *Call the draft an experiment or an exercise.* Good writing is always an experiment. Make a run at it. See if it will work. The poet Mekeel McBride is always writing "exercises" in her journals. Since they are just exercises and not poems, she doesn't get uptight about them, but of course if an exercise turns into a poem, she accepts it.

10. *Dictate a draft.* Use a tape recorder, and then transcribe the draft from it. You may want to transcribe it carefully, or just catch the gist of what you had to say. No matter how experienced you are as a writer, you are a million times more experienced as a speaker, and it's often easier to get started writing by talking than by simply writing.

11. *Quit.* Come back later and try again. You can't force writing. You have to keep making runs at it. Come back ten minutes later, or later that day, or the next day. Keep trying until the writing flows so fast you have to run along behind it trying to keep up.

12. *Read.* Some writers read over what they've written, and they may even edit it or recopy it as a way of sliding into the day's writing. I can't do that; I despair too much, and when I read my own writing I feel I have to start over again; it's worthless, hopeless. If you don't feel that way, however, it may be a good device to go over the previous day's work and then push on to the new writing, the way a house painter paints back into the last brush stroke and then draw the new paint forward.

13. *Write directly to a specific reader.* The too-critical reader can keep you from writing, but you can also get writing by imagining an especially appreciative reader, or a reader who needs the information you have to convey. If you can feel that reader's hunger for what you have to say, it will draw you into the text. Sometimes when I write, I imagine the enjoyment I expect Don Graves, Chip Scanlan, or Nancie Atwell to feel at an unexpected turn of phrase, a new insight, or a different approach. I read their faces as I write, the way you read a friend's face during a conversation.

14. *Take a walk, lift weights, jog, run, dance, swim.* Many writers have found that the best way to get started writing is by getting the blood coursing through the body and the brain. As they get the physical body tuned up, the brain moves into high gear. Exercise is also the kind of private activity that allows the mind to free itself of stress and interruption and rehearse what may be written when the exercise is done. Running, walking, bicycling, or swimming are great ways to let the mind wander while the body is working.

15. *Change the place where you write.* I write in my office at home, but I also write on a lap desk in the living room or on the porch. I like to take the car and drive down by Great Bay, where I can look up from my lap desk and watch a heron stalk fish or a seagull soar—the way I would like to write, without effort. Some writers cover their windows and write to a wall. I like to write to a different scene. Right now, for example, I'm looking at the green ocean of Indiana farmland and a marvelously angry gray sky as I drive west and write by dictation. In the 1920s writers thought the cafes of Paris were the best places to write. I don't think I could work on those silly little tables, but my ideal writing place would be in a booth in a busy lunchroom where nobody knows me. Yesterday morning I started writing in a Denny's in a city in Michigan; it was a fine place to

write. When my writing doesn't go well, I move around. I imagine that the muse is looking for me, and if she can't find me at home I'll go out somewhere where I may be more visible.

16. *Draw a picture, in your mind or on paper.* Take a photograph. Cut a picture from a magazine and put it on your bulletin board. When small children start writing, they usually first draw pictures. They do on paper what writers usually do in their minds—they visualize their subjects. Last summer I started my writing sessions by making a sketch of a rubber tree that stands on our porch. I wasn't writing about the rubber tree, but the activity of drawing seemed to help me get started and stimulate the flow of writing.

17. *Freewrite.* Write as hard and as fast and as free as you can. See if language will lead you toward a meaning. As I have said before, freewriting isn't very free, for the draft starts to develop its own form and direction. But the act of writing freely is one of the techniques that can unleash your mind.

18. *Stop in the middle of a sentence.* This is a good trick when the writing is going well and you are interrupted or come to the end of the day's writing during a long project. Many well-known writers have done this, and I've found that it really helps me at times. If I can pick up the draft and finish an ordinary sentence, then I am immediately back into the writing. If I've stopped at the end of a sentence or a paragraph it's much harder to get going. If I've stopped at the end of a chapter, it may take days or weeks to get the next one started.

19. *Write the easy parts first.* If you're stuck on a section or a beginning, skip over it and write the parts of the draft that you are ready to write. Once you've got those easy, strong pieces of writing done, then you'll be able to build a complete draft by connecting those parts. A variation on this technique is to write the end first, or to plunge in and grab the beast wherever you can get hold of it. Once you have a working draft, you can extend it backward or forward as it requires.

20. *Be silly.* You're not writing anyway, so you might as well make a fool of yourself. I've numbered the day's quota of pages and then filled them in. One of my writer neighbors loves cigars, but he won't let himself have a cigar until he has finished his daily quota. Reward yourself with a cup of coffee or a dish of ice cream or a handful of nuts. It is no accident that some writers are fat; they keep rewarding themselves with food. Do whatever you have to do to keep yourself writing. Jessamyn West writes in bed the first thing in the morning. If the doorbell rings she can't answer it; she isn't up and dressed. Use timers, count pages, count words. (You may not be able to say the writing went well, but you'll be able to

say "I did 512 words," or "I completed two pages.") Play music, or write standing up. (Thomas Wolfe wrote on top of an icebox, and Ernest Hemingway put his typewriter on a bureau.) Start the day writing in the bathtub as Nabokov did. Nothing is too silly if it gets you started writing.

21. *Start the writing day by reading writing that inspires you.* This is dangerous for me, because I may get so interested in the reading I'll never write, or I'll pick up the voice of another writer. I can't, for example, read William Faulkner when I'm writing fiction: a poor, New Hampshire imitation of that famous Mississippian is not a good way to go. The other day, however, when I couldn't get started writing, I read a short story by Mary Gordon, one of my favorite authors. Reading a really good writer's work should make you pack up your pen and quit the field, but most of us find reading other writers inspiring. I put down Mary Gordon's short story and was inspired to write.

22. *Read what other writers have written about writing.* I may not write as well as they do, but we work at the same trade, and it helps me to sit around and chat with them. You may want to start a "commonplace book," an eighteenth-century form of self-education in which people made their personal collections of wise or witty sayings. I've collected what writers have said about writing in my own commonplace book, selections from which are now published in my book *Shoptalk* (Portsmouth, NH: Boynton/Cook/Heinemann, 1990). Some of my favorite quotes from that collection appear in the section "In the Writer's Workshop" sections in this book as well as throughout the text. I find it comforting to hear that the best writers have many of the same problems I do, and I often browse through these quotes as a way of starting.

23. *Break down the writing task into reasonable goals.* A few years ago I watched on TV as the first woman to climb a spectacular rock face in California made it to the top. It had taken her days, and as soon as she got over the edge, a TV reporter stuck a microphone in her face and asked her what she'd thought of as she kept working her way up the cliff. She said she kept reminding herself that you eat an elephant one bite at a time. You also write a long piece of writing one page, or one paragraph, at a time. John Steinbeck said, "When I face the desolate impossibility of writing 500 pages a sick sense of failure falls on me and I know I can never do it. Then I gradually write one page and then another. One day's work is all I can permit myself to contemplate." If you contemplate a book, you'll never write it, but if you write just a page a day you'll have a 365-page draft at the end of a year. If you're stuck, you may be trying to eat an entire elephant at one gulp. It may be wiser to

tell yourself that you'll just get the first page, or perhaps just the lead done that day. That may seem possible, and you'll start writing.

24. *Put someone else's name on it.* I've been hired as a ghostwriter to create texts for politicians and industrialists. I've had little trouble writing when the work will carry someone else's name. Most of the time when I can't write I'm excessively self-conscious. Sometimes I've put a pseudonym on a piece of work, and the writing has taken off.

25. *Delegate the writing to your subconscious.* Often I will tell my subconscious what I'm working on, and then I'll do something that doesn't take intense concentration and allows my subconscious mind to work. I walk around bookstores or a library, watch a dull baseball game or movie on TV, take a nap, go for a walk or a drive. Some people putter around the house or work in the garden. Whatever you do, you're allowing your mind to work on the problem. Every once in a while a thought, an approach, a lead, a phrase, a line, or a structure will float up to the conscious mind. If it looks workable, then go to your writing desk; if it doesn't, shove it back down underwater and continue whatever you're doing until something new surfaces.

26. *Listen.* Alice Walker says, "If you're silent for a long time, people just arrive in your mind." As Americans we are afraid of silence, and I'm guilty too. I tend to turn on the car radio if I'm moving the car twenty feet from the end of the driveway into the garage. One of the best ways to get started writing is to do nothing. Waste time. Stare out the window. Try to let your mind go blank. This isn't easy, as those who have tried meditation know. But many times your mind, distracted by trivia, is too busy to write. Good writing comes out of silence, as Charles Simic says. "In the end, I'm always at the beginning. Silence—an endless mythical condition. I think of explorers setting out over an unknown ocean . . ." Cultivate a quietness, resist the panic that the writing won't come, and allow yourself to sink back into the emptiness. If you don't fight the silence, but accept it, then usually, without being aware of it, the writing will start to come.

These are some ways to get writing. You will come up with others if you make a list of techniques from other parts of your life that may apply here. A theater major may know all sorts of exercises and theater games that can spark writing. A scientist will be able to apply experimental techniques to writing. Art majors know how to attack a white canvas, and ski team members know how to shove off at the top of a steep slope. Keep a record of methods of starting writing that work for you.

─────── **DRAFTING IN THE DAYBOOK** ───────

I try to go to my writing desk every morning—writers write—but I know that I am writing when I am away from the desk. At the desk I just harvest what has been written in my conscious, my subconscious, and my daybook.

My daybooks have hundreds of leads or beginnings and almost as many endings that I try out in slivers of time when I am between periods at the hockey game, before the concert starts, while watching television. In the daybook I can quickly try different voices, difference points of view, different starting points, then polish again and again the lead that I have chosen.

I use the daybook as the forester uses a field book, the sales woman a contact list, the artist a sketchbook, to record what has been noticed and to note what should be noticed. I draft turning points when I am stuck in my daybook. I draft definitions of complex information. I use it to describe key people or places, seeing them from different points of view.

In the daybook I can write quickly and badly. It is essential for me to have a place where I can write badly. All of us can become slick, saying what we have said before in the way we have said it before. The daybook allows me to try out other voices, other points of view, other genre or sequences. It is the place where I rehearse so that my writing will seem spontaneous when the final draft is published.

─────── **HEAR THE DRAFT'S VOICE** ───────

I have drafted pages with the computer screen turned off. I look at the keys when I draft—or out the window into the woods at the squirrel circus that never ends. I hear the evolving text, and the music of the draft often tells me what I feel about the subject—hate, nostalgia, sadness, rage, anger, detachment, concern. I draft with my ear to understand the meaning of what I am saying. I want to recreate the music that will support that meaning as well as reveal it.

I also write with my ear because I have had much more experience with oral language than with written language even though I am a writer. I may write a thousand words or more a day and read many times that much, but I speak ten thousand words a day or more and hear even more than that. I want the language experience of my ear involved in the making of the draft.

Good writing is not speech written down, but it creates, in the reader's mind, the illusion of speech. The writing that readers most enjoy reading has the sound of a good conversation, the one you wish you had created at the party.

The voice of the essay on the melancholy of a sunny day I have worked on pages 8, 46, 81, and 111 is clear in my ear. Once I have that voice, I can carry it with me into a different genre—this could become a poem or a short story—

and a different context. This morning, in Florida, as I write my column for the *Boston Globe,* I hear that voice and it makes me see the world around me in a new perspective. As I write I feel I am riding this voice the way I imagine a surfboarder rides the waves or a Wynton Marsalis rides a line of notes as he improvises on his trumpet.

Boston Globe—Now and Then—January 23, 2001

I've been coming to Florida, off and on, for more than thirty years and each time there are more taller condos, more fancier shopping malls, more diverse restaurants, more larger drug stores, more sudden manicured landscapes with full size palms, unrolled grass, unexpected ponds, fountains, and waterfalls.

And each year I am more than a bit, well, snotty about Florida. Yet I return to rent the same condo that rises from an artificial island of Isla Del Sol with a delightful, manufactured landscape.

At seventy-six I am comfortable with contradiction, but the other day as I felt the warm sun on my arms and stood under a huge, neatly trimmed palm and looked at the view a landscape artist decided I would like, I was transported sixty-one years back to a New Hampshire forest.

Then I also felt the sun on my bare arm as I explored a New Hampshire forest alone. I had been told that if I studied the age of the trees and followed the younger, thinner ones, I may find I can follow a road through the forest abandoned almost seventy-five years before I was born.

It wasn't easy. The forest was thick with summer foliage and I circled about for an hour or so until I could see a double line of older trees separated by a line of younger ones.

I ran down this suddenly visible forest road until I heard a strange roar. I wondered if it was a train, then realized it was a river. I followed the curving road toward the sound and discovered another road crossed my road, then still another.

I looked around and began to see the moss-covered granite stones half-hidden by saplings, bushes, underbrush and could read the pattern. These fields had once been cleared. The rocks were walls. Then I found bigger rocks, great blocks of granite arranged in squares and rectangles, with a sagging in the middle. Trees grew right through the cellar holes of homes where once people lived.

In my imagination I raised the homes, barns, and at the edge of the roaring rapids, I grew the mill on the great stone slabs beside the river rapids.

I darted from what may have been a pig pen, to a small worker's house, to the one the mill owner must have built. I found the church and saw the outlines of the town common, running from place to place, shouting my discoveries to the silent forest.

Then I became quiet. These buildings had once seemed as permanent as my home, my church, my school. I took one of those bursts of mental and emotional growth that mark our travel to maturity. No building would ever seem as permanent again.

The people who had lived here were all gone. I knew my history and realized I had probably discovered one of those villages where everyone had packed up and left in the Gold Rush of 1849. I sat on one of the great mill slabs and watched them in imagination as they lived their lives in this village and as they packed up and left to follow a dream that may not have been fulfilled for any of them.

Then I was back in my condo, living the dream of a winter month in Florida that once seemed impossible. I traveled in memory to the great Indian cliff villages of our Southwest, to the ruins I had visited in Italy, Greece, England, Scotland, Norway, and near home. All had once seemed sure to last forever.

I felt the passing melancholy the way you feel the shadow of a cloud that makes the sun seem brighter, warmer when the cloud is gone. I will enjoy Florida all the more because I know these grand condo palaces will one day tumble into their own cellar holes, the way that village I discovered in the woods did so long, so short a time ago.

Note that the word melancholy doesn't appear until the last paragraph but it was there all the time in the voice of the essay.

IN THE WRITER'S WORKSHOP

How do I know what I think until I see what I say? E. M. FORSTER

Of The House of Five Talents, *I wrote the first draft in longhand, with a pencil, on Saturdays, Sundays, and vacations; had it typed, triple spaced; and then carried it around in a briefcase. Thus I was able to work on it very easily not only evenings but on the subway or any other time when I had a few minutes to spare. You have to be fresh for the first draft of a book, but I find that once I get to work on the second or third draft; it's like knitting.* LOUIS AUCHINCLOSS

I write the first draft quickly, as I said. This is most often done in longhand. I simply fill up the pages as rapidly as I can. In some cases, there's a kind of personal shorthand, notes to myself for what I will do later when I come back to it. Some scenes I have to leave unfinished, unwritten in some cases; the scenes that will require meticulous care later. I mean all of it requires meticulous care—but some scenes I save until the second or third draft, because to do them and do them right would take too much time on the first draft. With the first draft it's a question of getting down the outline, the scaffolding of the story. RAYMOND CARVER

(1) Do not wait until you have gathered all your material before starting to write. Nothing adds to inertia like a mass of notes, the earliest of which recede in the mists of forgone time. On the contrary, begin drafting your ideas as soon as some portion of the topic appears to hang together in your mind. (2) Do not be afraid of writing down something that you think may have to be changed. Paper is not granite, and

in a first draft you are not carving eternal words in stone. Rather, you are creating substance to be molded and remolded in successive drafts. (3) Do not hesitate to write up in any order those sections of your total work that seem to have grown ripe in your mind. There is a moment in any stretch of research when all the details come together in natural cohesion, despite small gaps and doubts. Learn to recognize that moment and seize it by composing in harmony with your inward feeling of unity. Nevermind whether the portions that come out are consecutive. (4) Once you start writing, keep going. Resist the temptation to get up and verify a fact. Leave it blank. The same holds true for the word or phrase that refuses to come to mind. It will arise much more easily on revision, and the economy in time and momentum is incalculable. JACQUES BARZUN

My "first draft" is it. I can't rewrite to any extent: I've tried once or twice, but I haven't the mental stamina and I feel all the time that although what I'm attempting may be different, it won't be better and may very well be worse, because my heart isn't in it. DICK FRANCIS

My first draft was 700 pages, not because I had so much to say, but because I had so much to find out. EDWARD HANNIBEL

I normally do three drafts, never more and seldom less. The first draft is long and kind of an exploratory draft, with a lot of guesswork involved in it, some of it unsuccessful guesswork. Frequently in the first draft of a book there will be an element of redundancy, and you will write the same scene several times, an important scene in the novel, and you won't recognize perhaps you're doing that. The second draft is basically a cutting draft, in which you eliminate the bad guesses, pure mistakes, redundancies, and overwriting of all kinds. In the first draft when you're trying to develop a character, you let conversations run on for pages if you want to. In the second draft you tighten that. The third draft is stylistic basically. I don't pay much attention to style in the first two drafts; I write fairly rapidly, and I'm trying to visualize the scenes I'm describing as intensely as possible. The third draft is the stylist draft. I may get down to two eventually. I never want to go above three, because in a sense you participate in the emotions of the book every time you do a draft, and I think three times is about as many times as you can participate in those emotions and keep them alive. It goes cold. LARRY MCMURTRY

Writing the first draft is the hard part, when you're actually trying to think of what happens next. That's quite painful but the rest is fun. JOYCE CAROL OATES

Writing a first draft is like ice fishing and building an igloo, as well as groping one's way into a pitch-dark room or overhearing a faint conversation, or having prepared for the wrong exam or telling a joke whose punch line you've forgotten. . . . TED SOLOTAROFF

The first draft is always scary to me. I can't risk interrupting it for long or I may lose it. The momentum is important; there's a sense of pushing off from one side. It's like building the Verrazzano bridge from one side, hoping it won't fall in on the way. You don't know if you're going to make it. MARGE PIERCY

—— QUESTIONS ABOUT DRAFTING ——

I can't write using an outline. Never could and never will. I freeze when I see one.

If you can organize your paper without an outline, don't make one. Some people never use outlines, and others only do when they're faced with an unfamiliar writing task. Many writers let their pieces shape themselves and then impose structures on them. Do what you feel is best for you, but don't be afraid to experiment either.

What if I have a teacher who wants me to stick to an outline when I want to change it after I begin writing?

You may want to talk to your teacher about your new ideas. Have your new outline on hand for him or her to look at. If your teacher still insists that you stick to your original outline, then you will have to explore your topic within certain perimeters; these perimeters may not be what you would like, but they will still allow you to think and write critically about your topic.

Some teachers fear that if their students deviate from outlines, they will write papers that are disorganized and hard to read. These instructors are concerned that their students will not learn enough about their topics by writing this way. Another teacher might want you to discover very specific information about a topic and so ask you to adhere to a specific outline.

Whatever reasons your teacher has for requiring a strict outline, you can still explore within those restrictions. You can draw information from a variety of sources, experiment with point of view and angle, and choose a focus within the perimeters of the outline.

What if I've got to write the paper tonight?

If you have an hour, take five or ten minutes to collect the information you will need to write. Take a few more minutes to be sure you have a focus, and then a few minutes to put the information in order. If you take ten minutes for each of those tasks, you'll only have invested half an hour. You'll have twenty minutes to write and ten minutes to check over what you've written. The planning will make your draft quicker, often longer, and better.

This kind of quick planning will come in handy when you have to write an essay answer to an exam question or fill out an application that requires long answers. If you have only a limited amount of time, don't give up on planning. Condense your writing process and put the time you have to good use.

I don't have any problem writing my paper once I get started, but it takes me hours to come up with a good lead or opening. How can I get beyond this?

By getting beyond it. Don't be a perfectionist with your openings. The process of writing will allow you to return to them later. Do what you need now to get going, even if you write an impossibly sappy, dry, or silly opening. Just plunge in and start to write. Put someone's name on it and start it as a letter, or write the closing before the beginning. Go with what works.

I don't write drafts; I just sit down and my writing flows. When I'm through, I've said all I want about my subject. So why should I change?

Because you have probably never found out how much more you have to say. If you never draft and revise, you won't ever see the complexities of the topics you write about. You won't know how much more depth you can bring to your subject. If you're still not a believer, try writing an exploratory draft anyway. See where it takes you. Go about it earnestly and record your progress in your daybook.

What if I have the opposite problem? I have a hard time getting anything down on paper. I worry before I even begin a writing project, and then I get knots in my stomach when I sit down to do it.

No deadline, assignment, or piece of writing is worth getting sick over. But sometimes it's worth getting mad over! I knew a writer once who used to get paralyzed when she sat down to write in front of an empty computer screen. She'd get sick to her stomach before she had written a word; then she'd get angry for getting sick! By that time she'd march back to her computer and chew it out. Then she'd just write.

But it's easy for other people to say "just write!" If I want to write something really good, it takes a lot of effort. Besides, my grade point average depends on how well I write.

These are valid concerns. Most writers want to write something good, and all writers have to take the consequences for writing well or poorly: Students know that good writing usually results in good grades. Professionals know that good writing results in paychecks.

The problem comes when you let the consequences of writing overshadow the process itself. It's the process of writing that will help you get beyond what is often a paralyzing perfectionism. As you sit down to that blank screen or paper, say to yourself: "This is just an exploratory draft; no one else has to read it. I can do what I want with it, and I can always change it later."

At this point in your process, expect to write badly if you need to. Write quickly, just get something down.

But what if there's absolutely nothing in my head when I want to write?

If you draw a total blank, it doesn't necessarily mean you are paralyzed from fear or an overdeveloped sense of perfectionism; it may mean that you need to go back and do more brainstorming, mapping, focusing, or planning. You may need more information to get you going or a solid angle from which to start. In these cases, you might want to return to some of the activities and suggestions in earlier chapters of this book and use them to jump-start your draft. If you still can't write, it could be that the conditions for writing are simply not good for you. Get up and walk away for awhile.

When I get stuck, I don't try to force the writing. I back up, stop, do something else, and try again, perhaps in ten minutes, perhaps the next morning. I'm a morning writer, and I find that if the writing doesn't come one time, it will come the next. But be assured that it will come.

But what if I have a paper due the next day? I don't have time to wait for the writing!

Then you will have to force the writing. Even the most well-organized professional at one time or another encounters a deadline bind. At those times, if the writing does not come easily, the writer works to get something, anything, on paper.

Look at some of the adjoining activities for ideas about drafting. In one of them I suggest setting your clock for a sustained period of time and making yourself write until the alarm goes off. Disciplining yourself like this doesn't mean producing gobbledygook. It means getting said what needs to be said within a given period of time, then going back to revise it. That's what all writers need to do when they are face-to-face with a deadline.

I'm more afraid of losing control of my paper than of having nothing to say.

The planning and focusing you do before beginning your draft will give you a certain amount of control over what you write. But it's not at all unusual for an exploratory draft to take on a life all its own. This may be frightening, but it's also good. When the draft starts leading you instead of you leading it, it probably means there is some real thinking going on. Since writing allows you to try on new ideas and perspectives, you may have to change your strategy as you articulate your thoughts. You can always go back and fiddle with your focus or outline so that it accommodates your new way of seeing and thinking.

But what if the draft is literally all over the place and doesn't make any sense?

This is still not a bad thing. It's the draft leading you back through a thinking process, getting you to clarify what you want to say. Use some of the suggestions and activities for focusing listed in Chapter 3. A writing partner or group will also be helpful here; other readers can sum up your major points for you, or you can jot down in the margins of your paper what you want to do with each section. That will give you a sense of direction. Then go back and make an outline for your draft and try to stick with it. You can always go back later and develop or pare down areas of your paper as you see fit.

Drafting Activities

1. Power through a draft. Read through all of the information, interviews, details, and facts you have collected for it, but don't consult them while drafting. Do as much as you can from memory, and leave a space or asterisk in the text wherever you think you want to insert more details. For the time being, don't get hung up on particulars.

2. Get a draft down, then write another draft without looking at the original. Include only what you remember or want to remember. Allow the draft to lead you into new areas. Do this again. Then go back to your drafts and select the one you like best, or revise by combining the best elements of each.

3. When construction workers build a new skyscraper, they erect boards and railings and elevators around it so that they can do their work without falling off. When getting through a draft seems as challenging as building a skyscraper, let your process become your scaffolding. Analyze your process in the draft itself: "I'm not sure what lead I want here, but I need to start with something, so how about this? . . ." "I thought I knew what to do at this point, but now I'm stuck." "This part of the paper is the suspenseful turning point, so I want it to be good." And so on and so on. When you are through, take down your scaffolding and let your draft stand by itself.

4. Compose your draft in vignettes rather than paragraphs. A vignette is a short sketch or portrait that stands on its own. Writing vignettes instead of connecting paragraphs will help you focus on details and get a sense of your major points; this method allows you to dip in and out of your story as you plan. Sketch out a list of scenes or incidents that you want to include in your

paper. Take one "corner" of each scene or incident, and explore it in detail: a description of your uncle's garden, for example, or the kind gesture of a stranger on the street. Then read your vignettes with an eye toward coherence and connection.

5. Cut up your draft according to ideas or major points and arrange them in "thought piles" on the floor, ordering information according to each idea or thought. Then use these piles to write another draft and to keep it under control.

6. During your most productive period of the day, set your alarm and write for a sustained amount of time, anywhere from one hour to three. Make sure that you are not interrupted during this period. Think of this time as a business or academic appointment and keep it!

7. Break up your writing time: fifteen minutes before breakfast, a half-hour after lunch, an hour at night, or fifteen minutes before you go to bed. Make sure to write fast and furiously, filling up every minute you have.

8. Think of your classmates as business colleagues, and schedule meetings with them twice a week to discuss your draft. Always have a new or revised chunk of writing to show them at the appointed time.

9. Start in medias res, which is Latin for "in the middle of things." Don't get hung up on finding a perfect lead, but jump in anywhere. Write a piece of description, a chunk of dialogue, or even the conclusion to your story. Develop an idea for the middle of the piece, or select one image or concept you know you can write about comfortably and start with that.

10. Write by ear. Compose sentences that have the right sound to them, the perfect rhythm and voice for the effect you want on your reader. Drum out a rhythm on your desk or daybook before drafting. Imagine what a reflective, inspirational, argumentative, persuasive, sarcastic, honest, or upbeat piece might sound like, and don't worry yet about how much information or sense your sentences convey. Let the sound guide your writing.

11. Experiment with genres if you get stuck. Write a poem instead of an essay; then turn your poem into a complicated recipe. Write up instructions for writing your essay. Make a "grocery" list of pertinent points. Write a letter to your friends telling them the story you are about to write. Turn your intended story into a play. Then turn your play into a story. Get writing.

12. Go ahead, break the rule: Tell, don't show! For the time being at least, forget about details, description, dialogue, and development. Write your draft in summary form as though it were an encyclopedia entry or an abstract. Then go back and fill in the details, showing rather than telling.

13. Draft directly to other writers on the Internet. Set a schedule to e-mail each new section of your draft to someone you meet in a writer's chat room, or post your draft in installments to a writer's bulletin board.

14. Set up a writers' Web page on the Internet as a class, or get one of your computer whiz friends to do it for you. Publish a schedule on the page that advertises the "publication" dates of parts or whole drafts. Then take turns as a class or in groups "publishing" pieces of your drafts.

15. Pretend that you're writing in your diary rather than composing a story or assigned essay. Don't try to be deep or complicated. Just get your draft going. Use plenty of time references and words that imply sequence, just as you might in a diary: "That morning . . ." "Later . . ." "After a while . . ." "Then . . ." Let these time words propel you forward; you can always remove them later.

16. Put on your favorite classical music—a waltz, prelude, concerto, or symphony—or any kind of music that takes you out of the moment and puts you into a reflective mood. Take a deep breath and "fall" into the music. Vow to write for the length of time it takes for the piece to play, and when it ends, leave your last sentence unfinished. Take a break. When you return, put on a new piece or repeat a melody that worked for you before. Pick up where you left off by finishing the last sentence you wrote.

17. Arrange with your teacher to set aside a drafting period in class, a half-hour or so of writing time once or twice a week. Write sections of your draft by hand during this time as quickly as possible. Commit yourself to having a substantial chunk of text to read aloud to your classmates when the period ends.

18. Make drafting part of a larger ritual of physical and intellectual well-being. If you're a morning person, meet the sunrise with t'ai chi, a cup of herbal tea, and a half-hour or more at your computer. If you work best at night, combine your drafting time with deep breathing exercises and meditation. Visualize productivity, and say no to anxiety.

19. If you have writer's block, get a change of scenery; take your draft and work somewhere other than your usual writing space. Move from space to space if you need to, making yourself comfortable in each and vowing to write a chunk of draft before moving on.

20. Commit yourself to a certain number of pages each day—whatever seems reasonable. Meet your daily quota and revise what you have at the end of each week.

21. Meet a daily paragraph quota. Determine to write a certain number of paragraphs each day, perhaps five or ten. If you finish quickly, write more or go back and hone your paragraphs. If you are having difficulty writing, push yourself to meet the quota anyway, knowing that you can revise later.

22. Take a significant piece of information from the writing you're working on and list all of the ways it can be documented: quotations, statistics, descriptions, anecdotes, and so on. Then develop it, using some or all of these elements.

23. Go back through activities for previous chapters and use any—or many—of the suggestions for collecting, focusing, or ordering to see if they will help you get a draft flowing.

24. Get an opening paragraph down, and have your partner or group brainstorm questions about what should follow. Write out detailed answers to these questions on your draft, and then decide what parts of these answers you want to keep. If particular questions get you rolling, go with them.

25. Jog, walk, swim. As you fall into the rhythm of your body's movements, think about the rhythm of your piece. Let words and lines unfold as you go. When you have finished, write your ideas down in your daybook. Don't be discouraged if they are incomplete concepts or half-finished leads and sentences; arrange them as potential headings for your paper's outline, and begin gathering information and details for each heading.

26. Draw a picture of your essay. Make it any shape you want, adding width where you want plenty of details and condensing where you want fewer details. Try drawing dark or jagged lines where you want your essay to reflect anger or other volatile feelings, or soft, thin lines for more benign emotions. When you complete your drawing, write one sentence in each part of the sketch that sums up what you want each section of your essay to do.

27. Ask your writing partner or group to brainstorm questions about your topic and then select at least ten questions they want answered in order of importance or interest. Make an outline for your draft using these questions as major headings.

28. Think of the effect you want each section of your paper to have on your reader, then make a checklist of each part. Start with the words: "With this title I want my reader to . . ." ("become interested in what I have to say," "laugh," "expect to be surprised," "expect a serious piece," "take me seriously," etc.). Move through each section of the piece as you envision it, and anticipate the reader's response.

CHAPTER 7

SHOPTALK: PREPARING TO REVISE AND EDIT

I can mark the day I became a writer. It was not when I scratched shapes I hoped were letters in the dirt by the kitchen steps of the house on Vassall Street in Wollaston, Massachusetts. Not when Miss Chapman in the fourth grade pointed an imperial finger at me and said, "You are the class editor," although that may have set the direction of my life. Not in a writing course, not when I became editor of my school newspaper, not that wonderful moment when Mort Howell, my freshman English teacher got an editorial of mine reprinted in the *Christian Science Monitor* and told me, "You'll be a writer when you come home from the war." Not when I got a job on a big city newspaper and read my byline on page one. Not even when I won the Pulitzer Prize.

It was earlier in that same year just before I won the Pulitzer at age 29. The *Saturday Evening Post* accepted an article of mine with a many-paged, single-spaced letter from an editor, Bob Johnson, packed with suggestions for revision. The letter was longer than the article—and then the editor sent Johnson from Philadelphia to Wellesley, Massachusetts, to spend the day teaching me how to rewrite.

I got up at 3:00 the next morning and rewrote the first half of the article, did the same thing the next day, met the forty-eight-hour deadline, and become a writer.

Until then I had been a first-draft writer, always able to write a first draft that was good enough to get me through the English course or published in the newspaper. If I had to rewrite anything I saw the request as a mark of failure. Sometimes I accepted that failure as mine but most of the time I thought it the failure of the teacher or editor to appreciate how talented, how spontaneous, how original, how creative a writer I was.

Of course I did edit my copy, making it as typographically neat as I could with my two-fingered typing skills. I checked the accuracy of names and facts, corrected the spelling when I could recognize a misspelled word, put in and took out punctuation, smoothed the surface of the first draft, but I didn't re-think or rewrite what I had written. My first draft was my last.

At the *Boston Herald* I was recognized as a fast first-draft writer, even occasionally assigned to rewrite with the master old pros of the city room, where we didn't rewrite but took stories from reporters over the telephone and turned their notes into quick first drafts. I met every deadline and delivered to precise space limitations: one paragraph, two, four, ten, twelve, even to the line—twelve, twenty, forty. I turned out an average of forty stories a shift, but when I read Bob Johnson's letter and sat beside him at my writing desk, I discovered I was not yet a writer.

——— THE REVISION ATTITUDE ———

Bob Johnson's demands were so detailed, so carefully crafted, so instantly recognizable as right that, for the first time, I didn't see the need for revision as the reader's failure or mine but as opportunity. In that one day my standards were raised from those of daily deadline journalism to weekly magazine standards, where there was time for revision and where the first draft was not the end but the beginning of writing. And the weekly standard opened the door to writing that had a monthly deadline and eventually to books where the deadline was a year or two away and there was time to rewrite and rewrite and rewrite again. I became a writer. I discovered what the best writers knew: Writing is rewriting.

I began to appreciate what writers said about their craft:

I love the flowers of afterthought. BERNARD MALAMUD

I like to mess around with my stories. I'd rather tinker with a story after writing it, and then tinker some more, changing this, changing that, than have to write the story in the first place. That initial writing just seems to me the hard place I have to go to in order to go on and have fun with the story. Rewriting for me is not a chore—it's something I like to do. RAYMOND CARVER

What makes me happy is rewriting. In the first draft you get your ideas and your theme clear, if you are using some kind of metaphor you get that established, and certainly you have to know where you're coming out. But the next time through it's like cleaning house, getting rid of all the junk, getting things in the right order, tightening things up. I like the process of making writing neat. ELLEN GOODMAN

When I see a paragraph shrinking under my eyes like a strip of bacon in a skillet, I know I'm on the right track. PETER DEVRIES

Rewriting is when playwriting really gets to be fun. In baseball you only get three swings and you're out. In rewriting, you get almost as many swings as you want and you know, sooner or later, you'll hit the ball. NEIL SIMON

I had believed in spontaneity. The first draft would be the best draft. Good writing was the result of two elements I could not control: natural talent and luck. Now I learned that the best writers rewrote to create the illusion of spontaneity. John Kenneth Galbraith explained,

> All writers know that on some golden mornings they are touched by the wand—are on intimate terms with poetry and cosmic truth. I have experienced those moments myself. Their lesson is simple: It's a total illusion. And the danger in the illusion is that you will wait for those moments. Such is the horror of having to face the typewriter that you will spend all your time waiting. I am persuaded that most writers, like most shoemakers, are about as good one day as the next (a point which Trollope made).
>
> In my own case there are days when the result is so bad that no fewer than five revisions are required. However, when I'm greatly inspired, only four revisions are needed before, as I've often said, I put in that note of spontaneity which even my meanest critics concede.

What a relief. I no longer had to wait for inspiration, no longer hope that I had talent, no longer needed luck. Writing was work, a craft, a process of making. I no longer resisted rewriting, but wrote badly and then went to work to revise until I discovered what I really needed to say and how to say it effectively.

As it became my ambition to sell more articles to the *Saturday Evening Post* and other magazines, it became my discipline to write a discovery draft, a development draft, and a polished draft. And I would revise each one at least ten times. That's right, thirty drafts in making that step from newspaper to magazine writing. I don't often revise that much forty-seven years after Bob Johnson's visit. This is only the forth—or is it the fifth?—draft of this chapter. The craft I developed practicing the thirty-draft discipline makes my early drafts better but I still write to find out what I have to say, revise to develop and document it, finally edit to erase all signs of effort, making the language clear, accurate, graceful and spontaneous—at least spontaneous appearing.

— THE REVISION AND EDITING PLAN —

To revise and edit effectively, the beginning writer has to disobey two truths that aren't true although they have the power of logic reinforced by the careful, authoritative instruction of traditional teachers.

THE FIRST TRUTH THAT ISN'T TRUE

To revise your draft, first identify every thing that's wrong.

Years into my magazine- and book-writing apprenticeship, I still thought the primary goal of revision was to discover error and correct it. Then I started teaching writing as well as practicing writing and found I could pounce on error with the best of them, but corrected error didn't make a poor draft good, it only made it correct.

I began to study the student papers that did get better to see what they were doing, and I printed out my drafts on large pieces of paper with huge margins so I could write down just what I was doing when I revised successfully. I found out that the best students and their old-pro teacher were doing the same thing: they identified what worked in the draft as well as what didn't work.

It might be the language, the voice, the point of view toward the topic, the supporting documentation, the narrative or logical order, the surprise in what the draft said or how it was said. No matter. The writer seized what worked and ran with it. As the writers built on what worked, the drafts got better and most of the errors disappeared. Those that didn't could easily be corrected in the context of a strong draft that knew what it had to say and how it must be said.

THE SECOND TRUTH THAT ISN'T TRUE

Start at the beginning of the draft and correct each error as you come to it.

My teachers and editors looked first at the type or penmanship, the spelling, the punctuation, the grammar and that was it. They worked first on what was most obvious and most superficial. They didn't look deeply into the piece to discover what may have caused the bad writing.

Then I received that letter from Bob Johnson. It was not the scratched-over draft I expected. He stood back and looked at the entire draft to see what it could become. He didn't just charge in and edit it line by line.

He looked first at the topic and how it should be focused. He examined the structure of the article and how each part needed to be supported. He considered the pace of the writing, the proportion of the parts and their relationship to each other. He listened to the voice of the article in relation to the subject and its readers.

I began a new way of revising. I wrote to frame the house, to make the larger vision of the piece work: the subject, the topic, the structure. I wrote as many drafts as necessary to build on these strengths.

Then I wrote to construct the interior walls, floors, windows, doors, stairs in the house, to make each section of the article work, to get those sections lined up so that the reader was drawn through the article and that each section answered the questions the reader was asking when it was being asked.

And finally I wrote to finish the trim, hang the windows and the doors, put in the door knobs, polish the countertops, paint the ceilings and walls, develop the voice of the draft in each paragraph, sentence, phrase, word.

REVISE THEN EDIT

Now I step back the way an artist steps back from a canvas and read the draft quickly and in an intentionally superficial way. I skim over the surface of the draft, the way a reconnaissance plane zooms over enemy territory, asking the large questions that will reveal the draft's strongest points:

- What is the subject?
- What is the focus?
- What is the best form or genre to explore and communicate the subject?
- Where is the highway that will carry the reader through the draft?
- Where is it too long or too short?
- Where is the evidence that will persuade the reader?
- Where do I hear a clear, consistent, and appropriate voice?

The large questions have to be asked and answered first. It is a waste of time to check the draft more carefully unless these questions can be answered.

Revision means to re-see the whole, and editing means to clean up after the house is built, taking down the scaffolding, picking up the sawed-off lumber ends, sawdust piles, bent nails, to paint and landscape, to remove anything that gets between the reader and the subject, to hide all evidence of the work that went into the writing, so that the reader is invited to move into the article and enjoy its reading.

A USER'S WARNING

Once I learned to rewrite, I had to learn how not to revise. Rewriting becomes addictive. It is so much fun to play with what I have rewritten that I had trouble learning the Art of Letting Alone. I have seen students, teachers, published writers, and myself become obsessed with changing what is better left alone.

I was a writer for many years who believed the first draft was the best. It had been delivered, like a pizza in an insulated box, hot and ready to eat. I could not change the given word. Then I changed every word. I wrote a poem about finding my father's glasses in a drawer after he had died—and I wrote eighty-eight versions of the poem. Worse, I became proud of having written eighty-eight drafts. I began to do what I have seen teachers and students do, brag about how many drafts they have written. That is as stupid as thinking the first draft is the best.

The purpose of rewriting and editing is not to rewrite or edit. The purpose of revision is to find a significant meaning and make it clear. Writers have to learn to revise to develop their craft, and revision means knowing what works and what needs work—leaving what works alone and working on what needs work until the need is gone and the entire piece of writing reads as if it was written the first time, without effort, riding forth on the easy breeze of inspiration.

CHAPTER 8

SHOPTALK: HELPING EACH OTHER

Writing is a private act with a public result.

Even when I have written collaboratively and shared a byline, produced as-told articles, ghostwritten speeches, articles, talks, company reports and books, I have had to withdraw and work by myself. That's the best part of the writing process for me. I'm a friendly sort of guy, start my days with my cronies at the Bagelry at 6:00 A.M., but am happiest when I go down to my writing room under the back porch and sit alone before the computer screen.

I relish the loneliness of the writing act because in an increasingly complex world that forces people to work together in committees, teams, panels, groups, I am on my own.

I have a writing task I can perform successfully or screw up on my own. There is no one right way, no one wrong way, but thousands of ways that will work and as many that will not. It is up to me and me alone to find the way that is effective for this task, purpose, and audience. My method is my own. I have no boss, at this blessed lonely moment, telling me what to do.

My acceptance of aloneness that grew in appreciation and finally delight began early. I was an only child and a sickly one at that in an era that allowed weeks of convalescence in a bed. No television, no computers, no computer games. I could read stories and I could tell myself stories; I could napdream and daydream. I lived my stories, enjoying the long days by myself. That was what I liked about my before-the-sun-was-up paper route even in the crystal cold of a New England winter.

Lonely responsibility is what I liked about making deliveries in the Miller's Market truck, delivering messages, taking shortcuts through the alleys of Boston, chauffeuring the Massachusetts secretary of state when I was in high school. In combat I volunteered for lonely duty, carrying messages through what might or might not be enemy woods, standing guard alone on a road intersection, volunteering for missions where I could make my own mistakes or small victories. The loneliness of the newspaper reporter on assignment was what I wanted until I graduated to the increased aloneness of freelance writing. I wanted no editor telling me what to do and I did not want to be an editor telling others what to do and how to do it.

For me the aloneness of the writing life is not lonely. My companion is my craft and the surprises it provides. After a long lifetime of writing, I am still astonished by what I find myself saying. I did not plan the sequence that runs through the last paragraphs. The obvious thread that runs back through my life only came clear to me in its writing.

———— GOING PUBLIC ————

Most writing should not remain private. It's purpose is to share, to explain, to persuade, to illuminate, to call attention, to entertain, to make the reader think and feel, or as Joseph Conrad said, "My task . . . is, by the power of the written word, to make you hear, to make you feel—it is, before all, to make you see." Writing is a way of joining and contributing to the human community.

I often found that my shyest students were the ones who said the most yet resisted publication. It is frightening to go public. Writing is self-exposure. We reveal ourselves—how we think, how we feel, who we are—when we write. We all stand naked on the page.

To make the transition from private to public writing, we need to share our writing in process, to receive the response of readers when we can still make changes in our copy. We know what we intended to say but until we hear the reaction of test readers, we can not be sure if we have been heard.

And revealing a draft in process can be dangerous. We need to find helpful test readers who can tell us what works and what needs work with kindness and candor and make us go back to our desks eager to write.

———— FINDING A GOOD TEST READER ————

In class we may be assigned to groups of test readers, but most of the time we must find our own test readers—and it isn't easy. The difficulty is that we cannot tell if someone is a good test reader for us until we ask them to read a draft and receive their response. We must make ourselves—our draft—vulnerable and we must be able to survive when it turns out that the reader is not helpful.

While searching for good test readers I have learned there are significant issues that affect my choice:

- *Does this reader write?* I find that the readers who help me the most are themselves writers. They know the writing process themselves. They do not just see writing problems solved, but recognize the problems when they are not solved, when the writer is faced with contradictory options. There are good readers, editors, teachers who do not write, who read and recognize good writing, but the test readers who help me the most when I am in the process of writing are those who look at my drafts as they look at their own.

- *Is this reader right for me?* This is a clear personality issue. There are many good writers I neither like nor respect and others I do like and respect that simply rub me the wrong way. It may be a matter of their personality or mine, their style or mine, their way of working or mine, but they simply do not help me. How do I know? Because when I leave them I do not want to write. The good test reader may have delivered an opinion that is difficult for me to accept but I still want to get back to work on the draft immediately. I am inspired to revise.

- *Can this reader help my drafts?* Many brilliant editors, teachers, and colleagues simply make the drafts they read their own. They know what they would do to the draft and how they would do it, but it may not be right for me or my writing task. The good test reader doesn't take over the draft and fix it; he or she is able to enter into my draft, my voice, my way of working and help me see how I can become more myself. The good test reader respects what I am trying to do and my ability to do it.

- *Is this reader right for this stage in my writing process?* I may need a reader who is good at reading a sketch draft or outline and suggesting research options, another who can really evaluate structure, and another who is great at line-by-line reading and questions of voice. I also have readers who are helpful with poetry and others who hate poetry but are good at reading nonfiction.

Tell the test reader the reading you need.

My friend, Chip Scanlan, a fine writer, is my best reader and he taught me to tell the reading I needed. Before that we would share tentative, early drafts and subject them to demanding line-by-line editing. It is vital that writers tell the readers what they need:

- "I know this is rough, but do you think there's a story here?"
- "Here's an early draft, where do you think I need more documentation?"
- "I've written this as a personal essay; do you think it would work better as an argument or, perhaps, a narrative?"

- "I'm not sure I've got this organized effectively. What do you think?"
- "I like the way this is organized and documented but do you think the voice works?"
- "Before I submit this, would you check the spelling, grammar, mechanics, accuracy, grace to see if I've done anything stupid or clumsy?"

I look for classmates, friends, or colleagues I respect and like, ask them if they will read what I have written. I listen, try never to be defensive—if they don't get it, readers won't—and go back to my writing desk. I don't follow every suggestion—writing isn't a military drill—but if the reader's suggestions are helpful overall and if they made me want to take another crack at the draft, I treasure their help and will return to them again.

—— BECOMING A GOOD TEST READER ——

Asked for a reaction to another writer's draft, most of us unholster a red pen and cut. We cruise above the page like a hawk and when we see something to correct, we dive down and do it.

This is what most of our teachers and editors have done. They immediately make right what is—in their opinion—wrong. They take over the draft and make it their own. It's as easy as sitting in the stands and saying the quarterback shouldn't have thrown the ball after his pass has been intercepted. Of course we may be wrong in the context of the game or the season, but we don't admit that.

I have found that the less writing a person has done, the more certain the critical opinion. For professionals, writing is a fascinatingly complex process in which what is wrong on one page may be right on the next. It may be ineffective to use sentence fragments during a paragraph of exposition, necessary to use fragments on the next page to recreate action.

Worse still is the fact that most inexperienced writers want this mistreatment. They believe that writing is a matter of simple right or wrong, that writers follow strict rules that cannot be broken. They expect a teacher, editor, or classmate to fix their drafts so it follows the rules.

"Be honest," they say. "Don't worry about my feelings. I need a tough read." And there may be times when drafts need to be "fixed" on deadline, but it is not the best way to help inexperienced writers learn how to improve their writing skills.

The good test reader invites the writer to set the agenda:

"How can I help you?"

"What do you need from me?"

"What concerns do you have about the draft?"

"What are you trying to say to whom?"

Test readers should not take over each draft and correct it by the readers' standards, but help writers think about their individual writing task and their writing processes so they can learn how to apply the lessons of this draft to future work.

If the writer refuses, at first, to set the agenda, just saying, "Tell me what you think" or "Tell me what's wrong," the text reader should say, "It's not my piece of writing, it is yours, and I want to help you make it better in your way."

There are a number of questions that can help test readers help writers see their own drafts and their own writing techniques more clearly.

"What surprised you?"

This is my favorite because it tells me where the writer is and what the writer is learning that I can reinforce with my reaction. What surprised the writer may be on the page or off, it may be a matter of the topic or the technique, no matter. We can help writers best when we know where they are, what is their learning point.

My next favorite question is, "What works?" This usually surprises writers but they need to know the strength in the piece because most effective revision works by identifying and building on the strengths that are in the draft or may even be outside the draft in their command of the subject or point of view towards it.

That question is usually followed by "What needs work?" This does not imply failure but allows writers, once they have identified what works, to deal with what needs to be done to support and develop what is working.

Of course our questions must fit our personality and the personality of the writer, but the test reader's responsibility is to help the writer see the strengths and weakness and make her or him realize she or he has the ability to solve the problems.

Remember the priority of issues to be dealt with is just the opposite of what most beginning writers expect because of what they have been taught in school. They think that revision means working from problems of spelling, typography, grammar, to questions of structure, documentation, and voice, and then to matters of point of view, audience, genre, subject. The publishing writer reverses the order. First looking at the larger questions of subject, genre, audience, and point of view. There is no point in dealing with the more detailed issues until you identify the territory you are going to explore and the method you will use. After that is dealt with, it is wise to examine the structure, documentation, and voice. Finally when all those concerns are dealt with the test reader can help find typos, misspellings, grammatical and mechanical details that confuse rather than clarify.

HELPING A WRITING GROUP TO HELP YOU

When I studied writing in college and graduate school years ago, the writing group was more a test of fire than anything else. A student would publish and then everyone would attack. The writer was not allowed to defend himself or herself, not even allowed to speak, simply hunker down and take it. It was a literary scrimmage in which everyone tried to break the writer.

I hated it. It didn't help me. Most of the time the group didn't even seem to be talking about my draft but projecting their own writing problems or standards onto my work. They didn't seem to know what I was trying to do or how I was trying to do it. They didn't even care. They wanted me to write like them, each in her or his own contradictory way. The only result was to make me feel I couldn't write.

And, of course, when we read the papers of others I behaved the same way at first, tearing into them like a hyena who finds a wounded lion. That was what I was supposed to do even though I realized it was not helping the writer, often even destroying the writer.

And then, years later I found myself teaching writing. I watched my own students being thrown to the lions and was appalled at the bloody massacre of drafts that had possibilities and the destruction of writers who slunk away, convinced they were hopeless. Then I overheard two writing teacher colleagues say of a wonderful woman writing student that "she didn't have the balls to publish." This was so anatomically incorrect, so sexist, so unhelpful, so revealing that they thought the writing workshop was a macho text, not a matter of instruction, that I said I'd have no more workshops in my classes.

That would have been a loss because writers do need to test their drafts by going public in a workshop. We all know what we hoped to say, but we do not know what our readers have heard and how it affects them until we face them in workshop. We need to know the problems that must be solved, solutions that may solve them, and, above all, to know what works. That's what's most helpful to me when I share in a writing group. They see things that are good where I had only seen bad. But I didn't want to sponsor a kind of critical gang rape of my students' drafts. I didn't know what to do.

Then I read that the poet and writer Kenneth Koch asked the question of the student, "How can we help you?" The next day I changed the rules and announced:

1. The purpose of sharing in a writing group is to help writers.
2. The writers were to set the agenda before the group read the draft. (If the draft was to be distributed before class, always a good idea, the writers would set the agenda in writing at the top of the draft.)

3. The writers would answer the question: "How can we help you?" Now I would add, because of my experience with Chip Scanlan, my favorite test reader, "What kind of reading do you want?" The writers were encouraged to say where they were in the writing process, what they were trying to do, what they thought worked and needed work.

The tone and the effectiveness of the writing workshop changed immediately. The class didn't stop being critical, but they read the draft in the context of the writer's purpose and phrased their responses in encouraging, supportive ways. Often they were more demanding than before, seeing what the writer could do and, in that process, setting the standards higher for a writer.

Even more dramatic was the fact that the writers were not defensive in body language and attitude. In fact, just the opposite: they could be tough, honest, demanding of their own work, and many times the writing group saw more value in the draft than the writer did. Remember that the writer needs to know what works for the reader, so that the writer can build the revision on what works, not on what has gone wrong.

BECOMING A HELPFUL WRITING GROUP MEMBER

To make yourself become a helpful writing group member listen carefully to what the writer says of the draft, its purpose, and the process of writing it. Do not read the draft as if it had to meet some abstract set of standards and do not read the draft as if it was your own.

Read the draft with empathy, as if you were the writer. Your job is not to make writers become you—or Joan Didion or George Orwell—but to become themselves, seeing their world in their own way and sharing what they see in their own voice.

GOING PRIVATE

After you have gone public by publishing before test readers, you have to return to the loneliness of your writing desk and consider what you have learned. This does not mean following the test readers' instructions blindly. In fact, that should be impossible. You are an individual speaking to a group of individuals. In a recent publisher's review of one of my manuscripts, the reviewers split down the middle, half thinking issue after issue should not be changed because it was so good, and the other half thinking it must be completely changed because it was so bad.

You have to weigh each comment. Here is my scale:

1. I pay close and immediate attention to what readers say that surprises me. Often readers find things in my writing that I didn't see; often they see strengths where I saw weakness. But good or bad, I consider unexpected responses first. They give me a new vision of the piece. I may or may not accept that vision but each one—profound, scary, stupid, weird—illuminates my draft.

2. I next pay attention to the responses I hoped I wouldn't hear. In writing the draft I had suspected I should do more research but had tried to get away without doing it. Or I had made an illogical leap, hoping my cleverness would carry the day. It never does. Or I had some tangled sentences that needed untangling. I hope to get them past a reader's eye.

   I pay attention to what the reader doesn't understand or appreciate. I used to fight to defend what I had written when the teacher, editor, or colleague was so stupid they didn't get it. I don't anymore. I was once egotistical about what I had written and defended it to the death. Now I am egotistical about the fact I can find a thousand ways to write anything. I'll find some way to get what I want to say by the editor.

3. I read the draft with fresh eyes, seeing it anew, and try to make it cleaner, sharper, clearer. My goal is to write with accuracy and grace and become invisible. George Orwell said, "Good writing is like a window pane." I don't want the reader to see me, but to see the subject. Writers are truly subversive and they want their readers to think they experienced what the writer has written, that the thoughts and feelings on the page are their own.

I need editors, teachers, colleagues, test readers, but I am my most important reader. It is my brain, my soul that is on the page and the final draft must be the product of my mind and my heart and mine alone.

CHAPTER 9

REVISE AND EDIT

In 1957 I picked up a new issue of *The New Yorker* and read an article by E. B. White, the great essayist, about his writing teacher Will Strunk and in that article, which later became the introduction to *The Elements of Style* (William Strunk, Jr., and E. B. White), he quoted Strunk the words I shared with you in Chapter 2:

> Vigorous writing is concise. A sentence should contain no unnecessary words, a paragraph no unnecessary sentences, for the same reason that a drawing should have no unnecessary lines and a machine no unnecessary parts. This requires not that the writer make all his sentences short, or that he avoid all detail and treat his subjects only in outline, but that every word tell.

I can still feel my excitement as I typed out those words on a three-by-five card and thumb tacked it above my typewriter. The card turned from white to yellow to tan. Its edges curled and the type started to fade before I threw it away decades later. By then it was printed on the inside of my forehead where I could see it every time I sat down to draft, revise, or edit. It is still there.

Those sixty-three words were more than good counsel for revising and editing; they contained, for me, the joy I experienced in the craft of revision and editing, two separate but closely related crafts. Of course these crafts overlap. Revision is necessary for the writer to re-see the subject; editing is necessary for the reader to see the subject. As I revise I sometimes edit and as I edit I sometimes revise. That is why we have combined these crafts in one chapter, not the separate chapters they were in the previous edition. It is by practicing these two crafts of rewriting and editing, that writers explore the world and share their discoveries.

At first I had a blank brain and a blank page. I felt the normal panic that I had nothing to say, at least nothing worth saying; then, the words started to come, flowing on their own momentum, revealing that I had something to say. Was it worth saying? Well, that was up to editors and readers. Now I had a draft, I had a message, and it would, by golly, be delivered. The more intangible processes of writing were completed and now I had a job of work, a practical task of working with the draft to discover its full meaning, develop and document that meaning through as many revisions as necessary, and then, by the craft of editing, remove all evidence of revision so the writing appeared spontaneous, as natural as conversation.

Few moments are more exciting for me than coming to my computer and putting on the screen a draft that needs work. I am a surgeon eager to get to the operating room, a lawyer going to court, a football player just before the kickoff, a farmer cultivating acres of corn. I have a job to do and it is a job that I both know and continue to keep learning.

I am going to produce a rough first draft in response to a real writing assignment I have been given, then introduce a strategy for revising it—a logical, easy-to-understand, and easy-to-use method of revising—that can be applied to any writing task: a term paper or critical essay, lab report or office memo, thesis or letter of sympathy, case history or poem, scholarship application or take-home exam. Poets and screenwriters, historians and Supreme Court justices, marketing executives and clinical psychologists, novelists and engineers all have to think by writing and rewriting—and then rewriting again.

This piece of writing starts with an assignment from Diane Koski of the University of New Hampshire Foundation, a fund-raising organization for the college where I am both an alumnus and a retired faculty member. She asked me to write a letter telling how the university has changed in the past fifty years that might inspire financial support from my classmates. This is exactly the sort of assignment that might be given to an engineer, lawyer, sales manager, grant-seeking scientist, hospital administrator, minister, priest, or rabbi, anyone who has to produce a piece of writing designed to attract money. I've done this sort of writing professionally, and I am doing this one as a volunteer—a reluctantly drafted volunteer. Out of guilt and a sense of duty, I agreed to a task I did not relish but felt I must do.

I always start the same way, talking to myself in my head and in my daybook. I'm a visual person, as most writers are, and I see in images or pictures: myself as a soldier climbing down from the train that no longer runs, marching down Main Street, coming back to Durham after the war, twenty-one and a streak of white in my hair; particular classrooms in Murkland Hall, teachers such as Gwynne Daggett and Carroll Towle and Sylvester Bingham and Bill Hennessey and their offices; and my first wife. I walk around with that movie running through my head, and then I begin to hear fragments of language—proper names such as T-Hall, the main administration building once described by a student of mine as "a Victorian missile ready to lift off"—and phrases—"an educated man can sit alone in a room and be happy." That was to me, a lightning strike in the middle of a boring lecture on this campus. Finally, I start to write a discovery draft, beginning with description as I usually do.

When I first returned to teach at the university, the English department chair, who was a literature teacher, not a writer, ordered me NOT to teach description in freshman English since it was not sophisticated enough for college students. But description, the mother of all writing in my opinion, is where I start writing if I have no obvious beginning.

In this case I am trying to discover what I find special about my educational experience as a student and a teacher at the University of New Hampshire. I train my memory's eye on the day I first arrived in Durham. I was on a troop train in 1943, during World War II.

> The train pulled into the station in Durham, New Hampshire, the one that is now an ice cream parlor. We were marched up Main Street where GIRLS AND MORE GIRLS, REAL LIVE CO-EDS lined the street. I didn't know then that my first wife was among them, and I did not know that Durham would be my home—with my second wife and our three daughters, one of whom would be buried in the Durham Cemetery when she was only twenty.
>
> I wanted to be going overseas, not to school. My father wanted me to have my war, and I did too. So did my church. "Onward Christian Soldiers, Marching as to War." I didn't know I would become a paratrooper and survive combat. That I would return to school, marry the co-ed. If we had lived together, as my daughters and their husbands did, before marriage, we would never have married.
>
> Before I graduated I was insulted when the head of the English department suggested I should become a teacher and teach six courses a semester for $900 a year. I didn't know I would become a professor at this campus. I don't remember the classes so much as the professors' offices, conferences with Carroll Towle, his corncob pipe and his enthusiasm as he attacked my drafts. (And my conferences with his son years later.) Gwynne Daggett, his sleeves rolled up above his knotty biceps, his hands clasped behind his head, and his delight in ideas, attacking and defending, questioning, doubting, caring. When I was a teacher years later, I don't remember the classroom as much as my office and meeting all my students every week. One on one. I remember my learning as much as theirs. My teachers, I realized then and now, were still learning with me.

Now I have a first draft, one page, 299 words. It is a jumble that jumps around in time and topic, an example of freewriting that isn't close to a polished letter to alumni, but I sense there is something there I can build on. I am an experienced detective. Sometimes the topic or approach is obvious. I see it immediately and that is it. Other times it is not obvious, and I follow an organized search plan I call a strategy for revision. It was, at first, instinctive, but now I have made it into a chart so I can share it with others. It provides a logical approach to revision. If you study the chart you will see that the writer first looks within the draft itself, then looks ahead to new drafts, finally looks back to the original assignment. Revision is, after all, thinking, a process of discovering new meaning.

—— THE STRATEGY OF REVISION ——

1. LOOK WITHIN FOR THE SURPRISING:	2. LOOK FORWARD FOR THE CHANGING:	3. LOOK BACK FOR THE EXPECTED:
Word	Purpose	Purpose
Line	Meaning	Meaning
Distance	Distance	Distance
Voice	Genre	Genre
Focus	Audience	Audience
Details	Evidence	Documentation
Sequence	Order	Logic
Purpose	Pace	Pace
Meaning	Proportions	Proportions
Genre	Development	Development
Audience	Voice	Voice

I move quickly through the strategy of revision, skimming over some points, lingering over others, moving back and forth between the three forms of revision, as you will when you are experienced with the entire process. But to understand the strategy, you should, at least once, examine an early draft, point by point, to see the full potential the strategy can reveal in a draft. That is what I will do to see if my discovery draft has the potential for me to fulfill the assignment of a fund-raising letter.

I scan the text, reading quickly.

LOOK WITHIN FOR THE SURPRISING

Word

I hesitate over "GIRLS!" I realize, now that my consciousness has been raised, that the word *girls* hearkens back to an era I could remember and explore in a column. No other word really sparks my interest.

Line

"Onward Christian Soldiers" catches me, because it was one of my favorite hymns when I was young. I didn't hear the irony of a killing, militaristic Christianity until I saw my first dead German soldier and his belt buckle, which proclaimed that God was with the Wehrmacht, Hitler's army. "I don't remember classes as much as the professors' offices" also catches my eye. That may lead to something.

Distance

I'm remembering my first view of the campus reflected through the many lives I would live in Durham. Should I stay at that distance—the assignment would seem to demand that—or would it be more effective to move in close, put the reader with me on campus in 1943?

Voice

"I remember my learning as much as theirs" has a certain melody or music I can imagine developing as I write.

Focus

The focus is on the meetings, one-on-one, with my professors. That may be the focus of the next draft.

Details

I need more details like Towle's corncob pipe and Daggett's pride in his biceps.

Sequence

I sense a sequence or implied narrative that could run through the piece: discovery that my students were learning with me and later discovering that I was learning with my students.

Purpose

To get alumni to see what is special about this intimate form of education, to encourage them to celebrate and support it—with cash.

Meaning

At a university, faculty and students learn together.

Genre

This piece looks like an essay, more than a letter, a personal reflective essay that puts our alumni experience in a positive educational context.

Audience

I could target a different audience—the readers of my column, teachers who read my articles and textbooks—but here the audience will be alumni.

It took me a few minutes to zero in on this draft and find the approach I can use to produce a fund-raising alumni letter. Writing is always a matter of selection, choosing the road to go down, and making choices all along the way. Today I have found, within my discovery draft, my approach to the assignment—I will write about students and teachers learning together—but I must, to avoid problems as I write this piece, at least check the other two strategies of revision.

Next, I look ahead to see what may need to be changed.

LOOK FORWARD FOR THE CHANGING

Purpose

In reading these 299 words, I might have decided to write about the relationship of men and women ("girls") in the 1940s, or a militaristic Christianity, or the importance and techniques of teaching writing by conference.

Meaning

Any of these issues may have a new meaning that I might feel the need to explore. In fact, I think I will celebrate—in a column—the benefits of feminism for an old man who now has women friends.

In fact, I am going to start next week's column right now, while the words are eager to flow:

> The other morning I marched down Durham's Main Street, which runs through the middle of the University of New Hampshire, and was both a retired professor taking his constitutional and an eighteen-year-old soldier marching down the same street in 1943.
>
> What I remember is not the itchy winter uniform, the green lawns and brick buildings, but the GIRLS! that lined the sidewalk.
>
> Today I do not see girls but women.
>
> The girls were mysterious, alluring, threatening, different. The women to whom I nod or wave, with whom I stop to chat today, are colleagues and friends.

Once I have this much written, I can go back and finish it when I have time.

Distance

As I get back to thinking about my fund-raising letter, I might zoom back and forth, almost line by line, from present to past and back, making a virtue of one of the weaknesses of the discovery draft.

Genre

I see poems and short stories in this draft that I may develop later.

Audience

There could be a general audience—old-timers who would be nostalgic, young people who would be astonished, feminists who might be pleased, old fogies who might realize the benefits—to them—of the feminism they have attacked.

Evidence

I could go to school records which might document curriculum arguments for or against conference teaching, or rules and regulations that would document the very different treatment of men and women at UNH then and now. I might interview women who have lived these changes.

Order

I might not start with my parade down Main Street but with the scene, after I returned, of the Military Arts Ball, which no longer takes place in Durham.

Pace

I might saunter through the past or speed from present to past and back.

Proportions

I will always have the question of how much past and how much present.

Development

I must have enough information—descriptive details, facts, documentation—to make the past clear to the young, the present clear to the old.

Voice

My voice must, as always, be appropriate to the subject, the audience, and myself. I must be aware of language—girls, dates, balls, curfews.

Again, let me remind you that these lists are just quick checklists to protect you from wasting your time on fruitless revision, allowing you to concentrate your energy where revision will be rewarded. Finally, it is important to look back to what was expected. If you are rewriting a novel, you may want to betray your expectations, but if you are revising a screenplay for a Hollywood producer, a marketing report for a corporate vice president, a thesis for an academic committee, or a fund-raising letter for an alumni officer, you'd better be sure you can fit your discoveries to their expectations.

LOOK BACK FOR THE EXPECTED

Purpose

My focus on individual education can fit the purpose of showing alumni a consistent strand that deserves their pride and their funds despite all the changes at their university.

Meaning

It is significant that university faculty continue to learn and share their learning with their students.

Distance

It is appropriate for me to move back and forth in time, as long as the time shifts clarify the meaning I am communicating for my readers.

Genre

The essay format of the letter will work, I think.

Audience

My audience is clear. Men and women who graduated fifty years ago.

Documentation

My documentation is personal and anecdotal, which is appropriate for this piece of writing.

Logic

The emphasis on individual learning is logical, it makes sense.

Pace

I shall have to make sure the readers are kept moving forward fast enough so they will continue to read, slow enough so they will absorb what I have to say.

Proportions

I will have to make sure there is little—but enough—of a fund-raising appeal, surrounded by mostly informative material. I will also have to make sure there is enough reflection to recreate the past but much more on what is going on at UNH today. That is what we hope they will support.

Development

I will have to develop each part well enough that the reader can relive or live it.

Voice

My voice should not be pushy. I should simply recount what I have experienced at UNH in a way that encourages them to support the school. (Fifty-two alumni responded with $5,265.)

Here is the revision I submitted:

> I first came to Durham in 1943 when an Army sergeant counted cadence as we marched down Main Street. I returned from Europe in 1946, surprised to have survived combat, and experienced an unexpected intimacy of learning with Carroll Towle, Gwynne Daggett, Bill Hennessey, and others who met with us in class, in their offices, in their homes and ours, in the corridors of Murkland, and on the sidewalks of Durham.
>
> I lived the glorious triangle of university learning:
>
> An individual teacher,
>
> a senior learner
>
> > A test to be understood,
> >
> > a question to be asked,
> >
> > a problem to be researched
>
> An individual student,
>
> a junior learning
>
> In 1963 I was invited to return to the university to set up a journalism program, and I reentered the triangle of learning as the senior learner, meeting with each individual student every week in the method of Carroll Towle and the pattern of freshman English which is still taught by class and conference.
>
> Since retiring from the faculty nine years ago, I have continued to live in Durham, observing the evolving university firsthand. I have cheered the hockey and football teams, applauded the academic honors won by faculty and students, watched the new buildings rise on a campus I still find beautiful, but most of all, I have celebrated the evidence I have found that the triangle of learning goes on: An individual professor and an individual student learn from each other as they confront a specific intellectual question.
>
> This individual learning is expensive but central to the university. It is the way that faculty continue to learn, that students discover how to learn, and that society benefits from their combined learning.
>
> Visit the campus and you see buildings, but if you are fortunate enough to live here you may catch a glimpse of what goes on in the seminar room, faculty office, laboratory: a belief doubted, an answer that finds a question, a principle challenged, a theory tested, a pattern explained, a problem solved that gives birth to a new question.
>
> In room _____ at the Whittemore School of Business and Economics, Dr. _____ meets with _____. They are fascinated with _____ and study the puzzling results of a survey that

contradicts expectations. Now they have a problem to solve that may change the way _____ look at _____ .

In a laboratory in _____ , _____ uses a _____ to test and retest a _____ taken from Great Bay the day before. She calls over Dr. _____ who runs his own tests, and then they sit down to study computer printouts that may some day lead to _____ .

[And so on for the School of Health Studies and Human Services and the College of Liberal Arts]

Four individual students and four individual faculty members focusing on four significant questions. Radiating out from them are the intellectual interactions of _____ full-time and part-time faculty members with _____ undergraduate and graduate students.

Of course there are large classes, but the center of what goes on at the University of New Hampshire is that grand triangle of individual learning. I give to support what happens when an individual instructor and student learn from each other, and I hope you will join me.

The alumni office did the research that changed, developed, and filled in my blanks, and the letter was published pretty much as I had drafted it. But it was not a first draft; it was a revision constructed after exploring a discovery draft.

Notice that I passed up many topics in that discovery draft: my desire to go to war and what happened when I did; marriage, divorce, remarriage; the births of three children and the loss of one; what I studied in school and how it affected my life; what it was like to return and teach where I had been a student; teaching my teacher's son; profiles of Towle or Daggett; an essay on what makes a good teacher—all those topics and more embedded in 299 words. But I had an assignment, and so I concentrated on what might help me fulfill that assignment.

Sometimes I practice an unconscious revision. Once we have written, we have captured a vision of the world. Several years after writing that letter I was invited to write a column for the university magazine on what goes on at a university, and this column was, in effect, a revision of the piece above although I never looked back and didn't realize the connection until I was rewriting this chapter for the seventh edition. Here is the "unconscious revision:"

· A LANDSCAPE OF WORDS ·

I live at the edge of that mysterious organism we call a university, nine-tenths of a mile from the classrooms in Murkland where I was a student, the same distance from Ham Smith, where I taught for 24 years. As I watch faculty and students apparently arriving late and leaving early, or read news stories about research grants I do not understand, or listen to anecdotes that illustrate

Henry Kissinger's statement—"Campus politics are so vicious precisely because the stakes are so small"—I, like so many politicians and taxpayers in this state, find myself wondering, "What does go on in Durham anyway?"

A few times, waiting to meet an old colleague, I've lurked outside a classroom in Ham Smith, hoping to observe what indeed goes on, even to catch a glimpse of the central activity of a university. Perhaps I will see on a student's face the look of surprise and delight when confusion comes clear. I may hear a question that hangs above a seminar table until it attaches itself to a student's mind for a lifetime. I may even find the mystery that is a university when a professor pauses during a lecture, surprised at a truth that has tumbled unplanned from her lips.

But of course, I do not capture, see or hear what happens in a university. The central act is invisible—a sudden, unexpected falling in love with learning that happens so quickly, so easily that neither the student nor the teacher knows that a life has been changed.

I came to UNH first as a soldier in 1943 and returned from combat in Europe three years later, surprised to be alive. I carried little with me but the dream of becoming a writer—a dream that seemed so wonderful, so removed from the ordinary person I was, that I imagined it to be impossible. Yet in Durham, I found professor Carroll Towle, who seemed to think my dream possible. Gwynne Daggett, Sylvester Bingham and others demonstrated lives lived in the landscape of language. Just as important, I joined a community of pilgrims who followed the same impossible vision.

I remember no moment of grand illumination, but in four semesters and two sessions of summer school, my dream became a vocation. I left UNH a writer and have, ever since, lived a life of words. It might have happened somewhere else, but I doubt it. It happened in the mixture of hope and knowledge and obsession that is not only tolerated but encouraged in a university.

I returned to UNH 15 years later to teach. I worked hard at my new craft, but the more I learned to teach, the more mysterious this central mystery of the university became. It seemed the longer I taught, the less I taught, and the more my students learned. In fact, I did not teach so much as encourage. In my classroom, my office and my home, students found themselves part of a community that did not laugh at their dreams and allowed them to teach themselves the craft to which they, like their instructor, would forever be an apprentice.

I never quite knew what worked on my page or in my classroom, but I am amazed, looking back, how many students left with a vocation for writing. I knew it was happening, but I could never quite see it, never be sure what had happened and when.

The other afternoon, I was invited by John Lofty to meet with his class on the teaching of English. The students and I wrote together, then talked our way across the landscape of words that had become their teacher's life and mine.

What happened? What did I teach? What did they learn? I do not know.

TWO KEY QUESTIONS • 195

What goes on in a university remains a mystery. I leave John Lofty's class and cross the boundary between gown and town. At home, I again observe antics of the university community with amusement, amazement and, often, a critical eye. But each morning, at 75 years of age, I return to the lifelong apprenticeship that began when I returned from war to the mystery we call a university. I still do not know exactly what happened to me at the University of New Hampshire, but I am grateful each morning that it gave me the courage to write what I do not yet know.

——— TWO KEY QUESTIONS ———

Another approach to revision is built on two key questions:

WHAT WORKS?
WHAT NEEDS WORK?

Years ago, before I had a computer, I would write at least three drafts for a magazine article and revise each by hand at least ten times. To discover what I was doing so I could teach it to my students, I pasted each typed draft on a much larger piece of paper, revised, then wrote in these large margins what I was doing, why I was doing it, and how. I surprised myself. I thought I was fixing failure and correcting error but discovered that, most of the time, I was strengthening success. I was building on the elements in the draft that worked, making them stronger, rather than correcting error.

Once I found what worked and developed those elements, I went on to what needed work. I found that many of the errors, problems, or failures in early drafts disappeared as I revised by focusing on developing the strengths of the article. Those that hadn't disappeared could then be addressed.

Let's see how this system of revision works. I will write a brief freewrite or discovery draft:

> I am going to a football game—NH versus Delaware—opening game of the season. We will sit on the fifty yard line, twenty rows up. Beside the Drouins who we sit with at hockey games. I went to my first football game in this stadium fifty-one years ago. It is named for a classmate of mine, Andy Mooradian, who was athletic director. He died of cancer, and one of his daughters was one of the best friends of my daughter's. I don't approve of football—it is a violent and militaristic game—but I love it. I played it and got to college on a football scholarship. My right knee still hurts from an illegal block on a kickoff, no substitutes then. That was fifty-four years ago. When I watch the game, I'll be on the field. The fat old grad will sit in the stands, and the eighteen-year-old will go in at right tackle.

Actually I'd like to play right defensive end. I feel I could. The illusion is worse than my wife believes. I know I could sack the quarterback. I'd be cool. Not jump around, simply point down with the first finger of my right hand. Cool. Cold. Tough. Mean. All the virtues.

A jumble—a badly written jumble, but what works for me is the illusion of the old man that he could play a young man's game—and the tension that he doesn't approve of the game and still loves it. Teachers and editors might see the contradictions as a failure, something that needed to be fixed—or abandoned. I see the contradictions as what works, what has potential.

What is failure to one writer is opportunity to another; what doesn't work for one writer may work for another. I am reminded of what novelist Fay Weldon said:

> What others say are your faults, your weaknesses, may if carried to extremes be your virtues, your strengths. I don't like too many adjectives or adverbs—I say if a noun or a verb is worth describing, do it properly, take a sentence to do it. There's no hurry. Don't say "the quick brown fox jumped over the lazy dog." Say, "it was at this moment that the fox jumped over the dog. The fox was brown as the hazelnuts in the tree hedgerows, and quick as the small stream that ran beside, and the dog too lazy to so much as turn his head." Or something. Writing is more than just the making of a series of comprehensible statements: It is the gathering in of connotations; the harvesting of them, like blackberries in a good season, ripe and heavy, snatched from among the thorns of logic.
>
> Having thus discouraged the apprentice writer from overuse of adjectives, I turn at once to Iris Murdoch and find she will use eighteen of them in a row. It works. What is weakness in small quantities is style in overdose. So be wary of anyone who tries to teach you to write. Do it yourself. Stand alone. You will never be better than your own judgment, and you will never be satisfied with what you do. Ambition will, and should, always outstrip achievement.

Remember Fay Weldon: Ask "What works—for you?" Ask "What needs work—from you?" Then ask what the reader needs.

THE REVISION CHECKLIST

Revision is not editing. They are two separate activities, and keeping them apart makes the task of preparing a final draft much easier.

The following diagram shows how the emphasis changes from revision to editing:

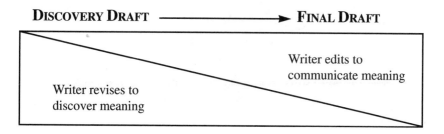

Revision is re-seeing the entire draft so that the writer can deal with the large issues that must be resolved before she or he deals with line-by-line, word-by-word issues involved in editing.

In reading for revision, it is important to step back and scan the draft so that you can see it as a whole. In this way, you will notice such things as the relationships between the sections of the draft that you cannot see when you are concentrating on the relationship between a particular verb and an individual noun.

Make your own revision checklist. Mine is in the list below. The list is long, but many of the questions can be answered in an instant. Because you have focused, explored, planned, and drafted, you have solved most of these problems in advance. This is a checklist to see if any problems remain that must be solved before the editing that produces the final draft:

CHECKLIST FOR REVISING

Subject
- Do I have something I need to say?
- Are there readers who need to hear what I have to say?

Focus
- Does the draft make a clear, dominant point?
- Are there clear, appropriate limits to the draft that include what needs to be included, exclude what is unnecessary?
- Do writer and reader stand at the appropriate distance from the material?

Authority
- Are the writer's credentials to write this draft established and clear?

Context
- Is the context of the draft, the world in which the story exists, clear?

Voice

- Does the draft have an individual voice?
- Is the voice appropriate to the subject?
- Does the voice support and extend the meaning of the draft?

Reader

- Can you identify a reader who will need to read the draft?
- Can you see a reader who will want to read the draft?
- Are the reader's questions answered where they will be asked?

Genre

- Is the form of the story the best one to carry the meaning to the reader?
- Does the draft fulfill the reader's expectations of that form?

Structure

- Will the lead attract and hold a reader?
- Does the ending resolve the issues raised in the draft?
- Is there a clear trail through the draft?
- Does each point lead to the next point?
- Does each section support and advance the meaning?

Information

- Is the reader's hunger for specific information satisfied?

Documentation

- Does the reader have enough evidence to believe each point in the draft?

Pace

- Is the reader carried forward toward the intended meaning by the flow of the draft?
- Are there points where the draft needs to be speeded up to keep the reader from abandoning it?
- Are there points where the draft needs to be slowed down so the reader has time to comprehend the meaning of what is being written?

Proportion

- Are the sections in appropriate proportion to one another to advance and support the meaning of the draft?

Quantity
- Where does the draft need to be developed?
- Where does it need to be cut?

Move through the checklist quickly, scanning the draft and then revising part or all of it as necessary until you have done all you can do—or until the deadline is upon you. Then begin editing the final draft.

——— EDIT TO CLARIFY MEANING ———

There are few satisfactions for this writer greater than editing a final draft—word by word, space by space, line by line. As Diane Ackerman says,

> Most of a writer's life is just work. It happens to be a kind of work that the writer finds fulfilling in the same way that a watchmaker can happily spend countless hours fiddling over tiny cogs and bits of wire. Poets also love to fiddle with a word here, a word there—small spaces for hours. And when I'm working on a poem, I'm working harder than I've ever worked at anything in my life—I'm concentrating harder. But it's enjoyable. Not something I would describe as fun—it's more like rapture, a kind of transcendent play.

Fiddling around with a piece of writing is so satisfying because the subject comes clear. I like to make my copy simple, easy—like the flight of the seagull. Each editing makes the writing more natural. Editing—ironically—makes each draft more spontaneous.

I'm going to write a few lines about a cliché topic—Father's Day—and then see if I can edit in the meaning.

> I never expected to be a father. My own father was at work or church most of the time. Even when he was home, he seemed at a distance a stranger in a house dominated by women—his grandmother and her daughter. I didn't really know what a father was supposed to do. Then I had a daughter, and I found I knew what to do.

Editing is simply a matter of adding, taking away, moving around, and making sure the result was clear. Do I have something to say? I can't edit until I have specified a topic, since all editing is aimed at developing and clarifying the topic. No topic, and editing is a waste of time. In my sample, I do have a topic—discovering how to be a father.

I also need a structure, a design and order. I have that. I have an embedded narrative—how I passed from not knowing a father's role to knowing. Now I can edit.

I move some of it around:

My own father was at work or church most of the time. Even when he was home, he seemed at a distance, a stranger, in a house dominated by women—his grandmother and her daughter. I never expected to be a father. I didn't really know what a father was supposed to do. Then I had a daughter, and I found I knew what to do.

I put in and take out:

My own father was at work on the road buying silk stockings, women's corsets, or ladies gloves or at the department store making sure they were sold at a profit. If he wasn't on the road he was at church, a deacon trying to fulfill the orders of the prophets. When I was young, I didn't know the difference between profits and prophets. Both ruled our life. Most of the time. Even when he was home, he seemed at a distance, a stranger in a house dominated by women. I never expected to be a father; I didn't really know what a father was supposed to do. Then a nurse handed me Anne, my first daughter, wrinkly red and howling. Then I had a daughter and I found I knew what to do. No thinking, just instinct. I held her against my shoulder and rubbed circles around her tiny back. Her howls became sobs, her sobs moans, her moans, silence. She slept, and I became a father.

That's all. In most cases, editing means putting in more than taking out, moving around, simply clarifying.

I have worked for the past few years with editors on some of the best newspapers in the country, and I've found that these editors make the same mistake most teachers—and their students—make. The mistake is to plunge in and start editing language first, working from the written line back to form and then to meaning. It simply doesn't work.

─── PROOFREADING AND EDITING ───

Proofreading is what most people think of when editing is mentioned, but it is only a small part of editing. It is important to correct spelling, to check facts and names and quotations, to conform to certain stylistic standards of mechanics and usage, to clean up typographical errors. But editing is that and much more.

Editing is the honing of thinking, making meaning rational and clear, accurate and graceful. Editing is the final clarification of meaning. You choose one word and reject another word in relation to meaning. If the meaning isn't clear, the choice will be arbitrary and often wrong. There are no rules for word choice unrelated to meaning. Also, when you choose to write a short sentence or paragraph, it is usually for emphasis, and unless you know what you want to emphasize you won't know whether to make the sentence or the paragraph long or short.

When you edit, you repeat steps from the revision checklist, but your reading is different. When you revise, you read to see what needs to be done in the next draft; when you edit, you are the reader's advocate, preparing the final draft for your readers.

———— EDITING PRIORITIES ————

Effective editing is usually the result of three separate and distinct readings, each with its own pace, strategies, and techniques. The highly skillful editor or writer may be able to perform all three readings simultaneously, moving from the large global questions of meaning to structural questions of order, and to line-by-line questions of voice. But those interrelated skills are best developed by separating the reading—reading first for meaning, next for order, and third for voice.

Of course in each case the writer has to keep an eye open for the audience, standing back and making sure that what is being said and resaid on the page is clear to the reader.

This seems to be a slow process, but the first reading is usually a very fast one—a quick flyover of the territory to make sure that there is a single dominant meaning and an abundant inventory of information to support that meaning.

If there is no subject, no dominant meaning, no inventory of information, it is a waste of time to do more revising and editing. Stop immediately. Find a subject. Find its meaning. Find the facts to support that meaning.

The second reading looks for form and structure. It is a bit slower, but not much. The piece is still read in chunks to see if the sections support the main point and appear when the reader needs them.

If there is no form to the writing, no order within that form that leads the reader to meaning, read no further. It will be a waste of time. Stop. Choose a form and establish an order within that form.

At the end there is the third reading, a slow, careful, line-by-line editing of the draft to be sure that it is ready for a final proofreading. Here the writer cuts, adds, and reorders, paragraph by paragraph, sentence by sentence, word by word.

The process of three readings may sound tedious, but it shouldn't be. In each case you'll have the excitement of discovery, of finding a meaning that you did not expect to find and defining a change to make it become clear. Writing gives you the satisfaction of craft, the feeling you have when you lean your weight into the corner and make your bicycle swing gracefully where you want it to go. Writing is similar to hitting a tennis ball, baking bread, building a sturdy shelf, sewing a dress, planting a garden. It is a process of making, and it is fun to make something well, to handcraft a piece of prose that will carry meaning and feeling to another person.

──────── EDITING MARKS ────────

Most computer editing is invisible, but those who work with typewriter and pen or pencil will find it helpful to mark up the copy according to the traditions of the editor's trade:

During the first two readings I sit away from the desk, if I

am not using a computer, in an easy chair and use a

clipboard or a bean bag lap desk. I read the draft quickly, as

a reader will, and do not mark anything within the text. I

do not correct spelling or typos, change words, revise, or

edit. Instead, I make marks in the left margin:

✓   A check for something that works,

✱   a star for something that works well,

C   a C for something that needs cutting,

↱   an arrow that suggests movement,

⤡   a two-headed arrow to indicate the need for expansion,

→◄—   two arrows pointing at each other to show what needs to be

tightened,

?   and a question mark for further consideration.

These marks allow me to move through the text quickly.

In the following list are some of the most helpful editing marks for the third, careful, line-by-line reading. If you are reading "hard copy" (manuscript pages, not a computer screen) you will find these marks helpful in editing your drafts or the drafts of a classmate in a peer-editing session.

---

paragraph	¶ The craft of editing depends on reading aloud.
capital	the craft of editing depends on reading aloud.
lowercase	The ₵raft of ₤diting depends on reading aloud.
close	The craft of edit ing depends on reading aloud.
separate	The craft of editing depends on reading aloud.
transpose	The editing craft of depends on reading aloud.
punctuate	The craft of editing depends on reading aloud⊙
insert	The craft of editing depends ᴼⁿ reading aloud.
take out	The craft of editing / depends on reading aloud.
cut	~~The craft of~~ editing depends on reading aloud.
restore	~~The craft of~~ editing depends on reading aloud.
move	⌜Insert A⌝ The craft of editing depends on reading aloud.

Large inserts should be numbered or lettered and an

arrow should be marked in the margin of the text

where it is to be placed.

⟶ (move Insert A here)

——— EDITING CHECKLISTS ———

The following checklists are built on the editing system that uses three readings—one for the topic, one for development of the topic, and one for language that communicates the topic. Of course the actual process of revising and editing will not be so neatly contained. Change of focus leads to change of language, and change of language can change the topic; still, the master list is a way of proceeding logically and efficiently through a series of confusing writing problems.

Each writer has his or her own strengths and weaknesses. Eventually you should adapt my checklist to your own style, problems, and solutions.

Many times writers edit against deadlines, without time to carefully revise and edit. Remember that you have to deal with the first item before going on to the second and the second before the third. Here is a checklist for that situation:

THE QUICK EDIT CHECKLIST

- State the single, most important message you have for the reader in one sentence.
- List the points that support the message in the order the reader needs to receive them.
- Read the draft aloud to be sure the text is accurate and fair, and that the music of the language supports the message you are sending to the reader.

When you learn that the first draft is not the end result of the writing process, you will plan to allow time—at least as much as comes before the first draft—for reading, revising, and editing. The quick checklist is designed to help in the three readings for subject, structure, and language, but don't be surprised when you have to move back and forth through the checklist as solutions breed problems, and new problems demand new solutions.

THE EXPANDED EDIT CHECKLIST

The list is long, but remember that many of your answers will come rapidly, in a second or less. You are scanning the text to catch the problems that have survived the writing process and must be solved before the draft is final, ready to face a reader.

- State the single most important message you have for the reader in one sentence.
- Does the draft deliver on the promise of the title and lead?
- Does your message have significant meaning you can make clear to the reader?
- Is the message important, worth the reader's time?
- Does your message contain the tension that will provide the energy to drive the reader forward?

- Is your message focused? Do you have a clear point of view toward the subject?
- Is the message placed in a significant context? Will that context be clear to the reader?
- Does the message have limitations that help you control and deliver the information?
- Do you have an abundance of information upon which to build the draft? Can you answer the questions the reader will certainly ask?
- Is that information accurate and fair?
- List the points that support the message in the order the reader needs to receive them.
- Is the form, the genre, of the draft appropriate to deliver the message to the reader? Will it contain and support the meaning of the draft?
- Does the structure within the draft support and advance the principal message?
- Does the order in the piece make the reader move forward, anticipating and answering questions as they arise?
- Is the structure logical? Does each point lead to the next in a sensible sequence? Is there a narrative thread that carries the reader forward? Will the sequence or narrative stand up to a doubting reader?
- Is the draft too long? Too short?
- Are the proportions of sections within the draft appropriate to the information they deliver? Are there sections that are too long? Too short?
- Is the draft effectively paced? Does it move fast enough to keep the reader reading, slow enough to allow the reader to absorb what is being read?
- Does the draft go off on tangents that take the reader away from its principal message? Does it include elements of good pieces of writing that do not support the current message but may be developed on their own later?
- Is each point supported with evidence that will convince the reader?
- Is the draft written at a distance that will involve the reader but also allow the reader to consider the significance of the message?
- Read the draft aloud to be sure it is accurate and fair, and that the music of the language supports the message you are sending to the reader.
- Does the title catch the reader's attention, and does it make a promise to the reader that can be fulfilled by the draft?
- Does the opening accomplish the same thing?
- Is each piece of information accurate and fair and presented in context?

- Does the reader need more information? Less? Can anything be cut? Must anything be added?
- Does the reader finish each sentence having gained information?
- Can the draft be heard by the reader? Does the music of the draft support and advance the meaning of the message?
- Does the draft reveal rather than tell whenever possible? Does the draft call attention to the message rather than the reader?
- Does each paragraph and each sentence emphasize the appropriate information?
- Does the sentence length vary in relation to the meaning being communicated, with shorter sentences at the most important points?
- Does the draft depend, at important points, on the subject-verb-object sentence?
- Is the draft written in the active voice whenever possible? Is each word the right word?
- Have all sexist, racist, and ethnic language and stereotypes been eliminated?
- Has private language—jargon—been replaced with public language the reader can understand?
- Has worn-out language—clichés and stereotypes—been replaced with language that carries specific meaning to the reader?
- Is the draft primarily constructed with verbs and nouns rather than adverbs and adjectives?
- Has the verb *to be* in all its forms been eliminated whenever possible? Excess *woulds*, *whats*, and *ings*?
- Is the simplest tense possible used?
- Are the tenses consistent?
- Are any words misspelled?
- Are the traditions of language and mechanics followed, except when they produce ungraceful language or change the meaning of the draft?
- Is the draft attractively presented, so that nothing gets between the reader and the message?
- Does the closing give the reader a feeling of closure and completeness, yet stimulate the reader to continue to think about the message that has been delivered?

Develop your own editing checklist, building on your own strengths and weaknesses in writing. Do not forget that this final stage of writing is still focused on discovery of meaning; as you edit, you learn more about your topic and make what you have to say come clear to the reader—so clear and easy to read that the reader may believe the writing was spontaneous.

—— REVISE AND EDIT IN THE DAYBOOK ——

Even when I have discovered an appropriate revision strategy, even when I know what works and what needs work, I often have to stand back from the draft, to get distance from what I have written and sketch what I may try in the next draft. That is when I return to my daybook.

I have learned to stand back the way an artist stands back from a painting. I do not look at the draft; I do not try to remember it. I simply play around with words, phrases, lists, diagrams, beginning paragraphs, fragmentary outlines. All are revisions, although they are only single words or selections a few lines long. Each shows me how the piece might be reworked.

I have to keep reminding myself not to get too serious, not to strain, but to play with the ideas in the draft, so that I can catch sight of the one that works out of the corner of my eye. The daybook allows me to do this in the traffic jam, on the bench at the front of the supermarket while once again waiting for my wife, while there are commercials on the television, in the doctor's waiting room. The daybook allows me a few moments of constructive play, and often, looking back, I find that it only took a minute, three, five to sketch out a revision I can complete the next morning—one that works.

My daybook becomes at the last stage of the writing process, a lab book in which I make note of references and facts I have to check in the library, illustrations and charts I have to locate and reproduce, reprint permissions I have to obtain. I also note problems that should be added to my personal checklist.

Most importantly, I make notes of questions, problems, conflicts that have arisen during the writing of a draft that may lead to new pieces of writing.

The computer is of enormous help in editing, making it possible to read the draft and fix problems with spelling, punctuation, diction, usage as you read.

—— REVISE AND EDIT YOUR VOICE ——

Revise and edit out loud. Listen to the music of the draft, and tune it so that each paragraph, each line, each word, each space between words creates a beat and melody that supports and advances the meaning of the draft.

Your ear has been trained since early childhood to listen to language and to use language to be heard. Your ear knows when the voice is honest or dishonest, graceful or clumsy, true or false.

When I sat down to write the final draft of the "melancholy" essay I developed on pages 46, 81, 111, and 159, I considered the many things that a writer has to keep in eye and ear at this stage of the writing process:

- The accuracy and power of the specific details
- The strength and direction of the narrative line
- The traditions of language, remembering George Orwell's counsel in his essay on "Politics and the English Language": "(vi) Break any of these rules sooner than say anything barbarous."

Most of all I listen to the music of what I'm saying, reading the text out loud to make sure the pace or rhythm, the flow, the melody that comes from the sound of the words and the tensions with the phrases and sentences, supports the meaning that has evolved during the writing of the drafts. I never forget that if the writing is effective readers hear as much or more than they see when they read.

I've been coming to Florida, off and on, for more than thirty years and each time there are more taller condos, more fancier shopping malls, more diverse restaurants, more larger drug stores, more sudden manicured landscapes with full size palms, unrolled grass, unexpected ponds, fountains, and waterfalls.

And each year I am more than a bit, well, snotty about Florida. Yet I return to rent the same condo that rises from an artificial island of Isla Del Sol with a delightful, manufactured landscape.

At seventy-six I am comfortable with contradiction, but the other day as I felt the warm sun on my arms and stood under a huge, neatly trimmed palm and looked at the view a landscape artist decided I would like, I was transported sixty-one years back to a New Hampshire forest.

Then I also felt the sun on my bare arm as I explored a New Hampshire forest alone. I had been told that if I studied the age of the trees and followed the younger, thinner ones, I may find I can follow a road through the forest abandoned almost seventy-five years before I was born.

It wasn't easy. The forest was thick with summer foliage and I circled about for an hour or so until I could see a double line of older trees separated by a line of younger ones.

I ran down this suddenly visible forest road until I heard a strange roar. I wondered if it was a train, then realized it was a river. I followed the curving road toward the sound and discovered another road crossed my road, then still another.

I looked around and began to see the moss-covered granite stones half-hidden by saplings, bushes, underbrush and could read the pattern. These fields had once been cleared. The rocks were walls. Then I found bigger rocks, great blocks of granite arranged in squares and rectangles, with a sagging in the middle. Trees grew right through the cellar holes of homes where once people lived.

In my imagination I raised the homes, barns, and at the edge of the roaring rapids, I grew the mill on the great stone slabs beside the river rapids.

I darted from what may have been a pigpen, to a small worker's house, to the one the mill owner must have built. I found the church and saw the outlines of the town common, running from place to place, shouting my discoveries to the silent forest.

Then I became quiet. These buildings had once seemed as permanent as my home, my church, my school. I took one of those bursts of mental and emotional growth that mark our travel to maturity. No building would ever seem as permanent again.

The people who had lived here were all gone. I knew my history and realized I had probably discovered one of those villages where everyone had packed up and left in the Gold Rush of 1849. I sat on one of the great mill slabs and watched them in imagination as they lived their lives in this village and as they packed up and left to follow a dream that may not have been fulfilled for any of them.

Then I was back in my condo, living the dream of a winter month in Florida that once seemed impossible. I traveled in memory to the great Indian cliff villages of our Southwest, to the ruins I had visited in Italy, Greece, England, Scotland, Norway, and near home. All had once seemed sure to last forever.

I felt the passing melancholy the way you feel the shadow of a cloud that makes the sun seem brighter, warmer when the cloud is gone. I will enjoy Florida all the more because I know these grand condo palaces will one day tumble into their own cellar holes, the way that village I discovered in the woods did so long, so short a time ago.

IN THE WRITER'S WORKSHOP

I've done as many as twenty or thirty drafts of a story. Never less than ten or twelve drafts. It's instructive and heartening both, to look at the early drafts of great writers. I'm thinking of the photographs of galleys belonging to Tolstoy, to name one writer who loved to revise. I mean, I don't know if he loved it or not, but he did a great deal of it. He was always revising, right down to the time of page proofs. He went through and rewrote War and Peace *eight times and was still making corrections in the galleys. Things like this should hearten every writer whose first drafts are dreadful, like mine are.* RAYMOND CARVER

I began to write essays, one a month for Esquire *magazine, and I am not exaggerating when I say that in the course of writing a short essay—1,500 words, that's only six double-spaced typewritten pages—I often used 300 or 400 pieces of typing paper, so often did I type and retype and catapult and recatapult myself, sometimes on each retyping moving not even a sentence farther from the spot I had reached the last time through. At the same time, though, I was polishing what I had already written; as I struggled with the middle of the article, I kept putting the beginning through the typewriter; as I approached the ending the middle got its turn. (This is a kind of polishing that the word processor all but eliminates, which is why I don't use one. Word processors make it possible for a writer to change the sentences that clearly need changing without having to retype the rest, but I believe that you can't always tell whether a sentence needs work until it rises up in revolt against your fingers as you retype it.) By the time I had produced what you might call a first draft—an entire article with a beginning, middle, and end—the beginning was in more like forty-fifth draft, the middle in twentieth, and the end was almost newborn. For this reason the beginnings of my essays are considerably better written than the ends, although I like to think no one ever notices this but me.* NORA EPHRON

I work not by writing but by rewriting. Each sentence has many drafts. Eventually there is a paragraph. This gets many drafts. Eventually there is a page. This gets many drafts. WILLIAM GASS

I write very impulsively, so terribly fast only I can decipher my scrawl. But only one-quarter of this first outpouring, at the most, is usable, so actually I work very slowly. It's mostly pacing, researching, brewing endless cups of herb tea while I think of how to annotate these terrible earlier drafts. Hours are spent figuring how to rewrite one single sentence—I've never managed to write anything, even a book review, in fewer than three or four drafts. FRANCIS DE PLEXIS GREY

There is a sort of basic law about everything for me, and that is that you have to pay attention. You've got to pay attention, as a writer, to the structure of language. You've got to pay attention to the sounds. BARRY LOPEZ

You have to keep working to find your voice, then have the grace or good sense to recognize it as your voice and then learn how to use it. JOHN GUARE

Write it out as verbose as you want. Have verbal Diarrhea. Then cut the unnecessary words, but keep the plot. Then rewrite and cut again. Then rewrite and cut again. After three times, you have something. DAVID MAMET

The American oral language is very musical, and if you read a lot and get involved with language, you can get a feeling for how the lines wish to proceed, how the words wish to follow each other, how the sounds work together in a kind of music. LUCILLE CLIFTON

The voice is the element over which you have no control: it's the sound of the person behind the work. JOHN HERSEY

Just to write a good sentence—that's the postulate I go by. I guess I've always felt that if you could keep a kind of fidelity toward the individual sentence, that you could work toward the rest. RICHARD FORD

The language must be careful and must appear effortless. It must not sweat. It must suggest and be provocative at the same time. TONI MORRISON

English usage is something more than mere taste, judgment, and education—sometimes it's sheer luck, like getting across a street. E. B. WHITE

Working at sentences and rhythms is probably the most satisfying thing I do as a writer. I think after a while a writer can begin to know himself through his language. He sees someone or something reflected back at him from these constructions. Over the years it's possible for a writer to shape himself as a human being through the language he uses. I think written language, fiction, goes that deep. He not only sees himself but begins to make himself or remake himself. DON DELLILO

When it comes to language, nothing is more satisfying than to write a good sentence. It is no fun to write lumpishly, dully, in prose the reader must plod through like wet sand. But it is a pleasure to achieve, if one can, a clear running prose that is simple yet full of surprises. This does not just happen. It requires skill, hard work, a good ear, and continued practice. . . . BARBARA TUCHMAN

(**i**) *Never use a metaphor, simile, or other figure of speech which you are used to seeing in print.*

(**ii**) *Never use a long word where a short one will do.*

(**iii**) *If it is possible to cut a word out, always cut it out.*

(**iv**) *Never use the passive where you can use the active.*

(**v**) *Never use a foreign phrase, a scientific word, or jargon word if you can think of an everyday English equivalent.*

(**vi**) *Break any of these rules sooner than say anything barbarous.* GEORGE ORWELL

QUESTIONS ABOUT REVISING AND EDITING

When I write a paper, I'm usually pretty satisfied with it the first time around. I figure that what I've written down is what I want to say. So why revise?

Writing well is thinking deeply. Real thinking, like thoughtful writing, happens in layers. We think on the surface, and then we dip below. Surface thinking helps us get done what needs to get done everyday. This kind of thinking is perfectly fine for routine writing tasks, such as making lists or composing notes to our siblings or roommates. This is superficial writing and there's no need to revise it.

But thoughtful writing requires a more complex analysis of ideas, images, and concepts. That's why we layer writing through drafting and revising, to get below the surface to the core of analysis. That's where the surprises and insights are; that's when and where we really start to see. Until you explore layers of thinking through writing and rewriting, you will never know exactly what it is you want to say or are capable of saying.

In the past when teachers asked me to revise, they just wanted me to clean up a few sentences and check my grammar and spelling. Why can't I do that now?

You can. Go ahead and fix mistakes, correct your grammar, be conscious of your spelling. A note of caution, though: Cleaning up and correcting are proofreading; they are cosmetic remedies rather than methods of thinking. They do not constitute revision, at least not in the way I use the term. Revision is just what it says: re-vision, or seeing again through rewriting. Seeing deeply means writing deeply, and to write deeply means to think deeply. This is what revision is all about.

Correct grammar and spelling are important, but it's probably no use fixing up what you've written in a first draft if your ideas and how you write about them are likely to change during the process of revising. While it doesn't really matter if you "clean up" earlier or later, it may make more sense to save this step until the end.

How do I know what needs to be revised in my paper? Where do I start?

If you are not used to revising, it is a good idea to roll up your sleeves and plunge right in. Move things around, change your focus, write from another perspective or angle. Experiment. As you transform your draft, you begin to see the various possibilities of each piece of writing. You also demystify your writing so that you aren't afraid to mess with it. This kind of mucking around with what once seemed solid and fixed will help make the revision process seem less daunting.

As you look for different ways to revise, you also want to work closely with a writing partner in class or read your drafts aloud in a group workshop. Ask for feedback, and practice giving feedback to other writers. This exposure will help you become a more apt critic of writing, not to mention a better revisionist.

What if I gather too much feedback? How do I revise?

Learning how to cull through comments and suggestions is an essential writer's skill. Different readers read differently. While there is often a consensus in writers' workshops about what needs to be done with a paper, it is just as likely that your readers will disagree in their suggestions. You will never be able to satisfy all of them. But you will have a sense of what you like or don't like about the suggestions you receive. Pick and choose from them; don't try to incorporate all of them into a revision. You'll only get muddled and end up confusing your readers.

Try to weigh feedback and suggestions against your own intentions as a writer. Trust your own intuitions about your writing and how your draft speaks to you. Ask specific questions of your readers about what you've accomplished and hope to accomplish in your draft. That way you will be sure to get feedback that is useful to you. You will also remain in charge of your writing.

My writing partner or classmates tell me that I don't have to change a thing, that everything is clear and makes sense to them. So I guess I don't have to edit, do I?

That depends. If you have edited thoroughly before asking your classmates to look at your work, it could be that your writing is ready to go. It might seem like an empty task to edit once more. Maybe you simply don't need to.

Or it could be that you need to imagine a wider audience for your work, a readership more varied than the one composed of your classmates. Imagine a magazine or newspaper that might publish your work, and think of the audience you might have. Is your piece ready for publication without further editing? Would your main images and ideas be absolutely clear to all of your readers?

Sometimes your classmates will understand what you write about because you share similar experiences with many of them: you may all be close in age, or live and work within the same school environment. For this reason, they may not need images or ideas clarified. They can simply "relate" to what you write. But someone who does not occupy the same realm of experience as you and your classmates may require more clarification. Keep these readers in mind as you edit.

Why can't I just run a grammar and spell checker on my computer?

Go ahead. These tools are useful. But they are no substitute for reading a draft for meaning. Your computer cannot do that. Sometimes it will even give you the wrong grammar suggestion for the meaning you want. You may purposely use long sentences to imply seriousness or formality, and your grammar-checking software will advise you to cut them in half. At other times you might want short, concise sentences or purposeful fragments, and your program will tell you to correct or lengthen your sentences.

Since you edit as much for the voice of the draft as for meaning and correctness, you will want to listen to your writing rather than depend on your computer to tell you if it's right or wrong. Spell check final revisions, but don't count too much on grammar checkers and other writer's programs to edit your piece. They make assumptions about what is standard writing and who are standard writers. You have your own voice, and your writing reflects that voice. There is nothing standard about it.

How do I know when I'm done editing?

When the deadline arrives. I once took a survey of all the people in my department at the university who had written books. They had all revised or edited their books after their manuscripts had been accepted. There is no natural end to the editing process. As Paul Valery said, "Writing is never finished, only abandoned."

What if I don't have time to edit?

Sometimes when you have to turn in writing that you do on the spot, you won't have time for extensive editing or revising. This possibility is particularly likely when you're writing answers to essay questions on exams. The trick in situations like this is to plan before writing.

With essay answers and other kinds of on-the-spot writing, you should take a few minutes to sketch out an outline or structure for your answer before you begin, since you will not be able to go back and reorganize when you finish. You will probably also want to edit as you write, or schedule a few minutes at the end of your available time to go back and make whatever changes you can while keeping your paper reasonably legible.

If you are in the habit of editing your work anyway, you will develop an eye and ear for what's right or out of place in your writing. Reading and editing closely while you have time will sharpen your editing skills for those occasions when you don't.

What if I have a teacher who won't let me revise my papers?

I know of no teacher who would be disappointed to receive writing that is well thought-out and thoroughly revised. No instructor in his or her right mind would out-and-out ban revision. Whether or not a teacher allows you to revise papers that have already been graded, however, might be a different issue.

You will probably be given many opportunities to revise in your writing class. You will be asked to take your work through a process of brainstorming, focusing, planning, drafting, rewriting, and editing. The goal of this process is to enable you to turn in your finest work at the end of the semester.

In other classes, teachers may expect you to revise on your own. When you turn in a paper they will expect you to submit a polished product that has already been rewritten and proofread. This does not mean that you have to give up the process that worked for you in your writing classroom. It only means that you will have to follow up your process on your own.

Develop a schedule of deadlines for each step in the procedure from brainstorming to planning, drafting to revising, focusing to editing. Give yourself time to go back and revisit steps as needed. Then when your deadline arrives, turn in your best-revised work.

Revising and Editing Activities

1. If you keep a diary or a journal, go back to entries that describe a significant period in your life. When you originally wrote these entries, you wrote them for

yourself alone; now envision a readership—your classmates or the readers of a newspaper column you might write. How would you change these entries for your readers? What would you keep and what would you omit? Consider how your own perspective on the events or period you wrote about may have changed with time: What do you know now that you didn't know then? What experiences have you had that allow you to read these entries differently than before?

2. Go to a favorite outdoor site and write about it, double-spacing and keeping wide margins. Put the piece away for two weeks and then return to the site, changing your perspective by sitting in a new place to write. Look again at your surroundings, jotting down any extra details that you may have missed the first time. Then note in the margins and between the lines of your paper what you would want to develop or change. As you re-see your environment, how might you revise your paper? How might your focus change according to your new perspective?

3. Give copies of the second half of your draft to the class. Ask them to write a couple of paragraphs each describing what they imagine the first part of the draft to be like. Then pass out copies of the entire draft and discuss ways that their readings of the draft's conclusion may help you revise the first part.

4. Hand out copies of your paper and read it aloud to your class. Then pass around a piece of paper and ask your classmates to compile a "What if?" list: "What if you dropped this opening paragraph and began here?" "What if you forgot this part about your aunt and wrote just about your grandmother instead?" "What if you took the wonderful sentence in the middle of paragraph five and made that your focal point?" Choose one or more of these "what ifs" and use them to revise your paper.

5. List at the top of a draft at least three of the seven writer's senses—seeing, hearing, touching, tasting, smelling, imagining, and remembering. Then go back through your paper and expand the areas that bring these senses into play, incorporating into your draft the details that pertain to each sense. As your paper expands, you may want to go back and pare down other sections where you summarize or tell instead of describe and show.

6. Ask a writing partner to pinpoint three or more techniques you might use to improve your paper. He or she might, for example, suggest that you use more dialogue, details, or documentation. Then layer your revisions, concentrating on one technique at a time. Don't try to incorporate everything at once. Pause between each revision and note how your draft changes with each layer.

7. Start with the first full paragraph on your second page, and drop your entire first page altogether. You may have to revise the opening sentence of this paragraph a bit, but use it as the start of your revision. If you wish, incorporate bits and pieces of your original first page into the rest of your story. Then reread your draft to see how it changes. Does your new beginning confuse the reader,

or does it invite her with an interesting lead? Do you still need what preceded your new beginning, or can the revised paper stand on its own without that material? What changes in the body and conclusion of the draft will you have to make in order to accommodate your new beginning?

8. Choose a significant scene or idea in your draft and copy it onto a new piece of paper. Expand that particular moment in your essay by examining it from every perspective and angle you can think of. Embody it with details. When you have finished, reincorporate the expanded scene or idea back into your paper and see how it changes the draft's focus. Try another scene or idea.

9. Work with a partner to re-see (re-vise) selected portions of your draft. Read aloud passages that are meant to convey specific images, and ask your partner to listen without reading along. Pause between selections and have your partner describe to you what he or she sees, or doesn't see from your reading ("I see . . ."; "I wish I could see . . ."; "I don't see enough of . . ."; "I don't get a full picture of . . ."). Have your partner jot down specific questions that will help you re-see portions of your draft. ("What color hair did your friend Tom have?" "What kind of furniture did the scary room have?" "How did the girl move when she was scared?")

10. Copy your draft onto a computer disk or hard drive, or photocopy it for safekeeping. Then take your original copy and drop a bomb on it! Demystify it. Break it up, fragment it, "discombobulate" it. Try a bit of dialogue here, expand description there, cut paragraphs or sentences in the middle, rewrite the conclusion as the lead, or the lead as the conclusion. Try different fonts. Incorporate poetry into the story. Rewrite whole scenes or incidents from another person's viewpoint. Take risks and have fun with your draft. (Remember: you still have a copy of your original version!) When you finally have a working draft—a fragmented piece in progress—share it with a group. Have each person pinpoint at least three new areas of your draft that intrigue him or her. Choose from these to find a basis for a more coherent revision.

11. Divide your draft into sections, leaving ample room between each. Write in the blank spaces between each section, answering the following questions: "What do I want to achieve in this section of my draft?" "What have I achieved?" "What more do I have to do to this section in order to reach my goal?"

Follow the same procedure above, but list only what you hope to achieve in each section. Then pass the draft on to a partner, and let him or her decide whether or not you've achieved your goal. Have your partner suggest ways of revising your draft to better accomplish what you want.

12. During the first week of class, write an essay about your impressions of college. Exchange the essay with a classmate to keep until later in the semester. Before the semester ends, have your partner read your essay aloud to you. As you listen, note what changes in perspective you have now as a seasoned college

student as opposed to someone who is brand new to campus. What things would you want to develop, downplay, or change in your original essay? How do time and space help you revise what you wrote earlier?

13. Collect troublesome sentences from your own work. As your writing partner, group, or teacher helps you recognize wordy, unclear, or grammatically weak sentences, add them to your list. Select one or two sentences from the list daily, and work with a partner to rewrite them.

14. Take a piece of writing, your own or someone else's, and cut it in half. Replace multiple words with one when one will do. Make war on needless adjectives. Cut back on prepositional phrases. Pare to the bone.

15. Choose a descriptive piece of writing with vivid and specific imagery and make it vague. Replace concrete adjectives (limp, sallow, square, sharp) with abstract adjectives (awesome, beautiful, boring, ugly). Then read the passages aloud to see how they change. Close your eyes and try to picture the images. Which adjectives work? Which don't?

16. As a class, list on the board as many vague or abstract sentences you can: "It was sure a bright day." "The room was really nice." "The poem was pretty boring." "It was the most exciting moment of my life." With a partner select five of these vague sentences, and make them vivid and descriptive. Read them aloud to one another to see if you get the picture.

17. Choose five sentences from any of your drafts, and rewrite them in at least five different ways: Make them concise, vague, descriptive, awkward, short, ungrammatical, whatever. After each rewrite, incorporate the sentences back into the drafts they came from, and discuss with a partner or group how they change the original paragraphs.

18. Exchange papers with a partner and edit each other's drafts. Make sure that you give your partner a clean, working copy so that he or she will feel free to mark it up. Read carefully, but edit boldly; don't be afraid to cross out words, pare down or clarify sentences, correct spelling, or identify grammatical errors.

19. Keep two verb lists in your daybook, one for strong, active verbs (yank, scoop, sweep, hurl), and the other for passive verb forms (was yelled at, is made clear, was held by). As you read textbooks, stories, poems, signs, essays, instructions, novels, drafts, or e-mail messages, write down strong, interesting verbs on the active verb list, and then write a sentence next to each using the verb in the passive voice. Jot down passive constructions on the passive verb list, and write a sentence for each changing the passive voice to active. Once a week, select two verbs from both lists and discuss them with your group. Explain how the active and passive voices convey different tones and meanings.

20. Brainstorm a list of clichés in class, and write them on the board. Then exchange papers with a writing partner and go through line by line in search of

clichés. Add more to the list on the board as you find them. Circle them and have the authors write replacement phrases or sentences.

21. Have a partner read through a couple pages of your draft and then write one sentence in the left margin next to each paragraph briefly summing up what the paragraph is saying. If your partner has trouble summarizing a paragraph or misreads your meaning, rewrite the troublesome passage, working to clarify each sentence.

22. Pass out copies of your final revision to the class and read aloud. Ask the class to put a check next to sentences that need clarifying or grammar that needs correcting. Keep the workshop focused on editing and clarification rather than major revisions.

23. Read your paper backward, sentence by sentence, starting with the very last one. This technique allows you to pick out mistakes you might normally gloss over when reading logically from beginning to end, front to back.

24. Refer to the editing checklist in this chapter, and personalize it with some editing tips of your own. Then go through each item one by one and scan your paper closely for errors. If you want, go through the first five or so points on your own, then pass it on to a classmate who can look at the next group on the checklist with fresh eyes. If necessary, keep passing it on.

25. Rewrite your title for different genres or different markets. Pretend that your piece is a newspaper column, and write an appropriate title. Make it an essay in a scholarly journal, and rewrite the title. Come up with a list of different kinds of publications and their markets, and rework your title for each market, making it as catchy to the reader's eye as possible.

CHAPTER 10

FIT YOUR PROCESS TO YOUR TASK

When you know how to write and revise, you are prepared to accept and complete a great many different writing tasks—some you never expected to perform.

A research paper, annual sales report, book report, scholarship application, poem, essay of literary analysis may look different when they are printed, but they are constructed of common elements and with similar skills.

When you have come this far in the study of writing, you have experienced all the essential skills you need to write effectively. If you now learn the basic elements from which writing forms are constructed, you can prepare yourself when a professor asks for a critical essay, a science teacher assigns a lab report, a history instructor demands a term paper, experience inspires a poem, the concert committee assigns you to write a press release, a foundation invites a grant proposal, an employer asks for a marketing memo, or a supervisor wants an analytical report on a manufacturing process.

The ability to adapt your writing process to new writing tasks will serve you well after college. One study revealed that electrical engineers do far more writing after college than English majors do. As you live and work in an increasingly complex and shrinking world, you will find yourself communicating in writing with supervisors, subordinates, colleagues, clients, customers around the globe.

Specific writing tasks may change, and the messages they produce may, in your lifetime, be sent and received by technological devices we cannot yet imagine—I never imagined a fax or modem—but the demand for clear writing will increase as we work with people over great distances.

_____ HOW TO RESPOND TO A NEW _____ WRITING TASK

There are logical steps to follow when faced with a new writing task. First, listen to the instructions, and ask questions if you do not understand the purpose of the assignment or what the person giving the assignment expects. It is helpful to study examples of similar assignments. Each writing form has its own traditions, but you may depart from them for reason; if you do not know the tradition the reader expects, however, you cannot depart from it in a way the reader will accept.

If you give yourself a writing task—a letter applying for a job, a note of sympathy, a journal narrative of an important event in your life, a memo re-defining your job, a poem—you need to listen to yourself and then, playing the reader, question yourself to determine your expectations.

Writing forms or structures may appear arbitrary, but they have all been constructed, as houses are constructed, in response to logical, predictable de-mands. Houses need roofs and walls, doors and windows, rooms and hallways to satisfy the needs of people who live in them. The design of the house will change if it is to be built in northern Maine or southern Arizona, if it is in Man-hattan or on a farm in North Dakota twenty miles from town. But each house is a variation on a common need.

The same elements occur in every writing. Traditions are simply the records of how writing has been constructed in the past to solve special problems, the way a house in Minnesota may have a peaked roof so snow will not collapse it, and one in Arizona will have thick walls and extended eaves to make it cool and keep out the noonday sun. If you look at the problems a writing tradition at-tempts to solve, you will understand the tradition and be able to adopt or adapt it to solve your writing problems.

The following sections review the questions to ask when you confront a new writing task.

WHY WRITE?

The writer needs to answer that TOUGH question. To choose, adapt, or de-velop a form, the writer needs to know the purpose of the writing to be done.

There are important general reasons to write. Writing is the most disci-plined form of thinking. Writers have to make the writing clear to themselves if they are to make it clear to readers. The act of writing demands content that is accurate, documented, authoritative, persuasive.

A written text can be read and understood over distances of time and place. It can be read and reread, shared, examined, revised, edited, considered, and re-considered by many people. It provides a continuous point of reference.

In most literary works the purpose for writing is less clear to the reader, sometimes even to the writer in the beginning—to celebrate an experience, to explore
an event, to understand a character, to examine an emotion, to tell a story, to entertain—but most writing does not produce literary works; it usually has a clear
purpose—to persuade, to inform, to explain.

The reasons people write vary greatly. The writer may want to get a passing
grade in history or share her historical research with other historians; the writer
may want to report on families who have multiple social problems for a course
in social work or persuade the government to concentrate all its services on a few
problem families; the writer may want to recruit students for a junior-year-
abroad program or to persuade an employer to adopt a new sales approach.

A good way to understand the purpose of a piece of writing is to define
what you expect the reader to think, feel, or do after reading it: "I want the
reader to respect our Franco-American heritage"; "I want our government to
concentrate on those few families in town who are the breeding ground for most
of our social problems"; "I want students to sign up for a junior year in Siberia";
"I want my boss to try a new sales technique."

A clear purpose helps the writer define, limit, and focus what the writer has
to say and often predicts the form that will fulfill the writer's purpose.

WHAT IS MY MESSAGE?

Writing is thinking, and writers discover what they have to say by saying it. The
message cannot be entirely predicted, and so the writer not only chooses the
form of writing according to the message, but adapts that form to fit the evolving meaning.

Some writing tasks, such as poetry, are highly inventive, with the message
discovered during the line-by-line drafts. But most writing tasks in the academic
and working world have a clear purpose: to identify, define, and develop an historical trend; to report on the results of a biological experiment; to analyze a
piece of literature; to explain a new software program; to suggest solutions that
may solve a traffic problem at the supermarket checkout counter.

Sometimes a word will reveal my message to me in the private way of a
writer's language—"advantaged"—or more likely a phrase—"the disadvantages of
being an advantaged student"—occasionally a sentence—"I came to realize my
disadvantaged students had an advantage." Too often an editor, early in a project,
will demand a clear, specific, conclusive statement of intent. Sometimes this is
called a *thesis statement,* but I do not like the term; teachers held me to statements
that I had to make before I had completed my research and before I had thought
about the topics by writing drafts.

The message statement is not a contract. It is a goal, a possibility, a target, a
starting place. Some such statements might be:

- To document the role of French Canadian priests in the exploration and mapping of North America.

- To argue that social services should concentrate on the families in a community that have the most physical, emotional, social, educational, and financial problems.

- To recruit students for a junior-year-in-Siberia program sponsored by the Russian department.

- To propose that an automobile dealer consider the no-salesperson approach, where each car has the final price posted and there is no negotiation.

WHO IS MY READER?

The message statement usually implies the audience: The first message above implies a history instructor or an audience of American historians; the next a sociology professor or a legislative group or agency that controls a budget; the third, college students who have enough money to spend a year abroad; the fourth, the owner or manager of an automobile dealership.

It is important, as you can see, to limit or target a specific audience. A sociology professor teaching an undergraduate course would require a different form and voice from a professor of social work in a graduate program. If the professor is in political science, still another form might be required. If the writer is appealing for a change in the law or a change in agency policy, the form of the appeal will again be different.

WHAT EVIDENCE WILL PERSUADE MY READER?

When you have decided on the purpose, the message, and the reader, you can anticipate the reader's needs.

Readers are hungry for information. Specific, accurate information gives your writing authority. The reader says, "This guy's done his homework; this guy knows his stuff." Readers need documentation; they need evidence to be persuaded.

Writers need to remember to write with information, no matter the writing task. Readers read, above all, to be informed.

WHAT VOICE WILL KEEP THE READER INTERESTED AND MAKE THE READER BELIEVE WHAT I HAVE TO SAY?

The reader responds, above all, to voice, to the individual who stands behind the page. We each have our natural voices that are reproduced in our writing, and we need to develop and control those natural elements that are composed from ethnic and family heritage, environment, and practice in speaking and listening. Voice is also a matter of intellectual, social, and emotional style.

Your challenge as a writer is to hear your voice then tune it to the topic and the audience. As you plan to write, you should compose fragments, perhaps sentences and paragraphs, in your mind and on your journal pages, listening to make sure that the music of the language supports your meaning and communicates to a stranger.

Effective writers hear, then see, their language appear on page or screen. They tune the language—word choice, pace, rhythm, manner or style to what is being said and to whom it is being said.

WHAT FORM WILL CARRY MY MESSAGE AND ITS DOCUMENTATION TO MY READER?

Finally the writer chooses the form, the vehicle that will carry meaning to the reader, or adapts the assigned form to the particular writing task.

To write this section, I looked in memory for the basic writing tasks I have done and came up with four tasks that have their own basic structures. You can do the same thing when faced with a writing task: Look within your experience and the demands of the job, then decide how to do it. Of course my "inventions" were discovered by the Greeks centuries ago, but we have to keep creating a rhetoric that serves our task, our audience, our time.

These are the basic writing tasks or problems the writer has to solve. The writer's purpose defines, in part, the solution or form, and these forms lie behind the writing in other genres—screenwriting, poetry, science writing, historical writing, business and political writing. The writer begins with the tasks writers most frequently face:

To describe
To analyze
To inform
To persuade

Of course, these forms overlap. Description may be necessary to persuade, informing may involve analysis, and so on. The writer creates the form that fits the task, adapting the formal elements to the immediate task, inventing each time from the materials that have been invented before.

Most writing tasks are not so neat that you can run into the warehouse and grab a pretested, prepared writing form. Each task is different, and you need to adapt traditional forms to the new task and sometimes design a new form. It is really a simple task.

──────────── **WRITE TO DESCRIBE** ────────────

Description is the basic form of writing, but when I first taught freshman English it was outlawed in our program as being too simple for academic discourse. Simple? That was the opinion of those who did not write. Description is not simple, but it is fundamental and the best way, I believe, to lay the foundation of the writer's craft. At first, you use description to capture a place or a person, then places with people, then people interacting with others, and you end up describing ideas, theories, concepts, thoughts and feelings, propositions and conclusions, speculations and facts. All forms of writing contain descriptive elements that make readers see, think, feel, react.

Writing description can introduce you to the discipline of recording information, ordering it into meaning, and communicating that meaning to readers. All the elements of effective writing—accuracy, concreteness, meaningfulness, context, development, form and order within a piece, emphasis, documentation, flow, grace, style, reader awareness, proportion, pace, voice—may be called upon when you write description.

TIPS ON WRITING EFFECTIVE DESCRIPTION

- *Be accurate.* The writer has to earn the reader's trust. A single error in fact or an accurate fact in the wrong context can cause the writer to lose the reader's trust.

- *Be specific.* Readers hunger for concrete details. The specific carries authority with it. Don't use words such as *beautiful* and *ugly* that carry no meanings out of context. What is beautiful or ugly to one person is the opposite to someone else. Give the reader specifics, and the reader will feel or think the reaction to it. Don't tell the reader what to think or how to feel; make the reader think and feel by using specific images.

- *Create a dominant impression.* Establish a focal point, and relate all your details to that point, developing and supporting it. If you walk into a trauma center, your eye goes to a stretcher or to a team of people working on someone or to parents sitting and waiting. Everything in your description must flesh out the dominant impression.

- *Establish an angle of vision.* The reader should see the trauma center from a particular angle: from the waiting room or the swinging doors of the ambulance bay, from the patient's bed looking up, from a nurse or doctor's eyes looking down. This position can move, but it should move slowly. Think of how a professional moves the movie camera and how the amateur blurs the screen by panning too quickly.

- *Determine the correct distance.* Stand at an appropriate distance to reveal what you want to say. Zoom in close for intimacy and immediacy; draw back to put the subject in context; move back and forth so that the topic is revealed effectively.

THE NARRATIVE ESSAY

Narrative—storytelling—is the most important form of description. Narrative allows the writer to describe historical and current events, processes and travels, searches and researches, biographies and autobiographies, reflections and investigations, actions and reactions that take place in the river of time.

We think of narrative as primarily a fiction technique, and when I first started teaching, narrative was not allowed in freshman English. Yet writing narrative is an essential skill for a nonfiction writer, too. In fact, all effective writing has an embedded narrative; the reader may not be aware of it, but the implied story keeps the reader's interest and moves the reader forward, toward the writer's meaning.

Narrative also satisfies the reader's fundamental hunger for story, chaos ordered into meaning. Readers who would not read about a subject on their own, will make the effort if it is told in the form of story: the boring financial or scientific story is un-bored if you read the account of a fiscal battle or a scientist's struggle to make a breakthrough.

TIPS ON WRITING NARRATIVE

- *Time in a story is not a clock.* The second hand does not move evenly, click by click, toward the minute; the minute hand does not move evenly, click by click, toward the hour. Time in a story is distorted, as it is in life. We spend a great deal of time telling of a moment in great detail then skip to the next moment that is important to the story. When I was in the infantry, we used to say that combat was days of boredom with minutes of terror. That comment also describes the use of time in a narrative.

- *Show, don't tell.* This fundamental rule of dramatic writing applies to any narrative, whether it is fiction or nonfiction. The reader likes to have the story revealed, and it takes a while for an inexperienced writer to show what is happening rather than telling the reader what is happening—and what to think and feel. Narrative makes the reader think and feel for himself or herself. I write fiction, and when I make the transition to narrative, I find myself seeing the event I am describing as a movie. I do not say the character is scared; I show his hand shaking, his eyes open wide and looking around, his hesitant step and quick retreat back through the door.

- *Build with scenes.* The basic narrative unit is the scene, just as in a play or movie. The scene includes character, action and reaction, and setting. At the end, at least one of the characters is changed.

- *Characters interact.* Character, not plot, makes the story go. One person says or does something—or says or does nothing. "I love you," she says. He stands up, nods to the people at the next table and leaves the restaurant. There is an action and a reaction, and now the story will grow as she acts or he returns and she leaves and so on. His response to her statement comes from the nature of his character and is a Revelation of his character. The action—his departure—is driven by Character. That is what interests the reader: not his leaving but how could he respond in this way? The reader wants to see how she will respond and her response comes from the nature of her character and is a revelation of her character. Story is built on character; story is driven by character; character determines action.

- *Dialogue is easy.* Beginning writers are often afraid of dialogue. I remember what Elizabeth Bowen wrote: Dialogue is action. It is what people do to each other. The only exercise I assign is one to teach dialogue. Here is the situation: She is meeting him to tell him she is pregnant; he is meeting her to tell her that he does not want to see her anymore. Write that scene entirely in dialogue. Not names, no he-said's or she-said's. Just speech in quotation marks, one speaker to a paragraph.

This is still description, the revealing of the world. All of the issues of description exist in other forms of writing, but they are especially clear in the writing of description. Read descriptions that help you understand a subject, make notes on the techniques the writer uses. Try them yourself.

———— WRITE TO ANALYZE ————

As we describe, we analyze. We cannot help but evaluate what we have seen, taking it apart to see what makes it work. Analysis is as important to the writer's toolbox as the wrench is to the mechanic. Analysis helps you understand an idea, an event, a feeling, a text. Analysis is a work of the mind more than the emotions.

Graham Greene once asked a profound question: "Isn't disloyalty as much the writer's virtue as loyalty is the soldier's?" Writers are blessed and cursed with this disloyalty. Disloyalty allows them to stand back from themselves—and their families, friends, churches, jobs, organizations—dissect what is happening to see what forces are at work. Writers suffer from this distancing, always standing back and questioning their motives, what they do and do not do, how they and their families, friends, neighbors, colleagues act and react. Writers question the world; nothing is sacred.

Writers are take-aparters. They x-ray, analyze, and look for causes and effects, theories, patterns, systems. The only defense of the writer's lonely trade is that writers are also put-togetherers. They construct their own analyses, new buildings of meaning that bring order, sense, and reason. These new constructions will face analysis from others as the intellectual world struggles to understand.

The principle elements of effective analysis include a clear and *fair* statement or description of what is to be taken apart, a logical process of dissection complete with evidence at each step of the way, a tone or voice that is appropriate and convincing, and a conclusion that constructs a new meaning.

TIPS ON WRITING ANALYSIS

- *Read the text.* The text may be a novel, documentation of a new personnel procedure, a sociological report, the film of a football game, a marketing plan, an environmental report. Read it quickly all the way through, then read slowly, step by step, to make sure you understand what you are analyzing—or what you don't understand.

- *Respond.* Respond to what you are analyzing—an essay, a manufacturing procedure, an historical theory, a medical treatment, an engineering report, a political speech, a movie—by taking into account your personal reaction. Too often, analysts stand back, not allowing themselves to connect what they are analyzing to their own experience, not realizing that emotion and personal thoughts are appropriate factors in analysis. When I analyze an historical account of a military event, I make use of my experience in combat; when I analyze a news story, I make use of my experience as a newspaper reporter.

- *Discover the focus.* To begin analysis, the writer should understand the central meaning of the process, event, discovery, law, theory, text to be analyzed. The writer works backward from the meaning or point of focus to see all that leads up to it.

- *Look for patterns.* Meaning is constructed of relationships. One thing leads to another. Look for those connections, the map of meaning the writer has drawn.

- *Be skeptical.* Use your common sense. Question. Doubt. Check the evidence the writer uses to support the meaning. Double-check the sources. Examine the author's chain of logic for weak links. Remember what

Ernest Hemingway said: "The most important essential gift for a good writer is a built-in, shock-proof shit detector."

- *Look at the context.* A piece of writing does not float free like a birthday balloon. Study what is written against the context in which it is written, the world in which the writing exists.

- *Write in an appropriate voice.* In most cases of analysis this means a professional, somewhat detached voice. The voice of a fair judge who is looking at the subject with a stern impartiality and analyzing in a way that is speaking to the subject, not the person or people behind the subject.

ANALYSIS IN THE BOOK REPORT

The book report is a common form of analytical writing, and the biggest mistake students make is to leave out the analysis. They limit their book reports to simply informing the reader that the book exists while the real purpose of the book—or article or short story—review is critical analysis. The reader wants an informed opinion of the information in the book, and the writer's success depends on presenting that information.

TIPS ON WRITING A BOOK REPORT

- *Include publication information.* The reader may want to buy the book or order it from the library. List the title and subtitle if there is one, the author, the publisher with principal city of publication, and the year of publication.

- *Be critical.* That does NOT mean being negative. It means evaluating the content and the presentation within the book.

- *Document each point with quotations.* The reader wants evidence to support what the reviewer says.

- *Compare.* Look at the book in the context of other books that have been published on the same subject, evaluating their strong and weak points.

- *Include biographical information about the author.* This background is helpful if it will help the reader to understand the basis of the writer's authority—or question it.

———— THE REFLECTIVE ESSAY ————

The reflective essay is a more sophisticated form of analysis. It often begins with a personal experience—the death of a loved one, the coach's instructions to cheat to win a game, the decision to get—or not get—an abortion. The essay finds meaning in its subject.

It is a common misconception that analysis is a cold, detached, scientific process in which the writer analyzes the thoughts, experiences, or writing of others. Of course, this assumption often holds true, but in reflective essays the writers analyze their own thoughts, feelings, reactions. A classic case of such an essay is George Orwell's "A Hanging" in which the real subject is Orwell's reflection upon his reaction to the event.

The personal experience is analyzed in much the same way as it is in the academic paper, but that experience is written about in a much more reflective manner as the writer focuses on a personal experience and finds meaning in it. The finding of meaning or significance is important. People who tell stories often just ramble on. The writer of an effective essay reflects, ruminates, considers, reconsiders, and takes the reader along on the adventure of thought.

That meaning may be thought out in considerable detail before the first draft is written. This is likely to happen when the writer attempts to explore a traumatic subject, such as the death of a loved one, because that topic has been rehearsed, thought over and over in the writer's mind.

The meaning, however, may be discovered entirely in the writing. The writer may be obsessed with a subject and have no understanding of it until the shape of the draft, what is in the act of being said, and how it is in the act of being said, reveals the meaning to the reader. This often happens to me. I plunge in, hoping that meaning lies on the blank page—or the blank screen—and it usually does, revealed in the words I do not expect to write. Most times meaning comes in a combination of prethinking and drafting. I have a hint, a clue, a sense of what I may discover, and then the writing defines and redefines, qualifies and clarifies that idea, gives it fullness and meaning.

In writing the reflective essay, you discover and develop the skills of critical thinking. You move in close and then stand back. There is immediacy and detachment, close examination and the placing of an event in perspective. There is compassion and judgment, feeling and thought.

An effective reflective essay is often personal, but it is not private. The reflective essay allows the reader to discover the subject—and the meaning of the subject—with the writer. The reader is invited to think along with the writer and to think against the writer, discovering in the act of reading the reader's own meaning in the essay.

TIPS ON WRITING THE REFLECTIVE ESSAY

- *Be personal.* The more personal you are, the more universal your readership. You should speak to the human condition—in specific terms. Your strength is your difference, your own peculiar vision of the world.

- *Allow your mind to run free.* Write fast so that you will discover what you didn't know you remembered, what you didn't know you thought and felt, what patterns and connections lay hidden in the experience.

- *Be critical.* The function of writing the personal or reflective essay is to find meaning in experience, not just to record experience. Be skeptical and critical, challenge your own prejudices, beliefs, your own knowing.

- *Put your vision in context.* Describe your vision of the world then place it in a context—historical, scientific, sociological, psychological, political. The personal experience should connect with a larger meaning.

- *Take the reader along.* Invite the reader to accompany you as you reflect upon experience. Allow the experience and the meaning that arises from it to unfold at a pace that encourages the reader to follow.

———— WRITE TO INFORM ————

One of the reasons to write is to report, to make others understand our knowing and our living, to explain. As the old hunter came back to the cave and described the mastodon, where it could be found, how it could be trapped, so we as citizens and scholars report back to the community so that what we each learn is shared with others, and the collective community knowing exceeds the knowledge of each individual.

To inform, you have to attract listeners by quickly showing them how what you have to say affects them. You have to make a connection with the reader, so that person has a personal stake in hearing what you have to say.

This is a tricky business. If you are too sure of yourself, too full of your own knowing, you will offend and put off potential listeners. You will call attention to yourself, not to what you have to say. On the other hand, if you are too modest, too shy, too unsure of what you have to say, no one will pay attention.

The best way to steer a middle course is not to say too much about oneself and not to say too much directly to the reader, telling the reader how valuable one's information may be for him or her. Instead, deliver the message, focus on the material itself, allowing its importance to grow in the reader's mind as he or she is informed by the facts.

Humans enjoy learning—and perhaps as much enjoy being authorities and informing others. You will be well read if you give the reader information the reader can put to use—and can share with others.

TIPS ON WRITING TO INFORM

- *Write with information.* Give specific, revealing details, concrete facts, accurate information. Build the piece of writing from information not language. Be direct, informative.

- *Anticipate your reader's questions.* Role-play your reader and imagine what you would need and want to know—and when you would want to know it. Good writing is a conversation with the reader in which the writer hears the reader's unspoken questions: "How come?" "What do you mean?" "So what?"
- *Answer your reader's questions.* In writing, the reader has no stupid questions. The reader must be accepted where the reader is. It is the task of the informing writer to serve the reader who does not know.
- *Connect the information with the readers' experience.* Give readers information in a form and context they can use in their thinking, in their lives, in their work.
- *Write in an inviting voice.* Do not preach, condescend, patronize, talk up or down to the reader. Just share your delight in the information with the reader in a voice that focuses on the information to be shared.

THE RESEARCH PAPER

One common way of informing is to write a research paper. In writing, revising, and editing the research paper, you must conform to the style in which research is reported in your discipline. Each scholarly discipline has its own form for the research paper. Not only are there significant differences in the way the physicists, literary scholars, sociologists, historians, botanists report their findings, but a single discipline such as psychology may have different styles within the field with clinical psychologists, social psychologists, and laboratory psychologists all conforming to different traditions. Discover the traditions and forms of the research paper appropriate to the discipline in which you write a research paper.

There are, however, important similarities in all research papers.

THE RESEARCH QUESTION

Good research is usually the product of a well-focused question. The experienced researcher spends time narrowing that question until it is one that can be answered within the limited time of a course or a grant and with the resources available to the researcher. Research is a discipline of accumulation, with each researcher adding to the increasing knowledge within a field of study.

RESEARCH NOTE TAKING

The researcher must have a consistent system of note taking appropriate to the discipline. Note cards—3 × 5, 4 × 6, 5 × 8—are still popular because each card can be ordered and reordered during research as the scholar explores the subject.

The biggest problem for the inexperienced researcher is knowing the difference between a direct quote and a paraphrase. A direct quote is precisely what is said or written. It is enclosed in "quotation marks." Paraphrasing is the technique of putting what you have read or heard in your own words; a paraphrase can never be put in quotation marks, but it should have an attribution so the reader can follow the quotation back to the source.

As the note cards are reordered, the information on the source of the information travels with the note. Write down *ALL* the details on where you found the information. For example, the title of the book, the author's name, the person quoted, the publisher of the book and the city where it was published, the edition or printing, the year of publication, the library where the material is stored, the chapter, page, paragraph, and line so that you can check the source, and so that other scholars can go to the source of your information.

PLAGIARISM

If you use another writer's words as your own, you have committed a major—perhaps *the* major—intellectual crime. I have been plagiarized, and I know what it feels like. A high school student won a national writing contest with a short story of mine until someone recognized it; a nun who ran workshops for writing teachers used almost one hundred pages of one of my books, distributing it as her own text, until another nun read it and identified it as mine. In both cases, the plagiarists had not changed a word. I felt as though they had broken into my mind and stolen my ideas and my language.

Plagiarism is a felony. Where I taught, students who plagiarized were given *F*s and made to take the courses over. I thought they should have been driven from the campus and banned from ever returning; or hung by their writing hands from the university flagpole for a month; or put in stocks in front of a dining hall so students could pelt them with old salad parts; or used as human football tackling dummies; or charged with theft in a court of law, as they would have been if they had stolen the computers or typewriters on which they had plagiarized.

The responsible writer—student or professional—gives credit for the specific words, information, and ideas that belong to someone else.

THE FORM OF THE RESEARCH PAPER

As I said at the beginning of this section, you must conform to the style required by your discipline. This is not a time for creativity. The form is designed to serve readers; they expect to find the information they need in a familiar form and place.

Footnotes

The research paper serves other researchers, and so you provide the sources of specific information *at the time you use that information* through a footnote system. A footnote tells the reader where you discovered the fact or quote you are using at the moment the reader reads it. This is easy if your notes are in order.

Bibliography

At the end of a research paper, you should provide other scholars with a list of your sources according to the style of the field in which you are working. Your note cards, if properly kept, make this a simple task.

Follow the golden rule: Serve your reader as you would want to be served yourself.

TIPS ON WRITING THE RESEARCH PAPER

- *Attribute.* Attribute. Attribute. The reader of a research paper not only wants to know the evidence you have to back up each point, but also where it came from. You should have a system of footnotes and bibliography that the reader can use to research the same area.
- *Define your terms.* Each discipline or profession has its own language or jargon that others may not understand. It is important to define any term that the reader may not understand, that others in a different branch of the same discipline may not understand, or that has a different meaning in normal, nonprofessional speech.
- *Use graphics.* Make charts, maps, illustrations that will clarify your research. Use typographical designs and type styles that emphasize what you have to say. If you have a list format, you may want to use a list, as I have here, rather than running information entirely in normal sentences.
- *Explain your methods.* Other researchers will want to know the procedures you followed to get your results. This part of the presentation may incorporate a review of the literature, or that review may be a separate section of the paper in which you reveal what you read and comment on how helpful particular articles or books were.

There are many forms of writing we use to inform: speeches and presentations, letters and brochures, advertisements and book reports. Each form has a similar purpose: to teach the reader the subject.

———— WRITE TO PERSUADE ————

One of the principal reasons we write is to persuade. In the academic world, this form of writing is often called *argument,* but most students hear that tone and imagine a fight. I use the term *persuasion,* which more accurately describes the form—and voice—of appropriate intellectual discourse in which writers attempt to persuade readers through a process of reason to reconsider their views on a topic.

In fact, I believe, academic argument is a term and a process left over from the days when the academic world was exclusively male. The training I received from my male professors—and all my professors were men—was similar to the training I received on the football field and in the paratroops. Truth was found by two men taking completely opposite sides and each trying to destroy the other. It must be a direct descendant from the tournament practice of two knights trying to knock each other off their horses.

When I taught a course in argument, I found the male students comfortable with this term to describe a form of writing that is designed to cause the reader to rethink a position. They had been socialized on the playground or hockey rink to appear as if they enjoyed battle: hurt and do not reveal your own hurt.

But the majority of students in the class were women, most of them far brighter than the males in the class (and the male who taught the class). They hated *argument* which they told me was a male activity. I think we need far more development of forms of persuasion which are not built on the concept of the knights with lances hurtling toward each other on horseback. I reject the term *argument* and use *persuasion* to describe the form of writing in which the writer attempts to make readers reconsider their views on a topic.

Persuasion is the basic form of intellectual discourse; it is the way that new ideas are introduced, that old ideas are discarded, and old ideas are adapted to new trends of thought.

TIPS ON WRITING PERSUASION

- *State your position.* This is no place for suspense. Make it clear what you intend to advocate. Define and establish your own issues and the context in which they are to be discussed.

- *Establish your credentials.* Let the reader know up front what experience you have had, what research you have done that should convince the reader to listen to your position.

- *Anticipate your reader's points.* You should be able to empathize with your opponent. Read that person's mind by imagining you are taking the other side, then make the best persuasive points you can.

- *Counter your opponent's points.* Now that you know your opponent's views, you can counter them right away, answering them before presenting your own views.

- *Appeal to reason.* Readers are rarely persuaded—at the least in the intellectual world—by emotion. Appeal to reason, base your position on documented evidence presented in a logical order.

There are many other forms of persuasion. A letter applying for a job or a grant tries to persuade others that you should be given a job or financial support. Again, you should role-play those people so that you will know what appeals to them, what questions they will ask, what information they will want to know, what tone of voice will persuade them.

TIPS ON WRITING A LETTER APPLYING FOR A JOB

- *Research the application process.* Talk to your college placement office for counsel in writing job-seeking letters. Study books and articles that describe the strategies and techniques of successful job seekers.

- *Research the company.* Look up the company at which you are applying in the business references in the library. Read the company's annual report and brochures, interview people who work and have worked there, who supply the company and are supplied by the company. Make sure you know what the firm does—provide advertising services or manufacture ball bearings—and how it does that job—specializing in mail-order advertising or selling ball bearings in the international market.

- *Say specifically what skills you offer a potential employer.* "I'm willing to do anything" doesn't entice an employer, but "I learned to get along with a great variety of people working as a waiter, then the head waiter, at a resort that attracted many tourists from overseas" or "I tested my courses in accounting against my experience in summer jobs, in serving as treasurer of the student union, and in spending a semester internship with the Internal Revenue Service."

- *Be specific about your goals.* Tell the employer what you hope to learn from the job, what additional skills you hope to develop, so that you may better serve your employer.

- *Anticipate and answer the prospective employer's questions.* Remember that the reader is looking for someone who fills the company's needs. Read the advertisement or job announcement carefully and respond to the specifics of the position.

- *Sound professional.* Write in a professional manner that demonstrates that you are someone who will do a good job and represent the company well.

E-MAIL AT WORK

The other day I received an e-mail message: "Didja?" That was the entire message and my complete answer was: "Yep."

I am an e-mail addict. I begin each morning by checking my e-mail and I keep checking it during the day. Much of my social life is conducted in my computer community and so is my professional life. All the planning, drafting, revising, and editing of this manuscript was done by e-mail. No snail mail at all.

There are no "didjas" and "yeps" as I correspond by e-mail with my editors and my agent. I delight in the informality of e-mail. I am amazed by the word choices people make on e-mail. Many people I hear from use words in e-mail they would never use in a letter, on the telephone, or in person. We write in fragments and incomplete sentences, pay little attention to formal paragraphing, frequently break the most fundamental rules of grammar, usage, spelling, and punctuation. A whole new informal e-mail rhetoric is developing which fascinates me with its vitality.

This casual style is dangerous in the workplace. It is a matter of etiquette and much more. Professional communications should be filled with specific, accurate information ordered in a logical, trustworthy, and persuasive fashion. Clarity is essential and to make yourself clear it is wise to follow the traditions of language which are understood by writer and reader.

I do not write e-mail notes to my agent, my editors, and my publishers. I write and rewrite my professional messages with great care, usually writing them before I go to the Internet. In this way I can clarify and reorder as much as necessary before I send it.

I also grammar check, punctuation check, logic check, and accuracy check. I do not go to get a bank loan in my under shorts. I dress so the bank will trust me, and if I write with the formal conventions of language my professional associates may trust me. When everything is correct, I then transfer the text to e-mail or attach it to an electronic message.

Writing live on e-mail is fine for informal conversations, but it is easy to send a message by accident before it is ready to be sent. And the ultimate horror is to accidentally send the message to the wrong person or distribute it by hitting an inappropriate list serve. In one corporation where I was a consultant, a new manager ordered his assistant to evaluate all the people in a department, including any health, alcohol, drug, or sexual problems they had that might effect their work. He did a good job, revealing each person's weaknesses with cruel accuracy—and then sent it by accident to the people he was exposing!

Remember while writing e-mail in the workplace that the informal language and rhetoric appropriate in communication with your close friends is not appropriate for professional communication.

QUESTIONS ABOUT FITTING
—— YOUR PROCESS TO YOUR TASK ——

I'm not planning on getting a job where I have to write. Besides, I'll probably have a secretary who can write for me. Why should I think of adapting my process to other writing tasks?

Many jobs do not require writing. But just as many do. Because so many companies are in the process of downsizing and reorganizing, you may find yourself performing a variety of tasks, including writing.

Keep in mind too that the personal computer has replaced support staff in many organizations. Because it is so easy and quick to compose, revise, and edit on computers, employers have cut back on clerical help who take dictation and write up reports and letters. Usually one person does it all. That means you.

Won't I have to worry only about the forms of writing for my particular position?

You might want to consider the advantage of good writing skills if you decide to change jobs or seek a promotion. Most people no longer stay in one job for life, but change careers several times before retirement. The more multi-skilled you are, the better prepared you are to meet any job demand. If you end up starting your own business, your writing skills will be all the more valuable. As your own employer, you may need to write grant requests, issue publicity statements, and correspond with clients all at one time.

If you learn now to adapt your process to various writing tasks, you will be prepared for whatever employment opportunity comes your way.

Why don't we learn how to write memos and reports in college instead of critical essays or personal narratives? It seems to me that learning these forms would prepare us more effectively for the "real" world.

You very well may write reports, memos, applications, letters, and other kinds of business forms in a business communications class or another writing class. But it's important not to lose sight of what writing's all about; it helps us communicate, and it helps us think.

Many top companies do not necessarily recruit students who come equipped with specific skills such as report or memo writing. They hope instead to find students who have learned how to think critically in college and can transfer their analytical skills to the work arena. They want workers who can analyze and solve problems as well as communicate. Your writing process will help you develop the analytical skills these employers seek.

You've stressed the importance of finding your own voice and topics when you write. Yet now you're saying that I have to fit my voice and ideas into a particular form or genre. How can I write like that and still be original?

It's true that certain academic disciplines or fields of work have established accepted forms of writing. But this does not mean that you have to give up hope of working creatively. Scientists have always written their findings in a strict format. First they state a problem and a hypothesis for solving the problem; then they describe the methodology they intend to use in their study; finally they write about their findings and conclusions. But no one accuses them of being unoriginal. In fact, we are most likely to classify scientists as creative problem solvers.

Besides, no matter what form you use when you write, and no matter what your task, you will decide what details and information you will include in your piece. Your word choice and style of composing will enhance a sense of your own voice and perspective in whatever you write.

Don't give up on originality when you must write within the perimeters of a particular genre. Make the genre work for you.

You haven't talked about length. Isn't that part of form?

It is. As you study the traditional forms used to solve specific writing tasks, you will get a sense of the expected length, but that doesn't mean you have to meet it. You should give the reader all the information the reader needs and no more.

In general, remember: Shorter is better. I have never had to cut a piece of writing without making it better. One famous writer said to "kill all your darlings." I don't entirely agree. Some of the writing you especially like may be effective, but there is a danger that many of the paragraphs we like really don't carry their weight of meaning to the reader. When that occurs, cut them. If you have writing that you really like, you can always save it for another piece.

This is just as true of literary writing as business writing. Poetry is the highest form of literary art, in part, because it says the most with the fewest words.

Peter DeVries said, "When I see a paragraph shrinking under my eyes like a strip of bacon in a skillet, I know I'm on the right track."

What if I mix forms? Can't you write reflectively and still do research? Or be persuasive and still write reflectively?

Absolutely. It's good to be aware of the different features of each form, but you certainly can mix them if the draft leads you in that direction.

If you are writing formal reports for another class, check with your teacher first to see if it's okay to mix forms. Some teachers will want you to follow a particular genre in order to learn certain things about a topic.

Activities to Fit Your Process to Your Task

1. Ask a professor to suggest a journal in your field of interest, or go to the library and ask the reference librarians to direct you to one. Copy an essay, study, or report from the journal and then outline it in your daybook. Notice how the author moves through the piece, what kinds of information he or she uses, and how it is arranged.

2. Collect at least three editorials, opinion pieces, or other kinds of persuasive writing from magazines or newspapers. Read each piece twice. After the first reading, write down your immediate responses: Did the piece persuade you? Did it help you change your mind about a particular issue or topic? During your second reading, jot down the author's major points. How does the writer establish himself or herself as an authority? How does he or she use evidence and information? In what ways does the writer account for opposing viewpoints? Decide from this reading which of the three pieces you found most persuasive and why.

3. Split up in groups of three or four and visit different offices on campus. Have each group member interview an employee in the office about the kinds of writing he or she is expected to do at work. Ask if you can get copies of various reports, letters, or memos that the employee is likely to write. Then come back together as groups and discuss the main features of the different forms or genres. Do some of them have standard openings, use formal language? Do any include pictures or graphics? How do they begin and end? Who is the audience for each piece of writing?

4. Have each member of your group select a piece of writing that represents a particular genre, and imagine the process the writer went through. Pretend you are that writer and plan the piece—what information you'll need, the kind of readership you anticipate, how you intend to focus, when you expect to have a draft, what kind of feedback you will get, how you will revise and edit it.

5. Compare and contrast two pieces of writing in different forms—a researched essay with a persuasive essay, for example; or a reflective essay with an analytical essay. Draw a line down a page in your daybook and outline the main features of the first essay on the left, the second on the right. Discuss your findings in class.

6. Select a piece of writing, and rewrite the opening in a form suitable for at least three of the following genres—the reflective, persuasive, analytical,

research, or narrative essay. Then write a couple of paragraphs describing the differences between the openings, the tone of voice you established, and what information you included in each. How do your different openings foretell the kind of writing that will follow?

7. Think of a career you might like to enter after college, and brainstorm a list of the forms of writing you think you would do in that field. Then arrange an interview with employees in the field, and ask them to describe in detail their writing tasks. Ask to see copies, and note down the main features of particular genres.

8. Brainstorm a list of all the writing tasks you've had to do over the past two to four weeks. Don't leave anything out; include application essays, exam essay answers, school excuse notes for children or siblings, memos, reports, lab observations, and so on. Then with a partner, talk about the context or setting for each form of writing. Where or why did you compose each? Who did you expect your readers to be? In what ways did the forms differ from one another? What might be appropriate to one form of writing and not to another? Did you feel that you were a novice with some forms and an expert with others?

9. If you had to write a college application essay, pull it out and review it. Recall the process of writing it and the kind of advice parents, teachers, friends, school counselors, or writing tutors gave you. What specific details did they want you to concentrate on? What did they think was appropriate to include or omit? What difference did the perceived readers of the piece make in the way you wrote it? How did you revise it? What features characterize this kind of essay as a particular genre?

10. Try your hand at a writing form you are unfamiliar with. If you have never written an analytical essay, for example, plan one from beginning to end, and take it through the steps of your writing process. Keep track of your progress in your daybook, and make sure to note what you had to do differently with this piece of writing than with others you have done. Refer to the tips in this chapter on writing the form of essay you have chosen.

11. Keep a notebook of writing you do for other classes. Include whatever instructions your teachers may give you, the pieces of writing themselves, and any notes and drafts. Insert a blank sheet of paper after each piece and write a short but detailed analysis of how you approached the assignment and wrote it.

12. Think of a writing assignment that proved to be particularly challenging to you. Pretend that your writing partner must complete the same assignment. Define the assignment, the form of writing it required, and how you completed it. Then write up a list of tips, similar to the ones in this chapter, that will help your partner.

13. Gather sample essay questions from exams you have taken or that other students in similar classes may have taken. Determine the amount of time you are

allowed to answer each question and then practice planning, writing, and editing the answers. In the margins of the text sheet or on a separate piece of paper, give yourself time to sketch out a thoughtful outline before you begin. Then write your answer and edit it. Work to complete all steps in the process within the allotted time. Keep practicing until you feel comfortable with the process and meet your time goal.

14. Join a group of classmates to study three or four genres of television shows (a sitcom, a drama, a detective or cops show, a documentary, a mystery, a made-for-TV suspense film, a magazine news program, etc.). Assign one kind of show to each person. Take notes as you watch. Think of the writer's role and what features of the genre he or she must emphasize. What kinds of elements characterize certain kinds of shows? Get together as a group and write up an analysis comparing and contrasting the different features of particular television genres.

15. Choose one of the essay forms featured in this chapter, and find a published essay that is most like that form. Using the writing tips I've given for each form, analyze the essay and describe how the writer incorporates these steps into his or her piece. Note also where the writer deviates from the "tips" or combines different forms.

16. Write a persuasive essay that's not so persuasive. In other words, disregard the tips for writing such an essay. Ignore your opponent's arguments, and don't back up your points with evidence. Ignore reason, and make only emotional appeals. Then read your essay aloud to a group and have them "workshop" the essay to make it better. Ask the group to give you specific details and to talk about their responses to the essay as you read it.

17. Choose a letter to the editor from your school or local newspaper. Analyze the letter and discuss why you think it is or is not effective. Make a list of suggestions for the writer that might help him or her write a more effective piece.

18. Ask a teacher in your major or field of interest what constitutes good student writing in that discipline. Have him or her give examples from successful student papers, or ask if you may have copies. What details of writing did the successful student writer pay attention to? Why are these details particular to that field or discipline?

19. Talk with someone who has created a home page on the Internet. Study other home pages, and note the features of this particular genre. What kind of writing is expected on a home page? What kind of writing would not be expected? How much of the writing is dictated by the technical perimeters of the home page itself? How does text interact with pictures or graphics in these pages? What other forms of writing does home page text resemble? Design your own home page.

20. Take a piece of writing, and draw up a plan for turning it into a research paper. You might, for example, study a letter to the editor in the school.

CHAPTER 11

LEARNING FROM WRITERS

Writing is not a mystical art; writing is a craft that can be understood, shared, learned. The best writers do have talent, but that talent is honed and developed. It is important for apprentice writers to join experienced writers at the workbench, to see how badly they write—good writing is the product of bad writing; the said that cannot yet be said—and how they find the good within the bad and develop it so that others can understand.

Fortunately there is a great deal of testimony by writers on how they write. The autobiographies and biographies of writers, their collected letters and published notebooks, their case histories and the reproductions of their manuscript pages, interviews with writers such as those published in the *Paris Review* and collected in the series *Writers at Work*—all of these sources document how writers work. You can also invite classmates to share their case histories, asking them to tell you how they have written pieces that you admire. Most of all, you should write your own case histories to discover what you have done when writing well, so that you can reinforce those habits and skills that work for you.

The case histories in this chapter reveal the narrative of writing samples, then the final drafts. You may want to skip ahead and read the final drafts, then go back to see how they were developed. Too few readers have had the opportunity to attend play or symphony rehearsals, watch artists or sculptors at work in their studios, and most of all—since writing is ordinarily a secret art—see writers alone with their pages. When Ernest Hemingway was asked where he worked, he reportedly said, "In my head." We can't open up the skulls of writers, but we can go into their workrooms and observe the process of "making" writing.

STUDENT CASE HISTORY: WRITING TO DESCRIBE—SARAH HANSEN

Sarah Hansen has written an excellent student case history that covers the entire writing process from finding a topic to completing a final draft. Her piece grew out of an assignment to write, with abundant detail, about a familiar place—her hometown.

···

HOW I WROTE MY ESSAY

Sarah Hansen

This descriptive essay is the result of eight drafts, conferencing, workshopping, journal writing, thinking, and sharing. It was hard work—sometimes frustrating but mostly rewarding. I have learned to have confidence in my own writing. But I still have not tackled procrastination, and wonder if I ever will.

To come up with a topic, I brainstormed places and people that I would like to describe and that I know a lot about. I picked my hometown, Birch Grove, Illinois, because I have a lot to say about it, and at that point I was confused about my feelings for Birch Grove. My English teacher, Bruce Ballenger, says confusing topics are the best to write about because by writing about them a discovery might be made that will help to end the confusion.

Before I began a first draft, I brainstormed another list of Birch Grove people, places, and events. The list I made ended up in two piles: one bad and one good. This was something I hadn't expected.

I circled the most controversial and the weirdest things on the list. Directly after this, I began to free write about the circled things.

I thought about the paper for a few days then went to the computer to type what I had written during the free write. I added more stuff to it that had been in my head and took the first draft to my conference with Bruce. He liked it. But the point I was trying to make was not clear, because I didn't really know exactly what the point was. Ideas about a hometown are complex. This was the most difficult part of writing this essay: trying to find the point.

Also, my first draft had too much description. I had to find the places where the description didn't fit the purpose of the essay. I actually used scissors and tape on the first draft to cut out unnecessary description. The second draft had less description but was no closer to realizing a point than the first. I was frustrated.

Our writing class had group workshops where we shared our pieces with three or four other students. I read the Birch Grove paper to my workshop group, because I needed fresh perspectives. I also needed some positive reinforcement. All three students liked my paper—that made me feel more motivated to work on it. One woman in my workshop agreed with Bruce and me that the point of the essay needed to be clearer. The most valuable thing I learned from the workshop was that the topic of the essay wasn't clear until the middle. They suggested starting the essay with a paragraph or idea from the middle.

With this in mind, I changed the first paragraph and fiddled around with various parts of the essay. But I was still frustrated with the meaning. I knew that the essay was slowly progressing with each draft, but from drafts two to six, I made little progress finding exactly what it was I wanted to say without sounding boring, clichéd, or obvious. I started to share the essay with a lot of different people. Most close friends tend to like just about anything you do and aren't objective enough and don't give much criticism. Older English majors and my parents and their friends, people that read a good amount of writing, turned out to be the most helpful.

With each successive draft, the second to the sixth, my English teacher and I became more and more discouraged. I couldn't reach exactly what it was about Birch Grove I wanted to say. Did I want to say how I felt; did I want to say something to the people of Birch Grove; did I want to make a point about all hometowns; did I want to make a statement about the world by talking about one hometown? My biggest mistake was not writing in my journal enough. I procrastinated writing about my feelings for Birch Grove, because it was too frustrating.

Around draft four or five, I couldn't look at the paper with objectivity anymore. I was too close to my subject and practically had the words memorized, as did my English teacher. Finally, after draft five, Bruce gave the draft back to me with questions written all over it about what it was I was trying to say. In my journal I wrote answers to his questions. It was this way, by talking to myself in my journal, and by answering questions, that I nearly found what I wanted to say.

I wrote that the good in Birch Grove I had realized by going away far outweighed the bad. The energy of the good things is what makes Birch Grove all right. When people realize this, then Birch Grove will be safe. We decided that this would be the final draft. I thought I was done.

But when my father read the essay out loud that night, I realized what I had wanted to come across did not. In the sixth draft it seemed I had forgotten the racism and the close-mindedness. I intended just the opposite. I wanted to say that I have realized the good in Birch Grove, but that the bad needs to be changed.

The biggest problem I had writing this essay was attempting to find exactly what the meaning was. I also needed to spend more time talking to myself about the essay in my journal. In hand with this, I needed to spend more time writing than thinking about the essay. A good idea can sometimes surprise me as I write, but that rarely happens when I think about my writing without a pen in my hand.

I learned to share my work with as many people as I could who were willing to take the time to read it and give their responses. It is motivating to hear fresh and new ideas. The conferences helped in that Bruce and I would talk about what it was I was trying to say. The discussions helped each draft to come closer and closer. It was also good to hear someone give positive comments about my writing.

Writing a descriptive essay can help with any other kind of writing. De-
scription is about saying things so that other people can see, feel, hear,
and smell what you have. These things are revealed through specific de-

tails. It is exactly the same concrete writing that is needed to critique a novel or write a term paper.

Sarah's daybook started out with the following entry:

I have to write a paper for a book—a descriptive essay—to be published. I have no idea what to write about—just knowing it's for a book makes me nervous. I've even been avoiding thinking about it. Dad—Heather—East H—commune—expectations—grandma—Birch Grove—Berry Farm—trip to France—second semester at UNH.

She starts out with a writer's apprehension and makes a list of possible topics. She did put a mark like a rising sun after "Birch Grove," and then she wrote a draft that plunged into the subject: "The round and friendly minister of the Methodist Church of Birch Grove, Illinois, was found in Sanderson's three-story department store stealing a large pair of light brown corduroys."

In her daybook Sarah wrote:

I showed my first draft of the essay for the book today. Bruce liked it. I was so relieved. He's really helped me to be more confident about my writing. We decided that the point of the paper wasn't too clear. He said that I need to "peel the onion." In class we talked about how the layers of the onion are like layers of ideas and points to an essay or a piece of writing. The deeper into the onion layers you get, the closer you are to your main point. I know a few things that I am pointing out but I don't know exactly how to say them. I think my main point is about how Birch Grove was all bad to me at first, and then, as I went to UNH, I realized the better things about it. But the better things don't excuse the bad things. I'm still confused about it. I don't think this paper is very interesting. I don't think it will keep the reader's interest. We also talked about how there are too many descriptions.

I find this sort of writing to myself important. It helps to put into words what you got from a conference and to identify your feelings about the text and about the process of writing.

The next page in Sarah's daybook showed a typical jumble of doodling and writing. She listed potential specifics as a form of recovering memories and discovering what she may write.

Later she wrote in her daybook:

I've decided to show my paper on Birch Grove to my workshop group. I don't know where to go with it. I have been thinking a lot about the focus of this paper and it's getting me nowhere. Hopefully, they'll have some insight to it that will get me motivated for revising this paper. I spend too much time just thinking—I should be writing in this journal more but don't have discipline—I procrastinate too much.

• • •

My workshop group really liked my paper. Lin said it reminded her of her hometown which is cool cause that's sort of a point I'm trying to make—every hometown for every person is both good and bad—end up blaming hometown for everything—have bitterness towards it. A love-hate thing. I don't know that's quite what I want to say though—seems cliché. Brian and _____ both thought that the beginning isn't clear—maybe begin with paragraph that starts, "I moved to Birch Grove, where life offers more, when I was four . . . ." They said as it stands now it's a little unclear what I'm talking about. So I'll try to rework that into the beginning and Brian thought that my point was perfectly said—that I shouldn't add more but said I should make my point clearer. I agree more with _____ cause at this point I don't even know what my main point is. I asked them if they thought it was boring and if it caught and kept their attention. They said it was interesting and kept their attention well so that made me feel better. Asked if there was too much description and they said no.

> *In all her daybook entries Sarah reveals the way a writer's mind—and emotions—work. I certainly feel the same way about my drafts as Sarah does about hers. To learn to write effectively you need to be open and realize your feelings and how to deal with them. Later in her daybook Sarah writes:*

I'm annoyed with my paper about Birch Grove. I'm sick of it. I'm too close to it and can't see it correctly any more. It seems so trite and boring and cliché. Bruce seems to not like it much either. That's really discouraging. I don't know what exactly I want my point to be that's creative and fresh.

> *These excerpts from her account reveal the writer at work, what goes on backstage that is essential to the creation of an effective piece of writing. Space limitations here preclude reproducing her drafts, sometimes marked up with her comments, other times with the comments of her readers, but they document the evolution of her essay. In the third draft, for example, Sarah begins, "When I was four, my mother, my dog, and I moved to Birch Grove, Illinois. I've spent all my time there minus the summers which I've spent with my father. Passing the town border a cheap billboard reads: 'Life offers more in Birch Grove.'"*

> *By the fifth draft her lead reads, "Passing over the town border into Birch Grove, Illinois, a billboard, paint peeling off, reads: 'Life offers more in Birch Grove.' When I was four years old my mother, my dog, and I moved to this Midwestern town. As I grew up, I'd pass the fading billboard* ~~faded as was along with~~ *and my tolerance for BIRCH GROVE,* ~~my bitterness and anger seen in a grimace as I thought, 'Life offers less in Birch grave.'~~ *faded along with it." By the eighth draft the lead was as it appears below. Writers have to learn by writing and by considering what they have written and how it can be improved.*

> *Here is Sarah's final draft as it was turned in:*

SIMPLE BIRCH GROVE

SARAH HANSEN

Passing over the town border into Birch Grove, Illinois, a billboard, paint peeling off, reads: "Life Offers More In Birch Grove." When I was four years old my mother, my dad, and I moved to this Midwestern town. As I grew up, I'd pass the fading billboard, and my tolerance for Birch Grove faded along with it.

The owner of Sanderson's three-story department store found the round and friendly minister, Donald Morison, of the Methodist Church of Sycamore stealing a pair of brown corduroys. Most of the bank presidents and company founders and Mercedes Benz owners of Birch Grove belonged to the Methodist Church on the corner of Third and Main. They put up a big fuss about having a kleptomaniac as a minister. There was great pressure on Don to leave. These influential people weren't seen at Sunday services anymore to listen to Don with his brown, shining eyes give the sermon. Only a few members forgave Don, told him so, and asked him to stay. One Sunday, a woman slowly stood up and told the churchgoers that the Bible says to forgive, and that we should forgive Don, and help him out, because his problem is a disease, just as alcoholism is a disease. Don left the Methodist Church two long months after the incident, and the members are now content to sit in the pews and sing out of the worn, red, cloth-covered hymnals.

Miss Gooch, the assistant counselor at Birch Grove High School, wears her thin, gray-brown hair in a tight curl perm. I was the student council president my senior year, and we were discussing some upcoming activities. Miss Gooch liked to gossip; she asked me how my friend Peggy was doing. Peggy has fair, freckled skin and blond, curled hair—like most other girls at Birch Grove High School. Her boyfriend is thin and has beautiful, chocolate brown skin. What Miss Gooch meant was, "How is she dealing with having a black boyfriend?" Miss Gooch said, "I am not prejudiced, but I don't think the races should intermingle . . . and I hate Mexicans." Sixteen black students and forty Mexican students attend Birch Grove High School, where Miss Gooch is the counselor and student council advisor.

At age eleven, my sister Traci walked to the Save And Shop, three blocks down Walnut Street from our house, to buy groceries. As she crossed the supermarket parking lot, a little girl, not over seven years old, was left alone in a beat-up station wagon. The girl rolled down the front seat window. "Nigger," she said to Traci, my adopted sister, now one of the sixteen black students at the high school. Traci is startled as she looks in the mirror to see her own black face. Her eyes are so accustomed to whiteness.

Sam Ritchel was salutatorian of my class. Now, when I come home for Christmas or Easter vacation, I see Sam wandering around Birch Grove, or staring off in a booth in the Coffee Shop. He's taken too much acid, refuses to get a job, dropped out of the University of Wisconsin, shaves his eyebrows, wears black lipstick, black eyeliner, and black clothing. He listens to Jim Morrison on his tape recorder, and says nothing but "black, melancholy, darkness, despair . . ." In the Weston Elementary School, Sam's nickname was Happy.

I hated everything about Birch Grove. I hated its conservatism, its hypocrisy, its ignorance, its racism, its close-mindedness, and its ugliness. I hated what it did to bright, open-minded people who could not escape. In Birch Grove, I could only think about itchy, depressing, angering things. Times when snotty Claire Saunders knocked over my newly painted three-speed bike in the fifth grade, when the whole of Birch Grove watched Top Gun perpetually for weeks after it came out on video, when high school students egged our house five times in two months because my stepfather is the assistant principal of the high school—a fair, kind man who must punish students for skipping a study hall, for smoking in the music wing.

But since I've been at college, far away from my hometown, I can remember eating macaroni and cheese on Kiersten's sunny, white porch with her mother and mine, enjoying the lunch hour before returning back to the third grade. I can remember the annual January snow sculpture competition in front of Prince's Restaurant across from Birch Grove Park. I remember my very first valentine in seventh grade from my very first boyfriend: shy, curly white-haired Jim Morse, a farm boy. The homemade card was caringly shaped and cut out of red, pink, and white construction paper. Two white rabbits kissed on the front; inside, pencil cursive writing read, "I'm glad that you're my valentine, Sarah."

I remember the annual Birch Grove Pumpkin Festival where all of Birch Grove competes in a pumpkin competition, decorating them as a scary monster with orange peels for hair and gourds for arms and legs or a pumpkin phone for goblins and ghosts to use. The Miller family won the grand prize one year and got to go on the Bozo Show. There was a pumpkin princess or prince award to the best essay in the junior high, and the grade-schooler with the best scary picture got to ride on the fire engine at the front of the Sunday Pumpkin Parade. I watched the parade from the Abbens' house on Somonauk Street with people from our church, eating warm carameled apples, and drinking hot apple cider sitting on fold-out chairs along the street. The huge oak, maple, and sycamore trees lining the street screamed autumn with their yellows, golds, reds, and oranges.

I remember Mrs. Munter, my junior and senior year English teacher, my most influential teacher, sneaking chocolate M&Ms out of the second drawer down. I remember her strong, clear, enunciated voice demanding and challenging us to accomplish more in her class than we ever had before.

I remember driving along the smooth and winding North River Road just after dusk on a hot summer day, windows rolled down and arms out waving, watching the thousands of tiny blinking lights of the fireflies just above the soybeans and wheat fields. Although I used to hate the flatness of the land, now as I return I appreciate the great big sky and lie in the middle of a cornfield with Steven and Pam, watching the silver-white shooting stars stream across the blue-black expanse.

I see Sean Allen in the store window of Ben Franklin, the five and dime, and wave back knowing he's still the same friendly, simple person he always was and will be. I know that every summer the woman with the wrinkled face will bring out her popcorn stand, and my mother and I'll buy sweet caramel corn and eat the whole bag as we walk slowly home in the hot night air.

Mom says Birch Grove is a good place to bring up children. Maybe it is in some ways. Friendly Sean Allen, the sun on a white porch that makes the skin hum, and Mrs. Munter's deep, resounding voice are as pure and warm as the wealthy churchgoers and close-minded Miss Gooch are tarnished and cold. But even as the sweet-smelling fields, the wide Midwest sky, the leaves of screaming colors that crackle under foot seek to balance this out, I know that Birch Grove still is no place to bring up my children.

PROFESSIONAL CASE HISTORY: ——— WRITING TO ANALYZE— ——— CHRISTOPHER SCANLAN

Christopher Scanlan is the writer I turn to first when I need help, diagnosis, encouragement, support, criticism, inspiration, comradeship.

He is a master writer of fiction and nonfiction who can write short and write long, write on hourly deadline and write over time. He can write on many subjects in many voices. He is—my greatest compliment—a pro.

He has been a staff member of the *Providence Journal,* the *St. Petersburg Times,* and Knight-Ridder Newspapers' Washington Bureau. His stories, essays, and articles have appeared in *Redbook,* the *Washington Post Magazine,* the *Boston Globe Magazine,* and numerous other publications. He has won sixteen awards for writing, including a Robert F. Kennedy award for international journalism.

He is also a master teacher of writing. He is director of writing programs at The Poynter Institute for Media Studies in St. Petersburg, Florida, where he teaches professional writers to improve their writing. He also writes journalism texts for Harcourt College Publishers.

Now Chip Scanlan takes us into his workroom, showing just how he wrote a personal essay.

HOW I WROTE MY ESSAY

Christopher Scanlan

ORIGINS

"We've got the O. J. 911 tapes," the morning drive-time DJ promised. "Coming up. After these messages."

Like other commuters on this July morning, I was hooked. When the playback finally came over my car radio, I heard Nicole Brown Simpson's voice—fed-up, frightened, resigned—but that wasn't what brought tears to my eyes sitting at the downtown stop light. It was the voice in the background—the shouts of a man out of control, choking on contempt and rage, spewing abuse. I knew that sound.

I've heard it echoing off the walls in our house. I've felt the lump of remorse that screaming at the top of my lungs leaves in the back of my throat, the pit of my stomach. "I have to write about this," I thought.

After twenty years reporting for newspapers, big and small, I don't need both hands to count the times the first person singular appeared under my byline: a deadline account about a stint volunteering at a mental hospital during a state workers' strike; a recollection of a year in the Peace Corps; a Father's Day message to my unborn daughter; a travel piece about the search for a soldier's grave in Europe; a brief stint as a fill-in columnist. But in most of these I stayed back, little more than a personal pronoun. Like most journalists, I feared the word *I*.

I knew the rules, unwritten but oft-spoken, by cynical colleagues and fearsome editors:

"Reporters don't belong in their stories."

"Nobody cares about your personal opinions."

"If your life was really interesting, we'd be writing about you."

Writing about yourself is often difficult for reporters and editors whose work focuses on others. But writing about yourself, honestly, even painfully, can make you not only a better writer but a better person. The personal essay trains its sights on the writer's own life and the writer's emotional, psychological, and intellectual reactions to the most intimate experiences. As Phillip Lopate says in his introduction to his anthology *The Art of the Personal Essay* (Anchor Books Doubleday, 1994): "The personal essayist looks back at the choices that were made, the roads not taken, the limiting familial and historic circumstances, and what might be called the catastrophe of personality."

The DJ put on a song. The light changed. "But I don't want to write about it." I drove on.

THE PROCESS

The story began with handwritten notes in my journal and an assignment to myself. Don Murray, who has written hundreds of personal essays in his column for the *Boston Globe,* had come to Poynter in July 1994 to teach in a summer program for college graduates bent on a career in journalism. The assignment: to write a personal essay.

"Make a list of what you think about when you are not thinking," Murray advised. "What makes you mad? What makes you happy? What past events were turning points in your life that you'd like to understand?"

I had my subject. Or more accurately, it had me.

"The place you come from and how you remember it matters," says writer Robert Love Taylor. "It is your territory." Writing the personal essay requires you to seek out the territory that is your life and to explore it as deeply and honestly as possible. It means subjecting your own life to the same scrutiny that you train on your sources. It's here, at the beginning of the process, that I almost chickened out. My wife and I have three daughters, including a set of twins, who are always doing and saying cute things. I could write about being the father of twins, scattering my essay with funny anecdotes and the darndest things kids say.

I certainly wasn't going to write an essay that let anyone in on my dirty little secret, that I too often lost my temper with these three little girls. And then I remembered my reaction to O. J. Simpson's shouting on the 911 tapes, and I knew I couldn't keep my distance anymore. I began scribbling notes in my journal.

Temper, Temper

911 tape in car—tears at stop light. I have been there. My voice too.

Temper school

Male anger

Melvin Mencher, a professor at the Columbia University Graduate School of Journalism, had a simple cure for writer's block: "Whenever you are blocked," he said, "just stop and ask yourself, 'What am I trying to say?'"

The next day, I sat in front of a computer terminal with my students on all sides in a Poynter Institute computer lab, fingers frozen until I asked that question and the first tentative words began to appear on the screen.

I began, as usual, by babbling. Some call this *freewriting;* putting words on the page without editing or even stopping to correct spelling or grammar. I prefer *Washington Post* feature writer Cynthia Gorney's description: "I start to babble, sometimes starting in the middle of the story and usually fairly quickly I see how it's going to start. It just starts shaping itself. I tell students, 'Don't think, write.'"

Don't think, I told myself. Write. Or rather, think but do it with your fingers. The idea is to race past the inner censor, the creature novelist Gail Godwin refers to as the "watcher at the gate." The next day, I put the notes aside and began typing. I began typing:

I do not want to write this.

I love my kids, but I have left my handprint, like a blush on the backs of their thighs.

I do not want to write this.

Like a child whistling by a cemetery, I typed as fast as I could, writing without thinking, trying to discover what I wanted to say by talking to myself on the page as honestly as I could. In thirty-seven minutes I wrote 960 words. And yes, I did count them. At this stage, that's the only way I can measure progress. First drafts are painful; I'm convinced every word is the wrong one. It's like the first time you ride a bike; there's a lot of wobbling, falling, scraping your knees. So I try to remember what Christine Martin, who directs the writing program at the University of West Virginia journalism school, tells writers: free writing is like turning on a faucet in an old house; you have to let it run a while to get the rust out.

The first draft was riddled with errors. Errors of fact. Errors of omission. I didn't let that stop me. When I wanted to include an entry from my journal, I simply wrote: "A sample entry: TK (for *to come*) and kept on typing. Spelling errors. Grammar. Syntax.

Any of the good newspaper copy editors I worked with would have been horrified. I didn't let that bother me. Like Frank O'Connor, the Irish short story writer, any garbage will do. "Get black on white," Guy de Maupassant, the French short story writer, counseled. "Get anything down," the legendary editor Maxwell Perkins told one of his authors (they included Hemingway and Fitzgerald), "then we can work on it."

I printed out the draft and read it over. The computer and word processing software, which allow constant revisions without having to make an entire new draft, has made me less of a "copy editor's nightmare," the way an early job evaluation described me. Even so, I like to make a hard copy after my first writing session. Changing the writing surface to paper makes it easier to spot mistakes and to read the piece the way it will be read. On the screen everything looks perfect, even mistakes, and it's important for me to know that it's not, so I can make it better.

I try to read the first draft as a reader but inevitably my hand begins to itch for a pen. I started marking up the page. One line read ". . . fed up with the thousands frustrations that stud the ordinary workday."

I crossed out "fed up with" and replaced it with "choking on." One less word. More important, a vivid image that suggested the inner rage work produced in me. Not surprisingly, much of my thinking was disjointed. I drew arrows connecting paragraphs and made notes to "move up" paragraphs. I could have started with an outline but I prefer to discover what I'm trying to say first and then see how I can rearrange things.

The real key to writing success is learning how to read your manuscript with a discriminating eye—and ear. You have to discover what you want to say by writing it and then be willing to jettison it all when it doesn't work. So I reread what I wrote. I read it aloud to my wife. I choked back my usual disgust at my first draft. I rewrote. I jettisoned entire pages. I worked over paragraphs until just one phrase remained. I made my endings my beginnings. I added new material. I gave them to readers I trusted—my wife, Don Murray, Tom French at the *St. Petersburg Times,* and my colleagues at the Poynter Institute. I listened to their reactions and cut and added and re-ordered and wrote again.

It was beginning to look like a story, but I knew it still wasn't there. It was time to risk ridicule, to confront the possibility that I had failed.

I submitted the essay to the *New York Times* "over the transom," as they say. They turned it down. Then I contacted *Newsday*. They liked the piece but asked for a few changes. The refrain "I don't want to write this" helped me get the first draft done, but it didn't work for the editor. She also wanted the piece to be more topical, more newsy. I rewrote the lead using material from the O. J. Simpson case and added a description of St. Petersburg in summer. The story appeared in *Newsday*, but I wasn't finished with the subject.

GETTING NAKED

"If you can't tell an honest story about yourself, you're a long way from telling an honest story about someone else," Walt Harrington, staff writer for the *Washington Post Magazine*, says in *The Complete Book of Feature Writing*, edited by Leonard Witt (Writer's Digest Books, 1991). All writers have a territory, a landscape of experience and emotional history unique to them. Like any landscape, there are safe havens and dangerous places. I could easily write a light-hearted piece about being the father of three girls. But the topic that needed exploring was my darker side: my temper with my kids.

"You can't write a personal column without going to some very deep place inside yourself, even if it's only for four hours," says essayist Jennifer Allen in *Speaking of Journalism*, edited by William Zinsser (Harper Collins, 1994). "It's almost like psychotherapy, except you're doing it on your own. You have to pull something out of yourself and give away some important part of yourself. . . . It's a gift you have to give to the reader, even if it's the most light-hearted piece in the world."

After the essay appeared in *Newsday*, I got a call from Evelynne Kramer, the editor of the *Boston Globe Magazine*, who invited me to submit an essay. When I mentioned the *Newsday* piece she expressed an interest—not about the Simpson case connection which wasn't timeless enough for a magazine's longer lead time—but on male anger. She'd like to see something on that.

Back to the computer, where I found myself writing about a starkly etched memory: It's late at night, and I'm screaming at my kids again. Yelling at the top of my lungs at three little girls, lying still and terrified in their beds. Like a referee in a lopsided boxing match, my wife is trying to pull me away, but I am in the grip of a fury I am unwilling to relinquish. "And if you don't get to sleep right now," I shout, "there are going to be consequences you're not going to like."

In this version, I also used passages from a journal I'd been keeping about my temper. In the *Newsday* version, I had mentioned my father, who had died when I was a boy, his drinking and his own angry outbursts. But most of the focus in this draft was on my children and me.

I can look at my favorite stories and tell exactly where and how an editor improved it. In this case, Evelynne Kramer of the *Boston Globe Magazine* liked my initial submission but added, "It doesn't seem resolved in a literary way." (There aren't many newspaper editors who talk this way.) My father played a role that she felt I only hinted at.

For me, that meant trying to recreate an unforgettable moment that occurred nearly forty years ago and which I became convinced held answers to my own battles with anger.

I am no more than nine, and I am standing just outside our family kitchen. My father has come home drunk again. He is in his mid-forties, (about the age I am today). By now, he has had three strokes, land mines in his brain that he seems to shrug off, like his hangovers, but which in a year will kill him. He has lost his job selling paper products, which he detested, and has had no luck finding another. He and my mother begin arguing in the kitchen. Somehow he has gotten hold of her rosary beads. I hear his anger, her protests, and then, suddenly, they are struggling over the black necklace. (Has he found her at the kitchen table, praying for him? I can imagine his rage. "If your God is so good, why are the sheriffs coming to the door about the bills I can't pay? Why am I broke? Why can't I find a job? Why am I so sick? Why, dammit? Why?") Out of control now, he tears the rosary apart. I can still hear the beads dancing like marbles on the linoleum.

Evelynne's questions led me to confront why I was so mad at him. Writing about my temper led me to an unexpected insight—and a new peace—about my relationship with my father, who died when I was a boy. Whatever psychic wounds my father's death caused when I was ten seem to have frozen over my recollection of him. I have few conscious memories; those I have are starkly etched scenes of drunkenness, grief, and rage that left me with a reservoir of unresolved anger. This limitless supply feeds the frustrations of my own life, as do my templates of parental behavior that I, the loyal son, can reenact with my own children. For many years, I thought that I hated the dimly remembered stranger who was my father. I believed that I hated him for dying before I could learn who he was, for scaring me when he was drunk, but now I realize I hate him only because he left me before I could say "I love you."

Evelynne is one of those rare editors who doesn't feel she has to take over the writing, but instead leaves that responsibility with the writer. It's a lesson that Michael Crichton, the best-selling novelist, says he's learned about working with editors. "Ask for their reactions to what they find wrong, and not for their suggestions for how to fix it."

I owe the power of this piece to two people, Evelynne Kramer, who forced me to discover its true meaning, and my wife, Kathy Fair, who not only encouraged me to publish it, but insisted I do so.

FEEDBACK

Some of my friends cautioned me against publishing this piece; people might get the wrong idea about me. But writing the piece has helped me understand myself better and, more important, treat my family better. Judging from the letters and phone calls I've received from readers grateful to see a painful issue in their life aired publicly, it's helped others, too. Explore a dangerous region of your writer's territory by writing a piece nobody can write but you. By reporting on the central issues of the human condition—joy, loss, birth, anger, fear, death, hate, and love—you will give voice to the unspoken feelings and thoughts of your readers and draw each other into the human community.

JUDGMENT DAY

Writing about my temper with my kids was the easy part. Going public was the biggest risk. After it appeared, several letter writers to the *Boston Globe Magazine* denounced me. "I am outraged that the *Globe Magazine* devoted space to a domestic-violence apologist," wrote one. "Temper tantrums are excusable for two-year-olds, not for grown men," another agreed.

Be ready to be judged, says my friend Mark Patinkin, a columnist for the *Providence Journal*. "When you use the letter *I*, for every supportive letter you get from someone who related to your one-year-old having a scene at a restaurant, you'll get another from a reader tired of hearing about your kid."

Their criticism was softened by other letters from parents who said they recognized their own family struggles with temper in my story. One mother from Maine planned to share the piece with her siblings "so they can tackle the trait sooner and hopefully more effectively." Another woman said she wished her father were still alive so he could read it.

Stylistically, recreating my parents' argument over her rosary beads and my father's anguished questions seems a bit risky. I make it clear it's a product of memory and imagination, though, and several people tell me they find it the most affecting part of the piece.

I have gotten more reaction—letters to the editor, phone calls, personal comments—from personal essays than from any single story in my entire career.

TIP SHEET

A personal essay is an attempt to understand. You don't have to find the answer. Like any quest, the experience of writing and rewriting will change you, whether or not you find the grail.

What do you need to understand?

About yourself?

About life?

What are you most afraid to write?

What is the story that nobody else can write but you?

This is the first and most important step. And if it's not close to the bone, keep looking. It's the willingness to explore something that is very personal and even painful that will serve you and the reader. I think it's best to write about something you feel deeply about but which you don't yet fully understand. Write what you don't know or know you don't know but which you need to know. The stuff of everyday life, meticulously observed and described, is what sets the personal essay apart. At Poynter, seminar participants have written haunting, wrenching, funny, and inspiring essays about a thirty-year-old prom dress, the minefield of personal relationships, a friend's suicide, the pain of racism, the trials of living with a pack rat, their children, their marriages, their parents' lives and deaths. "There are common human experiences, and journalists strike a chord when they write about them," says Ruth Hanley, an assistant city editor for the *Dispatch* in Columbus, Ohio.

I have written essays about my pathetic boyhood athletic career and how it made me a nonsports watcher ("Stupor Bowl" in the *Boston Globe Magazine*) and how my wife and I ask the parents of our children's friends if they have guns in their homes ("It's 10 P.M. Do You Know Where Your Guns Are?" in the *Christian Science Monitor*), as well as the story about my temper which appeared in the Sunday magazines of the *Boston Globe*, the *Detroit Free Press*, and the *Hartford Courant*.

At the *Boston Globe Magazine*, editor Evelynne Kramer, says she looks for writing "that plumbs a universal feeling that a reader can relate to on some level even though they might not have had that particular experience." Effective essays, she says, "explore universal themes although not necessarily experiences."

Recreate Pivotal Moments

Larry Bloom, editor of *Northeast*, the Sunday magazine of the *Hartford Courant* and author of *The Writer Within: How to Discover Your Own Ideas, Get Them on Paper, and Sell Them for Publication*, puts the form to a rigorous test. "You don't have a personal essay unless you have a religious experience," he says. "Then it's the task of the writer to re-create that moment."

Take Risks

The single most important lesson I learned in journalism school, from a taskmaster named Melvin Mencher, was a line he considered a throwaway: "Be counter-phobic." Do what you fear to do. In twenty-two years of reporting for a living, there were very few days I wasn't scared. Could I get the interview I needed? Could I write the story? Did I get it right? To succeed, counter-phobia was my only option. Imagine a tightrope, and every day walk across it. Who's the one person you're afraid to call? Where is the one place in town you've never been because you're afraid to go there? It may be a housing project, or it may be the top floor of the big bank. What's the riskiest way I can write this story? Ask yourself every day, "Have I taken a risk?"

Write

Writers write. It's that simple—and that hard. If you're not writing regularly (every day, three times a week, every Saturday, for just fifteen minutes before your day job), then you're not a writer. You're part of that vast universe of people who want to be writers, but don't want to do the work. (I'm talking to myself here, hoping I can start paying attention and stop procrastinating.)

Writers fail more than they succeed. Ask yourself, "How can I fail today?" Then give it your best shot. Get in the game. Submit your stories. Risk rejection or you'll never have a chance at success.

ROLE MODELS

My biggest struggle with writing is putting my butt in the chair. I keep reminding myself to swallow the bile that rises with the first draft and having faith that somewhere in a disorganized, unfocused, even sometimes deceptively coherent story there lurks the promise of a final draft. It's always easier to channel surf the TV or the World Wide Web.

I read for inspiration and motivation. Books, like this one, that introduce writers to the way professionals work are enormously helpful. *The Best American Essay* series and *The Art of the Personal Essay* are two ready sources of good writing and discussion of how the writing was made. Fortunately, personal essays are everywhere these days, in newspapers, magazines, and on the Internet. Start keeping your own collection of writing that makes you want to write. Every sentence you read is a writer's workshop. So is every sentence you write.

Go out and buy a blank notebook today and begin filling it with your ideas. Essays, like trees, begin with a single seed, nourished by time and effort.

We are deluged today by what novelist and short story writer A. Manette Ansay refers to as "public domain" images and language: clichés, commonplace descriptions, and derivative plots that blur any attempts at originality. Draw instead on your individual experiences by tapping the "private stock" of memory and feeling that is inside you. Search for the particulars, the telling details and observations that give resonance and meaning to your story and set it apart from all others, and the chances of producing a piece with universal appeal are strong.

We all have stories that only we can tell. Is there a message you think needs to be heard? A story in your "private stock" that needs tapping? One story that's telling you how it must be written? A dangerous territory worth exploring? An idea you've never lost faith in? Ask yourself, "What's the writing only I can do?" And then do it.

LOVE AND ANGER

CHRISTOPHER SCANLAN

It's late at night, and I'm screaming at my kids again. Yelling at the top of my lungs at three little girls, lying still and terrified in their beds. Like a referee in a lopsided boxing match, my wife is trying to pull me away, but I am in the grip of a fury I am unwilling to relinquish. "And if you don't get to sleep right now," I shout, "there are going to be consequences you're not going to like."

With that vague but ominous threat, I slam the door so hard that I hear plaster falling behind the walls, and I throw myself onto my own bed, out of breath, pulse jackhammering in my temples, throat bruised and burning, a tide of remorse and revulsion rising within. From the children's room, howls descend into sobs and then sniffling whimpers as my wife murmurs a lullaby of explanations. "Daddy loves you very much," I hear Kathy tell them, a bedtime story in which I appear as a monster whose true, kinder side is obscured by fatigue and worry. "He's just tired, and he wants you to go to sleep. No, you're right, he shouldn't lose his temper, but sometimes parents get upset and they do things they shouldn't."

All my life I have struggled with anger, and its manifestations in fits of temper.

In college, I once punched a kitchen cabinet in anger, and, while I no longer recall what I was so frustrated about, I have never forgotten how, for months afterward, I couldn't shake hands without wincing. But it was only after I became a parent—we have a seven-year-old and five-year-old fraternal twins—that my rages grew worse and more frequent.

I have never hit my wife, but I have punched walls during arguments with her.

I love my kids, but I have left my handprint, a faint blush, on the backs of their thighs when I've spanked them. I have seen them recoil from me in terror.

At the office, I'm friendly, easy-going, generally considered a nice guy. It's only at home that I display this vein-popping, larynx-scraping rage. It's not just that I never show this secret, ugly side of my personality to others; I don't even seem to feel it in any other spheres of my life. Why must loved ones bear the brunt of anger?

It's 6:15 A.M. Two of the kids are slurping their way with a solemn determination through their Ripple Crisps and Cheerios. The laggard remains in bed, curled under her comforter, thumb planted firmly in her mouth.

"I'm counting to three," I call up from the landing. Silence.

"One."

The whiny protest is muffled, by the blanket and the finger. "Don't count!"

"You're going to miss the bus. You can't be late. Two."

Nothing.

"If I get to three, no 'Scooby Doo' tonight." Denying them this inane cartoon, their latest favorite, has proven a potent threat, and from the howl it sparks, I know I have hit a nerve. She doesn't move. Inside my head, some unseen force is unleashed, and my anger spews forth, like a race car's fiery exhaust. "That's it," I roar, my anger all out of proportion to the offense. "THREE-EEEE."

With that, the recalcitrant child is howling, and her twin joins in, while the eldest begins berating me. The peaceful breakfast is now a war zone.

I didn't want to believe anything was wrong. I shrugged off my wife's complaints that I had become the out-of-control parent her father had been. "I don't want my kids to have a father they're afraid of," she said after one of my outbursts.

"Wait a minute," I countered. "The kids know I love them." Didn't I always apologize after my anger had spent itself? Wasn't I unstinting with hugs and kisses?

"Maybe you should talk to somebody about it," she said, but I rebuffed that gentle hint. Everybody loses his temper sometimes. People get angry. Kids can drive you crazy. It's not as if I beat my wife or kids.

Kathy began clipping the occasional newspaper article about anger and pinning it to the refrigerator door. Eventually, she told me flat-out that she wouldn't tolerate any more verbal abuse. Her ultimatum, along with a particularly awful late-night screaming assault on the kids that left me ashamed, and, most of all, afraid, finally broke through the wall of denial. I did what I always do when I'm trying to get hold of something elusive: I wrote about it. Two years ago, I sat down in front of my computer and began what became a series of meditations. I called it my Temper Log.

I didn't write in it every day or every week, not even every month. But a pattern emerged from the sporadic entries. I was then working as a newspaper reporter in Washington, D.C. I constantly felt under the gun of deadlines at work, worries about supporting a family of five on a single paycheck, and the incessant demands of the children. I seemed to lose it most often early in the morning, in the rush to get sleepy children to school, or at the end of a long day and a deadening ride home on the Metro. I was usually tired, hungry, overwhelmed by the frustrations that studded my workday, beset by the responsibilities of a family. Half of me wanted to be Super Dad; the other half wanted to be left alone. And for the first time, I had someone I could yell at without immediate consequences—someone who wouldn't fire me, or hang up and give the story I was after to a competitor, someone who loved me so much that they took this crap that they shouldn't have to take.

FROM THE TEMPER LOG:

"Tuesday night, shortly before midnight. The last two days, I have lost my temper with the children as I got ready for work and tried to get them up. Today I got so furious with Michaela when she wouldn't put on her OshKosh jumper, I picked her up and dropped her on the bed against the bunched-up comforter. This is how 'normal' people wind up on the child-abuse hot line, accused of mistreating their children. I am sick at heart for acting this way. I love my children so much, and I don't want them to remember bad things about me, the way I remember Daddy breaking the rosary that night in the kitchen."

I am no more than nine, and I am standing just outside our family kitchen. My father has come home drunk again. He is in his mid-forties (about the age I am today). By now, he has had three strokes, landmines in his brain that he seems to shrug off, like his hangovers, but which in a year will kill him. He has lost his job selling paper products, which he detested, and has had no luck finding another. He and my mother begin arguing in the kitchen. Somehow he has gotten hold of her rosary beads. I hear his anger, her protests, and then, suddenly, they are struggling over the black necklace. (Has he found her at the kitchen table, praying for him? I can imagine his rage. "If your God is so good, why are the sheriffs coming to the door about the bills I can't pay? Why am I broke? Why can't I find a job? Why am I so sick? Why, dammit? Why?") Out of control now, he tears the rosary apart. I can still hear the beads dancing like marbles on the linoleum.

I don't want to make this another one of those "It's all my parents' fault" stories, the convenient apologia of the Adult Child of an Alcoholic. Like me, my father was the product—and the victim—of his own upbringing: the only child born to a mother who had numerous miscarriages before him and a second-generation Irish-American father who squandered several fortunes and ended up alone with his memories in a furnished room at the YMCA.

While my own memories of my father are fragmentary, my mother's stories describe a vibrant, winning man, rich with an aura of promise that became deadened by alcohol and the burden of supporting a large family on a salesman's uncertain salary. No wonder he was angry.

Whatever psychic wounds my father's death caused when I was ten seem to have frozen over my recollection of him. I have few conscious memories; those I have are starkly etched scenes of drunkenness, grief, and rage that left me with a reservoir of unresolved anger. This limitless supply feeds the frustrations of my own life, as do my templates of parental behavior that I, the loyal son, can reenact with my own children. For many years, I thought that I hated the dimly remembered stranger who was my father. I believed that I hated him for dying before I could learn who he was, for scaring me when he was drunk, but now I realize I hate him only because he left me before I could say "I love you."

FROM THE TEMPER LOG:

"I told Caitlin that I am trying to control my temper because I don't want to frighten her and Lianna and Michaela. Last night, she angered me because she didn't want to go to bed, but I tried to put myself in her shoes and realized she was worried because Mommy wasn't home yet. So I lay down with her until she fell asleep.

"It's a balancing act, I see now, between my needs and theirs. Sometimes mine will have to take precedence. And sometimes, like last night when Caitlin just wasn't ready to sleep because she was afraid, I have to let the anger go and focus on what they need."

They read like confessions, these recitations of my outbursts, and the act of setting them down, however painful, has helped me. I've also gotten better, with my wife's help, at recognizing the flashpoints; like an early warning system, she can detect the first signs of a blow-up—the edge in my voice, my impatience with the bedtime-delaying antics of the children—and steer me clear.

I've finally begun to take her advice to just walk away, shut the door, go for a walk, without feeling guilty. Unlike, or perhaps because of, my father, I rarely drink. I talk about my temper with the kids. They know Daddy has a problem and he's working on it. I'd like to be able to say that I never lose my temper anymore, but I can't. Kids are constantly testing you, and often, I know now, they can inspire deserved anger.

The night my father broke my mother's rosary, my younger brother and I lay crying in our beds. The door opened, and light spilled in. In the placid cruelty of what passes for reason in a drunk's mind, he told us, "Don't worry, boys, your mother and I are getting a divorce," which, of course, sent our wails even higher. There have been moments when I have remembered that scene, and the memory has checked me from saying something equally terrible to my own children huddled in their beds.

Even then, I knew that he was terrified of something, and now I see that my worst anger seems to come when I am most deeply afraid—about work, about money, about whether I will amount to anything or if I will die as he did, bitter and unfulfilled. I don't want my children to remember me the way I remember my father, as this looming, frightened man.

"At every corner," the poet Robert Lowell wrote, "I meet my father, my age, still alive." The other morning, the barber who cuts my hair stood behind me with an oval mirror to show off his handiwork. I found myself looking at the same bald spot on the back of my head that I used to stare at from the back seat of our family Ford, when my father was at the wheel. There are mornings when I wake up afraid and wonder: How many mornings was he afraid? How many nights was he squeezed to the break-ing point?

I meet my father now in the dark of my children's bedroom, hearing in my shouts the echoes of his rage, the legacy of anger passed from father to son. As our children have grown from cribs to their own beds, I have begun to hear myself in their outbursts: temper tantrums from the oldest, impul-sive slaps from the youngest. Rivers of rage run from one generation to an-other, and it may be impossible to staunch the flow. But I have to keep trying. One breakfast, one bedtime, one day at a time.

STUDENT CASE HISTORY: ——— WRITING TO PERSUADE— ——— EMMA TOBIN

....

HOW I WROTE MY ESSAY

EMMA TOBIN

It all started with a letter. Donald Murray wrote to me one day, asking if I'd be interested in writing a piece for the new edition of his book *Write to Learn.* Thrilled by this proposal, I immediately responded with an enthusiastic "yes."

Don asked me to come up with a list of topics and a somewhat sketchy outline for each. Really having no idea what I wanted to write about, this proved to be harder than it at first sounded.

It took a while, but I did get a list. The topics included: comparing gay and lesbian rights to other minority groups' rights, animal rights, how contemporary music affects teens, rock musicals, and age discrimination on the Internet.

A few days later I got an "OK" from Don to go ahead on any of these topics, but he was leaning toward the one on age discrimination on-line—mostly because all the communication we had done was on the computer. I considered this. I had written a more developed paragraph outlining what I would write about on this particular topic, and I felt I would be able to continue writing about it. So I did just that; I had my topic.

I'm an Internet user from pretty far back. I use it for research, communication with friends, and, yes, I do go into chat rooms more than I probably should. But it's from being in these chat rooms that I've noticed the incredible amount of discrimination that goes on. There is almost always someone who is hating someone else about something. It can be anywhere from one fourteen-year-old who is trashing another for being a skateboarder or an entire chat room ganging up on one individual for being a different race. But whatever it is, it's almost always there, in one form or another.

I had lots to say the first time I sat down at the computer to begin writing my paper . . . maybe a little too much. After about a half-hour of furiously pounding away at the keyboard, I finally stopped, looked back, and realized I had three pages filled with jumbled opinions, terrible spelling, some random punctuation, and not a single paragraph. This, I realized, was definitely NOT my essay.

I made several more lame attempts at starting a draft on this topic, until I sat back, realized this wasn't working, and took a new approach. I probably wouldn't have come to this conclusion so quickly if it weren't for Don, actually. After e-mailing him all of my first attempts, he told me that, while I did have good ideas, they were totally disorganized and not very well focused. Organization has never been a strong point for me, but I was determined to improve.

Don's advice to organize my thinking got me sitting down in front of the screen the next day with a plan just to write a good, solid lead. And that's what I did. I wrote a clearly focused, organized lead, went back, edited it, spell-checked it, and saved it. "There," I thought. "There's the first part of my essay I will actually be able to use."

My paper progressed. I kept writing. I discussed every aspect of age discrimination I could think of. Problem was, I couldn't really think of a whole lot. Where it had seemed that I had a lot of ideas on the topic in my original outline and in my first writing attempts, when I actually decided to get organized, there didn't seem a whole lot to say. I only got about three pages. Dead end. From that point on, I could not think of one, single thing to add, and the only thing I could think to blame was my topic. It was time, I realized, for sane reconsideration.

It was then, in my first exasperated stage, that I came to an on-line article about the law that the government had passed but that had been blocked by the courts in 1996. The law would have made it impossible for teens under eighteen to access a lot of information on the Internet. This, quite honestly, outraged me. I consider myself an adult, and the fact that the government was going to keep one from ANYTHING on-line had me furious. (But also a little thankful because I then had more to add to my piece.)

The first draft was the most difficult. After discussing the law the government was working to pass, I ran out of ideas again and rambled my way through another couple of pages. But there were definite sections that were usable, definite paragraphs, sentences, words even that I liked. So even before I sent the first draft off to Don, I began making changes. I was so embarrassed in fact by my first full-length attempt that I decided to wait until I had a second draft complete to send along with the first, including a note that I knew the first one was not exactly up to par.

But even in the second draft, it again seemed that organization was the key problem. Nothing was in any kind of order that made sense. That's when I decided to come up with a detailed outline that I could follow for the whole essay. I already had the sections written, even if they were a little sketchy. But before I could work on improving them, I needed them to be in place.

Basically, my outline divided my paper into three sections, the first being "What are parents, teachers, and politicians doing to limit teenage [Internet] access?" The second was "Why they shouldn't limit teenage access, and what's wrong with the way some adults view teen Internet use." That was the section that needed the most revision. When I start going off about something I feel strongly about, there's really not much stopping me. I'll ramble for pages before I realize I'm doing it.

The third section was "What I'm proposing." It took me a while to get this one done. To be honest, I didn't know what I was proposing. I wasn't sure what I thought should happen in the end. I guess maybe if I were more sure from the beginning, the piece would have been easier to write.

The main thing I learned about while I was writing this essay was the importance of revision. I certainly did enough of it anyway. Something that I wrote that sounded good one day would sound awful to me the next. An opinion that I had at one point would seem outrageous to me later. I not only had to revise to make the writing better; I had to revise to make my actual opinions different. I kept changing my mind so often on so many issues that it really became difficult to revise my piece.

One thing I changed my opinion on fairly drastically was the issue of pornography on-line. I kept shying away from the topic to begin with. I didn't want to discuss it in a way that made me sound inhuman, just reciting facts and figures, but I also didn't want to get into too many details and make it too explicit. Finding a place in the middle was kind of difficult.

When I started writing this paper, I was sure it was hard to get pornography on-line if you were a teenager, though I really hadn't tried to find out. But when I actually began letting other people (besides Don) read my work, they would read that section, look at me critically, and say "Is that true? Isn't it easy to find pornography on-line?" I would tell them it was in fact true, hoping and hoping that I was right. One day I made the decision to find out for sure.

This is what I discovered: If you want pornography on-line, you can get it regardless of your age. That's when I had to almost totally rewrite that section of any paper. My position changed from "It's difficult to get porn," to "Most teenagers don't really spend their time doing that kind of thing on-line anyway." In general, this is true, but I feel I would have made a stronger point if pornography really WAS difficult to come by . . . which it's not.

The pornography issue definitely tested my revising skills. I was stretched to make a good point, where maybe there was not such a good point to make (or at least not a point in my favor).

It was around this time that I met with Don. Before now, we hadn't conferred in person, only on-line and on the phone. By then, he had read my first and second drafts, and he came to the conference prepared with a list of changes to be made. But, his were very open-ended suggestions. Nothing was "And this part should be more like this . . ." It was more like him telling me how to look for what didn't work, instead of showing me what he thought didn't work. It turned out that, in Don's opinion, my lead didn't work. It had consisted of a sort of sketchy picture of what a typical day for me on-line looks like. "This piece is about safety issues on-line," he said to me. "There has to be some element of danger. Some feeling that something COULD happen." It turned out that he was absolutely right. Conveniently, my second paragraph worked very well as a lead, with a few changes. So in the end, it turned out that the first thing I wrote that I thought could be used really couldn't be used at all.

After working through and reworking an entire essay more times than I can count, I came up with my "third draft" which was really more like my tenth. If I had printed it out and sent my piece to Don every time I made drastic changes, he would have gotten far too many drafts in the end. I was sure that this was it; I had finally produced an essay worth reading.

HOW I HELPED EMMA TOBIN WRITE *HER* ESSAY—DON MURRAY

I invited Emma Tobin to write a freshman English paper for me for entirely selfish reasons. I wanted to work directly with a student assigned to write a college freshman paper. I never expressed any doubts that she would do a good job, because I did not feel any. I found that most students see themselves—and their potential—reflected in the teacher's eyes. Confidence on the part of the teacher and writer is as important as confidence in the writer. Another word for this is *faith*. I had faith that Emma Tobin would produce a good paper.

Teachers who hold opposite views think that such confidence—the student is capable of good work until proven guilty of poor work—pampers the student, that the method is touchy feely. I disagree. My confidence that Emma would produce a publishable paper put extraordinary pressure on her.

I had two principal approaches I would apply that appear contradictory. First, I would give Emma a lot of room to teach herself. I wanted her to find her own subject so that she would be motivated to pursue it. I also wanted her to write *without* instruction so that I would not waste time teaching her what she already knew. I would, however, reinforce her natural writing abilities so that she would know she possessed those skills. Then I wanted to give her a chance to learn to write on her own, knowing that what she taught herself would be truly learned and would remain with her all her life.

I would be available to nudge, encourage, direct, support, rescue, stimulate during her own learning if necessary. When she produced a draft, I would respond with a candid, professional response that would encourage her to solve the problems I spotted in her own way.

She first showed me a long list of topics. Her first one seemed the most likely. It was better thought through, a significant topic that would interest readers of my textbook and could be completed in a few weeks. I nudged her toward this topic, revealing my interest in it, but emphasizing she had to make her own choice; she was the one who had to live with the topic.

Here is her proposal:

....

AGE DISCRIMINATION ON THE INTERNET

From my experience, the average person in a chat room is a teenager or young adult. Many of us spend more time on-line than adults, and understand how it works better than they do. But still, we are considered "the lower level being" on-line. For example, we are thought to be less intelligent, unimportant, even silly or annoying. Some adults even go so far as to imply or suggest that we "leave the area."

It's a type of discrimination that is not considered "bad" or "unkind" because the ageist person uses the excuse "I was young once too." By saying this, it means they believe that they have the right to dislike us, because they were in our place once. Ageism shows through in everyday life, but much more strongly on the Internet. I believe I could produce a good paper defending teens on-line, but taking the adults point of view, and trying to understand it.

Hands-off criticism can be frustrating for most students. They are used to being told exactly what to do, but instruction external to the piece often doesn't work. Each writing situation has its own context. The writing has its own focus, the point of view of the writer, its own meaning, and a specific form and order that carries that meaning to the intended audience. The writer doesn't just apply rules; the writer thinks, defining the subject and its writing and solving problems that vary with the writer, the writing task, and the writer's experience with the task. My job was to create an environment that gave Emma the confidence to discover and solve her own problems, certain I would be on hand if she needed me. We all know the basic model for teaching and editing: When a baby starts to walk, we hold out our hands close enough to help, far enough to encourage—and we laugh when the baby falls, cheer when it doesn't, and keep increasing the distance. I gave Emma room, hid my impatience, and waited while she wrote several drafts before she gave me one.

Now I had to give her a professional response. I read the draft quickly and phoned her that it was good but needed work and we made a date to get together. Then I read the draft carefully, doing some line-by-line editing on page two. I did not want to "correct" the entire piece because I would make it mine, and it was her subject and her language. I wanted to show her what I would do but make it clear she had to find her own way to solve the problems I saw in the piece.

Here is her draft:

···

TALKING TO STRANGERS OR AT-RISK ON-LINE? TEENS IN CYBERSPACE

It's been a long day, and I drop into the chair in front of the screen with relief. Point-and-clicking my way through folders and files, I find what I am looking for right where I know that it would be. After following seven "quick and easy" steps, I hear the familiar voice.

"Welcome. You have mail!" No surprise. Clicking into the mail center, I open my personal America On-line "mail box" to reveal the list of letters that await me . . . all twenty-four of them. No joke. Scanning the list, I figure out that only about ten of them are real or of any importance to me, and the rest are junk mail: "Make a million dollars in six months!" "Lose ten pounds a week!" I quickly delete them.

After responding to letters from friends I've met off- and on-line, I head my way into "Instant Novelist" to get some feedback on my latest short story. I have four responses; three please me, one doesn't. After a moment of consideration, I decide to tell "Mr. Critical" just what I think of his latest story. I quickly type up my thoughts and post them for him to find later. I've had enough of this for one day, and almost without even looking at the screen, I have myself into a chat room—"Lobby 216"—within seconds. I settle back to chat.

And so goes another average day on AOL.

HOW ADULTS PERCEIVE AND
RESPOND TO TEENAGE INTERNET USE

A newspaper article headline jumps out at me from the page. "Girl Kidnapped from Home by Internet 'Romeo.'" Immediately dropping the comic I was just starting, I turn my attention to the story. . . . Same old stuff. Thirteen-year-old girl leaves her home willingly with a strange man she met online. Girl is underage, becomes sexually active, police get notified by parents, strange Internet guy gets found, girl returns home, admits she made a stupid choice. Story ends with parents saying the problem is solved because their daughter "No longer has Internet access."

This type of story convinces many non-Internet using adults that the Internet is not safe for their kids. Right there is a huge reason why parents don't want their kids hanging out unsupervised on-line. They believe that they are going to get molested or sexually harassed by some screwed up forty-year-old guy lurking on the Net. And if they have no other way of knowing what the Internet is like, then they will become certain that it is a dangerous or risky place for their children to be.

Now I mark up this page.

Pornography. ~~The word certainly catches your attention, doesn't it? It's also a word~~ comes up ~~fairly~~ often in discussion of teens and the Net. Even

I cut here to show Emma how to get out of the way of the text. She was running around, waving her arms, calling attention to herself, getting between the reader and the text. I find that I only have to do this a few times for the writer to understand.

adults who don't worry that teens will encounter sexual predators on-line worry that they will be exposed to inappropriate and disturbing images and information.

I wrote in the margin: "Good direct sentence." It is important to point out what works as well as what doesn't yet work.

Finally, there are some adults who think of the Internet as a big computer or video game which teens waste their time and energy on.

I wrote: "Good but that's another point," followed by some words I can't translate. My bad handwriting was an asset; my students had to figure out what I meant. They had to think.

So what actions are these adults taking to limit teenage access to the net?

In the margin I wrote, "Let's discuss rhetorical sentences." Inexperienced writers try to make a connection with the reader in this way but it doesn't work. The questioner knows the answer. It is insulting. Questioner doesn't listen to answer. Nurse: "We want to take our shot don't we."

Many kids and teens whose families own computers are not ~~even~~ allowed to use chat rooms or the World Wide Web when there are no parents home. Some parents ~~even~~ insist ~~that~~ they sit by the computer and supervise their kids.

I cut some unnecessary words and suggested she start a new paragraph below.

The other place where a large population of teens can use the Internet is at school. ~~Many schools across the country have net access so students can use it for research on the Web and for communication with other classrooms in other schools. Of course, teens could get themselves into the same kind of situation just as easily at school as they could at home. This being what teachers~~ [*I inserted*] BECAUSE OF CYBERFEAR ~~students have~~ many schools limited access, ~~and many schools~~ block all chat room use completely, and strictly ~~limit~~ control [?] Web use.

Here I wrote: "Let's talk about transitions—not needed if information is in the right place."

~~These are some of the reasons that parents and teachers don't want kids on the Internet, but it goes to an even higher level than that I~~ In 1996 the state of Pennsylvania passed a law, the Communications Decency Act, that would make it illegal for any one under eighteen to obtain or access anything online that is considered offensive.

I wrote: "Develop. Clarify."

That obviously includes sexual images and sexual text. Fortunately for teens across America, the law was challenged,

"What was challenged?"

argued before the Supreme Court in the spring of 1997, and eventually overturned. But this does not mean that the government is through. The law was not adopted because the court thought that it was too vague. ~~It is safe to assume that I~~ In the near future, HOWEVER, a more specific law ~~will~~ MAY be proposed and passed in other states.
~~The point is that~~ Adults are making decisions to limit Internet access to teens . . .

I did not mark up any more pages, but I did give her the following written response, telling her these were just suggestions:

Response to Emma Tobin's draft, August 21, 1997

As I said in the e-mail last night I am glad you are doing this. We have something to work on. I am going to give this a professional, line-by-line reading, and I will be specific about what I think needs to be done. I think it is important for me to be directive at this time. But I want you to have room to disagree, to solve the problems in your own way. I want to be clear so you will understand my concerns but I do not want to be dictatorial.

As I used to tell my students, this kind of careful response is a compliment. Most drafts, my own included, do not deserve this attention.

I will have marked the draft in spots to show how I might do it. Do it your own way.

1. *Title.* You're getting there, but I think it will be helpful if you sharpen the title with some tension or at least an implied conflict.

   Why Parents Should Fear Cyberspace

   Why Should Mom and Dad NOT Fear Cyberspace?

   Should Mom and Dad Fear Cyberspace?

   Should Cyberspace Be Off Limits for Teens?

   Is ~~Parents'~~ Mom and Dad's Cyberfear Justified?

   Is Cyberfear Justified?

   Are Teenagers at Risk in Cyberspace?

   Play with some more as a focusing device, trying to get to the central issue in as few words as possible. This is too important to be taken seriously: Play.

2. *Lead.* The lead is well-written but it would not compel me to read on. Nothing happens. If that's your message, the reader has to go on with the fear that something may happen. The first paragraphs may be scaffolding, what you needed to write to get to the lead, and it may be a scene you can use later to allay fears about cyberspace.

   Your lead may be in paragraph beginning "A newspaper ~~article~~ headline jumps ~~out at me~~ off the page: "Girl Kidnapped . . .""

3. *Orwell's pane of glass.* Get out of the way of the information. This is hardest to learn, but you are right on the verge of learning it. Let the information speak. George Orwell said, "Good writing is like a window pane." You should see the subject, not the author.

   I'll point out what I mean on page two. Good writers always do what you do, writing about what you are going to say. You'll learn just to say it.

   You have to write with authority, in specific terms with specific evidence.

4. *Answer the reader's questions.* Anticipate the questions the reader will ask and answer them when they ask them.

5. *Line-by-line editing.* When your draft is finished—you have your topic, a sequence or order that carries the reader from point-to-point, and you have provided evidence for each point—then you should read line-by-line:

Are my nouns specific?

Are my verbs active?

Are my sentences, sentences—usually subject-verb-object?

Is each word the right word?

Is everything clear to an uninformed, intelligent reader?

Is my voice clear and tuned to support what I am saying the way a movie score supports the action?

Have I emphasized what is important, usually placing the most important information at the end or the beginning of the paragraph or section?

Do I move fast enough to keep the reader reading, slow enough to allow the reader to absorb what I have said?

Have I given the reader enough or too much information?

Do I break tradition only when it's necessary for clarity or emphasis?

Also, I gave Emma the George Orwell and Will Strunk quotations cited on page 183 and page 184.

Here is her final article:

WHY TEENS SHOULD BE ALLOWED IN CYBERSPACE

Emma Tobin

A newspaper article headline jumps off the page. "Girl Kidnapped from Home by Internet 'Romeo.'" Immediately dropping the comic I was just starting, I turn my attention to the story . . . Same old stuff. Thirteen-year-old girl leaves her home willingly with a strange man she met on-line. Girl is underage, becomes sexually active, police get notified by parents, strange Internet guy gets found, girl returns home, admits she made a stupid choice. Story ends with parents saying the problem is solved because their daughter "No longer has Internet access."

This type of story convinces many non-Internet-using adults that the Internet is not safe for their kids. They are convinced that their children are going to get molested or sexually harassed by some screwed up forty-year-old-guy lurking on the Net. And if they have no other way of knowing what the Internet is like, then they will become certain that it is a dangerous or risky place for their children to be.

Of course, there are other reasons why parents might limit their teenagers' access to the Internet. Some think of computers the way they think of video games or television--as a giant waste of time and energy. But for the majority of parents, it is pornography that dominates their thinking about teenagers and the Internet. Even adults who don't worry that teens will encounter sexual predators online worry that they will be exposed to inappropriate and disturbing images and information. For this reason, many kids and teens whose families own computers are not allowed to use chat rooms or the World Wide Web when there are no parents home. Other parents insist they sit by the computer and supervise their kids.

Teens have even less on-line freedom at school. Many classrooms and libraries across the country have Net access so students can use it for research and for communication with other classrooms in other schools. But teachers and librarians worry that teens could get themselves into the same kind of situation just as easily at school as they could at home. Because of cyberfear, many schools limit access, block all chat room use completely, and strictly control Web use.

Many politicians have the same idea: In 1996 the United States Congress almost unanimously passed and President Clinton signed the Communications Decency Act, a law that, among other things, criminalizes "the use of any 'interactive' computer service to 'see' or 'display in a manner available' to a person under eighteen any communication that 'depicts' or describes, in terms patently offensive as measured by contemporary community standards, sexual or excretory activities or organs" ("Complaint," 2). Fortunately, for teens across America, the law was challenged, argued before the Supreme Court in the spring of 1997, and eventually overturned. But this does not mean that the government is through. The law was not adopted because the court thought that it was too vague and that limited adults' freedom of speech. In the near future, however, more specific laws limiting teenage access to information on the Internet may be proposed and passed.

Adults are making decisions to limit Internet access to teens partially out of a misunderstanding of what the Internet has to offer and partially out of an overreaction to sensational stories they've read or heard. Most of these adults just don't have a realistic idea about how most teens spend their time on-line and about what are the relative dangers of an on-line life.

Let's start with the risk of sexual molestation and kidnapping. Even if we admit that there is some risk of meeting a dangerous sexual predator online, is this danger greater than the one teens face every day in "real life"? This same parent who won't let a child go into a chat room may let a son or daughter walk to the convenience store two blocks away, where their child may not just talk to a child molester through a screen, but actually encounter one. When looking at the things that can happen to kids and teens on the Internet, some adults seem to forget that these same--or much worse--things can happen off the Internet just as easily. There are dangerous people in the world; there are people on the Internet. Therefore, you are going to end up with some dangerous people on the Internet. It is fine for parents to take that into account, but they need to understand that most Internet interactions are positive and completely safe.

Of course, that's not the impression you get from reading newspapers or magazines. For example, a 1997 People magazine story described case after case of teenagers who left their homes to meet up with on-line correspondents. If you read the piece carefully, you see that a majority of the stories were about teens who met up with other teens who turned out to be perfectly safe and friendly. Of course, there were also some stories of teens who met up with middle-aged sexual predators, but in those cases, is the Internet to blame? It's really just juveniles making unwise, uninformed decisions. When a person goes somewhere on their own will, it does not mean that they were kidnapped. Teenagers can make a bad decision to leave home with someone they meet in person just as easily as with someone they meet on-line. Something is definitely wrong in these cases, but the Internet is not the source of the problem. Teenagers who have a desire to run away with someone they have never met must already have a pretty good motive for wanting to leave home.

Adults who want to limit teen use of the Net because of the easy access to pornography also have several misleading beliefs--that pornography is forced on children, that teenagers spend all of their time surfing erotic Web sites, and that older teens would be as traumatized by sexual material as young children are. There is no denying that pornography is available on the Net. There are hundreds or even thousands of Web sites featuring explicit photographs, videos, and stories ranging from soft-core erotica to hard-core child pornography. And even though a teenager has to go through an "age check" and waiver statements to enter most of these Web sites, pornography is pretty easy to get your hands on, if one chooses to do so. But "chooses" is the key word there. When one does end up with sexual content, it is almost always deliberate. You could erase every letter or ad that porn sites send out, you could simply not reply to any on-line users who are looking for someone who wants to "trade pics" (send and receive pornographic pictures), and you could leave any chat area where the topic is sex. If you did not go out of your way to get pornography, you probably never would.

But pornography is not the reason most teenagers go on-line most of the time. While some teens spend some of their on-line time looking at porn, the average seventeen-year-old doesn't come from school, sit at their computer, and start searching for pornographic pictures. Some adults seem to believe that since there is access to pornography on-line that every teenage person in the entire world is going to do all they can to get to it and is going to end up using the computer for nothing else.

But let's assume that some teenagers are spending most of their on-line time viewing pornography. We could still ask what harm is taking place? Is there any evidence that proves that teenagers are hurt by talking about sex with other teenagers in chat rooms or by looking at pictures of naked people on Web sites? Many teens are actually having sex themselves. One would think that if a person could actually have sex, then they could write or read about it. Same thing with pictures. If a teenager has seen (or done) off the Net all the things they see on it, then the Internet is not the problem.

The law that Congress tried to pass in 1996 would keep a person under eighteen from getting their hands on anything even vaguely related to sex. If an eighteen-year-old person can vote, serve in the armed forces, and drive, then certainly a seventeen-year-old can surf the Net. In fact, many seventeen-year-olds are sexually active, some are married, most have jobs, and some are freshmen in college. If our culture gives teens the freedom and responsibility to do adult things, then it's ridiculous to deny them full access to everything on the Internet.

If the Communications Decency Act had been adopted, then it could have been illegal for some teenager to get information on AIDS and HIV, because it is sexual material. It could have been illegal for a homosexual teenager to get any information that they may not feel comfortable asking someone for in person. It could have been illegal for a pregnant teen to get information about pregnancy or abortion. Teens suddenly would have been cut off from a whole world of valuable information.

Let's imagine there is a fifteen-year-old girl named Ann who has just had her first sexual experience. And let's say that she soon begins to worry that she may be pregnant or may have picked up a sexually transmitted disease. Let's assume that she doesn't want to talk to either of her parents about it or anyone at all, for that matter. The thought of going to a doctor or to Planned Parenthood has her terrified, so she looks into the only anonymous source she knows: the Internet.

If the 1996 law had not been overturned, Ann would find once she was on-line that she might not be able to get access to any information on STDs or pregnancy or AIDS. There would be barriers to "protect" her from this information. While adults may think that they are helping Ann by denying her this information on-line, I do not think they understand how wrong they are. Of course, this is exactly the kind of argument that the plaintiffs in the Supreme Court case made to overturn the law. Groups including Planned Parenthood, the Queer Resource Directory, ACLU, and American Library Association all argued that teens have a need for as well as a constitutional right to this information.

The other problem with adults' perceptions of the Internet is that they not only point out everything that's wrong and exaggerate those points, they also seem to ignore all of the good things that the Internet has to offer teenagers. For example, you never see a story written up on the thirteen-year-old girl who puts out a newsletter every month on animal rights. Or an article on how two fourteen-year-old kids meet twice a week to discuss poetry. And you'll never see anything on the sixteen-year-old boy who has started his own successful graphic design business on the Net. You only see the stories of destruction the Internet has caused.

And what about that side of teenage Internet use that no one could have a problem with: the academic side. It's eleven o'clock at night. You have a paper due the next morning. Frantic for information on the Spanish Armada, you turn to the Internet. There in front of you is an encyclopedia article, plus many other write-ups. You take the notes and produce a good paper without setting foot inside a library. Now, of course, I am not saying this is the best way to get a paper written. One should look in many places and sources of information for a well-rounded piece. But it is a life-saving way to get something done when you have no time. And even when you do have the time, the Internet is an excellent source. They will have information on all the aspects of what you're looking for. What could be better?

Some adults believe that there is no educational side to chat rooms such as those found on America On-line. Totally wrong. Just to get the basics out of the way first, there is really no better way to learn typing than being in an interactive conversation where you have to respond quickly, or your chatting partner will quickly be bored with you. One learns how to argue maturely and effectively and how to relate to people through the written word. Then we come to chat rooms that are especially designed for learning, such as AOL's "Thinkers," a room for pondering life--or really--whatever else is on your mind. Next are chat rooms where you are able to work one-on-one with a teacher on the subject you need help with. Many times I have tackled complicated math work I never thought I could do using someone I found on the Internet as my tutor. The flow of information coming from the Internet is endless. There are so many sides to it, so many possibilities.

For someone like me who has a great interest in writing, the Net has been incredibly enriching. For instance, through AOL's "Instant Novelist" site, I have had a chance to be part of a writing community. You can respond to anything you read, both positively and negatively. When you post a story of your own, it is read by hundreds of little editors across the country, all there to help you improve your work. Many participants develop e-mail relationships with fellow on-line writers. I, personally, do not see one thing that could be considered dangerous about this and most other Internet sites. What I do see are a million ways to learn, to find useful information, and to connect to other people.

When ten-year-old children wind up with pornography in their grasp, we have a problem. But when seventeen-year-old young adults are not allowed access to information that they may need for their education and even health, then we have another problem. Many schools, government agencies, and computer companies are all working now to develop guidelines and new technology to keep kids away from dangerous material on the Internet without limiting adults' freedom to information. Parents can buy "smut-blocker" software, like "Cyper Patrol" or "Net Nanny," which restricts and records a child's use of the Internet. And libraries can now buy Web software and search engines that keep children "from turning up unwanted risqué sites while looking for information on that report on The Chile Pepper through History" (Powers, 2).

But as Boston Globe columnist Ellen Goodman has said, the key is to "protect children, without shackling adults." And, in this area, teens ought to be treated as adults. Parents, teachers, and politicians have a good motive: protecting young people from the dangers of the Internet. But they need to step back and distinguish between children and teens. Again, if a seventeen-year-old can work, drive, and attend college (not to mention, have sex and even have children), how can you keep full access to the Internet off that list?

WORKS CITED

Electronic Privacy Information Center, "Complaint," U.S. District Court, Eastern District of Pennsylvania, Civ. No. 96–963, http://www.epic.org./free_speech, p. 2.

Goodman, Ellen. "'The Boston Solution' to Pornography on the Internet," Boston Globe, July 24, 1997.

Powers, Kate. "DO YOU Know Where Your Children Are Surfing?" Parent Soup: Family and the Internet, http://www.parentsoup.com.

Rogers, Patock. "Snared By the Net," People 48, No. 6, August 11, 1997: 48–53.

STUDENT CASE HISTORY: WRITING TO INFORM—TINA WINSLOW

The research paper is the fundamental building block of academic discourse—and it is the composition assignment most dreaded by the students who have to write research papers and the instructors who have to read them. Most research papers are dull, because the students have not yet done research on a topic important to them and the form becomes more important than the message.

Yet students need experience in gathering information, building the information into a significant meaning, and presenting it so that the reader not only understands the message but has access to the sources of information the writer used.

Tina Winslow demonstrates that a student can prove a knowledge of academic research conventions while writing a lively, interesting report that places scholarly material in a human context.

Her assignment was to "Inform readers by completing a five- to ten-page [1,500–2,500 word] research report that will demonstrate your ability to use scholarly techniques to investigate a topic and reveal its significance to them."

She was told to keep a journal that would reveal her writing problems and how she solved them. The student was given time to find a territory, then a topic, sharpening her research question in consultation with the instructor and classmates, then to write several drafts. She was to have at least a dozen sources with footnotes and a bibliography that follows Modern Language Association guidelines. Tina was also referred to the "Tips on Writing to Inform" (pp. 000–000).

The case history shows how she moved from the vague and general to the specific, finding a way to combine several aspects of her topic so that the final article had a clear, documented focus. She moved toward this clarity of vision while achieving an increasing grace. Her work is a demonstration of good thinking as well as good writing, as all effective prose should be.

In her journal she first brainstormed (pp. 277–283) on animal rights looking for a focus line (pp. 278–279) that contained enough tension to spark a research report:

- Animal rights--where is the line?
- Who decides whose rights get to be violated--the chemical industry at odds with the natural order or is it the natural order?
- Would people buy the products if they saw the process it goes through?
- Do animals have rights--historical/religious implications--meat industry--health implications
- Pumping poultry, beef with hormones
- Is the meat industry lying about the health requirements and how far down the line does it go?
- Feel passionately about not eating meat without bias, why?
- No meat has helped achieve my goals to trim down--why? What does meat do psychologically or physiologically that slims people?
- Moods are evened out--hormones in meat?
- No guilt with eating healthy, cheaper
- In small way have stopped poor treatment of animals
- Read a book that describes the process
- People live too much of their life with spurts of unrealistic violence or softened reality
- Would you enjoy chicken if you watched the man rip his feet off because the nails had grown around the bars of the cage back into his feet?

This is an excellent way to begin. Tina doesn't worry about the writing, she is scouting the territory to find a way into her subject, and the journal entries show her ranging across the whole area, looking for the most important material—the material she needs to explore and that her reader needs to know. Her final topic is deeply hidden in her list, and the approach that makes her final paper distinctive does not appear. But this step was essential to her thinking process.

Now let us listen in as she continues talking to herself in her journal. Remember that the direction in which she thinks she is headed is not the direction in which she will go. Elizabeth Bowen said: "The writer . . . sees what he did not expect to see . . . . Inattentive learner in the schoolroom of life, he keeps some faculty free to hear and wonder. His is the roving eye. By that roving eye is his subject found. The glance, at first only vaguely caught, goes on to concentrate, deepen; becomes the vision." In Tina's journal, we catch a rare but important glimpse of the writer in the act of thought, catching her unexpected vision.

JOURNAL

When I think about animal rights many issues shoot through my head. My two kitties waiting on my bed, waking up with a lazy stare that pretty much lays out the law--"You have the right to scratch my ears and why you are at it the bowl in the other room is a bit empty." Those are their rights but they are lucky cause I'm a sucker for a good mew and milk breath. Society's definition of animal rights extends more into our comfort zone as human beings. Not only my comfort zone about what I will use on my body but what goes into my body and the realities that went into mundane things I take for granted. My true experience in this issue began when my roommates a year or so ago were very much into the movement of animal rights. They were adamant about how cruel vivisection was and that it should cease immediately for all products. While I struggle as a compassionate human who has done volunteer work with animals to comprehend the exact reality of vivisection, which in essence needs a proper definition this issue becomes one of limits. Flipping in the handy Miriam-Webster the definition alone of vivisection bothers me inside--"the cutting of or operation on a living animal usually for physiological or pathological investigation" or worse, definition two, "animal experimentation especially if considered to cause distress to the subject." Who gave us the power to take that animal's life? Or worse keeping it alive to test it's reactions. I understand the theory that it's an us or them kind of world but in reality where people are just vain creatures how much does it matter if the deodorant and the makeup don't look just right or don't exist especially when everyone will not be wearing it. It's just a layer of protection anyway.

Tina's final paper will not focus on animal rights, but she needs to start here to find her ultimate focus. Her journal reveals the writer talking to herself, and what some people might describe as bad or sloppy writing is good writing here, appropriate to the task. It is courageous of Tina to allow us to see a good writer doing the rough, pre-draft writing that is essential but not usually revealed to a reader.

Let's listen further to Tina talking to herself. She is at once the appropriately floundering writer allowing her evolving text to carry her toward meaning and the draftsperson standing back and watching herself working. This split vision—being in the writing act and observing and standing back watching herself in the act—is essential for good writing.

The paper I want to write needs a focus line. Something that creates a tension. I think if you take the normal person who wasn't attacked by vicious dogs as a child and who was socialized with animals normally and show them the process from start to finish they will understand the brutality of the process. To take something living and breathing and warp it for our needs doesn't seem right. Do the end results, a juicy piece of chicken or tube of lipstick, really make the process OK? In a world filled with lawsuits on product liability, companies are scrambling to find proof that this product when accidently swallowed, poked in an eye or applied incorrectly won't adversely affect humans. If there is so much concern with humans why aren't humans used to test these results and why is there such a lack of concern with humans when their food is concerned. If they don't want to harm people why would they pump pesticides onto the eventual food of cows and poultry, pump hormones into animals for better growth, keep them in deplorable conditions and then wonder why Americans are getting fatter, madder and sicker. It all comes back to a basic respect for other things.

This paper will be about the realities involved in everyday products that involve animals. It could go two ways right now. With vivisection you have the brutality of pictures and there is a plenty of tension about it with animal righters and research industry. When I visited a pharmaceutical company my friend worked in she told me not to even joke about freeing the animals. They had them locked up in a special room you had to have four keys to get into. When I asked her why she didn't mind testing on them she was like well they throw poop on me and are mean but ultimately her argument was humans first, everything else "bah." She didn't realize that if someone put me in a cage and shot me full of drugs I would have a very similar reaction. Mean as spit and proud of it. The other direction of the paper could be on when we eat, what is the process of the food. The chickens and cows we eat aren't exactly running around the yard, they are chemicals through and through from the minute they are born.

Focus lines--potential:

Chemical food--what are we eating? Whose rights are they anyway?

Food industry--provider or killer?

In consultation with her classmates and a conference with her instructor, Tina came to realize she didn't really have anything new to say about animal rights but that she had strong feelings about her new decision to be a vegetarian, a decision that was tested on a cruise with her parents and confirmed two weeks later when her mother—a life-long meat eater—suffered a heart attack. Tina felt uncomfortable about using her personal feelings and her personal experience in a research paper but was encouraged to try to find a way to combine objective research information with personal experience.

Writing is often like a tunnel that is wide at the beginning but narrows as you follow it. Here you will see Tina as the tunnel narrows and she finds her focus and begins to work within it.

OK, focus line:

Solidifying Vegetarianism--the hard way. Or why I am still a Vegetarian today. Or Taming the Taco Urges.

But really the focus although it doesn't sound focused is that the after shocks of my Mom's heart attack solidified never eating meat again for me. I guess I need to trim it into a more readable state but basically this issue to me is like a spark to gasoline. For the record, when I shared this topic with my parents they were not exactly thrilled. To defend my mother, who really wants to know that an incident in her life scared everyone down to their belief foundations. To defend my father, well he just likes to argue. Basically, he wants to vent that you can't be a vegetarian for purely health reasons because he believes that you can be unhealthy, heartwise, and eat no meat. For instance, chicken and turkey and low fat/cholesterol meats can be eaten and still be healthy or did you hear the one about the vegetarian who died of a heart attack. He maintains you are a vegetarian for ethical--not health reasons. My point for my focus is that although I was a brand new vegetarian before the heart attack (Wait till I tell you the taunts that a week cruise with my family brought me a week and a half before my mother's run in with her arteries), the material I read after the scare solidified that I will never again put meat in my mouth. I guess the ethical part is there as back up but after what I learned I see meat and the industry as killers and beyond that totally unnecessary.

(Title)

- Momma, Me, and Meat
- Scaring the Meat out of Me
- Meat Stinks
- A Tube in the Nose Is Meat out of Me
- Vegetarians Unite
- You Don't Get a Chest Pain Eating Broccoli (Unless You Swallow a Stalk)
- Reeducation of My Mouth and My Mom
- Liar, Liar Heart on Fire
- If It Had a Mother I Won't Eat It--Mom
- Moo Cow and Then Shoo
- You Don't Have to Beat Me with a Carrot to Make Me Give Up Meat
- Thicken Your Clogged Arteries with Lies

(Lead)

Understand what will stop me from ever putting meat in my mouth again, was my mother in an ICU bed after her heart attack.

• • •

Well that's part of it. But after reading up on heart attacks and what they are about, I realized she didn't have to be in that bed and that keeps me focused in my non-meat eating habits.

• • •

(Lead-2)

Nothing made being a vegetarian easier than realizing that my mother having a heart attack didn't have to be a reality.

(Trail)

- mother has heart attack
- already a vegetarian but very new
- in learning more about heart attacks read book after book which detailed what meat is and what it isn't both from heart aspect as well as healthy living aspect
- realization it's a lie--meat industry
- based on what it does to your body, what is in it and the benefits of other types of protein--meat stinks
- I realize this isn't an ethical attack on meat eater's way of life but I personally feel betrayed

(End)

You don't have to not eat meat to be heart healthy but after realizing what goes into the process and how close you are to being a vegetarian why would you eat meat.

(Possible first paragraph)

Through the mist that are tears unshed, I look wildeyed at my mother in an ICU bed with slightly green, thick tubes in her nose. ICU has no room for deep personal talks with the doors flung wide open and everyone's heart-beeps beating loud enough for the staff behind the desks to hear. Her nails are purple as well as her lips. She looks an off color like someone walked in and sucked the oxygen out of her skin. Pale and tired, with wide brown eyes, she pleads with me not to be scared--it's just a minor life threatening procedure.

Good writing is promiscuous; writers do not write one draft but many. We do not have the space to show each of Tina's drafts, but we can listen to her journal as she reacts to completing her first draft.

OK, the first rough draft is out. It's weak in some areas admittedly but I feel better having the thoughts in a rough diving board for better work. I just hate, hate, hate showing other people work that I don't consider finished. The hardest part for me in this critique sessions is admitting that I have to write just like everyone in stages and that the first things out of my typewriter/computer look just like everyone else's. I guess I want to be brilliant and perfect on the first shot. "BULLS EYE! the crowd roared as they tossed the first draft writer roses." But alas, I need more work on the quotations and the integration of paraphrases not to mention documentation style at this early stage is enough to make MLA come out and personally tweak me on the nose. But at least I have exorcised the demons onto paper at this point all while on Tylenol for sinus and cold.

Better flow and tighter in beginning paragraphs, Smoother flow in Paragraph 2. More quotes, direct in Paragraph 3, check for logic flow LOGIC FLOW in paragraph 4 with more sources, more sources and another quote or two. Summary needs more bite.

So . . . round two is done but I have to cut cut cut.

• • •

I guess I am going to have to cut the chemicals paragraph but I do this under duress.

It was not cut. She found a way to keep it in the piece by making it support her focus on why vegetarianism is important to health. Later, in her journal, Tina debates a cut her peer readers suggested. Ultimately the decision has to be the writer's but she expresses the insecure response to a critical suggestion that is natural in a writer.

I like that paragraph, I feel it has merit and geez, it grosses me out and I wrote the thing. I was hoping to get my punch in quick and well I guess as a being with somewhat rational thought I realize it doesn't fit in with the mom-had-a-heart-attack motif. I really like the mixture of personal vignettes mixed in with writing of a more research nature. I find it really interesting the process this had been. I started out with animal rights and have it nuzzled, pushed and CUT it down to just vegetarianism.

For next draft:

- Finish getting the references pinned down to MLA style
- Re-arrange the chemical paragraph out of the paper and work out the flow
- Go through with a fine tooth grammar comb and get all of it laying down without obvious cowlicks (pun intended)

A complete case history would reproduce draft after draft, and space prohibits reprinting each one of them. Also, it would probably be boring to all but the most interested students. The important element in the process is the astonishment expressed by the writer in her journal at what she has written, discovering that writing is not recording previous thoughts but thinking by writing. Her understanding of the subject changes as she captures and clarifies meaning through language. This is the most important lesson of her writing course.

Man, oh, man. Whew! Done, finis, end of papyrus! OK, so I feel guilty at being relieved that I'm done with the paper. It is not what I would have conceived at the beginning but it wound it's way down the paper trail to completedom. I wanted a paper that bit and nickered at lies and then spit it out in a huge cavalcade of burning all consuming truth. What I got was a paper that resembled "What I Did over the Summer" tone with a vegetarian twist.

Now, now, I can hear that voice now. (How come this voice always resembles my mother's voice?) "If you aren't happy with the paper then change it." The truth is I will never be happy with the paper. I can put it in my treasure box and dig it up 10 years from now and say (in my knowing and critical tone, of course) "This seems so pedantic and stiff," "What was I trying to say here?"

"Why did I pick that word or phrase?" Hopefully, buried in that chest is also my good critic who reads it and nods her head and whispers, "Because that's where you were. The paper is done I can look at it and see the legitimate course it took. I started off worried by what I would write, how to say it perfectly, WHERE AM I GOING TO FIND THE TIME and now I can look at it and realize I created something.

> *Each of Tina's drafts clarified what she had to say and allowed her to say it in with increasing liveliness and fluency. At first, she wrote each paragraph separately, moving the information to a position that answered the reader's questions. Then she had to consider the pace and proportion: How much of her mother? How much research information? Throughout the process she had to listen to her peer readers and her instructor but make her own way.*
>
> *Compare the drafts of the lead in her journal with the final, disciplined example of good writing. She had to go from the bland statement of her first effort ("Understand what will stop me from ever putting meat in my mouth again, was my mother in an ICU bed after her heart attack.") to purple prose ("Through the mist that are tears unshed, I look wild eyed at my mother in an ICU bed with slightly green, thick tubes in her nose.") to the fine, professional beginning that moves the reader ("I look at my mother in the Cardiac Care Unit bed with pale green, plastic tubes in her nose.")*
>
> *In her first draft, Tina moved from her mother to this paragraph:*

Defining what a heart attack is, how it occurs and how to prevent it/takes research it's not as cut and dry as eating to much fatty fried stuff, arteries clogging and then the next moment you are grabbing your arm and clutching your chest calling for an ambulance as you go down. In essence, it is an artery clogging that causes heart attacks but as more and more research is done, it's about a whole lifestyle. Several papers can be written on the technical medical reasons behind a heart attack, why meat is morally wrong, what is wrong with the meat industry but the focus for this paper is on why eating meat and dairy products is unhealthy for the body. Every fork of meat and dairy product have harmful chemicals present, a meat and dairyless diet automatically trims weight off people and a vegetarian diet makes having a heart attack hard to do. Accordingly the premise that being a vegetarian while only one aspect of the whole heart attack chain reaction and still a controversial one, is one worth merit and consideration.

As Tina said in her journal, she is embarrassed at readers seeing her early drafts, but it is important for students who imagine that others write well the first time to observe how real writing emerges, draft after draft, until the final draft has this excellent paragraph:

The first step is to look at meat and dairy products for what they really are. Meat and dairy are primarily vehicles for fat and cholesterol. Most of the established health organizations, as well as the Surgeon General, recommend reducing the fat in your diet to 30 percent (Robbins, *May All* 89). Studies indicate that this number should be even lower to prevent cancer, strokes, diabetes, hypertension and heart disease risks, and to eliminate or drastically reduce cholesterol (Robbins, *May All* 89). But Dr. T. Colin Campbell, director of one of the most comprehensive and informative diet and health studies ever undertaken (Chen et al.) and on the committee that set the 30 percent guideline, states it would have been impractical to recommend less than 30 percent, as most people would have to drop the animal foods from their diet and go vegetarian (Robbins, *May All* 90).

Every piece of information, whether it comes from personal experience or library research, moves the meaning of the paper forward. The result is a moving, significant, well-documented research paper that both pleases and educates the reader. Here is her final draft:

....

TAKE A BITE OF LIFE

Tina Winslow

I look at my mother in the Cardiac Care Unit bed with pale green, plastic tubes in her nose. CCU has no room for personal whisperings with the doors flung wide and everyone's heartbeeps beating loud enough for the staff behind the desk to hear. Her nails are purple as well as her lips. She looks an off color as if someone sucked the oxygen out of her skin. Pale and tired, with wide brown eyes, she pleads with me not to be scared: it's just a minor lifethreatening illness.

The initial prognosis was a minor heart attack, which calmed everyone until the tests revealed three of her arteries were more than 65 percent blocked. This new prognosis, terrible and threatening, was the one thing that would force change into my Mom's life so dramatically and so thoroughly. Having married a Nebraska "meat and potatoes man" her response from the beginning was not one of compromise but rather pouty resistance to a new way of life forced upon her.

Even with a monitor recording her heartbeat she was upset by the chicken and pasta they gave her for lunch.

"It is so bland."

"Mom, you're in a hospital."

"But you think they could put some cheese on this stuff."

"Mom, you just had a heart attack."

I had just become a vegetarian shortly before my mother's heart attack and I discovered through the research I did--both before becoming a vegetarian and after my mother's heart attack--that a diet with no meat and dairy products automatically trims weight and reduces the chances of a heart attack. I also learned that a vegetarian diet prevents the harmful ingestion of chemicals that are present in meat and dairy products and provides a good defense against disease. With benefits like these, being a vegetarian seems the only logical choice for a healthy life.

The first step is to look at meat and dairy products for what they really are. Meat and dairy are primarily vehicles for fat and cholesterol. Most of the established health organizations, as well as the Surgeon General, recommend reducing the fat in your diet to 30 percent (Robbins, May All 89). Studies indicate that this number should be even lower to prevent cancer, strokes, diabetes, hypertension and heart disease risks, and to eliminate or drastically reduce cholesterol (Robbins, May All 89). But Dr. T. Colin Campbell, director of one of the most comprehensive and informative diet and health studies ever undertaken (Chen et al.) and on the committee that set the 30 percent guideline, states it would have been impractical to recommend less than 30 percent, as most people would have to drop the animal foods from their diet and go vegetarian (Robbins, May All 90).

Even chicken, the most common alternative consumers choose when trying to cut fat from their diet, derives 35 percent of its calories from fat and that's without the skin (PETA Guide 1). Beef, on the high end of the scale, has about 22 grams of saturated fat in an average 8-oz. serving (PETA Guide Compassionate Living 17). And as Dean Ornish points out in his book Reversing Heart Disease, "eating fat makes you fat" (255).

Why does eating vegetarian naturally cut weight and reduce the chances of a heart attack? According to Martin and Tenenbaum, authors of Diet against Disease, most of the fat we eat is in the form of meat and dairy products, so reducing our fat consumption in these areas will reduce the total fat and saturated fat in our diets (16). Conversely, vegetarian foods are primarily complex carbohydrates and are hard for your body to convert into fat (Ornish 257), so the less cholesterol you eat, the lower your risk of developing coronary heart disease (Ornish 263). As advised by the Physicians Committee for Responsible Medicine, a diet without meat and dairy products makes low cholesterol easy "since cholesterol is found only in animal products such as meat, dairy and eggs" (2). Your body also makes all the cholesterol it needs naturally so "it's the excessive amounts of cholesterol and saturated fat in the diet that lead to coronary heart disease" (Ornish 263).

Two months after becoming a vegetarian and two weeks before my mother's heart attack, my entire family went on a cruise. I guess on a cruise, where every meal is supposed to be about reckless abandon without regard to waist size, waste or what you're eating, a vegetarian feeling uneasy isn't going to be the most popular topic.

"What do you mean the French onion soup made you sick?"

"Mom, once you don't eat meat, your body gets used to not having it and I didn't think about French onion soup being made with beef broth."

"There is no way broth can make you sick."

My mom, looking concerned but unbelieving, eyed me suspiciously and tried to make light of it.

"Look, honey, I just ate a whole side of cow, tail and all and I'm fine. How can a soup broth made of beef make you sick?"

The vegetarian target on my forehead grew as my mother's tone drew my entire family's attention at the dinner table. That week spent with my family trapped on board a floating buffet table, just two weeks before my mother had a heart attack, was a study of open hostility at the mention of not eating meat or cheese. My mother--at the head of that committee--was unbelieving that meat could be so harmful. "My quirky daughter, what's next?" seemed to be the question asked without realizing she was less than fourteen days away from a full-blown heart attack--not realizing that it was also the same thing making us both sick.

But it is not just the fat and cholesterol we need to be aware of in meat and dairy products: "Most of us, with images in our minds of the cows of yesteryear, could hardly believe the extent to which the meat industry today relies on chemicals, hormones, antibiotics and a plethora of other drugs" (Robbins, Diet New America 109). The image of a cow chewing on grass in a field is an image of the past as is the pecking and scratching chicken of the barnyard, and the loving mother cow letting the farmer squeeze milk into the pail. They are all misconceptions of what meat and dairy consumers are actually internalizing each time they consume these products. Today's cows used for meat are fed a diet with the strict purpose of fattening them up the cheapest way possible (Robbins, Diet New America 110). "It is impossible to raise animals in intensive confinement without continual reliance on antibiotics, sulfa drugs and other substances" (Fund Facts 2).

Chickens are also fed a diet of chemicals to produce more fat and thus more profit. With "over 90% of today's chickens" fed arsenic compounds (Mason and Singer 56–58) and virtually every chicken raised in the United States being fed a diet of antibiotics, it is hard to believe chicken is being sold as a health food (Robbins, Diet New America 65). Furthermore, "up to 90% of federally inspected poultry is infected with salmonella bacteria" (PETA Guide 1). Chicken is not health food as presented to Americans everyday.

The ad campaign "Milk: It Does A Body Good" is also a lie. With the introduction of the Bovine Growth Hormone (rBGH), milk, cheese, butter, ice cream, yogurt and infant formula are now being contaminated without the U.S. Food and Drug Administration testing the long-term health effects on consumers (Vegetarian Voice 12). Furthermore, the FDA admits that "use of rBGH in cows may lead to increased amounts of pus and bacteria in milk" and that "powerful antibiotics and other drugs used to fight increased disease in rBGH-injected cows may lead to greater antibiotic and chemical contamination of milk and dangerous resistance to antibiotics in the human population" (Vegetarian Voice 12). And because these drugs present in these forms of meat and dairy products "form toxic residues in animal tissue, they pose a harm to human consumers" (Fund Facts 2). In other words, what they eat, you eat.

After her heart attack, I tried to help my mother understand the vegetarian lifestyle--which means no meat and dairy products of any kind.

"Tina, you can pick the chicken out."

"WHAT!? Mom, it's tortilla soup with shredded chicken not to mention it's in a chicken broth."

"Well it's got lots of vegetables in it. Maybe you can pick those out."

"It's OK, Mom, I'll just make a cucumber sandwich and be fine."

"But I did put in extra veggies for you."

"And for you, too, Mom, you get the benefits, too."

Since the heart attack she has resigned herself to retiring the Cooking Beef: A Recipe a Day cookbook and has even had lessons in low-fat cooking, but it hasn't occurred to her that as she moves away from fat and cholesterol she is also moving into vegetarianism. We are making progress, though. After realizing that fat and cholesterol make eating meat and dairy so bad for us, she also understands what makes them a double jeopardy for everyone.

Meat and dairy products add chemicals, saturated fat, and cholesterol to a diet. So what will vegetarian foods add to a diet? Beyond reducing fat and cholesterol as previously discussed, a diet without meat or dairy products will reduce cancer risks, reduce protein levels, and add fiber. A vegetarian diet higher in fiber than meat-based diets "helps to dilute, bind, inactivate, and remove many of the carcinogens and toxic substances found in our food supply" (McDougall 120). Due to these properties and other considerations involving fiber "a diet high in fiber helps prevent colon cancer as well as cancers of other parts of the body" (McDougall 120). "An additional benefit of a [vegetarian diet] is that it contains generous amounts of substances with 'anti-cancer' properties" (McDougall 128). Some of these include Vitamin A, Vitamin C, Vitamin E, and minerals. Thus a vegetarian diet, "complemented with vegetables and fruits, provides a multitude of overlapping mechanisms for preventing cancer and keeping us healthy" (McDougall 130).

According to Martin and Tenenbaum, "there is no known nutritional need for the amount of protein we eat" (27). Americans typically eat roughly twice the amount of protein as the Recommended Dietary Allowance sets for healthy people (Martin and Tenenbaum 27) and much of this protein comes in the form of meat and dairy products. Too much protein lowers the body's ability to naturally absorb calcium and "as surprising as it sounds, one major culprit in osteoporosis may be protein" (Barnard 19). Furthermore, high protein "intakes have been found to contribute to progressive kidney damage" (Barnard 24). Through eating more whole grains, fruits, and vegetables, which naturally reduces saturated fat--and maintains the same level of protein intake--an alteration in the ratio of animal to vegetable protein inevitably will occur" (Martin and Tenenbaum 26). The shift allows more reasonable protein intake without the fat.

I couldn't believe it. My mother was defending my beliefs to my aunts. It was a humorous and satisfying scene.

"Tell them, Tina, what is that Bovine Hormone thing you were telling me about. GROSS, pus in my milk."

"Well, the milk farmers put . . ."

"And what about McDonald's cows eating the rain forests" she interrupted.

"See to support the cows used in . . ."

"And the chicken, Tina, tell them about cholesterol in chicken. The whole industry of meat has hoodwinked us all. It's all a mass market sell."

I know she hasn't eliminated meat entirely but I have watched her over the past four months gently guide herself and our family from taco salad, hamburgers, and sausage to red beans and rice, lentil soup, and other vegetarian meals as she discovers the hidden benefits of vegetarianism on her own.

The choice of a vegetarian lifestyle with all the perceived sanctimonious philosophy can be traced back to the simple fact that eating meat and dairy products is bad for you. A constant reminder to me is remembering someone I love with a monitor on her heart now sitting across from me laughing as she puts another bite of life into her mouth.

WORKS CITED

"Altered Bovine Hormone Makes Milk, Dairy Products Even Riskier." Vegetarian Voice 20.3 (1994): 12.

Barnard, Neil, M.D. Food for Life: How the New Four Food Groups Can Save Your Life. New York: Crown, 1993.

Chen, J., et al. Diet, Lifestyle, and Mortality in China: A Study of the Characteristics of 65 Countries. New York: Oxford UP, Cornell UP, and the China People's Medical, 1990.

Fund for Animals, The Fund Facts: Animal Agriculture Fact Sheet #2. Houston: Fund for Animals, 1992.

Martin, Alice A., and Frances Tenenbaum. Diet against Disease. Boston: Houghton Mifflin, 1980.

Mason, J., and P. Singer. Animal Factories. New York: Crown, 1980.

McDougall, John, M.D., and Mary McDougall. The McDougall Plan. Piscataway: New Century, 1983.

Ornish, Dean, Dr. Dr. Dean Ornish's Program for Reversing Heart Disease. New York: Ballantine, 1990.

The PETA Guide to Animals and the Meat Industry. Washington, D.C.: PETA, 1993.

The PETA Guide to Compassionate Living. Washington, D.C.: PETA, 1993.

Robbins, John. Diet for a New America. Walpole: Stillpoint, 1987.

Robbins, John. May All Be Fed: Diet for a New World. New York: Avon, 1992.

STUDENT CASE HISTORY: ———— WRITING TO ANALYZE— ———— JULIE SCHUM

Read the following student paper by yourself, ignoring my commentary, then read it with me as I demonstrate what a writer reads in the writing. It was written in an undergraduate course in critical analysis of literature for Dr. Brock Dethier when he was on the faculty at the University of New Hampshire. The student, Julie Schum, is a science major who wants to be a writer concentrating on science and environmental issues.

KATE'S RESISTANCE TO DOMINANCE BY PETRUCHIO IN *THE TAMING OF THE SHREW*

JULIE SCHUM

I had one strong response upon reading Kate's submissive speech at the end of Shakespeare's *The Taming of the Shrew:* I don't buy it.

This is an academic paper, an excellent literary research paper, but the writer's voice is established in the first sentence. The writer has a strong point of view and her own unique way of expressing it. I hear her voice as a promise of a strong and lively point of view.

Something seemed funny about the strong female character, who had been the star of Shakespeare's play, her scalding wit an equal match for any of the male characters', suddenly forsaking her independent nature and calling upon all women to become submissive to men. I didn't believe her. I wasn't convinced. Her words were telling me one thing, while her actions and the fact that hers is the voice delivering the critical and longest speech in the play seemed to contradict that message.

> *The author makes a statement, then immediately documents it. I sense an order that will take me through a reading of a play I haven't read in decades. I feel I will have a guide that will make each point clear and give me time to consider it.*

My reading of *The Taming of the Shrew* left me with the feeling that Shakespeare's purpose in the play was not to encourage men to dominate women and women to be submissive to their husbands. Shakespeare was dealing with an issue facing his audience at the time. The play seems to be a reflection of the cultural change from a time when women kissed their husbands' feet as part of the wedding ceremony to a time when many women chose not to marry and to speak up for themselves in the patriarchal society. To the audience of the 1590s, Kate's final speech would have sounded old-fashioned, possibly reminiscent of the good old days, but would not be interpreted as a message to women to be submissive or for men to abuse their women into submission.

> *The author puts her topic into literary, historical, and social contexts. I feel sure that she has something important to tell me and that she will satisfy my hunger for accurate, specific information that will stimulate my thinking.*

Lynda Boose points out in her article "Scolding Brides and Bridling Scolds," . . .

> *I'm relieved. This isn't just going to be the author's opinion off the top of her head. She is going to cite objective, scholarly authorities to support her position.*

. . . that Kate's statement,

> . . . place your hands below your husband's foot.
> In token of which duty, if he please,
> My hand is ready, may it do him ease" (V.2 176–178) . . .

> *Good. I do not have the play in front of me, but I am going to be given evidence from within the text so I can hear the lines and see if they support the writer's thesis.*

. . . is an allusion to an actual pre-Reformation marriage ceremony in which the bride must kiss her husband's feet in an act of submission and obedience, a ritual which was removed from the Book of Common Prayer in 1549.

> *The lines from the play are put in context. My guide through the piece— the author—is answering my questions as I ask them.*

Boose believes Shakespeare used the patriarchal, outdated reference in Kate's speech because, "on the one hand, it inscribes the concluding Kate and Petruchio marital relation as an anachronism; and yet, on the other, by idealizing and romanticizing that model, it imbues it with the nostalgic value of a vision of social order imagined as passing away" (195–6). By this interpretation, the audience would have taken the taming of Kate as exaggerated, an old-fashioned ideal of submissive women, not as a model Shakespeare was encouraging them to follow. Men in the audience may have cheered Kate's final speech, but most would have done so with a sense of fantasy and nostalgia, knowing that they would never see their wives making such a speech. Seeing Kate's speech in historical context gives me a different perspective on the injustice of the speech and its impact on women's role in society. Knowing that the audience was probably not convinced by the explicit theme of taming women allows me to see beyond the blatant sexism of the plot to the more implicit themes of the play.

> *Here the author skillfully leads me to her conclusion and then, in the next paragraph, establishes and defines—definition is very important—an important theme.*

One of these themes is the importance of language and the ability of women to have power through speaking. Kate is considered a shrew because of the language she uses and her disregard of what is socially acceptable for her to say. Bianca, on the other hand, plays the role of the socially acceptable woman--she is silent. Karen Newman makes the observation in her article "Renaissance Family Politics and Shakespeare's *The Taming of the Shrew*" that, ". . . Kate refuses her erotic destiny by exercising her linguistic willfulness. Her shrewishness, always associated with women's revolt in words, testifies to her exclusion from social and political power. Bianca, by contrast, is throughout the play associated with silence" (90).

> *Each point is made clearly and then documented. I am instructed in writing and rewriting this chapter by the author's skill in this process.*

The contrast in the speech of the two sisters is shown clearly by comparing Petruchio's courtship of Kate to Lucentio's courtship of Bianca. In the first exchange between Kate and Petruchio (II.1 182–271), Kate is the instigator of the quarrel and gets the better of Petruchio through puns which mock his attempt to treat her as an object of exchange. She uses words to resist his efforts to dominate her. Newman agrees that, "[Kate] takes the lead through puns which allow her to criticize Petruchio and the patriarchal system of wooing and marriage" (94). In the exchange between Bianca and Lucentio (III.1 31–43), Bianca simply repeats the words Lucentio says to her. Newman feels that Bianca is conforming to the accepted role of women by not speaking. She says, "[Bianca's] revelation of her feelings through a repetition of the Latin lines [Lucentio] quotes from Ovid are as close as possible to the silence we have come to expect from her" (94). Kate is considered a shrew because she uses wild language and linguistic wit to resist being treated like a commodity. Bianca is favored by suitors because she is quiet, complacent, and submissive. In this instance, language is the tool Kate uses to break away from being traded among men by her father.

> *Go through the rest of the research paper by yourself, with a partner, or with several of your classmates, noting just what the author is doing, paragraph by paragraph. Read it aloud and hear the writer's voice. Outline it to see the logical trail she carves through the material. Write out her thesis and the points she makes to see the significance of what she is saying.*

As Petruchio tries to tame Kate, a major tactic he uses is intentionally misunderstanding what she says. By changing the meaning of her words, he takes away her power to be independent. After the quarrel when Petruchio and Kate first meet, Petruchio negates Kate's power by telling Baptista that Kate has agreed to marry him and that she loves him when they are alone (II.1 278–310). Baptista believes Petruchio, and Kate is powerless to fight against being treated like an object by her father and Petruchio. She must marry Petruchio, who forced himself upon her and defeated her independence by ignoring her ability to speak.

Petruchio intentionally misinterprets the meaning of Kate's words again when she wants to stay at the wedding feast (III.2 198–238). Kate clearly tries to resist his power to control her by saying,

> "The door is open, sir, there lies your way,
> You may be jogging while your boots are green.
> For me, I'll not be gone till I please myself" (III.2 209–211).

Petruchio ignores her will, and the fact that she's angry about being humiliated at the wedding, and claims that he is rescuing her from thieves, saying,

> "Fear not, sweet wench, they shall not touch thee, Kate" (III.2 237).

He says this in the same breath that he calls her

> "my goods, my chattels, she is my house,
> My household stuff, my field, my barn,
> My horse, my ox, my ass, my any thing" (III.2 229–231).

His tactic of dominating Kate in this scene is to rob her of her independence as a human being by ignoring her words.

Petruchio's strategy continues when they reach his house. Newman says, "Kate is figuratively killed with kindness, by her husband's rule over her not so much in material terms--the withholding of food, clothing, and sleep--but the withholding of linguistic understanding. As the receiver of her messages, he simply refuses their meaning; since he also has material power to enforce his interpretations, it is his power over language that wins" (95). Kate still struggles to maintain her independence through words. In the scene with the tailor, Kate tells Petruchio that she will not be silenced:

> "Why sir, I trust I may have leave to speak,
> And speak I will. I am no child, no babe.
> Your betters have endured me say my mind,
> And if you cannot, best you stop your ears.
> My tongue will tell the anger of my heart,
> Or else my heart concealing it will break,
> And rather than it shall, I will be free
> Even to the uttermost, as I please, in words."

As Petruchio withholds food and sleep from Kate, she becomes more willing to be civil to him, realizing it's the only way she'll stay alive. Still, she doesn't lose her wit and her confidence to be outspoken and contradict Petruchio.

The conversation between Kate and Petruchio on the way to Padua is a relief to me. It shows that Kate has not been conquered in the sense that she still has her wit and her ability to speak. Newman says this exchange shows Kate is having fun playing along with Petruchio's games (95–96). She refers to the pun Kate makes when saying to Vincentio,

> "Pardon, old father, my mistaking eyes,
> That have been bedazzled with the sun" (IV.5 145–6).

"Sun" in this case, is a pun referring to Petruchio, who referred to himself as his mother's "son" earlier in their conversation.

Kate retains her sharp verbal abilities through the end of the play. Even when Kate gives her monologue on how to be a good wife, it is Kate who is speaking and telling the audience what she feels. She has retained her individuality at least to the extent that she contradicts the other two wives and addresses the audience with the longest and most climactic monologue in the play. Newman says, "Kate's having the last word contradicts the very sentiments she speaks" (99). Newman also notes that even though one shrew is tamed, two more reveal themselves: "Bianca and the widow refuse to do their husbands' bidding, thereby undoing the sense of closure Kate's 'acquiescence' produces" (100).

Because Kate does not lose her power to speak, it seems that Shakespeare is showing us that Kate is not ultimately defeated by Petruchio. The play leaves the audience with an uneasy feeling that the conflict of men not being able to dominate their wives is not resolved. This is further supported by the historical context of Kate's final monologue and how the contemporary audience would have responded to that as a fantasized, unrealistic basis for the situation to wrap up. Historically, this play reflects the feeling of English society in the 1590s. According to Newman, "The period was fraught with anxiety about rebellious women" (91). Other historians have identified the era as a "crisis of order" which was based on a fear of women rebelling against their submissive role in the patriarchal culture (Newman 90). Boose adds that there was a sudden increase in witchcraft trials and other court accusations against women documented in this time period. There was also an increase in the instances of crimes that are typically female, "scolding," "witchcraft," "whoring," "brawling," and "dominating one's husband" (184). These historical records of punishment show the strength women were showing in beginning to overcome their submissive role in society and the magnitude of the threat these women posed to men.

Boose observes, ". . . what is striking is that the punishments meted out to women are much more frequently targeted at suppressing women's speech than they are at controlling their sexual transgressions" (184). This social phenomenon is reflected in *The Taming of the Shrew*, when Kate is considered a shrew because she speaks freely, and in the way Petruchio tries to dominate her by suppressing her ability to speak.

Also in the play, there are several references to Kate that could imply accusations of witchcraft. After Kate yells at Baptista for making deals with Bianca's suitors, Hortensio says,

"From all such devils, good Lord deliver us!" (I.1 65).

When Baptista scolds Kate for attacking Bianca, he says,

"For shame, thou hilding of a devilish spirit" (II.1 26).

Kate is associated with the devil, probably like many women in England at that time, because she is a threat to male authority.

The punishments that Kate receives from Petruchio—public humiliation at her wedding, humiliation at the wedding feast—also resemble the historical customary punishment of "scolds" and "shrews." Boose refers to these as Kate's "shaming rites" (192).

Looking at the play from this historical perspective shows that Shakespeare's purpose in *The Taming of the Shrew* was to reflect what was going on around him in society. The audiences who saw Shakespeare's play probably recognized Kate's outspoken, shrewish behavior in women of their time and identified with Petruchio's quest to dominate them and restore the order that society once knew. Many men probably cheered Kate's final speech wishing their women would adopt such attitudes. But, by showing the audience Petruchio's inability to truly dominate a shrew, the play showed the present and future of the gender struggle--that for one tamed shrew there were two more untamed, that the days of a woman professing her submission and inferiority to her husband were gone. Despite the content of Kate's final monologue, it seems the primary theme of *The Taming of the Shrew* is that men should beware because the shrews will not be tamed.

Note the strong ending written not with rhetorical flourishes but with solid, specific information that weaves all the strands of the research paper together and leaves at least this male thinking about women today and the women in his life—his wife, his daughters and granddaughter, his

women friends. Shakespeare speaks to us today because he dealt with the fundamental issues of men and women, then and now.

WORKS CITED

Boose, Lynda E. "Scolding Brides and Bridling Scolds: Taming the Woman's Unruly Member." Shakespeare Quarterly 42 (1991): 179–185, 194.

Newman, Karen. "Renaissance Family Politics and Shakespeare's The Taming of the Shrew." English Literary Renaissance 16 (1986): 86–100.

Shakespeare, William. The Taming of the Shrew. Ed. G. R. Hibbard. London: Penguin Books, 1968.

....

The author's teacher, Brock Dethier, wrote at the end of the paper: "*A.* Excellent. Best research paper I've seen this semester." It is a superb example of academic writing that is more than that—simply good writing—and we can all take instruction and inspiration from good writing.

CASE HISTORY OF A TURNING POINT—CARMEN SARKISSIAN

This essay by a student of Armenian descent at Glendale College in California captures that miraculous moment all young writers experience when they first connect with an audience. It is worthy of celebration and consideration.

We all feel we are alone, that we don't have anything to say, and that no one would listen if we did. And then we cast out words as we might put a note in a bottle and toss it in the sea with little hope the note will draw a response. And then it does. As the student reveals, the audience inspires more writing. The audience is waiting to hear me. It's a connection central to the human experience.

....

THE SPONTANEITY OF WRITING

Carmen Sarkissian

My family has always struggled to carry the heavy luggage of traditions on its shoulders. According to one of these traditions, the family celebrates the occasion of the appearance of the first tooth in a baby's mouth by surrounding the baby with a number of tools and gadgets. The one it picks up first will supposedly determine what the child will become when it grows up. Despite the heavy influence of superstition in our culture and family life, I myself am inclined more toward reason. However, when my mother mentioned one day that I had picked a pen during my "first tooth" celebration, I started viewing superstition with respect. For years later I had indeed developed a love and fascination for "the pen." Of course I would never become a writer. However, I would become an ardent reader, endowed by a strong imagination. As a young girl an incident occurred that made me wonder for an instant whether the predictions of that tradition were actually coming true.

I was a teenager then and was struggling with the idea of why I had to go to school. I considered all the subjects boring and a waste of my precious teenage life. One day in class, while experiencing a true "dictatorship" by a teacher, it happened. During the lesson, my classmates and I did not dare move, cup our chins, play with our books and pens, or even take notes. It wasn't long before I found myself floating in the carefree and comforting world of dreams. The teacher's voice had become the monotonous chant of a psychologist hypnotizing his patient. A lovely warm feeling had started to embrace me. I was dozing off. The outcome, however, could be disastrous and I had to find a distraction, something to help keep my eyes open. But what? Miraculously, I spotted it. Lying under my shoes was a torn, blue envelope flap. Getting it from under the desk without being seen did not prove to be hard. One swift move and I was in possession of my ticket out of boredom.

Staring at and scribbling on the little parchment alternately, I gradually found myself enveloped in an image that I typically created in my mind in situations of utter boredom. This image started to materialize on the blue envelope--my blank canvas.

Somehow it grew and evolved, and I found myself writing so fast, as if I were possessed. A plot was blooming amidst its scenes. For the first time in my life, I was experiencing the spontaneity of writing. My imagination had taken off and at the same time it was keeping me awake and out of trouble.

It seems that the expression on my face had started to betray me. Driven by her curiosity and being equally bored herself, my friend had turned her questioning gaze towards me. She grabbed my note and started reading. To my amazement, traces of boredom on her face were gradually replaced by a curious and surprised look.

She had liked it! She had really liked it! I could not believe it.

Before I knew it, my story had taken its memorable course through the hands of all my friends. I examined everyone's expression in detail. It seemed as though my story had tickled their curiosity, and they were becoming restless in anticipation for the continuation. Now I had to come up with the rest of the story.

Writing on a regular-sized paper was dangerous, for it would be visible to the teacher. My friends then came up with a solution. They would hand me little pieces of paper on which I was required to supply them with the rest of the story. I thus kept on writing and writing. The journey I was led on was determined by the characters in my story, which was in essence a reflection of a teenager's life, and was fueled by the expectations of my classmates.

As more and more papers started circulating, I further aroused my readers' curiosity and eventually found myself responding to their needs. After all they had become my audience. There were moments I realized I was losing their attention. Right then I would come up with a turning point and captivate them once again. It was as though I was taking them for a ride. They depended on me until I finished the story.

I could sense the feeling of satisfaction writers enjoy as they succeed in captivating their readers. In fact, it was a wonderful feeling to have become the center of attention. I was enjoying an episode of popularity and self-confidence. I knew I could do it again, and could one day even become a writer. That was not the path I ultimately chose for myself. However, the memory of the experience would linger in my mind, reminding me of the trace of a mysterious truth existing in that old "baby's first tooth" tradition.

———— CASE HISTORY OF AN ESSAY ————

DONALD M. MURRAY

Friday, December 15.

At 5:00 P.M. I am given the assignment to write an essay that will interest college students "seventeen to forty-five."

My first reaction, as it always is—that I have nothing to say. Then I feel those subjects that first come to mind—the Battle of the Bulge in the winter of 1944–45, my wife's and my unequal aging, the role of caretaking in a forty-nine-year-long marriage—do not seem appropriate for this audience. They reflect my immediate concerns: the snow outside reminds me of my first battle, my concern for my aging wife and my lack of qualifications as a male nurse. All those are and will be legitimate subjects for my "Now and Then" column in the *Boston Globe,* but they do not seem appropriate for this assignment.

I make myself remember that the subject will come, in my case, not by forcing, by hard, focused thinking; but it will rise from a dreamy corner of my brain if I assign it to my subconscious; what topic can I explore that may interest seventeen-to-forty-five-year-old college students?

I notice that I say explore. I "write to learn" and I want to discover something by this and every writing task. The topic may not be new to me, but I hope to write something more than I have written—or thought—before.

As I drive with Minnie Mae to Applebee's for dinner I realize that a corner of my mind is asking itself what did I need to know. The word failure drifts by but a car is cutting me off, so I pay attention to my driving. After ordering, while Minnie Mae goes to the restroom, I allow my mind to drift and find I'm back in school as a high school student, failing, and realize no one taught me how to fail. In writing down these notes the idea is more developed than I want it to be. I don't want my conscious telling my unconscious what it has already said. I want to allow that important, dreamy kind of thinking, to take place before I write. I take out the three-by-five card I always carry with me and write "failure." That is enough to remind me of the potential topic.

Saturday, December 16

I get up at 5:30 A.M. On Saturday morning I pick up two old friends and we go out to breakfast. I feel the idea of failure being turned over like compost in the back of my brain and recognize I have a topic: importance of failure . . . still learning to fail . . . can't write unless willing to fail . . . risk and failure . . . ought to teach failure . . . hurt children only teaching success. I could interview my friends, one is a sculptor, the other a scientist, and both teachers. That would be a good way to approach the subject but I choose to keep it to myself, to play with the ideas in my mind without interference from anyone else. We talk hockey, the cost of health care, politics, and engage in our familiar male banter.

I have the choice of following what I call a linear or straight-line approach to the topic or a nonlinear, circular, approach. Using a linear approach I would:

- Look for quotations on failure.
- Seek articles and books on failure.
- Interview people who I think would have something significant to say about failure.
- Search the Internet.
- Make formal notes on my failures and what I have learned from them.
- Start playing with sketch outlines.

I have done all those things in the past and may do many or most of them later, but I have learned to follow the advice of the novelist Virginia Woolf who wrote, "As for my next book, I am going to hold myself from writing it till I have it impending in me: grown heavy in my mind like a ripe pear; pendant, gravid, asking to be cut or it will fall." I will go on to other work, other living, and allow the topic to ripen.

Sunday, December 17

It is a good topic but I realize that I have dealt with the topic too often. I feel I will discover new things to say, but I have to consider other topics.

I am working within restrictions. My audience is college students "seventeen to forty-five." I want to write a personal essay, an internal exploration of what I don't know I know rather than a formal research paper, since I may be able to use it as a column or publish it in a local journal that welcomes my essays. And I am restricted by the life I have lived. This will be nonfiction although I write fiction and poetry.

I brainstorm:

- Why I write fiction? Fiction truer than nonfiction, imagined more realistic than reality?
- The older I live the more I wish I had known my grandfathers who died before I was born—and their four grandfathers, and their eight grandfathers, and their sixteen grandfathers who lived far back in the mists of Scotland. I think I am more influenced by them than I know.
- I have just edited a memoir. The stranger in the mirror.
- My secret childhood, a healthy schizophrenia that saved me.
- A quote I want to explore:

From THE ART OF POSSIBILITY, Zander and Zander, Harvard Business School Press, 2000

"Frank Sulloway, a former research scholar at the Massachusetts Institute of Technology in the Department of Brain and Cognitive Sciences, [*Born to Rebel* (New York: Pantheon Books, 1996)] suggests that we think of 'personality' as a strategy for 'getting out of childhood alive.' Each child in a family stakes out her own territory of attention and importance by developing certain aspects of her character into 'winning ways.' One child may be sociable and outgoing, another may be quiet and thoughtful, but both are aimed at the same thing: to find a safe and identifiable niche in the family and the community and to position themselves to survive. Anxiety regulates behavior and alerts the child to the dangers of being one-down, unattended to, or at a loss.

"The survival mechanisms of the child have a great deal in common with those of the young of other species, save for the fact that children learn to know themselves. They grow up in a medium of language and have a long, long time to think. A child comes to think of himself as the personality he gets recognition for or, in other words, as the set of patterns of action and habits of thought that get him out of childhood in one piece. That set, raised to adulthood, is what we are calling the calculating self. The prolonged nature of human childhood may contribute to the persistence of these habits long after their usefulness has passed."

- How I survived childhood?
- Did I survive childhood? Still trying to escape.
- Try to look back and see myself as a teen-ager.
- My Tilton year. The person I became my freshman year in college.
- What I learned from my war.

- Good war. Term used about my war that I hate, but there was good for me in what I learned about the world and myself.
- One trait. Desperate risk taker. Confronted the dragon.

My subconscious is back on the hunt. It will continue tomorrow as I drive to Boston to see a doctor and back. (Another topic: Seventy mile-per-hour writing. The writing before writing.)

↓

The danger of having an imagination.
The imagined reality.
- And that circles back to the imagined self.

Monday, December 18

I come to my desk harried and harassed. I have to go to Boston to a doctor. I have a number of Christmas tasks and errands to do and an alp of correspondence that needs answering. And I can't even remember what I've been writing about here. This doesn't worry me. I have it written but I need to make myself calm, quiet. We have to make ourselves ready to receive writing. I take deep breaths, I make my body relax, perhaps my mind will follow.

Now I can look at what I had written yesterday to see if anything surprises me. Is there a line I have to follow? No, but . . . Writing often lies in the buts. In this case: No, but I see an image of a skinny kid with glasses in a maroon woolen sweater with a striped stocking hat and—can it be?—corduroy knickers, turning off Hancock street in Wollaston, Massachusetts. There is a trolley car screeching past in the background. He would be sixteen in 1936 and allowed to wear long pants so it must be before that. He is coming home to tell his parents he's gotten a job. They will not care. That isn't the problem but what I find mysterious is why he went to apply for the many jobs he worked as a teenager. How did he, an almost pathologically shy kid, have the nerve . . . [My globe editor calls to go over a column and I do some rewriting, making three phone calls to get it right. No problem with interruptions. I have stopped in the middle of a sentence. I'll be able to tune to the voice of that draft.] . . . to march in and ask for the jobs, acting, he hoped, confident that he could do a job he didn't know he could do. What did he learn? How much has it, did it, mark his life since? What was his peculiar self-image, a bookworm who thought he was stupid in school, one boy at home and another on the street? What was held back, what is held back?

This has, of course, become interior freewriting, a sort of pre-discovery draft that may lead me to what I need to write. And I notice that in writing this I have grown calm, patient, lost to the world in following the words that may lead me to a territory to explore.

Tuesday, December 19

A distracted morning of care for Minnie Mae, responding to the editor of *Twice Lived Life,* responding to the editor of *Write to Learn,* seventh edition, and being interrupted by phone calls, and the pressure to pack up a complete office to send to Florida so I can work in the rented condo there next month, yet I have a feeling from two notes I made on my three-by-five card at the doctor's in Boston yesterday that I can plunge in.

The note was: *How I saw myself*

"see"

I watch a skinny 15-year-old kid with glasses running for home. Hancock street in Wollaston, Massachusetts. It is 1939, at the end of the Great Depression and months before the Germans invade Poland and World War II begins. A yellow-orange trolley car screeches by in the background as he turns at the Amoco gas station and climbs the stairs, two at a time, to the second floor apartment his parents rent in the two decker.

He checks in on his grandmother who lies paralyzed in the middle bedroom. Her eyes are closed and her mouth gaps open. He steps close to her. She is still alive and goes to the kitchen where is mother sits by her cup of tea staring at some world in which she lived.

He tells her he lost his paper route because he had been sick and had to spend so much time in bed. But now he has a job at Miller's Market after school on Friday and all day Saturday. He knows she heard him, knows she will use this information to order fancy food she cannot afford, but is not surprised by the silence. They hurt each other with not speaking, turning away, going in the next room as he does to escape into a library book.

His sleeping porch bedroom has a ceiling of National Geographic maps. The Arctic is right over his head. That is where he will go if he does not have his war.

This is how he sees himself.

shy

dumb (bored)

introverted

ugly

weird

confident

writer

(football plays and girls)

I have to stop and meet someone for lunch, but I hear a voice and see a direction I will take when I get back to the draft. Then I will start by layering, writing over what I have written and pushing on, loosely following the trail I have made in my list.

[later] Driving this afternoon I hear my parents and my teachers criticizing my lack of concentration, one of my strongest points.

Wednesday, December 20

My mind keeps wandering back to this piece with a change:

1. how I was seen
2. how I saw myself then
3. how I see myself now

I don't formally outline but I do note potential sequences as I have here.
Now I want to plunge in, writing over or layering what I have written and moving forward.

I watch a skinny 15-year-old kid with glasses, darting between the cars on Hancock Street in Wollaston, Massachusetts and he races home. It is 1939, at the end of the Great Depression, months before the Germans invade Poland and World War II begins. A yellow-orange trolley car screeches by in the background as he turns the corner by the Amoco gas station and climbs the stairs, two at a time, to the second floor apartment his parents rent in the two decker.

He checks in on his grandmother who lies paralyzed in the middle bedroom. Her eyes are closed and her mouth gaps open. He steps close to her. She is still alive and he goes to the kitchen where his mother sits by her cup of tea staring at some world in which she lived.

He tells her he lost his paper route because he had been sick and had to spend so much time in bed. But now he has a job at Miller's Market after school on Friday and all day Saturday. He knows she heard him, knows she will use this information to order fancy food she cannot afford against his 50-cent a full day salary, but he is not surprised by the silence. In his family they hurt each other by what they do not say, by turning away, by suddenly standing up and going to the next room.

He goes to his sleeping porch bedroom has a ceiling of National Geographic maps. The Arctic is right over his head. That is where he will go if he does not have his war. He opens again Admiral Byrd's book *Alone* in which he tells how he survived winter in the Antarctic in solitude.

I am this boy and I remember how others saw me and how I felt about myself. Mother criticized my posture, my enunciation, my clothes, my hair and my overall ugliness. And I agreed with her, feeling I was unattractive.

She joined my father, my uncles, and my teachers in calling attention to my lack of concentration and I thought that my principal moral flaw.

People worried about my being an introvert, a loner, shy. So did I. I preferred reading to hanging out on the corner by the drugstore, I was self-conscious and self-centered, awkward at meeting strangers.

My vulnerability to childhood sicknesses made me feel weak, not strong. My uncles led the chorus that said I was spoiled. My mother told me again and again I was lazy. My father, mother, ministers, teachers, classmates and streetmates were critical of my weirdness, thinking my sense of humor unfunny and certainly unpolitic.

I was funny looking, awkward, clumsy, scared, stupid, lazy, strange: a teen-ager. And I believed that the way I was seen was accurate.

But now, sixty years later I see that skinny kid hustling work, motivated by what I am not sure. He is not lazy and deep down he knows it. He does think he is stupid, but he'll make up for that by good work habits and he does.

dumb in school—reader—bored

concentration

meeting people

strong—man's work

snapshot photo store "hunk"

Thursday, December 21

My stomach is in knots with all I have to do this morning before we drive to New York. I need to have a quiet moment writing. This serves me as prayer or meditation serves others, a calm out-of-the-world moment in which I concentrate or focus on a quiet task of making or discovering. I can either layer again or pick up where I stopped.

Writing is, above all, a matter of faith, and reading this over I have lost faith in it. It seems a dung pile, nothing less. But I have learned that the solution to this feeling is to enter into the writing task, forgetting the grand angst for the moment of line-by-line making.

This evening at the moment of melancholy as the sun goes down but the evening dark has not closed in I hear the voices of my childhood from the grave. My mother, of course, is the loudest telling me to stand up straight, to enunciate clearly, to dress properly, to be obedient.

My father stands at a distance, watching me to see if I will stand up to mother as he cannot; my uncles telling me I am spoiled, to grow up and be a man; my teachers telling me to concentrate not to stare out the window; my classmates thinking—I think—I am not only funny looking but weird.

I am surprised to be writing a new beginning. I heard it and allowed it to write itself. It may frame the piece better, it may be a new piece, it may be . . . what I do not know. I am involved in the frightening fun of writing, saying what I do not expect, what may be what I do not want to hear or what may clarify the confusions of a long-lived life.

I decide to focus on this kid to which the voices are directed, to make him come clear in my mind's eye by description. I pick up the draft, writing over it if necessary.

I watch a skinny 15-year-old kid with glasses, darting between the cars on Hancock Street in Wollaston, Massachusetts as he races home. It is 1939 at the end of the great Depression and only months before the Germans invade Poland and World War II begins.

A yellow-orange trolley car screeches by in the background as he turns the corner by the Amoco gas station and climbs the stairs, two at a time, to the second floor apartment his parents rent in the brown shingled two decker.

He checks in on his grandmother who lies paralyzed in the middle bedroom. Her eyes are closed and her mouth gaps open. He steps close to her. She is still alive and the boy goes to the kitchen where his mother sits by her cup of tea, staring at some better world in which she lives in memory of imagination.

He tells her he lost his paper route because he had been sick and had to spend so much time in bed, but now he has a job at Miller's Market after school on Friday and all day Saturday. He knows she heard him, knows she will use this information to order fancy food she cannot afford against his 50-cent a full day salary, but he is not surprised by the silence. In his family they hurt each other by what they do not say, by turning away, by suddenly standing up and going to the next room.

He goes to his sleeping porch bedroom that has a ceiling of National Geographic maps. The Arctic is right over his head. That is where he will go if he does not have his war. He opens again Admiral Byrd's book *Alone* in which he tells how he survived winter in the Antarctic in solitude.

He dreams the escape I know now he made to a life far better than he dreamed, yet he [I?] still hears the voices, but now he [I?] must answer them.

The world intrudes and I must stop, but I am impatient to see how the piece will now turn from description to reflection.

I am this boy and I remember how others saw me and how I felt about myself. Mother criticized my posture, my enunciation, my clothes, my hair and my overall ugliness. And I agreed with her, feeling I was unattractive.

She joined my father, my uncles, and my teachers in calling attention to my lack of concentration, and I thought that my principal moral flaw.

People worried about my being an introvert, a loner, shy. So did I. I preferred reading to hanging out on the corner by the drugstore, I was self-conscious and self-centered, awkward at meeting strangers.

My vulnerability to childhood sicknesses made me feel weak, not strong. My uncles led the chorus that said I was spoiled. My mother told me again and again I was lazy. My father, mother, ministers, teachers, classmates and streetmates were critical of my weirdness, thinking my sense of humor unfunny and certainly unpolitic.

I was funny looking, awkward, clumsy, scared, stupid, lazy, strange: a teen-ager. And I believed that the way I was seen was accurate.

But, now, sixty years later I see that skinny kid hustling work, motivated by what I am not sure. He is not lazy and deep down he knows it. He does think he is stupid, but he'll make up for that by good work habits and he does.

dumb in school—reader—bored

concentration

meeting people

strong—man's work

snapshot photo store "hunk"

December 22

It is a busy day with computer problems but riding home after a family dinner at a Japanese restaurant, I thought I could take a quick look at a possible ending.

They were wrong and I am grateful they were. What people told me I was made me work hard to prove they were wrong. It might have taken only a few A's, a couple of hugs at home, to satisfy the hunger that has driven me toward a life better than I could have imagined when I raced home to tell mother I had a job at Miller's Market.

Many novelists say they know the end before they begin. I don't usually work this way and certainly this ending has only come after I had pretty much completed the draft. Tomorrow I will get up early and finish it.

What I've learned:

- *Much writing is done away from the page.*
- *Once I have the tension and the voice I can stop and return at any time.*
- *Writing can be done in small fragments of time during a busy and distracted life.*

December 23

This has been one of those hours-on-1-800-numbers-with-computer-problems days and now I will try to do a complete layering draft as much as to calm me down as to complete the assignment.

~~This evening at the moment of melancholy as the sun goes down but the evening dark has not closed in I hear the voices of my childhood from the grave. My mother, of course, is the loudest, telling me to stand up straight, to enunciate clearly, to dress properly, to be obedient.~~

~~My father stands at a distance, watching me to see if i will stand up to mother as he cannot. my uncles telling me i am spoiled, to grow up and be a man, my teachers telling me to concentrate not to stare out the window. my classmates thinking—I think—I am not only funny looking but weird.~~

*I have been worried about using a frame—my experience is that it is bet-
ter just to get to the story, and that opinion was reinforced when my possible ending referred back to the material after the frame. The frame also
tells too much while showing too little and expands many issues rather
than focusing on one issue.*

I watch a skinny 15-year-old kid with glasses, darting between the cars on
Hancock Street in Wollaston, Massachusetts as he races home. ~~it is 1939 at
the end of the Great Depression and only months before the Grmans invade
Pland and Wrld Wr II begins.~~

*I'm not sure the depression and war stuff is necessary, not sure it moves
the essay forward.*

I am that boy, now a 76-year-old man, and I hear a yellow-orange trolley car
screeche~~s~~ by ~~in the background~~ as ~~he~~ I turn~~s~~ the corner by the Amoco gas
station and climb~~s~~ the stairs, two at a time, to the second floor apartment
his parents rent in the brown shingled two decker.

He checks in on his grandmother who lies paralyzed in the middle bedroom. Her eyes are closed and her mouth gapes open. He steps close to her.
She is still alive and the boy goes to the kitchen where his mother sits by her
cup of tea staring at some better world in which she lives in memory of
imagination.

He tells her he lost his paper route because he had been sick and had to
spend so much time in bed, but now he has a job at Miller's Market after
school on Friday and all day Saturday. He knows she heard him, knows she
will use this information to order fancy food she cannot afford against his
50-cent a full day salary, but he is not surprised by the silence. In his family
they hurt each other by what they do not say, by turning away, by suddenly
standing up and going to the next room.

I enter into that boy I was so long ago and am surprised by how he sees
himself. He believes what his parents, his uncles, his teachers have told him:
that he is lazy, that he lacks the ability to concentrate, that he is a shy introvert who cannot meet people, that he is unattractive, even ugly.

The fact is that part of him still believes what had been drilled into his
head with unceasing repetition. Yet that boy racing home is clearly not lazy.
He has sought work on his own without the support, counsel, or suggestion
of his parents.

At Miller's Market he will work long hours—often from 5 am on Saturdays when they go to market until close to midnight and Mr. Miller, going
outside and looking up and down street for potential customers, sees none
and reluctantly shuts the store.

This skinny, bespectacled boy will do a man's work, hauling in huge bags
of potatoes, staggering under sides of beef, lugging in large boxes of canned
goods. He answers the phone and takes orders, sells at the vegetable bins
and behind the counter, takes over the canned goods inventory, arranges the

fruits and vegetables displayed on the sidewalk and in the store, becomes the maker of Scots all-beef sausages.

His teachers, well most of them, tell him he is dumb yet he reads far beyond the assignments . . .

December 24, 2000

[picked up the next morning while waiting to go to breakfast with son-in-law and grandsons.]

His teachers tell him not to read beyond the assignments, not to look out the window and daydream but to concentrate, to pay attention, to focus, not to let his mind wander.

He believes them although he reads fat adult books when he is in elementary school, carries on a game of monopoly with his friends that last months, develops a stamp collection that includes hand-drawn colored maps of each country, starts a collection of sayings about the writer's craft that will become a book 52 years later.

In fact, as a writer he has lived on his ability to daydream, to look out the window and see what others didn't see, to find the unusual in the commonplace. And his power of concentration, his ability to write in the city room and anywhere else, to shut out the world beyond the story is amazing—and sometimes painful—to those who live close to him but on the other edge of his consciousness while he writes at the computer or in his head at the supper table.

I switch back and forth between the boy I was and the old man I am, remembering how I felt because I carried many of the childhood beliefs all my life. Others saw me as a risk taker, a paratrooper, a freelance writer while having a family, a job switcher who gambled on his future. Yet I saw myself as a conservative, a person who played it safe.

I was told I was weak and I was seen as a coward on the playground because my mother told me that if I really believed in Jesus and did not hit back the bully's hand would be stayed. It wasn't, and I played football, boxed, fought in my war yet still felt I was weak and a coward until the young trainers at the health club are amazed at what I can lift at my age and I accepted that I could do what had to be done in the face of danger.

I stop and do a word count: 798. I should be closer to 700. I add that ending I had drafted and read the piece to see what I can cut or sharpen and to see if the fragments I have written at different places hold together as a logical, consistent essay that says something worth saying.

They were wrong and I am grateful they were. What people told me I was made me work hard to prove they were wrong. It might take only a few A's, a couple of hugs at home, to satisfy the hunger that has driven me toward a life better than I could have imagined when I raced home to tell mother I had a job at Miller's Market.

Now for the final line-by-line reading:

I watch a skinny 15-year-old kid with glasses, darting between the cars on Hancock Street in Wollaston, Massachusetts as he races home.

I am that boy, now a 76-year-old man, who ~~and I hear a yellow-orange trolley car screeches by in the background as he/I turns the corner by the Amoco gas station and~~ climbs the stairs, two at a time, to the second floor apartment his parents rent in the brown shingled two decker.

He ~~checks in on his grandmother who lies paralyzed in the middle bedroom. Her eyes are closed and her mouth gapes open. He steps close to her. She is still alive and the boy~~ goes to the kitchen where his mother sits by her cup of tea staring at some better world in which she lives in her imagined memories.

He tells her he lost his paper route because he had been sick and had to spend so much time in bed, but now he has a job at Miller's Market after school on Friday and all day Saturday. He knows she heard him, ~~knows she will use this information to order fancy food she cannot afford against his 50-cent a full day salary, but he is not surprised by the silence. in his family they hurt each other by what they do not say, by turning away, by suddenly standing up and going to the next room.~~ but she says nothing and the boy feels the familiar disappointment. She thinks he will lose the job as his father has lost so many jobs.

I enter into that boy I was so long ago and am surprised by how he sees himself. He believes what his parents, his uncles, his teachers have told him: that he is lazy, that he lacks the ability to concentrate, that he is a shy introvert who cannot meet people, that he is unattractive, even ugly.

The fact is that part of him still believes what had been drilled into his head with unceasing repetition. Yet watching that boy I was racing home I realize he is not lazy. He has sought work on his own without the support, counsel, or suggestion of his parents.

At Miller's Market he will work long hours—often from 5 A.M. on Saturdays when they go to market until close to midnight and Mr. Miller, going outside and looking up and down street for potential customers, sees none and reluctantly shuts the store.

This skinny, bespectacled boy will do a man's work, hauling in huge bags of potatoes, staggering under sides of beef, lugging in large boxes of canned goods. He answers the phone and takes orders, sells at the vegetable bins and behind the counter, takes over the canned goods inventory, arranges the fruits and vegetables displayed on the sidewalk and in the store, becomes the maker of Scots all-beef sausages.

His teachers, well most of them, convince him he has a serious problem of concentration. ~~is dumb. Yet he reads far beyond the assignments. His teachers tell him not to read beyond the assignments, not to look out the window and daydream but to concentrate, to pay attention, to focus, not to let his mind wander.~~ He believes them although he reads adult books when he is in elementary school, carries on a game of monopoly with his friends that last months, develops a stamp collection that includes hand-drawn colored maps of each country, starts a collection of sayings about the writer's craft that will become a book 52 years later.

In fact he has astonishing~~, as a writer he has lived on his ability to day-dream, to look out the window and see what others didn't see, to find the unusual in the commonplace. and his~~ powers of concentration, ~~his ability to~~ writes in the city room and anywhere else, shut outs the world beyond the story in a way that is amazing —and sometimes painful—to those who live close to him but remain on the other edge of his consciousness while he writes at the computer or in his head at the supper table.

I switch back and forth between the boy I was and the old man I am, remembering how I felt because I carried many of the childhood beliefs all my life. Others saw me as a risk taker, a paratrooper, a freelance writer while having a family, a job switcher who gambled on his future. Yet I saw myself as a conservative, a person who played it safe.

I was told I was weak and I was seen as a coward on the playground because my mother told me that if I really believed in Jesus and did not hit back the bully's hand would be stayed. It wasn't, and I played football, boxed, fought in my war, yet still felt I was weak and a coward until the young trainers at the health club are amazed at what I can lift at my age and I accepted that I could do what had to be done in the face of danger.

They were wrong and I am grateful they were. What people told me I was made me work hard to prove they were wrong. It might have taken only a few A's, a couple of hugs at home, to satisfy the hunger that has driven me toward a life better than I could have imagined when I raced home to tell mother I had a job at Miller's Market.

Another reading before I send it off to my editor:

I watch a skinny 15-year-old kid with glasses, darting between the cars on Hancock Street in Wollaston, Massachusetts as he races home.

I am that boy, now a 76-year-old man, who climbs the stairs, two at a time, to the second floor apartment his parents rent in the brown shingled two decker. His mother sits by her cup of tea at the kitchen table staring at some better world in which she lives in her imagined memories.

He tells her he has a job at Miller's Market after school on Friday and all day Saturday. He knows she heard him, but she says nothing and the boy feels the familiar disappointment. She thinks he will lose the job as his father has lost so many jobs.

I remember how the boy sees himself. He believes what his parents, his uncles, his teachers have told him: that he is lazy, that he lacks the ability to concentrate. Part of me still believes what had been drilled into his head with unceasing repetition. Yet watching that boy I was racing home I realize he is not lazy. He has sought work on his own without anyone's encouragement.

At Miller's Market he will work long hours—often from 5 A.M. on Saturdays when they go to market until close to midnight when Mr. Miller, going outside and looking up and down street for potential customers, sees none and reluctantly shuts the store.

This skinny, bespectacled boy will do a man's work, hauling in huge bags of potatoes, staggering under sides of beef, lugging in large boxes of canned goods. He answers the phone and takes orders, sells at the vegetable bins and behind the counter, takes over the canned goods inventory, arranges the fruits and vegetables displayed on the sidewalk and in the store, becomes the maker of Scots all-beef sausages.

His teachers convince him he has a serious problem of concentration. He believes them although he reads adult books when he is in elementary school, carries on a game of monopoly with his friends that last months, develops a stamp collection that includes hand-drawn colored maps of each country, starts a collection of sayings about the writer's craft that will become a book 52 years later.

In fact he has astonishing powers of concentration and is able to shut out the world beyond the story with a painful detachment from those who live close to him when he writes at the computer or in his head at the supper table.

I switch back and forth between the boy I was and the old man I am, remembering how I have carried the myths of childhood inside me all my life. Others saw me as a risk taker, a paratrooper, a freelance writer while having a family, a job switcher who gambled on his future. Yet I saw myself as I had been seen as a child, a boy paralyzed by fear.

I was told I was weak and was seen as a coward on the playground and believed my reputation even when I played football, boxed, fought in my war, and impress the young trainers at the health club at how much I can lift at my age.

I am angry at all who made me feel inadequate when I was young and angry at myself for believing them so long. Then I remember how hard I worked to prove them wrong. It might have taken only a few As, a couple of hugs at home, to satisfy the hunger that has driven me toward a life better than I could have imagined when I raced home to tell mother I had a job at Miller's Market.

I do a word count: 617. That's more like it. Compare this draft from the last one and you will see how much I have cut and changed, but what you will not see is the joy I felt as I worked at my craft, using language to clarify my relived life.

Would I have preferred to write a draft of the essay at one sitting without interruptions?

Yes. But my life intruded. My wife had some serious medical problems I had to deal with. We had to pack and travel to visit a daughter and her family. I lost control over the time I had to write and I had two major computer problems that have yet to be solved. I can't use the CD drive that I need to use and the screen frequently flickers and goes blank.

Would it have been better if you had not had to write it this way?

I don't know. I think it would have been different because it would have not had as much rehearsal time in my head.

What have you learned?

1. I have learned about my life, exploring how the opinions of others affect our image of ourselves.
2. I have learned once more that I can write in small fragments of time despite distractions and interruptions.

QUESTIONS ON WRITING A CASE HISTORY

Will writing a case history really help me with the kind of writing I will do in other classes than my writing class?

Writing case histories means reflecting, analyzing, and interpreting. Since writing is learning and thinking, a case history is a microcosm of the educational process itself. It replicates everything you do in school: taking subjects apart, examining their components, holding them up to the light, exploring them, and then putting them back together and viewing them from an enlightened perspective. You follow this process in almost any class—whether it be math, science, English, history, or economics.

But won't picking apart my writing ruin my spontaneity? If I analyze my writing too much, I'm afraid I'll start to sound boring and stilted.

Athletes play hard, putting body, soul, and mind into their work. Writing a case history is like being an athlete who reviews videotapes of a game in order to improve his or her performance. Fast forwarding, rewinding, or pausing at crucial points in the tape, the athlete analyzes key parts of the game and reflects on what he or she sees, taking stock of what went right of wrong in a game, what worked and what didn't. This kind of analysis does not ruin the athlete's ability to enjoy him or herself on the field; it allows the athlete to act spontaneously while engaging the mind.

When you write a case history you are like the informed athlete. The more you analyze and reflect on the process of writing a piece, the more informed about your own skills you will be as you approach writing tasks of different kinds. You will know what you do best and what you need to work on. You will know what methods work with one type of writing and not with another. This knowledge will make you a more confident writer, one who can adapt skills to almost any assignment. The more confidence you gain, the more spontaneous and creative you will be.

How can I write a case history if I haven't kept track of the way I wrote the piece?

Often we tell or write stories about ourselves or others from memory. In fact, writing itself is a way of reclaiming memory and bringing it into the present. While your case history may not be "scientifically" accurate if based solely on memory, it will still allow you to reflect, to think back on how you write and what you have learned.

I can remember some details, but memory alone won't help me write a complete history.

That may be true. As you sit down to write your case history, you will probably find that you have much more to go on than memory alone. If you have followed this text and completed some of the activities in previous chapters, you will have a variety of sources to interpret and analyze. You may also have kept a daybook or journal, or your writing partner may have kept notes on stories and essays you have written. If you have worked extensively with a partner or writing group, you might want to interview them to get their perspectives on your writing process and the pieces you have written throughout the semester. Look also at any comments your teacher has written on your papers. If you have had conferences with your teacher, you might want to think back on those conversations, as well.

Case History Activities

1. Reflect in your daybook about writing a particular piece. Don't go back yet to your notes or conversations with your writing partners. Instead, write from your "gut." What were your strongest feelings about the piece? What did you love about it, hate about it? What in it pleased you or frustrated you? Where did you get stuck and how did you move on? How did you feel as you started the piece? Continued it? Finished it? How do you feel about the piece in retrospect?

2. Research your own case history as a writer of a particular piece. Consult your daybook and go back to comments your classmates or teacher wrote on earlier

drafts. Interview your writing partner, your groupmates, your dorm neighbors, friends, or parents—anyone and everyone to whom you talked about your piece. Ask them what they remember about your writing process and what you told them about your topic. Review the activities that you completed in this text that may have helped you as you wrote your piece. Sort through outlines, maps, brainstorming lists, and freewrites as ways of tracing your writing process.

3. Write a collaborative case history with your writing partner. Trace how you helped each other as you wrote, what kind of feedback you got, and how sharing your writing influenced your final draft. Interview one another and share notes from your daybooks, drafts, outlines, and free writes. Vow to be as honest as possible with each other about what worked and what didn't.

4. Compile a booklet of case histories with your writing group. Have each member write a history about an essay he or she composed in a particular genre—a reflective essay, a persuasive essay, a research essay, and so on. Don't let any two members select the same genre. When the case histories are finished, exchange them within the group, read them as editors, and prepare them for "publication." Make sure to include final drafts of each member's genre essay with his or her case history.

5. Select one of the case histories in this chapter—Sarah Hansen's, Chip Scanlan's, Emma Tobin's, or Tina Winslow's—and make an outline of the steps each writer took while reflecting on his or her writing experience. Jot down the questions each writer asked while compiling his or her history. Use this outline and these questions as starting points for your own case history. Add your own steps and questions as you proceed.

6. Look back through this text at the steps you followed in writing a particular piece, and organize your case history around them. You may, for instance, want to begin with brainstorming as your first point, and then move on to focusing, exploring, planning, and so on. As you address each point, go back through your notes and drafts to find the information that best reflects how you approached each step. Organize this information under the appropriate headings.

7. Visit a writer's bulletin board on the Internet, and trace one writer's journey through a single essay or story. Read all of the writer's posts, and keep a list of the writer's main concerns and how she or he resolved particular problems. Think of the writing process and outline in this text, and ask yourself how each concern relates to a particular step in that writer's process. Then use this list to begin compiling your own case history.

8. Write a case history of one particular step in your writing process (brainstorming, focusing, planning, drafting, revising, etc.). Choose a step that you always have difficulty with, no matter what you write. Using your notes and conversations with classmates, reflect on the ways you approached this step, the obstacles it presented, and how you negotiated those obstacles. Interview

classmates about their own experiences with this step and then reflect on what you have learned about it.

9. Compare and contrast the first draft of a paper you wrote with a final draft. Make a copy of your first draft on your computer or word processor and triple space between lines. In the margins and spaces, note where you made significant changes to the draft as you revised it. Retrace the steps you took to get from the first to last draft. How and why did you make the changes you did? What effect did those changes have on the final draft? What did you learn about your writing process while revising the original draft?

10. Find an interview with a writer in the Paris Review or the series Writers at Work. Write a case study about that writer, focusing on the writer's particular composing process and how he or she goes about revising. Then compare that process with your own.

11. Write a case history of an editorialist or columnist for a local or school newspaper. Ask if you can sit in on meetings in which editorials or columns are discussed. Then interview the writer several times over a period of weeks and at every stage of writing. Ask the writer to save drafts and proofread copies of his or her work. Interview the writer's coworkers—other writers, editors, support staff, and so on—about the writer's process and what they know about how the writer works.

12. Use the headings of your original outline to build a case history. Under each heading retrace your steps in writing the paper, and review how you adhered to or digressed from your outline. Explain why. Did feedback from your writing partner or group influence your decisions? How many revisions did you do before you made the changes? At what point in the outline did you become stuck? Where did you find it easy to move forward? Think of your outline as a series of stepping stones to your final draft; explain how you used, or skipped these stones or moved them around as you wrote.

13. Draw lines down the centers of two sheets of paper in your daybook. At the top of the first sheet write, "Things that Worked." On the left-hand side of this sheet, list the parts of your essay that you had fun writing or that you found easy to compose. On the right-hand side, reflect on how and why you went about composing these sections. At the top of the second sheet, write, "Things I Found Difficult." On the left-hand side of the page, list all the parts of your essay that seemed hard to write or that frustrated you. On the right-hand side, reflect on the reasons for your difficulties and how and when you overcame them. Use these observations as the basis for your case history.

14. Write a case history of writing projects by your roommates or friends. Ask to see drafts of essays they have written for their classes. Interview them about the steps they took in writing their essays. Observe them in action and ask them to reflect—either by talking or on paper—about their writing processes. Have

them tell you what they liked or disliked about writing their essays, what worked and didn't work, and why.

15. Choose someone you know who absolutely hates to write, and study his or her process of composing a single essay for a class. Ask the writer to describe the difficulties he or she has with writing. What obstacles did the writer encounter? Did he or she overcome them? If so, how? If not, why? Using the writer's drafts and interviews, compose a case history.

16. Choose someone who is in love with writing, and repeat Activity 15. Then write a case history comparing the avid writer with the frustrated writer. See if you can pinpoint specific features of both writers' processes that made writing particular pieces good or bad experiences for them.

17. Write a case history of a laboratory problem you have solved in a science class. Trace your steps in the procedure, and recall how you thought the problem through, where you got stuck, and how you finally resolved it. Adapt the same procedure to a successful essay you have written, tracing your journey from draft to draft. Then write a few paragraphs examining the similarities and differences in the two case histories.

18. Choose several observations from the writers whose case histories are included in this chapter that sum up aspects of your own writing. Use them to make an outline for your own case history, and make sure to bring in examples and details from your writing.

19. Ask your partner to write a case history of you as a writer. When he or she finishes it, alter the case history as needed so that it more closely reflects how you think of yourself as a writer. Select one essay or story you have written to use as the central piece in this case history.

20. Go back to the activities you have completed for each chapter in this text, and use them as the basis for your case history.

AFTERWORD

....

THE JOY OF A CRAFT THAT
CAN NEVER BE LEARNED

You have explored a craft that can never be learned. Be grateful—writing will bring you a lifetime of discovery and surprise. I have been writing for more than sixty years, but each morning at my writing desk, I still face the page with enough fear to make it exciting and enough confidence that I will write what I do not expect.

Writing has allowed my voice to be heard. I have been able to participate in our society, arguing for new ways to teach writing, arguing against old ways of resolving differences and against war, speaking out on the satisfactions and concerns of my generation. At my writing desk, I have been able to discover and explore the mysteries of life and survive the tragedies that enter each life—hurt and loss, sickness and death. I have been able to complain and to celebrate, mourn and laugh, imagine, and learn. Writing has also brought me the gift of concentration as I become lost in my craft, searching for the right word, creating the phrase that gives off sparks of meaning, constructing sentences that flow and paragraphs that satisfy, tuning the music of my voice to my evolving meaning. Writing has been my therapy and my craft.

Writing began as play and it remains play. I hope you will be as fortunate and find a lifetime of play, fooling around with language, and finding yourself surprised by a meaning that clarifies your life.

INDEX